The Personal Correspondence
of Sam Houston

Volume III: 1848–1852

edited by
Madge Thornall Roberts

University of North Texas Press ∽ Denton, Texas

Manufactured in the United States of America

10 9 8 7 6 5 4 3 2 1
Requests for permission to reproduce material from this work should be sent to:

Permissions
University of North Texas Press
PO Box 311336
Denton TX 76203
940-565-2142

The paper used in this book meets the minimum requirements of the American National Standard for Permanence of Paper for Printed Library Materials, Z39.48.1984.

Library of Congress Cataloging-in-Publication Data
Houston, Sam, 1793–1863
The personal correspondence of Sam Houston / edited by Madge Thornall Roberts.
p.   cm.
Includes bibliographical references and index.
Contents: v. 3. 1848–1852
ISBN 1-57441-063-6 (alk. paper)
1. Houston, Sam. 1793–1863—Correspondence. 2. Governors—Texas—Correspondence. 3. Legislators—United States—Correspondence. 4. Texas—Politics and government—1846–1865. I. Roberts, Madge Thornall, 1929– . II. Title.
F390.H833   1994   95-36738
976.4'04'092—dc20   CIP

Cover art by Dana Adams

TABLE OF CONTENTS

Preface

Volume III of the Houston correspondence begins in the fall of 1848 as Senator Sam Houston returns to Washington for the second session of the Thirtieth Congress after the close of the Mexican War. His first focus was on settling the Texas boundary dispute and other problems relating directly to the welfare of his state. Once these things were solved he seriously considered resigning his senate seat. He sensed the coming Civil War, however, and seemed to feel he should do all in his power to prevent it. Houston's letters reflect the nation's political activities during the time he struggled to maintain a strong Union stand against radicals such as John C. Calhoun, who favored Disunion. Houston voiced his despair as "one by one the bright lights of the Senate" went out. His personal unhappiness is evident in his continued expressions of longing to be home with Margaret and their growing family.

Many of the letters in this volume reveal how difficult it was to manage a farm during the decade before the Civil War. Houston gives Margaret written instructions to pass along to the field hands and overseers. The letters also contain information on methods of childhood education, medical practices, clothing styles, finances, and social life in Texas during this time period.

Of special interest in Volume III are intriguing new details concerning the plot to distract Houston and perhaps get him out of the Senate with an attack on Margaret's character. I am grateful for the information on the incident furnished by the descendants of Virginia Thorn and Thomas Gott. Mrs. Virgie Looney was extremely helpful to my understanding of the problem, and she agreed with me that it appears Virginia and Thomas were pawns in the hands of Houston's enemies. Also helpful were Joe Weldon Sneed, who shared his Thorn-Gott materials, and Ruth Grant, a Birdwell relative who gave me information on the Birdwells and Wilsons and the devastation the incident wrought on the women of those families. I am also grateful to James Patton, Walker County Clerk, for his help in finding materials on the subject.

I found Houston's correspondence concerning the 1852 presidential election particularly interesting. While obviously wanting the Democratic nomination and feeling that he was the best man for the job, he refused to actively campaign. When Pierce was nominated, Houston seemed to harbor no grudges, and he continued to work for the best interests of the Democratic Party.

Houston's recounts of his journeys to and from Washington give the researcher insight to the problems of nineteenth-century travel. His habit was to seek routes which would allow him to visit relatives along the way to his destination. While tracing his routes, I traveled to Marion, Alabama, where the people of Perry County and Judson College were eager to help me research the people and places mentioned in the letters. My Lea cousins, Ruth Sandlin, who served as my hostess, and her sister, Elizabeth Hall, shared family records with me. A visit to the site of the Lea farm gave meaning to the term "cane brake" which Houston so often used. Historian Eleanor Drake graciously took me on a guided tour of Uniontown (which Houston referred to as Woodville), and presented me with books on the history of Perry County.

In Washington, Houston regularly attended church, often as many as three times on Sundays. He very rarely went out otherwise, preferring instead to remain in his quarters answering his voluminous correspondence. Ironically, his letters are filled with colorful reports of the Washington social scene of which he was not a part. He did attend some of the presidential levees, and when official duties dictated that he attend the social functions, he reported that he usually "looked in" and left as soon as possible. One exception to his reclusive tendencies was a class in mesmerism which he attended with Thomas Rusk, studying clairvoyance and phrenology.

The same editorial procedures from the first two volumes are followed in this work. However, if a person has been previously documented, the full name is given only for clarification and the reference is omitted.

As in the previous volumes, unless specifically identified, the letters are from the vast Franklin Williams Collection of Houston correspondence at the Sam Houston Memorial Museum in Huntsville, Texas. I continue to be indebted to the fine staff of this institution, especially to Dick Rice and Mac Woodward. The process for identifying other collections is as follows: The phrase "Houston Letters" identifies a collection of letters written solely by Houston. "Houston Correspondence" identifies collections of letters written by Houston as well as letters to him written by friends and family. The phrase "Papers" identifies collections which may include Houston letters and correspondence, secondary sources of correspondence concerning the Houston family, newspaper clippings, and various documents. The term "files" identifies information on a specific subject or person.

As in the previous two volumes, letters are mentioned that have not yet been found. In May of 1852, for instance, Margaret alludes to a letter she received from Houston announcing his resignation from the Senate. No such letter has been located, which is frustrating for the researcher because something happened during the summer to change Houston's mind. Even more tantalizing are the pages missing from the legal records of Margaret's assault trial. Historians must still speculate on what information was in them and how they disappeared from the Walker County Courthouse.

Madge Thornall Roberts
San Antonio, Texas

Chapter I

November 9, 1848–November 4, 1849

November 9, 1848: Sam Houston to Margaret Houston
November 10, 1848: Sam Houston to Margaret Houston
November 11, 1848: Benjamin S. Wilson to Sam Houston
November 16, 1848: Margaret Houston to Sam Houston
November 18, 1848: Sam Houston to Margaret Houston
November 18, 1848: Margaret Houston to Sam Houston
November 22, 1848: Sam Houston to Margaret Houston
November 28, 1848: Margaret Houston to Sam Houston
December 5, 1848: Margaret Houston to Sam Houston
December 6, 1848: Sam Houston to Margaret Houston
December 12, 1848: Margaret Houston to Sam Houston
December 16, 1848: Sam Houston to Margaret Houston
December 19, 1848: Sam Houston to Margaret Houston
December 19, 1848: Margaret Houston to Sam Houston
December 20, 1848: Sam Houston to Margaret Houston
December 25, 1848: Sam Houston to Margaret Houston
December 26, 1848: Sam Houston to Margaret Houston
December 26, 1848: Margaret Houston to Sam Houston
December 27, 1848: Sam Houston to Margaret Houston
December 29, 1848: Sam Houston to Margaret Houston
January 1, 1849: Sam Houston to Margaret Houston
January 3, 1849: Sam Houston to Margaret Houston
January 3, 1849: Margaret Houston to Sam Houston
January 8, 1849: Sam Houston to Margaret Houston
January 9, 1849: Margaret Houston to Sam Houston
January 10, 1849: Sam Houston to Margaret Houston
January 13, 1849: Sam Houston to Margaret Houston

January 16, 1849: Sam Houston, Jr., to Sam Houston
January 16, 1849: Margaret Houston to Sam Houston
January 20, 1849: Sam Houston to Margaret Houston
January 20, 1849: Sam Houston to Margaret Houston
January 25, 1849: Sam Houston to Margaret Houston
January 30, 1849: Sam Houston to Margaret Houston
January 30, 1849: Margaret Houston to Sam Houston
February 1, 1849: Sam Houston to Margaret Houston
February 2, 1849: Sam Houston to Margaret Houston
February 3, 1849: Sam Houston to Margaret Houston
February 4, 1849: Sam Houston to Margaret Houston
February 6, 1849: Margaret Houston to Sam Houston
February 8, 1849: Sam Houston to Margaret Houston
February 11, 1849: Sam Houston to Margaret Houston
February 13, 1849: Margaret Houston to Sam Houston
February 15, 1849: Sam Houston to Margaret Houston
February 16, 1849: Sam Houston to Margaret Houston
February 16, 1849: Sam Houston to Sam Houston, Jr.
February 18, 1849: Sam Houston to Margaret Houston
February 19, 1849: Sam Houston to Margaret Houston
February 20, 1849: Margaret Houston to Sam Houston
February 25, 1849: Sam Houston to Margaret Houston
February 27, 1849: Sam Houston to Margaret Houston
March 2, 1849: Sam Houston to Margaret Houston
March 2, 1849: Sam Houston to Margaret Houston
March 3, 1849: Sam Houston to Margaret Houston
March 7, 1849: Sam Houston to Margaret Houston
March 11, 1849: Sam Houston to Margaret Houston
March 29, 1849: Margaret Houston to Sam Houston
April 11, 1849: Sam Houston to Margaret Houston
April 14, 1849: Sam Houston to Margaret Houston
May 7, 1849: Sam Houston to Margaret Houston
June 14, 1849: Sam Houston to Margaret Houston
November 4, 1849: Sam Houston to Antoinette Lea Power

The second session of the Thirtieth Congress opened on December 4, 1848. Houston left Huntsville for the nation's capital, traveling north to the Red River, in late November.

Nacogdoches
9th Nov 1848

My Dearest,

They were not ready to start when I came here. Until now I have been detained. In a few moments we will start. All your slips will be sent by February. Mr Chevellier[1] will send a Box of cuttings of many sorts, and some flowers or roots of them.

I have employed my time in part in looking into my land cases here, and must gain them. They will be valuable. I will write from San Augustine, and say much I hope.

I have only time to send my love to all. I am very well, tho' my trip was unpleasant.

Thy devoted Husband
Sam Houston
with a steel pen!!!

[1]Charles Chevellier. Identified in V. K. Carpenter, trans., *1850 Census of Texas*, vol. 1 (Huntsville, Arkansas: Century Enterprises, 1969).

Sabine Town
10th Nov. 1848

My Dearest,

This evening we came here in good time, from San Augustine, and on tomorrow, we intend to set out early, on our way to the mouth of Red river. It will require six, or seven days, to reach there. With the exception, of the day I started, our travel has been, pretty pleasant. On my way every one inquired for you, and the reason, why you were not with [me]. I did not render the usual excuse, that you were not "in travelling trim," but that you would not risk the winter of the north.

Thus far, I have attended to my business very well, in passport. I can tell you, as I know it will gratify you much, the Sons of Temperance, are increasing in every place by scores. The youth, or those who are eligible to admission, are joining in large proportions. To night I saw, and was offered, some of the best looking <u>Cider</u>, that I have seen for years, and had I not been a member of the <u>order</u>, I should have taken a good drink of the beverage, but as I was, I did not touch it, nor even allow myself to desire it. So you see my Dearest, that the Temperance pledge causes total abstinence!!!—from all drinks, and of every character. The restraints, upon an honorable mind, are as binding, when alone, as they wou'd be, were a man in the midst of the members of the <u>order</u>!

It is now very late at night, and for the reason, that where, and when we stop, we are surrounded by company. When we arrived here it was about sunset, and so soon as they could do so, they began to fire cannon, and how often, I do not know, but it continued for some time. I found Thos Palmer here. He has been in Louisiana, and his family are at Mrs P's[1] Fathers. He will soon return home, and will call and see you!

I did not direct at leaving home, for a sufficiency of cotton seed to be <u>hauled</u>, for the winter, though I mentioned it. You can direct it to be done. I want Mr Gott[2] to have some dubbin got at the Tanners,[3] & have all the carriage, & Buggy harness cleaned, and greased with it. And I wish the carriage, & Buggy so protected, that the weather cannot injure them. There are many things which I did not direct, and arrange, that I will not trouble you with, but write to Mr Gott. I hope my Dearest, the servants will behave well, and that you will have no perplexities with them, nor any thing else!

My mind, or my heart, is continually recuring [sic] to <u>you</u>, the <u>children</u>, and the association of home. Had it not been so, I would have thought the journey more unpleasant than I did. I have made up my mind to submit to absence, if spared, for the time, though I really think the sacrifice, more than, all my success, can ever repay, no matter how great that success may be. I certainly give in advance that which nothing pecuniary could ever purchase of me. Every thing recalls home to me, with all the pleasing associations, and with them are blended, all my regrets, of absence. The balm of hope, then rises in my breast, and casts a ray of delight, in expectation that we will all meet again, and be happy, in the embrace, of pure affections. I will try, and deserve, of our Creator, all that, and [sic] unworthy object can hope for, from a kind, and merciful God! I will not my Love, depart in any thing which you know, I regard, as appointed means, in the path of duty. I will not have it in my power to write again for several days, as we will be on no direct mail route. Give my love to Mother. Kiss the children, and present me to all. Salute our friends. If you think well of it, get Wilson to bring you Mess Pork, and such things as you may wish, or get Messers Smiths,[4] and tell them, to let all be of good quality. Mr Gott will be a good judge, of the articles brought, & if they are not good, do pray let them be returned, and not used. I will try, and send you from New Orleans, "Sugar cured hams." I do not yet know whether, or not we will go by Alabama.

Thy ever devoted
Houston

[1]Rachel Palmer.
[2]Thomas Gott, the Houston's overseer. Llerena Friend, *Sam Houston: The Great Designer* (Austin: University of Texas Press, 1954), 204.
[3]Houston may be referring to the tannery of William S. Dun. Carpenter, 2008.
[4]Huntsville merchants Sam R. and J. C. Smith. Carpenter, 2012.

The following letter from Huntsville merchant Benjamin Wilson is in the Andrew Jackson Houston Collection of Houston Materials at the Texas State Archives Library, Austin, Texas.

Huntsville
November 11th 1848

My dear General

I enclose you our newspaper in which you will see Col Hatch's[1] just remarks touching the speech made by Genl [Memucan] Hunt on the morning of our Presidential Election—You will there also see the result of the Polls. We had no excitement, whatever the Democracy did not turn out, in their strength, being confident of victory they slumbered upon their oars.

Genl Hunt touched upon your "<u>role in the Senate</u>" whereby you thought to render yourself a Southern man with Northern principles with a prospective view to occupying the White House,—But J. M. Maxey Esq. [blurred] him off [blurred].

Our Son, Born last Sunday morning 3:00, has his name registered in our old family Bible, that lays on the stand as follows.

Sam Houston Wilson
(named for Genl. Sam Houston Ex: President of Texas
and Prospectively of the U. S.)
their Son At Huntsville, Walker County Texas
Born November 5th 1848.

Your excellent wife, is well, also all the rest of your household.

Very truly
Benjamin S. Wilson

[1]Francis L. Hatch was the editor of the *Huntsville Banner*. The newspaper clipping has not been located.

Huntsville
Nov. 16th, 1848

My beloved husband,

On monday the 13 inst, I recd yours from Nacogdoches. I rejoiced greatly to learn that you had borne the trip so well, for I had many apprehensions on your account. The bundle came safely to hand. Sam was delighted with his knife, and I with my shoes, but I found it necessary to change them for a larger pair. I am not without fears, that you needed your blanket on the way. The caps fell to Mother, and she was much pleased.

We have been kept closely within doors, for several days, by the rain which had been almost incessant for a week. The children have been noisy prisoners, I assure you, and I have concluded with your consent to have two shed rooms added to the south side of the house. With an entry between, I think it would make the house very pleasant. As it is, we are very much crowded, but I will not think of it, unless I can have it done on reasonable terms.[1] My health is just as it was when you left, except that my cough is considerably increased by the cold damp weather. Sam has had a severe attack of croup, but is now very well. Nannie's cough is better, but she is quite as mischievous as when you left, and you must not expect to find her improved in this respect, when you return, for I think she will always be a perfect romp. Little Maggie improves every day. She seems to have a sweet temper, and I hope she will make us very happy. Sam's care of her is quite fraternal. Mrs Wilson's boy[2] is a noble looking fellow, and appropriately named I think, for he is exceedingly like you. You must be very proud of the name. Her health is uncommonly good. Your friend Gen'l Hunt spent the election day in Huntsville. I presume some of your correspondents in this place have given you an account of it, but lest they should not, I will merely mention that he made a speech in which he handled your Oregon vote rather unceremoniously, and that he was answered by Mr Maxy[3] and exceedingly well lashed. The citizens were very indignant at his insolence. Capt. Fletcher[4] a friend of yours from New Hampshire called on us since your departure, and seemed quite distressed to find that you were gone.

Our home matters seem to be doing well. I think Mr. Gott will be a good manager. He is good tempered I think, but seems positive with the servants. I enclose a note from Mr Wilson to me, not to annoy you, but to put you on your guard. Don't lend any more money, if you can avoid it. Please write to the editor of the "New York recorder," for me, and tell him you will pay his account except for one year. That has been paid. I suppose it was Judge Johnson's[5] fault that the paper has not come to us regularly.

When I think of the waste of months between us, I feel as if I had a dreary pilgrimage to perform, but when I compare it with our last seperation [sic], the time seems to diminish, and I feel as if we would soon meet again. Mother and Sam send thier love to you, and Virginia[6] sends howdy. My love to Mrs [Jane] Graham and your relations, Mr [John] Houston's family. If you get any news from sister Polly,[7] I pray you, let me have it.

Thy ever devoted wife

M. L. Houston

[1]This refers to the Houstons' Huntsville home, still standing, which has two small rooms in back, one behind the bedroom and one behind the parlor. One was Nancy Lea's bedroom and the other was a storage area for china, etc., and was called the dining area. The entire house is part of the Sam Houston Memorial Museum.

[2]Sam Houston Wilson, the son of Benjamin and Jane Wilson, mentioned in the previous letter. Carpenter, 2011.

[3]James Maxey. Identified in Carpenter, 2021.

[4]John Fletcher. Carpenter, 49.

[5]Judge Robert Johnson of Galveston.

[6]Virginia Thorn, (also spelled Thorne), Vernal Lea's ward now living with the Houstons.

[7]Mary Houston Wallace, Houston's sister.

Mouth Red River

18th Nov 1848

My Dearest,

A few hours since we arrived at this place. A part of our journey we had much rain, and this morning it snowed a little. We will wait here in pleasant quarters, until tomorrow morning, and then go by New Orleans, on the Southern route, to the city.[1]

Since we came here we are assured, that Taylor has beaten Cass, and is elected.[2] Well! It can't be prevented, therefore it must be cured!!! We have it to bear, & will not let it distress us. It will cause us, to be laborious, & vigilant, in the discharge of our duties, as Senators, and members of the Party. I will write to Young Royston,[3] and tell him to take out Teen,[4] to stay with you, and mother. If there is any one from Texas in Orleans, that I can trust, I will send you sugar, coffee, Hams, and Mess Pork, If not, you will have to order these things, & such others as you may need, or want. I will send you apples, if they can be sent. If you want things, in the mean time, send by the stage to Houston; they will be obtained there at any time.

I send you some magnolia seeds which you will please have planted in some safe place. I also send you some locust seeds, of a peculiar character—let them be planted carefully. They are a pretty tree. I send you some grass of which you heard me speak. Let it be planted, by covering the roots, or root end of the stalk. I will try, and send you some slips of crape myrtle[5] and mulberry. If they go safe, let them be soaked in water, for twelve hours before planting them. I send you two locks, which I hope will suit you!

I will write to you from every place, where, I make any stop. I wish I were again with you, at our own fireside, with our little ones, and friends around us, and enjoying the society of our friends. Then I could again be happy, and would remain with them!

I wrote to you of my dream, and since then I was fearful that you might think I was in danger of violating my pledge. This I can never do, while I have <u>honor</u>, and my <u>affection</u> for <u>home</u>! My wretchedness, was indescribable, in my dream. Rusks, was rather an amusing dream, than mine.

I want you to say a great deal for me to Sam, and tell me what he says in return. I think my Dear, you will find my papers which I lost in my Big Book, or "Journal of my Administration."[6] If they are, send them to me. Take care of the Book, my Dearest.

Present my love to Mother & kisses, and caresses to the children. Salute Jenny & Mr Gott. Tell the servants, that I hope, they will all do well, and be obedient.

Thy Husband
Houston

[1]Washington, D. C.
[2]General Zachary Taylor had defeated Lewis Cass in the presidential election.
[3]Margaret's nephew, the son of Varilla Lea Royston.
[4]Young's sister, Serena Royston. Her nickname is also spelled Tene in some of the letters.
[5]For a description of where Margaret planted the crape myrtle trees, see Amelia Williams, *Following General Sam Houston* (Austin, Texas: The Steck Company, 1935), 171.
[6]This journal is in the Sam Houston Library and Research Center, Liberty, Texas.

Huntsville
Nov. 18, 1848

My dear Love,

Dr. Carr[1] called today, while I was in town, and left word for me, that he expected to leave early in the morning, and would take pleasure in bearing a letter to you. I did not get home until late this evening, and it is now after supper and excessively cold, but I must say a few words to you, although the present mail contains a letter from me of the 10 inst.[2] After I had mailed my letter, I recd yours from Sabine town, and it was so much more cheering than mine to you, that I thought once of taking it out of the office, but there are times my Love, when I write under such great depression of spirits, owing to my seperation from you, that I can not say any thing cheerful, and the very effort to conceal my feelings seems to chill every thing I write. So if I should be so unfortunate again, as to write in a melancholy mood, you must just take it for what it is worth, and I will try to be cheerful dearest, for I have much to make me so, although I am deprived of my greatest source of earthly happiness, my husband's society.

The "sons of temperance" are to have a celebration here on next saturday, and the ladies are to present them with a flag. I expect we will fix on Mary Rogers to present it. I rejoiced to learn from you, that the cause is so flourishing. I was delighted at what you said about the cider. If you should deliver a temperance address, notice the 31st and 32nd verses of the 23rd chap. of proverbs, and see if you can not make a pretty application of them to cider. You must let me know how the society is progressing in Washington.

We are all well with the exception of colds amongst the children. My own health is much improved since the atmosphere became dry. Sam says "tell pa I am almost reading." As usual he is almost my constant companion. He is so much with me, that I am afraid sometimes he will inherit my <u>nerves</u>. If it should be so, I think he will hardly ever fight a battle.

Speaking of the book of "Proverbs" have you ever noticed the [blurred] verse of the 16th chap.? Read it dearest and reflect upon it every day. As it is late, I will take leave of you. May our Heavenly Father unite our hearts in his love, and may we spend many happy days together in his service.

Thy devoted wife
M. L. Houston

P. S.

The church accepted bro. Creath's[3] resignation today, and agreed to call bro. Talliofereo.[4]

[1]Dr. William Kerr. Carpenter, 438.
[2]No letter from Margaret for this date has been located.
[3]Reverend J. W. D. Creath. Identified in Carpenter, 2011.
[4]R. H. Taliafero. Identified in Z. N. Morrell, *Flowers and Fruits in the Wilderness* (Dallas: W. G. Scarff & Company, 1886), 258–59.

New Orleans
22nd November 1848

My Dear,

To day, I was to have left here, for the City[1] by the Southern route, but was disappointed, owing to my clothes not returning from the washerwomans. This I regretted, because I fear it will prevent me from calling to see our kindred on the way. I will yet do so, if I can! If not I will write, as I said I would do.

I have been quite busy, since I arrived here, and among other things, I sent you some seeds. The Bois d'arc, I want you to have soaked twelve hours, and then planted about two inches deep. Let the Blue grass seed, be planted in a neat bed some where, in the yard, when it is damp or wet weather, and do the same with the clover. Keep the other seeds where the Rats, and Mice can not get to them, until Spring.

Next! I have ordered, for you a Barrel, of fine sugar, (Excellent) one sack coffee (Rio D. Jenairo [sic]) one Bll of apples, one bll sugar cured hams, one bll mess pork, half bll, fine syrup, one dozen jars preserves, one keg Lard, etc. Indeed I do not recollect all but you will get a Bill of them. I send them to Mr Jesse McCreary of Houston. I will write to him, and get him to send them by a safe waggon [sic] with a cover, and a careful hand, that will not steal one half of them. The coffee when you parch it, ought to be made the colour of light mahogany, but not parched so as to burn it. You will get some of the articles spoken of in this letter by mail. I mean the seeds. You will get a piece of oil silk, to <u>use</u> as you may think best. I will send you a pair of shoes, to the care of Mr. McCreary. They are "nice." I hope my Dear, you will be pleased with them all, and I only regret that I can not return with them, my self, and see you in a good humour! If I could only return from here to embrace you, and the dear children, I would be willing to risk the Gulf, and that I do not like.

I need not tell you that Taylor has beaten Cass, by a fair majority. We will bear it calmly, and make no fuss. It is over, and I am content. The Generals troubles, are just beginning. His Cabinet has to be selected, and he can't select one, that will satisfy one half of his friends. The whigs, will be "Tylerised" or I am mistaken. Another matter will be that Mr Clay[2] will again be sent to the Senate, and will not take the best feelings, with him for Gen. Taylor. You may be assured my Dear, that I will "keep cool," and good tempered. Now, about home business, I have something to say. If you have a chance, to make sale of corn, you may sell, as much, as can be spared, if the prices will warrant it. Or it may be well, to let it be, until spring, if the weevils do not injure it. I will send you some arborvile seed, which you can plant. They will grow well, in Sandy land. Soak all your seed, from 12 to 24 hours, if you plant in the spring. In winter they may not require it.

My Dear, I came off, and did not take Sam's measure, for the boots. Send me the measure of his boot sole, <u>exactly</u>. I will close for to night, and retire!!

My Dear, It is thursday morning, Nov 23rd. I have been running about this morning, and will be off in two hours. I have met with Col

Bagby,[3] and by him I will send your shoes. There is no one here from Huntsville, or any of the adjoining villages, so I must rely upon those more remote, to get such articles sent on I may need, for the family. So soon as I reach the city, I will write to Mr Gott, about the Farm. Whenever I can command time, on the way, I will write to you, not that I expect to have any thing of much interest to write, but it will satisfy you of one truth, and that is, that you are hourly, and constantly present with me. Yes, and the children too. I retain the perfect image of all, but Maggy Lea seems, to cling most closely, and tenderly about the heart. It may be that she is most helpless, and therefore had higher claims on nature. I do hope Mr Gott, has had the roof patched, and the seams to the north lathed. I pray for your comfort. By the last steamer I sent you a pair of beautiful French Blankets, to the care of Rice & Nichols.[4] They were Boxed up neatly, and can be sent by the Stage to Huntsville. As to the articles, which I send to Jesse McCreary, Houston, it may be well, to get Col. Birdwell[5] to have them bro't by his waggon. If he shoud [sic] send down, you had best write or get Wilson to write, for McCreary to keep them, until you send an order for them. I hope you will get them all safe, as they are the best, or are to be, that have ever crossed the Gulf.

I have hourly anxieties about home, and would fly there if it were possible to do so. If possible I expect to feel more anxiety, this time than I have done before. It will be some relief to me, if I can call to see our relations,[6] on my route to the city. If I call at all, I will try, and see them at Marion as well as the Cane Brake.[7] If I do not call to see them, I do not intend to intermit one hour on my journey. I wish to be present, at the meeting of Congress.

I have called here to see your Dear Friend Mrs Christy.[8] She was delighted to hear from you, & desires to be presented most kindly to you. I just thought how happy she wou'd have been, if I could have told her, that you had a namesake for her. I suppose now there is no chance! Dont you recollect of what Mother said about Mrs Gray?[9] That almost alarmed me. When I arrive at the city, I will expect to hear something about matters. I have been so long distanced, that I hope to meet several letters from you!

13 : NOVEMBER 9, 1848—NOVEMBER 4, 1849

I will just note in conclusion that I have sent to Cuba for some pure tobacco seed! Tell Mr Gott that I will want it planted in the new ground between & town [sic], and the negroes have an equal amount, for their patch in some part of the field, where it will be more rich, and the sandy soil will be the best for Cuba Tobacco. The new ground will be enough for the potatoes, and Tobacco. There should also be in the Garden, some potatoes. But I hope to be at home in time for them!! A thousand kisses to our dear little ones. Love to Mother, and my regards to all friends. Do write every week!

I am faithfully thy devoted husband

Sam Houston

[1]Washington, D. C.
[2]Henry Clay of Kentucky.
[3]Thomas M. Bagby, a Houston merchant.
[4]A Houston merchant firm.
[5]Thomas Birdwell. Carpenter, 2020.
[6]Members of the Lea family still living in Alabama.
[7]The plantation home of the Roystons, located about twenty miles from Marion, Alabama.
[8]Catherine (Mrs. William) Christy of New Orleans.
[9]Houston is probably referring to Hannah Gray, a neighbor of the Moore family. Carpenter, 2029.

Huntsville
Nov. 28, 1848

My ever dear Love,

Since I wrote you last, I have recd yours from Hinestown, L. A. [sic] I thank you for your three welcome letters, and I feel humbly grateful to my Heavenly Father, for taking care of you thus far. I was greatly pained at your departure, and our family board and fireside seem desolate indeed without you, but the Lord sustains me, and I will put all my trust in Him. My friends as usual during your absence use every effort to comfort me and cheer me. Mr and Mrs Maxy,[1] Mrs Birdwell,[2] and Mrs. Evans[3] dined with me today and your name was not forgotten I assure you. I have many kind words for you, from your friends, but I can not attempt to repeat them all. Mrs.

Simms[4] requested me to say to you, that she regretted very much that she and the Capt[5] had not an opportunity of coming over before you left. Mrs. Branch[6] and Mrs. Wadkins[7] who have each spent an evening with me since you left, both requested to say the same to you for themselves and husbands.

The sons of temperance had quite a celebration here on last saturday. The ladies presented them with a flag and bible, and but for some dissappointments [sic] it would have been a joyful occassion [sic] to all. It was an understanding with the ladies, that Mary Rogers (our beautiful little Mary) was to present the flag and Arianna Simms the bible, but on the day that it was to have been arranged, Mrs. Parish[8] invited Isabella Moore to present the flag and Kate Banton the bible, who immediately accepted, and the result was they officiated.

That was an unpleasant dream of yours. Thank Heaven it "was all a dream." I have no fears that such a reality will ever blast our happiness and that of our children. But I must not forget to tell you that amongst other speeches that were made on saturday, your friend Wade,[9] delighted every body. It was fine I assure you. He ought to be an eloquent advocate of temperance. I had prepared a speech myself for Mary [Rogers], but as you will infer, it did not get a hearing. To quote a certain friend of ours, "It was the best thing I ever wrote!" But the world knows not that it had lost any thing, for I had never written it down.

I am afraid you have been troubled lest I should undertake the addition to our house, and thereby involve myself in perplexity. When I found what it would cost, I gave it up. It was impossible too, to get lumber at this time. Our paling is nearly finished and add[s] much to the appearance of the yard.

I hope you will not be greatly distrest [sic] if Taylor should realy be elected. If [Mirabeau B.] Lamar had not skill enough to ruin poor little Texas, have no fears of what Taylor can do, but I am so poor a politician, that an argument that would comfort me entirely could probably seem like the prattle of a babe to you. Do you remember my dream about the map?[10] I believe that will yet be realized. One thing is certain. There is a great and wise being, who holds the nation in his hands, and directs thier councils to the ultimate promotion of his own glory. This is my politics, and I want no better.

We are all enjoying fine health. I am improving daily, and lest I should have alarmed you about my lungs, I will say something on that subject. As to my being consumptive, in my own opinion it is not so. Therefore my presentments for the present are at an end. Mother is well and cheerful and often speaks of you most affectionately. Nannie has just been with me and says in good english, "let me write a letter to Gen'l Houston." Maggy is a perfect little charmer and begins to say "papa." Sam is still grave and thoughtful, not very pretty—but to me very interesting. Do write often and as much as you can conveniently.

Thine affectionately
M. L. Houston

P. S. Virginia sends howdy.

[1]Virginia (Mrs. James) Maxey. Carpenter, 2021.
[2]Tirza (Mrs. Thomas G.) Birdwell. Ibid., 2020.
[3]Manura (Mrs. J. W.) Evans. Carpenter, 2023.
[4]Mary Sims. Carpenter, 2018.
[5]T. S. Sims. Ibid.
[6]Mariah (Mrs. John) Branch. Carpenter, 2010.
[7]Cloana (Mrs. Henry M.) Wadkins. Carpenter, 2021.
[8]Katherine (Mrs. W. A.) Parish. Carpenter, 2020.
[9]John W. Wade. Carpenter, 2011.
[10]The editor continues to be puzzled by references to Margaret's "map" dream, because the original letter explaining the dream has not yet been located.

Houston reached Washington on December 2, 1848. The next day he wrote Margaret describing his difficult journey. In that previously published letter, he spoke of mail received including a letter from Benjamin S. Wilson informing him that the Wilsons had named their son Sam Houston.[1]

[1]For the text of this letter see *Writings,* vol. 5, 62–63. See Wilson to Houston, November 11, 1848.

Huntsville
Dec. 5th, 1848

My dear love,

It is a cold and rainy day, and I am compelled to sit closely in the corner and write in my lap, but I know you will make every allowance for my almost illegible writing, for such I fear it will be. I imagine that every kind of weather would be delightful, if you were here to share it. Sitting together by our own fireside, we could draw something interesting, even from the cold dark clouds and the deep-toned thunder whose distant mutterings are heard occassionly through the pattering rain. But such is not the will of him "who seeth not as man seeth," and we must "be still and know that he is God." We are all enjoying good health at this time. After the chill that I mentioned to you, I took a course of medicine, by which I was much benefited. Sam is growing finely, and as he insists so much upon it, I suppose I must tell you, that he is beginning to read a little. He is by no means a close student, but I do not wish him to study long enough at one time to weary him. He says "Ma, if you will tell pa that I am a good boy, I will be good." Nannie improves in mischief daily, but she is very affectionate. Our sweet little Maggie, the little violet, is so lovely, that I know not how to describe her. We have lately recd letters from Cany,[1] and I expect from them that Antoinette and Charles [Power] will make us a visit next month.

Mr. Jo Ellis arrived yesterday from Liberty. All well below. Amanda Smith (Carrol's sister) is with me at this time, and I expect she will remain several days with me. I am at no loss for company I assure you, and some of the girls I expect will always be with me. Col and Mrs Birdwell and thier daughter Elizabeth spent night before last with us. The latter is much improved since she left home, limited as her opportunities have been. She is very sensible and sprightly. I expect I shall remain quietly at home, the greater part of the time that you are away, for I am growing more and more timid and nervous. Could you not get some of the Yankees to invent me an automation horse and buggy? I fear it is the only chance for me.

I learn from the "Recorder" that your friend Mr Sampson[2] is returned to Washington. I am glad of it, for I know that it will add to your happiness, if your public duties will allow you time to converse with him. Do if you please hint to him as delicately as possible how delighted I should be, to see something from the Holy Land, though it be but a withered leaf or flower. Sam is delighted with his description of the caves at Bethlehem, and says when he gets to be a man, he hopes he will go there himself.

Thursday 7th

It became so cold that I was compelled to lay aside my writing, and hover over the fire. I have never seen such weather in Texas. The ground is covered with snow an inch thick, and the trees are hung with icicles. It is still snowing and sleeting alternately, but the sun peeps out occassionly, and promises better times. Yesterday your truly welcome favours of the 22nd and 23rd arrived. I can not tell you how happy I was to recieve [sic] them. The garden seed came to hand, and I suppose the supplies which you were so kind as to get will soon be here. I had sent for the same things by Mr Wilson, (and a good many others as you will suppose by the amount which the draft calls for,) but I expect he will meet with yours in Houston, and will only get such things for me as you have not sent. By the Bye—I will give up my share of presents this winter—to little Sam Houston Wilson (vous comprenez!) He is an extraordinary boy, and you will be delighted with him. We are all well. Nannie says "tell pa come home," and Sam says "now ma would you tell him sure enough?" Maggy calls for you more frequently than any one else, and very earnestly too.

Thy devoted wife,
[M. L. Houston]

P. S. Once more dearest please write a line to the New York Recorder for me and pay him only for one year which has been paid and if you think well give pay for next year. (which will make four years, to be paid for.) Refer him to Mr [James] Huckins who obtains the receipt for me. *[In margin:]* Think of Dr. Jones[3] now.

[1]Grand Cane.
[2]Reverend George W. Samson of the E. Street Baptist Church.
[3]Anson Jones.

Senate Chambers
6th Dec. 1848

Dearest,

We are in the onset of business, and so far as things have been developed, we are to look for a good humored session. Except so far as I am to attend to my letter matters, with Mr Calhoun,[1] I feel that I will have a peaceful time of it. Variety wou'd help to beguile my time, but I must assure you, that it is pleasure to me to reflect, that one fifth of the time of my contemplated absence has already transpired. You have some idea my Dearest of my devotion to home. You may, & do suppose that your anxieties are more, & greater than mine, but this, I will controvert if we live to meet again. You are at home, and enjoy the presence, & prattle, of our dear little ones. And you enjoy the pleasing task of instructing our dear Boy, and inducing his mind, with high moral, and intellectual feeling. This is a task, more noble, & more worthy, than I have to perform in the discharge of my official duties. And I assure you my dear, that I would be much more happy, than I now am, if I could share with you the delightful employment. I will be pained until I can be released from matters here. The Democrats, are very quiet, and say, "If we had only run Houston, we would not have been beaten." Such are the speculations, and even these my dear, do not create in me a single regret. Nor will I even desire the place, if it can by any means, diminish the prospects of my domestic happiness, or impair your health. I reflect on the chilling contrast, between your embrace, the embrace of a wife, and the chilling embrace of a Norther, which I had to encounter, when parting with you, the next moment. It was a sad, and unpleasant day, for me, nor had I much cheerfulness, on my journey. If there is any thing amusing or entertaining in the city, I can not tell you of it, for I was not even at the Drawing Room last night, nor have I presented my homage to Mrs Polk.[2] This I should have done, and must before long do so. I am sorry that I have not yet received a letter from you, since my arrival. I hope I will in the course of to day. I hope you will write to me, at least once every week. I will not fail to write to you, and as often, as I can I will write to our dear lad!

I think often of our dear little daughters, and my heart melts, at the helplessness of our little Maggy Lea. Indeed, I do not think it extravagant when I say, that more than one half of my waking hours, are given to meditation about you, and the children! I know that according to your notions (at one time) I ought to think all the while, or it wou'd be evidence, that I did not love you, as I ought to do. I will write no more on this subject at present, but hope to settle it amicably when we meet!!! Sam, poor fellow will think, that I ought to regard him a double portion. As I go to my room I must procure, and send him a pictorial Paper. I will send you any, and every thing that may be in my power, which I think will gratify, or be useful for you. As for Miss Nannie, she dont care about any thing, long at a time. I will send you soon some seeds, as you know, you talk of apples, and fruits. Every fine apple, or orange that I eat, or can get, I will send you the seeds of. Others, I will also send, so that they can be planted, during winter, in some suitable place for a <u>nursery</u>. You can make choice of the place, and when I send grapes to sow, that can be done by Mr Gott.

To day, I will send you the Presidents message,[3] but I am fearful, you will not read it, or would even do it, without annoyance, if it were mine. It is <u>so</u> long, (as Sam would say,) that you will think it tedious. Do by all means, hand it over to Mother, for a half hours amusement, of an evening.

Ever thy devoted
Houston

[1]Senator John C. Calhoun of South Carolina.
[2]Sarah Childress Polk.
[3]For information on Polk's message see James K. Polk, *Polk: The Diary of a President, 1845–1849.* . . . Allan Nevins, ed. (New York: Longman, Green and Company, 1929), 355.

Huntsville
Dec. 12, 1848

My ever dear Love,

After a long spell of cold and gloomy weather, the sun has shown out again, and we are all as cheerful and happy as we can be without you. The snow was on the ground several days. Sam was quite ambitious to make tracks upon it, and he enjoyed it finely I assure you. He had heard you talk about running in the snow when you were a boy, and I think he had taken up the idea that he could never be a man until he had done the same. His mind develops so rapidly, that I sometimes feel alarmed on account of it, but if it were a settled thing that remarkable genius foretold an early death, I suppose all parents would be unhappy. I for one, must confess that I would expect soon to become childless.

Dearest, you can not imagine what a feast you were preparing for me, when you brought me "D'Aubigne's history of reformation."[1] In the days of girlish romance, I never poured over any tales of fiction with so much delight. If you can possibly find time to read it, do get another copy. (we can present it to some poor family you know,) and please mark the passages which strike you most, as I am doing, and when you return we will compare them. I am inclined to think they will be the same. Some of Luther's trials were so similar to your own, though in a different field, that it accounts to me in part, for the interest with which I read this work. I know you will be so delighted with it, that even while I am reading it, I feel as if you were at my side and sympathising with me. I recommend it to you as an antidote against Sunday visitors. If any persons call, read it aloud to him, and I dare say the most of your visitors would soon excuse themselves.

The [blurred] piety and holy austerity of Luther would soon repulse a fashionable trifler. Read it my love, and I have great hopes, that the same spirit which brought the great reformer out of darkness into marvelous light, will dawn upon your soul and fill your heart with Heavenly peace.

I recd the package of seeds and will comply with your directions. I searched in the record book for the papers which you mentioned, but could not find them. If you can think of any other place in which they may be, mention it, and I will continue the search. You left some land matters for me to attend to, but no one has yet called to see me about them. I presume they will do so, in due time.

I think you will be pleased at Mr Gott's attention to business. He is industrious, pious and attentive to his duties. There is not the least difficulty with the servants, but every thing moves on like well ordered machinery.

Betty Culp[2] spent a night with me last week on her way to Galveston. She gave me a glowing account of the few minutes you stopped with them. Dearest, why did you not wait and go up to San Augustine in Mrs. Terril's[3] carriage? What a want of gallantry. But I will forgive you Love, as you were in a great hurry!

Sam grows more interesting every day. Nannie is more humourous and amusing, and Maggie seems to me lovelier every moment. To my eye, it is a rare assemblage of genius and beauty and I am quite sure that thier dear papa would not [sic] agree with me. Mother still thinks Nannie the beauty of the family, and perhaps she is. It is a difficult thing for a mother to decide.

The sons of temperance expect to celebrate your return with a great feast.[4] It is to be a rare thing, and some of the ladies wish me to get you to purchase the materials in Washington for a flag to be present on the occasion. It will be easily paid for as every one will wish to have a hand in it. We want crimson, blue and white satin with silver fringe. But you need not trouble yourself about it for some weeks yet. Before you return, I will make out a list of what we want. Since I commenced writing, I have heard that Harrison[5] will not survey the Palmer League until he recieves a hundred dollars for it. Had you not better let it rest until you return? Write often dearest. You may expect a letter from me once a week.

Thine ever
M. L. Houston

Mother sends her love to you.

[1] The location of Margaret's copy of *The History of the Reformation* by Jean Henry Merle d'Aubigne is unknown.

[2] Elizabeth Thilman Culp, the daughter of Margaret's friend Eugenia Andrews.

[3] Ann (Mrs. George Whitfield) Terrell.

[4] The celebration was held July 4, 1849. For Houston's acceptance of the invitation see Houston to H. Yoakum, William Lehr, and G. W. Rogers, May 10, 1849. *Writings,* vol. 5, 93–94.

[5] Margaret is probably referring to William Harrison of Danville. Identified in Johnnie Jo Dickenson,*Walker County, Texas 1850–1860 Census* (Huntsville, Texas: Dickenson Research, 1989), 117.

Washington
16th Dec 1848

My Dearest,

For three days, I have waited for a letter from you, as a second one. It has not reached me, but I hope, more than one, or two, are on the way for me. It is a month to day since your last was dated at home. I feel all the anxiety, that a Lover can do, and if possible, more than I did, before, I called you mine.

I send you a news paper from Memphis, in which you will find quite a Romance about Parson Maffitt.[1] I have marked the two chapters. I do not ask you to read it. That is as you may please! In high life they have some envious fancies, that I do not admire. These "marriage settlements" are not the best family (as Sam would say) "quieters," in the world!

Well, in the same paper you will see a ridiculous piece, about your dear Husband. "Three score"—just think of that!!!![2] The fellow is a simpleton, but does no harm. Every one declares that I look, as young, as I did fifteen years ago. My health is finer and my complexion better, than you have ever seen me wear. It is because, I take nothing but water as a beverage. Not even Cider, nor will I, so long as I have sense, or reasons. You may if you please quarrel with me, for I have been economical, and saved all that I can, and then just went and laid it all out in purchasing a pretty cloak, for my dear wife, and hope in two days to send it to you, by Mr. Cordova[3] of Houston. Now you may scold if you will, until I come home, for you know I wont hear you. I hope you will be pleased with it. It was my own fancy a man milliner made it, and I do not know that a woman ever saw it. I intended it to be plain, neat, convenient, useful, and comfortable. What else could I have designed than these enumerated points? I may by the time I can send it, find some other little matters for you! Oh my Love, I would be so happy, if I could only be present when, you put on the cloak for the first time. It is, as you will perceive quite roomy, and the arms, will not be confined. These expressions (accidentally), are all technical, and dont snub me, for their use, my Love!!!

No doubt, you have seen "my friend Anson Jones' late developments."[4] I pray you not, my Dear, to think any thing of them, or of his course. It does not injure me, but it will ruin him. For myself, I am glad, that it has come out at this time, as it will be of use to Texas, in adjusting her boundary. Jones intended to injure me by it, and has tried to play a base, dishonorable part. All the merit which he claims, is from his perfidy to me, in not executing my order, as he was bound to do, and I will be able, without trouble, to show that it was one of the most statesmanlike acts, of my whole career in official station.

I will be in no hurry, about the matter. If comments here are made, in the papers, I will send them to you as they appear! Some say "Jones was affraid [sic], that he would be forgotten," and others say that "his only wish was to attain immortality by associating his name, with that of Genl Houston." And all believe, and many say, that "Houston made him President of Texas, as much so as Genl [Andrew] Jackson made Mr [Martin] Van Buren President of the U States."[5] You will see, that he is a ruined man, in Texas. He never had much substantive character in Texas, and this will throw him, on his own resources. I am fearful that you will have seen his publication, and be distressed by it, supposing it will affect me. I suppose he was like Henderson,[6] thought he was <u>stout</u> enough to stand at putting me down! He is not the fortieth man, that tried that in Texas, and I really think, he will find that a common fate, awaits those who are less honest, and less "<u>lucky</u>" than myself! Poor Miller[7] will be in a sad state of mind about the matter. Tell Sam all of it, and write to me what he says! I mean tell him, of the ingratitude, and malevolence, of the Doctor [Jones], in your own way, so that he will understand it. I think Sams relationship a part [sic], has manly, and honorable perception, and principle enough to condemn the act! I think he (Jones) will run for Congress, and it is probable, that he was displeased with me, because I did not unite in his favor, to beat Genl Rusk[8] for the Senate. If this is not the cause, I can assign none other. I will dismiss this subject for I declare to you, it has not even provoked me to anger. You will be gratified, at this, I am sure!!!

I have spun you out a long yarn, and as winter evenings are long, and you will have time to read it, you can bear with me! So I have now only to tell you, how dearly, and devotedly I love you, and how anxious I am to embrace you, and the <u>little treasures</u> of life. Since I can not see you all, my greatest happiness, is to hear from you, and to pray for you, in this world, and that which is to come. My love to Mother, & all.

Thy ever devoted husband
Houston

Our friends here all send love to you, and a thousand enquiries, are made for you, and the "little fellows!"
My Love, I have a beautiful purse to send to you. I have not heard from the Roystons.

[1]Reverend John Newland Maffit.
[2]This paper may be quoting an unidentified story from the *New York Sunday Times* which is said to have reported, "He is a fine looking man, and would not be taken for more than 50 years of age, although he must be near 60." See *The Houston Chronicle*, July 23, 1939, "Many a Story is Found in These Old Papers on Famed Leader."

25 : November 9, 1848—November 4, 1849

[3]Jacob de Cordova, a land agent from Houston. Carpenter, 938.

[4]Jones, in a letter to the editor of the San Antonio *Western Texian* published November 17, 1848, complained of misrepresentations on the subject of the annexation of Texas, claiming for himself the credit for its accomplishment and accusing Houston of conniving with England and France to the prejudice of Texas interests. Friend, 192.

[5]For information about Jackson's relationship with Van Buren see Paul I. Wellman, *The House Divided: The Age of Jackson and Lincoln from the War of 1812 to the Civil War* (Garden City: Doubleday, 1966), 182.

[6]Governor James Pinckney Henderson. For a biography see *Handbook of Texas,* vol. 1, 795–96.

[7]Washington D. Miller, Houston's secretary.

[8]Thomas Jefferson Rusk, Senator from Texas.

Washington
19th Dec 1848

My beloved,

Your favor of the 28th of November has just reached me, and I am happy. I had looked for a letter every week from you, and I was to write, as often as I had time, or opportunity. You will by this time have seen that I have complied, in all sincerity, writing from every point on my journey, and since my arrival here. I was sure that you were ill, or that some sad calamity had fallen upon you, and was greatly depressed. I had nevertheless, gone with Mr De Cordova, & purchased a trunk, to put your cloak in with some trifling articles—a purse with a 5$ gold piece in it—a knitting ring, with a hook to hitch in the Ball of yarn, and one in clothes—put the ring on the wrist. I send you two silk caps, to keep, or dispose of, as you please. I send you some butter nuts to plant, or if not all a part of them. Let them be soaked eight & forty hours, and then not planted more than four inches deep. Then I have sent you a few yards of gutta percha, in which your cloak is folded. You may keep it for <u>another</u> occasion,[1] or use a part of it, now. Believing as I do, that you will be gratified with an appropriate present, I have selected for you a tasty "Box"[2] as a Christmas present. As it is a <u>box</u>, you will not I am sure fall out with the present, if you do not fall out with the manner of presenting it. I am greatly hurried, and must soon cease writing. Mr De Cordova will set out in a few minutes. I will write until time to seal my letter.

I have been called on, by the Sons of Temperance to make a speech in their Hall, but as yet I have not consented, altho I am sure no one is more zealous, than myself. I dreamed the other night, that by some means, which [I] could [not] understand, I had violated my pledge, and was in the greatest agony of mind. At last, I thought I wou'd commit <u>suicide</u>, as my only relief, when I awoke,—in perspiration, but to my great joy, as you may suppose! I have [no] wish, nor have I any fear, but I am rather, an enthusiast, in the cause, and whenever I can do so, I laud the Institution, as one, only second to Christianity, on earth, and it is a bright path, to that high estate of mortals! I would not taste one drop of cider, or any thing containing alcohol, for the honors of this world, or all the "Gold of California." Nor while Heaven grants to me reason, and my faculties, I do not fear that I ever will be less than I am, or have been in morality, and propriety of conduct.

My Dearest, I have noted your Temperance celebration matters, and wish that I could have been there, but I assure you that I would not have in any way interfered, with the prerogative of Mrs P.[3] in her arrangements. I am only sorry, that I have a niece [Isabella Moore], whose qualities render her a favorite of the Lady. Poor silly souls. Now [what] will be the consequence? Why, Sims family and Rogers' will both be mortified, and become hostile to our kindred, and Mrs P. is to be the agent, of all mischief, in the neighborhood. As for Miss Kate,[4] <u>she is a hardy</u>, and <u>sound</u> Gal. I have nothing to say, as I hope they will not be able to induce our niece to go to the stage. Tho' I assure you, I will not let her know that I do not wish it lest she should do it to mortify me.—and you also! The Dear little Girls, it would have been so obliging, and merited to them. It would have been a cheerful, and happy image to have dwelt up. Of all <u>simpletons</u> the greatest are overgrown Simpletons. Pray who was the Gentleman, who received the Flag? That may account for the freak, and officiousness of Mrs P. as the friend, of the young Ladies.

Do my Dearest, keep our <u>scion</u> from that Ladies wild olive tree, and its branch!!!!

I will my Love soon write more fully on this matter, and others. Look my dearest in the 6th chap. & 3rd verse of 1st Corinthians, and there you can <u>answer</u> Sam's question! As to the Agents being judged! My love to all. Tell Virginia, that I have a present for her, if I live to reach home.

Tell Mr Gott, that I wish him a Happy New Year.

Tell the Servants howda, and salute our valued friends.

I send a Book by the mail.—a Patent office Report. You [will] find it useful, for many things. Love, will you write once a week?

Thy affectionate Husband

Sam Houston

P.S. I have not had time to look over this letter. You have not yet said to me that a certain matter "is so," or "not so."!!![5]

Thine Ever

Houston

---

[1] Houston is referring to the fact that gutta percha, an insulation material made from the gum of a Malaysian tree, was used to clothe infants.

[2] This box, described as "Margaret Houston's workbox," is now in the Texas Memorial Museum, Austin, Texas.

[3] Katherine Parish. For information concerning the Sons of Temperance celebration, see Margaret's letter of November 18 and 28, 1848.

[4] Kate Banton.

[5] Houston is asking if Margaret is pregnant.

Huntsville

Dec. 19 1848

My beloved husband,

It is my regular day to write to you, and I take great pleasure in acknowledging the reception of yours from Charleston.[1] On last night, it came to hand, and I was delighted to learn that you were so near the end of your journey. Long before this I suppose you have entered upon your arduous duties. I feel deeply for you, when I think of the tiresome routine that awaits you day after day. How much happier you might be with your little band at home! Ah will it ever be our blessed privilege to enjoy each other's society without the painful consciousness, that it must be but for a few days! My loneliness is greatly relieved by the prattle of our little ones, but you have nothing but the great world about you, with its heartlessness and mockery of joy. I refer to worldly comforts, but I am enjoying the sweet belief dearest, that you will draw from the word of God, from prayer and meditation, rich consolation, which "the world can neither give nor take away." Oh what would I be without those blessed privileges! The more I examine myself, the more I see my own worthlessness! Oh my Love, let us never suffer a day to pass without employing the means which the Lord has given us to advance our souls in holiness.

Have you heard of Lucy Ann Lea's[2] conversion? A brother[3] of Mr Parish's[4] lately from Marion states that he saw her baptized before he left, but we have not yet received a letter on the subject. I had forgotten in my two last to notice your request not to interfere in Mr Creath's case.[5] A request from you is second only to a duty enjoined by my Heavenly Father, but your letter came after the conference was over. I had determined to take no part in the matter, but strange as it may seem, a large number of the new members determined to take things into thier own hands and retain him in the face of all the members could say. Thier sympathy had become excited for him, and it required a powerful effort of the part of them who disapproved his course, to get rid of him, for I can use no milder expression. Bro. [R. H.] Talliaferro was called, but almost without hope of his coming. It was done merely to keep out the other. My heart is deeply grieved for my beloved church. I can now understand the sad feelings of Jeremiah when he mourned the desolation of Zion. But the Lord will not suffer the cloud to rest upon us always, Ah no, there are too many praying spirits amongst us.

The temperance cause is still flourishing. Mr. Jo[seph] Ellis is to be initiated tonight. He has been waiting several days partly on that account, and partly to ascertain if there were any truth in the reports that Miss McMillan[6] and Mr W. Reeves[7] were soon to be married. We are all in good health. Dear little Maggy has been very low with the winter fever, but through the blessing of God she is now convalescent. Nannie says "I want my pa come home." Sam says I must tell you he will do all you say. Mother sends her love.

Dearest farewell
Thine own
M. L. Houston

[1] No letter from Charleston (probably the last week of December, 1848) has been located.
[2] The daughter of Margaret's brother Henry Lea.
[3] Elam Parish, who lived near the Henry Clinton Lea family. For more information on the Parish family see Perry County Historical and Preservation Society, *Perry County Heritage,* vol. 2 (Marion, Alabama: Published privately, 1991), 64.
[4] W. A. Parish. Identified in Carpenter, 2020.
[5] The Baptist Church was in a controversy over replacing the minister.
[6] Caroline McMillion. Identified in Carpenter, 2012.
[7] William Reeves. Ibid. They were married on December 28, 1848. Carolyn Reeves Ericson and Frances Ingmire, *Walker County, Texas Marriage Records 1846–1856* (Nacogdoches, Texas: Ericson Books, 1985), 5.

Washington
20th Dec 1848

My Dearest,

I was just about to retire to bed, when I opened a letter from our friend Wilson, which I will return to you to keep until we meet. My Love, I ordered Groceries and every thing, (or such things as I supposed you would want,) except flour, from Orleans. Let him take his articles when they come, and do you draw on Rice & Nichols, for $175.00 in favor of Col Wilson. I can not pay the Draft here, but my dear Love, I do not blame you, in the least. I have to ride hard two, or three miles to the Steam Boat, to see and overtake Mr De Cordova to send this letter by him. I may be to blame for all this. Wilson will not <u>do</u>, but I will not fall out with him. If you can avoid it, my Love, do not buy a pennys worth from him. Draw in his favor on Rice & Nichols as I above stated. They wrote to you to draw upon them, and the letter came to me, and tomorrow I will send it to you by mail.

I am troubled by Wilson very much, but I pray you my Dear, not to mind it. Since I wrote in the early part of the night, I received another letter from you of the 18th Nov by Dr [William Kerr], and another is refered [sic] to of the 10th not rec'd. I am in great distress, about your indisposition as stated in your note, on Wilson's letter. It is in my papers, on the table, and there is such a bundle that I cannot lay my hand on it now, as I have no time. It has a date on [sic] 3rd Dec since your last letter to me, on its back. You can not trust our friend Wilson in money matters of buying for you.

Don't be unhappy. I will do nothing wrong in these matters.

Thy devoted Husband
Sam Houston

1 o'clock A.M.
This is written in great haste. Excuse the scroll [sic].

H.

Washington
25th Dec 1848

My Dearest,

I salute you, with all the affection of a devoted husband, and with our dear children, embrace you in my hearts core. I would with my whole heart be with you in person, if it were possible, but as I can not do so, I will (if possible) dedicate more of my thoughts to you than usual. If this can be done, it is because I will not allow business to intrude upon my meditations, & recollections of home.—Yes, my Dear, our Woodland home. This is a day of excitement, and much <u>cheer</u> in this place, as I am told. It is now past one oclock, and I have not been out of the house to day. I was in the <u>parlor</u>, and was greatly insisted upon, to take egg <u>nog</u>, or apple <u>toddy</u>. Well my Dear, you can imagine my reply. "I am a Son of Temperance, and will not drink any thing." So strong, is my resolve, and my purpose so firm, that I would as soon, take <u>arsenic</u>, as any thing containing alcohol! The weather is harsh, and cloudy, or rather, it is drisling [sic] rain.

I have promised to dine out to day with Mrs. [Elizabeth] Watson,[1] and the company will be Gen'l Rusk, & myself with the family. *[An*

X *is inserted here with the notation* "26th" *placed in the margin.]*
There is, and I am sorry to see it, much dissipation, in the city. Since this time last year, there has been, and no doubt will continue to be, much reformation. I am not a zealot, my Love, but if I do speak, as I have been requested, I will try all that is in my power to make converts to the cause, for really I do think, it the greatest auxiliary, to human happiness, save the Christian Religion! To it, we may regard <u>Temperance</u> as a hand maid! Here, there never has been any enthusiasm, about the subject. If it is once started, there is a glorious field for it here.

You may be assured my Love, that so long as I live, I will omit no proper occasion, to influence, so far as may be in my power, the cause of Temperance, and if I may be worthy, the cause of Religion! For some days I have not received a letter but hope, that some of <u>those</u>, on the way, may reach me soon! I can only offer to you my dear, the assurance, that I love you, (if possible) more than I ever did before. I will write soon again. I will send you some Lavender, and some seed of the same! Soak the roots for forty eight hours before planting, and the seed twenty four. My love to all, and many happy Holidays.

Thy ever devoted
Houston

[1]The widow of Thomas Watson, one of Andrew Jackson's advisers.

Washington
26th Dec 1848

My Dearest,

I finished a letter to you, this morning in which, I mentioned the Lavender enclosed with this note. The seed did not come, as I expected. When it does, I will be happy to send it. I will get a great variety of flower seeds for you, if I can, and I advise you always to soak them from 24 to 48 hours, in water a little warm, or not cold. In the sun shine in a pleasant day, would make it warm enough. If you would like them my Dear, you can plant almonds, and they will do well in Texas. I will try, and get you some english walnuts to plant. They will grow as well in our country as the black walnut. If the Lavender should not live, no matter, it will stand but a poor chance, to do well, as it will be so long, without moisture.

I have no interesting news to write you, since morning. If any news occurs, I will try, and so economise [sic] my time, as to be able to write you, on all interesting occasions. I have enforced my rule, so as to command my evening and admit no one to my room, only in the morning. Rusk says he will do the same. My Love, I state with pleasure, that he intends to join the "Sons of Temperance." He did not taste any thing during the recess, while in Texas, nor has he tasted a drop since his return to Congress. This is private! For if I were to say any thing about the matter, it might be thought, that there had been formerly, some ground of complaint! He is a noble, & useful man! You will see that there is some excitement, on the subject of slavery in Congress.[1] You may rest assured that I will not inadvisably, involve myself in any foolish scrape. Calhoun[2] is mad, and vicious, on the subject. I will watch him, as I would an adder! He is a bad man, and all his views are selfish. I trust there will be enough, of good men, and true, to save the Union! I do see something of your dream,[3] beginning to shadow forth, its interpretation. I will apprise you, of any important phase, if any should take place, so soon as it results!

I assure you my dear, that I have a right good will to write you a love letter some time, and at this very time, if I were now at the commencement of this letter! But I am fearful, it would make you sad, from sympathy. You once were pleased with them, in part, and now we would have threefold reasons, to sanction, a long correspondence. These reasons my Love are so manifest, and so plausible, that I hope you will approve of them, if now others were adduced, which if desirable may yet be done!!! My highest earthly wish, my Dear, is to see you happy, and whatever, will conduce to that end, will be my pleasure. Present Mother my best regards. Love to all.

Thy devoted

Houston

[1]Abraham Lincoln was proposing to restrict and gradually abolish slavery in the District of Columbia. Friend, 194.

[2]John C. Calhoun in August had advocated that South Carolina take the lead in organizing a Southern party to deliver an ultimatum to the North, and follow that action, if necessary, by secession. Ibid., 193–94. For Calhoun's views on slavery see Margaret L. Coit, *John C. Calhoun: American Portrait* (Boston: Houghton Mifflin Company, 1950), 453–54.

[3]Houston is referring to a previously mentioned dream concerning a map of the United States.

Huntsville

Dec. 26th 1848

My Love,

How has this hallowed season found you? In the enjoyment of health, I trust, and with a heart full of humble joy and gratitude to God, for the gift of his precious son. Yesterday was a quiet day with me, but a pleasant one. I know you will suppose I had some agreeable conversation with our dear son, and you are not mistaken. Dearest his questions astonish me. I hardly know what to make of him. Two days ago, I was reading to him the 18th ch. of exodus, and he was delighted with the account of Jethro the Midianite. "Ma" said he, "When Jethro offered his sacrifice, did he think the Lord Jesus would come down some day and die for his sins?" I felt reproved for the indifference with which I had read the narrative, and I do not believe I will ever again think of that wilderness offering, without discerning the Lord's body. It may be that the Lord will honour his poor servant by allowing me to train a labourer for his vine-yard, and it may be that his genius is to ripen in Eternity. May I have no will but that of My Heavenly Father!

The things which you sent from New Orleans arrived last night, all in excellent order.[1] The apples were almost entirely sound, and the children enjoy them finely, I assure you. The boots suited me exactly. I am glad to see that you remember the size of my foot so well. Every thing that you mentioned came to hand.

There is nothing new or interesting in our vicinity, except that several weddings are to take place shortly. Your poor friend Joe [Ellis] is to have his prospects blighted on next thursday if Miss McMillan and Mr Reeves are to be married. It is said Miss [Kate] Banton and Roundtree[2] will soon marry. I am not acquainted with the others. We will soon be looking for sister A[ntoinette] and Mr [Charles] Power with thier boy.[3] Oh how much your presence would add to the enjoyment of our circle. Dr. [William F.] Evans has not yet returned, but Mrs [Jemima] Evans's only sister Mrs Henry has arrived with her children and her husband. Judge Henry[4] expects to come out with the Dr. Jerome McCown was also detained by the preparations to bring a wife with him. Before this it is supposed he is married to a Miss Jones. James McCown sold the land which you were bargaining for to Col Grant[5] for four hundred and fifty dollars.

Col Birdwell has been dangerously ill for several days with an abscess on the lungs. It has broken and he is much better, but it has not been in my power to go and see them since you left. Today I have an opportunity of going out, and I know my dear husband will excuse a short letter when my duty calls me to visit the sick. We are all in better health than usual.

My dear love yours of the 3rd Dec.[6] at Washington has this moment been handed to me. My heart is pained when I think of your exposure and sufferings. Dearest take good care of yourself. The same mail brought me a letter from Antoinette enclosing one from Lucy Ann [Lea]. It confirms the news of her baptism. She seems to be rejoicing with joy unspeakable. Mother sends her love to you.

Thy affectionate wife
M. L. Houston

[1]For a list of things sent see Houston to Margaret, November 22, 1848.
[2]Margaret may have been mistaken in the name. Catherine (Kate) Banton married E. D. Renfro on May 11, 1849. Mary E. Vick-Rainey, *Marriage Records of Walker County* (Huntsville: Walker County Genealogical Society, 1979), 6.
[3]Thomas Power.
[4]Judge John K. Henry. Willis Brewer, *Alabama: Her History, Resources, War Record and Public Men From 1540 to 1872* (Spartanburg, S. C.: The Reprint Company Publishers,

1975), 148.
[5]George W. Grant. Identified in Carpenter, 2029.
[6]See *Writings,* vol. 5, 62.

Washington
27th Dec 1848

My Dearest,

I declare to you, that it is now half past two in the morning, and I have been engaged the live long night at my table in my room. The last letter, which I opened, was one from Young Royston, and as I hope, it will gratify you, I will not retire to rest, until it is on its way to you. You can infer from it what I wrote to Young. I am glad that our Niece will soon be with you, and hope it will add much to your happiness, as well as Mothers. I will soon write to Young, and express my pleasure, as well as the familys, at the prospect of the visit. I have no news, only that there was a Ball, in the house, in which I am located, last night, and I was neither, in the room, nor did I even look in. I mention this for your satisfaction.

I have much business to do, and seldom retire until 2 oclk A.M. Every day I resolve to quit such habits, and retire at 10 oclock. Present my love to Mother, to Sam, and tell Nannie that I thank her for wishing to "write a letter to Genl Houston."

Kiss all the dear children, and tell Mr Gott, and Virginia howda for me.

I am thy devoted & faithful husband
Sam Houston

P.S. Not time to read the letter or correct it. H.

Washington
29th Dec 1848

My Dearest,

For two days we have had snow, and rain. The weather is not cold, but cool & damp, as you will imagine. We have adjourned over from to day (friday) until Tuesday, the second of January. This evening, I dined out, and I assure you my Love, that I am happy, yes truly happy, that I am a Son of Temperance, not that there was any excess, but that I have come home, as a man ought ever to do with a mind, as calm, and unexcited, as it was before I left my rooms to attend the dining! This was the second one, which I have attended this season, and I intend it will be the last, unless some very good reason, for a different course. I have not the least wish, to go into company, as I can not see <u>you</u> there! Now if I were at home, I would be perfectly willing to ride out to our friend Birdwells, and stay, a day and night! There we could all be happy, and rational, & peaceful—no envy, no watching, nor any cause, for the indulgence of mean passions, of this poor world! There is much talk [and] many prayers about <u>sleighing</u> in this city, and really it does not seem to me, as any thing desirable, or elegant!

Many persons come here, without employment, and time hangs heavy, on the idlers hands, always. Their great study is how they can <u>waste</u> it, in the most agreeable way, but never, how they can best improve it. I will try, so long as I feel, that I am making a great sacrifice, in being here, from all that I love, and the only thing left for me, is to act in such sort, as to soothe myself, that my absence has not been in vain, & of no avail to my family, myself, and mankind!

Just as I had finished the above sentence, the mail came and bro't me your welcome letter of the 7th Inst. I am happy to hear of your recovery, and pray for the entire restoration of your health. You gratified me extremely, in writing about the children. I do not by any means, reproach you my dear, but if Sam had learned nothing of Books, I would have been glad, but as it is the case, he may go on, but pray let it be at his option! I may be wrong about these things, but I can never change my notions. I hope it may be useful to him, and I think, [it] is natural for you to wish to hear Sam read.—I fear that he will know too much of Books, and too little of men! His gravity of disposition ought to be regarded, as an indication of a studious mind!

I hope my dear that you have long ire this received your stores! I sent more than I mentioned to you! If Wilsons Draft, is yet in the Bank here, I will pay it, but I am certainly displeased with him, and so soon as I can settle with him, I will trade no more in <u>his way</u>. I will say nothing about him, nor do I wish you to be <u>distressed</u>, about it. If I do pay the money here, I will have trouble to get it back, I am sure! When I come to settle with him for the am't which he has, you will see that he will afford me cause of dissatisfaction, with him. He can not avoid it. It is not in his nature, to act and feel, different from what he does. You need not my dear suppose that I will do anything to break off our agreeable intercourse with Mrs W. and our <u>other friends</u>![1]

Every letter which you have written to me, I have looked anxiously to see, the expression, that <u>it is so</u>, or <u>it is not so</u>. Well, I cant help it! It is your health my Love, that I am concerned about, and in either event, I could make some calculation, and my mind would be more easy! I pray, whatever is, may be best!

I am happy to hear that our little Nannie is <u>affectionate</u>, and that our dear Babe Maggy Lea, can lisp "papa." I know when she does it, that Sams, as well as his Dear Ma's heart, tingles with pleasure! You have not mentioned Mother. What is the matter my Dear? You say that you have no lack of company, and of this I am glad, for it will enable you, to pass your time more agreeably, than you cou'd otherwise do. I apprehend, that our relations from Caney, will not have time to visit you before spring. My Love, why do you not write to our friend Mrs Woods?[2] She will I fear, think hard of it!

As to the presents, I will not forget them, for Sam Houston Wilson, but you will have time, to write to me what to get, for the Boy! I will try, and take home a horse *[An X is inserted here with the phrase* "not 'automation' exactly!" *in the margin]* and buggy, to suit you my Love!

When you wrote last, all the letters, which I had scattered on the way for you, had not reached you. The last on the road was from Branchville,[3] so I presume by this time you will be tired reading this letter, as I fear you will not be much delighted with its contents. I will do as you suggest, with Mr Samson. In a former letter you will see, that I have met him since his return!

You did not tell me my Dear, how Mr Gott, and the Boys, or Servants were getting on, with the Farm and business! I am fearful, that I did not leave you so comfortable at home, as I ought to have done. My time was so short, and I was so much absorbed with you, and the children, that I thought of little else, but the present. If we ever meet again in health, and the blessings around us, which I left, I will be most truly happy, and not envy the most fortunate Gold finder in California!!!

Do not my Dearest, let Sam know, that I am not so much gratified, as he supposed I would be, at his reading!

Tell him that my heart is full of joy and happiness, to know that he is a good boy. Give my love to Mother. Kiss all with a new years kiss. Give howda to Virginia, and Mr Gott. Salute our friends all.

I am thy devoted husband

Houston

P.S. You forgot to sign your name to the letter—the last one

H.

[1]Houston is referring to the Birdwells.
[2]Almira (Mrs. Alva) Woods of Rhode Island.
[3]This letter has not been located.

Washington
1st Jany 1849

My Dearest Love,

The day has passed, and another year has begun, and I am most happy to salute you with the expression of my devotion, & my affection. To day has been a day of bustle. We have asked to visit the President[1] and Heads of Department, William Scurry[2] was in from Texas, and he and myself attended Mrs [Jane] Graham, and a (widow) cousin of his, the round of visits. As the Ladies are each about forty years old, I am sure you will not have any fear, of being supplanted by either of them, in my affection. I saw no one there, in all the room, whose brightest smiles, would ever compensate me, for a frown of yours. The reason is palpable. If you had in your power to inflict a frown, I would have to be present with you. If it were so, I would, by all, and every means try, and provoke a smile, to chase away all memory, of the uneasy look, and change it with the Spring of affection.

You believe in mesmerism. To night Gen'l Rusk, and myself are going to an exhibition, of experiments, which are said to be wonderful, and conclusive as to the truth, of the science. Rusk you know, is a believer, and I will make up my mind on the subject.

I have promise of some relic of Bethlehem for you, and so soon as I receive it, I will either forward it, or give you a description of it. I do not yet know what it will be, but it will be "a sure enough memento" from your friend and mine.[3]

The time has come, for us to go to the lecture. A happy new year to all the dear family.

Thy ever devoted Husband,
Houston

[1]James K. Polk.
[2]Scurry was the editor of the *Austin State Gazette*. *New Handbook of Texas*, vol. 5, 946.
[3]Reverend George Whitfield Samson, (also spelled "Sampson") the pastor of E. Street Baptist Church.

3rd Jany, 1849

My Dearest,

By the enclosed draft, which I have paid to day, you will see that I would not let it be <u>dishonored</u>, because your name was on it. You were not to blame, and I wou'd not for any [blurred], that you should think I did. If you have paid him, make him fork over to you, the amounts of the draft, in Gold or Silver, and if he offers you anything else, do not touch it. I have paid the draft in Gold.

I write in most haste as it is past mid night. I can tell you no news. The cholera has not reached here, but we hear of its terrible ravages in New Orleans. If it should visit you, my Love, you must use red pepper, and keep the patients warm, sweating if it can be brought about, will be a great thing, & put mustard plasters, on the stomach, on the back of the neck, and on the legs. Indeed whenever you can.—I pray that you may escape the scourge.

Give my love to mother, Sam, and kiss the children. Howda to Mr Gott, & Virginia.

Thy devoted Husband
Houston

P.S. If the cholera should visit you, let all be kept as dry as possible, and none exposed to wet, or cold.

Thine
Houston

Huntsville
Jan. 3rd 1849

My beloved husband,

On returning yesterday evening from a visit to Col Birdwell's, I was greeted by that sweet letter of yours dated the 6th of Dec. It proved a true comforter, I assure you, for it found me in a melancholy state of feeling. Our dear friend Mrs. Birdwell has been almost deranged on account of her husband's situation, (which I mentioned to you in my last.) He is considered out of danger by his friends and by Dr Keenan,[1] but you would not think so, if you could see him, and if he should die, I have scarcely a hope that she would survive him long. I need not tell you, how deeply I am grieved on her account, for you know that her sorrows are to me, the sorrows of a sister. But the Lord directs every thing, for the good of those who love him, and I hope we will all be enabled to trust in his mercy. There is considerable excitement in Huntsville on account of the cholera in Houston and Galveston. Indeed it is a terrible thought, but let me fear no evil, for pestilence itself moves at the bidding of him who rules the universe, and let us "be still and know that he is God." If it should visit

Washington dearest, I hope you will have your botanic remedies at hand, and go just now if you can, and find some well informed botanic doctor, and speak to him in time. I pray you, do not think of mercury in any form.

I do hope dearest that you will never leave me again, for I find that my fortitude decreases with my years, and I feel that I can not endure much longer, the anxiety that your absence entails upon me. It is true that the care of our little flock, is an absorbing thing with me, but even thier merry prattle can not banish my loneliness and gloom. Our little lamb[2] has become one of the merriest of the flock. Oh how I wish you could hear her sweet laugh. It is so musical. Nannie is said to be perfectly beautiful by all who see her. I think she will have an excellent mind and that gratifies me more than her beauty. Yes dearest, I do wish you were here to share with me the delightful task of instructing our noble boy. I have never engaged in any thing, that expanded my feelings and elevated my thoughts so much. Indeed it is a task without toil, for his active mind seems to search so diligently for truth, that so soon as it is presented to him, he understands it. I have given him a sheet of paper and pencil to amuse himself at my side, while I am writing to you, and I am half tempted to pry his <u>sketches</u> from him and enclose them to you. They would amuse you, but I hardly suppose you would imagine that we were raising a young Raphael.

I hope you will be pleased with our improvements when you return. My Love, I wish you to send me a great quantity of the blue grass. (I mean the yard grass.) I have heard a great deal of it, but have never seen it. It must be very pretty. Mrs. Branch[3] tells me, they have a pretty grass in Virginia for bordering walks, called the fringe grass. I wish you would be kind enough to get me some of the seed. By the bye, your <u>musket</u> (am I correct?) grass is coming up beautifully over the yard. During the snow and sleet and frost, it looked forth cheerfully and smiled on the desolation around. To one it is a sweet emblem. I leave you to imagine how I construe it.

My Love, I am pained when I think you had not received my first letter when you wrote. I thought it would certainly reach Washington before you could do so, but it seems that I was mistaken. I did not receive the president's message, which you sent me. If you send any paper, which you wish me to read particularly, I expect you had better write some thing on the back of it to the post master, for my papers are often taken out by other persons.

I would be glad for you to write to Mr Gott so soon as you can do so conveniently, and tell him what you wish to be done, particularly your regulations about the conduct of the servants, thier going to town at night, entertaining thier visitors, gambling, drinking, and things of that kind, and also the meat that is to be weighed for them and how much. He is a good man, but Prince and Joshua[4] I fear will soon have him blinded. It will not take you many moments to write him your laws, and I hope you will do it. We are all well. Mother sends her love. A few more weeks, and I trust we will be happy, my own Love.

Thy devoted wife
M. L. Houston

The Moores[5] and Creaths have united and Miss Isabella[6] heads the case. I am not in the least alarmed, I assure you. Bro. [James] Maxey says they talk largely, while you are away, but as soon as you return it will be "rats to your holes!" Mary Lehr[7] seems to be very violent against you. That letter dearest, was an unfortunate business. You will remember I opposed it. I was right my Love. You have heaped thereby the bitterest malice upon yourself, but your motives were good and that is comfort enough.

[1]Dr. Charles G. Keenan. Identified in Carpenter, 2010.
[2]Maggie Lea Houston.
[3]Mariah (Mrs. John) Branch. Identified in Carpenter, 2010.
[4]Houston slaves.
[5]Houston's sister and brother-in-law, Eliza and Sam A. Moore.
[6]Isabella Moore.
[7]Mary Moore Lehr, Houston's niece.

43 : NOVEMBER 9, 1848—NOVEMBER 4, 1849

My Dearest,

I have but a moment to write to you. I have to meet a committee this morning, to present an important measure to Congress.[1] You will see it soon. Your letters of the 12th and 19th came by land mail. They made me very happy. Your own health being good, and our children, also gave me the greatest of earthly pleasures. I will write tonight, and send some remarks about matters, and things in general. Sent you a pair of shoe soles, by Mr. Cordova, but did not tell you, that they were to be put inside of your shoes. If they are too long, you can cut them, so as to fit your shoes. By cutting them off at the toes, you will find them [sic] keep your feet warm, and may be of benefit to your cough. I rec'd of Bro. Henry [Lea], a long, and interesting letter. I will send it to you, so soon as I have perused it again. It is political, and highly intelligent in its character. He is fearful that I will make a blunder, in relation to the "Wilmot Proviso!"[2] The letter shows the deep interest which he feels for me on your account, in no small part, as I suppose. I appreciated the letter highly.

He had been to the Cane Brake, a few days before, and left all well. He said nothing about Lucy Ann's conversion, but on this subject, he may have felt a delicacy. He is a noble man, and I am proud of him. He spoke of Bob[3] and Teen going out west. Said the cholera had prevented them from starting, but I understood that so soon as it subsided, they would go, to see you.

I send you some seed to day sent to me by the public Gardener. I hope you will like them. I am so very happy to hear that our children are so smart! Don't, my Love, be afraid of the old Ladies prognostics, about children of genius. I do not suppose that your mother, and mine, had any fear of you, and myself, or if they had, we have both been reared. It is but fair to suppose that our weans may stand about the same chance, that we did, to be reared! I wish they may be smarter, but I doubt it. I will get a copy of the history of the Reformation, as you desired.

I must close, as my time to meet the committee is at hand. The reason that I did not write yesterday was that, I attended church, three times in the day, and night. The Sacrament of the Lord's Supper, was administered at half past 3 o clock. It was by Mr. Samson, who told me on yesterday, that his Boxes, and Trunks had just arrived, and that you should have some handsome present. Miss Elizabeth Watson (Sister to Mrs [Jane L.] Graham) has given me a beautiful <u>shell</u>, from Jerusalem carved neatly.[4] It is pure pearl, and as large as my two hands. I will have to <u>take</u> it, to you.

My Love to Mother, and Sam. Kiss the Babies, and give howda to Mr Gott, and Virginia.

Thy ever devoted,
Houston

I am happy the servants are behaving well. Tell them howda for me.

---

[1]See *Writings,* vol. 5, 65–66, Resolutions concerning a railroad to California, January 8, 1849.

[2]Houston was opposed to the Wilmot Proviso, which stipulated that slavery should forever be excluded from any territory acquired by treaty with Mexico. A letter in which he stated that he would continue to oppose it would later be published in the *Texas State Gazette.* Friend, 197.

[3]Robert Royston, Margaret's nephew.

[4]This shell may be seen in the Sam Houston Memorial Museum, Huntsville, Texas.

Huntsville
Jan 9th 1849

My dear husband,

By yesterday's mail, I recd your favours of the 18th and 20th ult. By saturday's mail, I recd one bearing date of the 11th of dec, and a day or two previous Dr Evans arrived from Ala, and having met on the red river, the gentlemen with whom you entrusted yours of the 9th he took charge of it, and brought it to me.[1] And now dearest, I owe you so many thanks, that I can not express them all in one letter. I know that I am remembered by you with affection, and that means that I am happy. I feel much relieved since I have recd your assurance that you will use the botanic medicine in case of cholera. I am distrest about you, but my faith is strong that the Lord has work for you to do in this little world of ours, and I am cheered by the hope of happy years together.

I laid Dr Jones's case[2] before Sam in the following manner. "My son there was a man named Anson Jones, and your pa talked to the people of Texas about him, and told them to make him president and because your pa said so, they made him president, the greatest man in the country, and now he has turned against your pa, and writes letters about him, and tries to make it appear that he is a greater man than your pa." Sam paused a moment and then looking up very suddenly he said, "Is that envy?" "Yes my son," I replied. "What do you think of him?" "I think he is a very bad man," exclaimed Sam with a great deal of energy. "don't you!" It was a question that admitted of no arguments between us, so that it was soon settled, but I was struck with Sam's view of the case. I had thought of ingratitude, meanness, selfish ambition and every thing but envy, and I think it very probable that Sam gave it the right name. Que pensez vous? You were very close to the truth, when you supposed that I might be excited by the Dr's letters. It has been a long while since I felt so much inconvenienced by my Irish blood. I apprehended no injury to your reputation. (On the contrary, I felt a little malicious pleasure to see how quietly he was laying himself on the shelf, for the rest of his days,) but I felt indigence at myself for dreaming such a creature into existence, for indeed dearest, he is the offspring of your superstition.[3] I will try to dream to better purpose next time, if you intend to convert my phantoms into realities.

I am truly glad that you have met with my old friend Aureliea F.[4] I am not afraid of her charms, for you have been so long accustomed to the humble pretensions of your wife, that I do not believe you could be attracted by any thing brilliant, or showy. I would be glad for you to see her often, and talk to her about her sister, my sweet friend Maria.

I rejoice to percieve [sic] your enthusiasm in the temperance cause. I am incomparably happier myself, since the order was instituted, because I believe my husband and son will be saved by it, and if our daughters should ever have husbands, I hope it will be a safe-guard to them. This you say is looking considerably ahead. True, but none save a mother can know a mother's fears. I must also tell you my Love, that it gratifies me to learn that you still attend your own church—that is the one that holds your tenets, and I sincerely hope that you will continue to do so. Our church here is still in a melancholy condition,[5] and my heart is filled with grief on account of it, but I will "Wait on the Lord" believing that he will give me the desire of my heart, which if I know myself is the prosperity of Zion. It is generally believed that no decision on the church will induce Mr. C[reath] to leave Huntsville. I intend to say nothing on the subject myself.

Sam has taken up the cause of temperance with great zeal, and says "Tell pa, I am a son of temperance, now won't you ma!" I have tried to convince him, that he is not initiated, but I suppose he thinks that he inherits the title from his father. By the bye, as you ask the name of the gentlemen who received the flag and bible, they were Dr Renfro[6] and Mr Branch.[7]

I will take your advice about our friend Wilson. I think I see into his late transaction, but he is such a perfect sophist that I shall never understand him. You remember dearest, that you told me, before you left me, that he had promised to get our supplies at Galveston and deliver them to me, without any profit. You did not say how he was to be paid, and I supposed it was to come out of the loan, but when I presented my memorandum to him, he said to me that you had told him that I must draw upon you for the amount of our supplies and also for what we are owing him previously, and for Royal's[8] and Samuel's[9] bills. I told him that you said nothing to me about a draft of that kind, and that I thought you had paid our old bill. He assured me that you had never paid him a dime, and spoke with such an air of truth, I suppose I was taken in, but I do not understand yet exactly what you have done. One thing I know, that if our business affairs are left to me, I should soon make beggars of myself and the children, but the Lord has hedged in his poor weak creature in such a way, that our helplessness will be provided for. I would write Sam's reply to you, and also to his young cousin,[10] but it is one of the coldest days I have ever seen, and I fear you can not read what I have written, so you must receive his apology from me, and present one to his young cousin for him. I will try to write both by next mail.

Thy devoted wife
M. L. Houston

P. S. The cloak has not been received, but I know I shall be delighted. Do send me the yard grass. We are well and send love to you.

[1]Houston's letters of December 9, 11 and 18 have not been located.
[2]See Houston to Margaret, December 16, 1848.
[3]This refers to Houston's feelings concerning Margaret's dreams.
[4]Aurelia (or Aureliea) Blassingame Fitzpatrick. For a photograph of Mrs. Fitzpatrick see Ada Sterling, ed., *A Belle of the Fifties: Memoirs of Mrs. Clay of Alabama* (New York: Da Capo Press, 1969), 27.
[5]Margaret is referring to the conflicts resulting from the hiring of a minister for the Baptist Church.
[6]Dr. E. D. Renfro. Identified by Carpenter, 2013.
[7]Anthony Branch.
[8]Peter Royal, a Huntsville builder. Donald R. Walker, *A Frontier Texas Mercantile: The History of Gibbs Brothers and Company, Huntsville, 1841–1940* (Huntsville: Texas Review Press, 1997), 31.
[9]Alan Samuels. Identified in Carpenter, 2011.
[10]James Houston.

Washington
10th Jany 1849

My Dear,

I have not written, as I proposed in my last letter. I had hoped that a letter might come from you, and that I might again have the pleasure to say how much happiness I enjoy in perusing your letters, again, and again. You, dear Love, can not realise the pleasure, which I feel when I receive your dear, & precious letters. When you receive letters from me, you are in the midst, of our little ones, and can talk of me, which will claim sympathy, from a part of your auditory, but you have to divide the pleasure. When I receive a letter, I have no one to sympathize with me, and enjoy the exclusive pleasure, of embracing all the treasures of home. When you tell me, that you are well, and comparably happy, and the little urchins are all well, & promising, I am more than happy, & [blurred] I can indulge, the pleasing anticipation, that when we shall <u>not</u> be, our places will be filled by those who will be useful to their fellow beings, and at the same time, impress posterity with the fact (so little regarded) that the mother, has it in her power, to form the character, of the offspring. This is too little regarded in the great world. Nothing is so important to the offspring, as the care of the Mother, not only to their mind, but their bodies also. I will send you a Book to day, or tomorrow, which I think you will be pleased with. I have only perused a portion of it. I call your attention [to] it and if it is valuable read it, but if not burn it. The education as I understand it, is physical, as well as intellectual & Moral. There is a book, which I have sent for only from its title, for I have not read it. It is something about making the <u>married state happy</u>. I wish to see, if it will teach me the means of improving my "<u>conduct</u>," as Sam would say. I know it needs it much, & I will catch every truth, & try to improve, upon them.

To day I must write to Bro Henry. I declare to you Love, that the pressure of business upon me, is so great, that my whole time, sleeping and waking were it resolved into business hours, I would have no time left to me.

I had sent to you, my Love, various articles which I had hoped would have reached you before the date of your last letter. However, I hope you will get them all safe, and that they will be agreeable to you. You will not forget to write me, what I ought to take to Sam Houston Wilson. I will try, and please you, as <u>you are so generous</u> as to solicit, in <u>behalf of a child</u> which <u>resembles me</u>. But my Love, I believe I had not been at home within some ten months previous to Sam H. Wilsons birth. I certainly, from what you say of him, am anxious to see the Boy.

I would just mention when speaking of boys, that you, and I have an understanding, that you were, without any explanation, to say that a certain matter, "is so, or it is not so." By your next letter, I hope to learn the truth. If I do not, I will not complain, if I am even disappointed. If I were a darky, there would be some excuse for my curiosity!—as it is, I am not sure, that I have a proper one.

This letter is written in all the talking—speaking, and confusion of the Session of the Senate! If there is any want of sense in it, you must impute it to <u>surrounding</u> <u>influences</u>.

My love to Mother, and Sam. Kiss Nannie for me, and tell me what she says. To our little violet give a hug, and a kiss. Tell all howda. I intend to write to Mr Gott soon.

Thine Ever,
Houston

Washington
13th Jany 1849

My Dearest,

The last mails from the south have failed, and no doubt have detained at least two interesting epistles from you. I can be candid in saying to you (and you will no doubt believe) that I regret their not arriving.

At this time, if I could only know that all were well at home, and happy, at a later date that the 20th ultimo, it would add much to my felicity. My friends can, and do go to the Theater openings—a thing which I have not done, nor do I intend to visit one, until you may ask me to do it. So well have you drilled me, that with the practice, I have lost the inclination to go. I was at my <u>last</u> <u>party</u> at the house of an old friend, and met your devoted friend Mrs Gov Fitzpatrick, and was her Beau for most of the evening, (<u>in part</u>) because she spoke of you, and Mother, and "Master Sam." She says that she will, if she can induce the Governor to go, and see you, (all the way to Texas). I said to her, that you would "be too appie." The Gov has told me, they have been unfortunate, with a child, but how I did not ask. I inferred, that she had miscarried. She now looks better than she ever did. I have been to see her but once, & she as well as the Governor reproached me with neglect. My excuse is, that all leisure time is employed in writing to you. So my excuse must be admitted as sufficient, for all neglect.

I have procured a handsome copy of the Reformation. It is very pretty, and when I can, I will read it. Mr Samson is to deliver four lectures on the subject of his travels in the East. If possible, I will hear them all, and esteem it a great deal. He preaches, more ably, than he ever did, before his travels.

You will see, my Love, that I have introduced a Resolution for a common road, as well as a railroad, from the Atlantic to the Pacific.[1] It must, & will be done, but whether, at present, or a future day, I can not now determine. The start is mine! I intend in a few days to call them up, and make a speech due them!

Give love to Mother, & Sam, & kiss him, as well as the dear Girls. Give howda to all.

My Love, please say to Mr Gott, that if tobacco seed has not reached him by the 10th of March, I will send some from here that will be there in time. My friend Hayden,[2] of New Orleans was to send some.

The servants would as soon, or sooner, have black land than that between Mothers field, and town. That wou'd be best, for if they have a truck patch there every thing will be stolen out of it. They may have their patch of equal size with it, in any part of the field where Mr Gott may think proper. They have my consent if they chuse it, in the middle of the field, or the spot where it will be most secure from Rogers.[3] I am satisfied that the sandy land is best for Tobacco (Cuba), for Major Cartwel[4] once raised some in Washington, on a sandy bank equal to any from Cuba.

Today (and why I don't know) a Gentleman, presented me the handsomest copy of Burns work that I have ever seen! I intend to send you two Books soon. One is "Parents' Gide" [sic]. I have looked into, but not read either. Indeed I have not time to read, only my Testament, which I do, every night before I sleep, if it is 3 or 4 oclock A.M. and remember you in my prayers to God our Father.

If I happen, my Love, to see any interesting Books, which I feel assured will add to your happiness, I will get them. You will see that

I have sent Sam, quite a Library. I am fearful, my Love, that I have in former letters said something which has given you pain. If so, forgive me. I did not intend it. I was vexed at Wilson, but have <u>mended</u> all! I afford you an opportunity, now to charge me, with <u>provoking</u>, Sam to learn Books. So if there is any blame, I will take it all upon me.

I hope to go to church tomorrow. I am ever

truly thine,
Houston

[1]For Houston's speech of January 8, 1849 see *Writings,* vol. 5, 65–66. Houston's personal map with the route he drew in red may be viewed at the San Jacinto Museum of History on the San Jacinto Battlegrounds, a donation from Charlotte Williams Darby.
[2]J. H. Hayden. Identified in Ronald Vern Jackson and Gary Ronald Teeples, *Louisiana 1850 Census Index* (Bountiful, Utah: Accelerated Indexing Systems, Inc., 1978), 112.
[3]Houston is probably referring to a neighbor, John Rogers. Identified by Carpenter, 2026.
[4]H. R. Cartwell. Identified in Johnnie Lockhart Wallis and Laurance Hill, *Sixty Years on the Brazos* (Waco, Texas: Texian Press, 1967), 40.

The following two letters were misdated 1848, but they were written in 1849. The letter from Sam to his father is in Margaret's handwriting.

Huntsville
Jan 16th 1848 [1849]

My ever dear Father,

As Mamma has offered to answer your dear little letter for me, I will try to tell her what to say. Oh that precious letter, it did make me so happy, and dear papa, I will try to do all you tell me. I will try to be a good boy and to love my Saviour. I know I ought to love him for giving me so kind a father. Sister Nannie is beginning to talk very sweetly about God. Yesterday Mamma spread a little dinner for Sister and myself, as a reward to me for a good lesson, and sister Nannie said isn't God good to give us apples and raisens [sic] and ammons

[sic]? Ma thought this was very sweet, and I thought so too. Oh pa, sister Maggy is growing so beautiful! And she looks so saucy, just as if she knew every thing. Mamma says she is quite large too. As to sister Nannie's peculiarities, I believe I am getting accustomed to them. Indeed papa she has an excellent heart, although she is a little self-willed sometimes. Mamma says she has never seen a child so easily subdued.

Mr Gott says the pigs are doing finely. I believe there [are] 31 young ones. My dear pa, as I have no suitable envelope, I enclose to you my letter to cousin James B. Houston,[1] that you may inspect it and enclose it to him.

Thy devoted son
Sam Houston

[1] The son of Houston's first cousin, John Houston.

Huntsville
Jan. 16th 1848 [1849]

My ever dear Love,

The two last mails have been kept back by the high waters of the San jacinto, and as you will readily suppose, it is a serious matter with me. Yes I am deprest indeed, and yet I am comforted, for my beloved husband is in the hands of that Almighty Being, whose providence withholds from me, the intelligence of him so near at hand, and I am greatly cheered by the trust that no evil will befall him. Oh, my love, daily and hourly I realize more of the wisdom of our Saviour's admonition to "lay up for ourselves treasures in Heaven." A little cause may blast our brightest hopes on earth, but the joys which are there, no disappointment can reach. Oh let us fix our thoughts from that Heavenly inheritance which "eye hath not seen, ear hath not heard nor hath it entered into the heart of man's conscience!" Oh my husband when my thoughts and feelings are drawn out upon this exalted subject, I long to see you cast off the weight of political cares and turn away from the unhallowed influences about you, that in our quiet home you may be enabled to seek with your whole heart, the only thing worthy of our affections.

Yesterday, I was reading with my usual pleasure that sweet book, "D'Aubigney's reformation," and on turning the presentation leaf, I discovered that it was presented on the 9th of May. My thoughts were these—"thus be remembered our wedding day? Perhaps this dear book may be the means of uniting our spirits for eternity." Dearest I have told you what I thought, but I can not tell you what I feel. Language can not express my feelings on that subject, but with heart felt sorrow, do I remember that I have given evidences of this deep interest in my husband's salvation. Oh where are the christian forbearance, the Heavenly mindedness, the patience and fortitude by which I have led him to glorify my Father in Heaven? With bitterness of spirit do I recall many instances of impatience and restlessness, ill becoming one professing godliness. We are told to confess our faults to one another. Here do I confess mine, resolving with the help of God to struggle against them.

A few more weeks, and I trust our little circle will be enlivened by the presence of him, whose name diffuses joy amongst us. I wish you could look in upon us occasionly [sic] and observe the influence of those magic words "my pa." Miss Nannie, I think prides herself on being her papa's favourite, and exhibits with great pride the different articles which she says "her pa" bought for her. Sam speaks of you with great fondness, but with manly gravity and respect, except when some one remarks that Nannie looks more like you, than he does, then his face contracts immediately, and he loses all self-command. Even little Maggy looks and chirps very knowingly whilst the animating theme is going on. I endeavor to rejoice with my little ones, but with me, it is but the semblance of joy. And must it be ever thus? Are your duties always to call you away from your family? If so, mine must be a lonely destiny. My advice to you would be to take leave of Washington now and forever, but there is much selfishness in it I admit.

I will lay this aside until the mail comes in, trusting to hear some-thing from your pen.

Jan 21st

Yours of the 20 ult. is just rec'd. A thousand thanks my dear love. It is the sabbath or I would write you a long letter by tomorrow's mail.

Thine

M. L. Houston

Washington

20th Jany 1849

My Dearest,

For more than a week, I have seized every mail, & looked for a letter from you, but in vain. Tomorrow is sunday, and another south-ern mail will arrive. I will hope until then, and expect again to hear from you. I would have been constantly unhappy if it were not that with Gen'l Rusk, and some other Gentlemen, I make a class of stu-dents, to a teacher on <u>mesmerism</u>. We are all greatly interested in the science. I have not a shadow of doubt on it, nor in Clairvoyance. I have seen such experiments, since I commenced attending the Lec-tures, that it entertains with confidence. One thing, my Dear, that will delight you much is that it throws, or casts light upon many parts of the old as well as the new Testament. I know you will be gratified by this assurance. Were I to tell you some experiments, which I have seen and others, which I have performed, I am sure you could not believe me. If we live to meet again, I will have much to say, and only a small part of which I expect you to believe.

I have told you of my beliefs, and I will now tell you of one experiment only. I saw a Youth, who I suppose was never out of this District, in a Clairvoyant state, taken to Nacogdoches, and he was asked as to the general appearance of the place—streets, etc., of all which he gave an accurate description. He described the Catholic church, and other houses in the place and noted any thing remarkable. Well, neither the Preceptor, nor any one present but Gen'l Rusk, and myself knew anything about Texas. I could instance many cases, quite, or even more remarkable than, this instance. I was affraid [sic] to send him to my home, for fear that something unhappy, might be presented to my mind, that I might not wish to believe, and yet could not disbelieve it! Gen'l [Alexander] Anderson of Knoxville, had him sent to his house, and he described his place, his buildings, and such of his family as were at home—their dresses, and eyes, & persons— also the part of the House, they were in, at the time, which he was there (the Clairvoyant). I asked him if he would answer me, to which he assented. I asked him for a description of Sam's Donkey, when he described his color, and appearance, as accurately, as if he had been standing present. If you please, dont think I am crazy, and so sure as we live to meet, I will satisfy you of the art, if I can not give you the reason for it. You once had a disposition to believe in it, when I had none.

After you have once seen it, you will read the scripture with more pleasure, than you have heretofore done, if possible. Imperfect as I am, in the science, I assure you, it has given me some insight into portions of holy writs, which before I could not essay to understand. This must for the present suffice, except to say that, phrenology is a great aid to the science, or rather a part of it.

My Love, now to house matters. By next mail I intend to send some Tobacco seeds. I hope you will have the goodness to tell me of, the little matters which I have sent, as they arrive. You do not, I fear my Love, intend to send me the measure of Sams shoes, or boots. I want the length of the sole, heel, and all at once. Since I first came to Congress, I have never had so much business on hand as at this time. I will have to make, one or two important speeches, this session, if not three, or more perhaps.

I have not seen your fair friend, from Alabama.[1] I see the Governor[2] every day. If you were here, Alabama would be <u>Fairly</u> represented. Dont you think so? I certainly do! I have been so busy, that I have not written to Mr Gott, but will when I send the Tobacco seed! Nor have I yet written to Col Wilson, or Madame, but I sent them news papers. I will write as soon as I can to the Colonel. I wrote to Brother Henry, and by this time I hope he is satisfied that I will not be a nullifier, or a Calhoun man. Calhoun's failure I fear will break his heart. If it does not, I have to score him, before I leave the city. But little will be done this session. It will be, I fear, that we can not get off, before the 10th of March, or there will be a called session of the Senate, to act upon the nominations of Gen'l Taylor's cabinet, and other appointments. It is midnight, and when I began to write, I did not intend to write but a few pages, and I am on the eighth. You must be tired, and I will have to tell you how much I love you, as I have no one else to tell it to. I assure you, if I were sole possessor of the "Gold Regions of California," I would give three fourths of them to be with you, and the children, but if I were with you, I cou'd send for them, you know.

It will yet be two months, ire I hope to see you, or upwards. Until we do meet, you will abide in hearts core! Give my love to Mother, & Sam, kisses to the Babes. Say kind things to all, and salute my friends.

Thy ever devoted husband,

Houston

[In margin:] My Dear, I am electioneering. I send news papers to many of your friends—Ladies. Houston

[1] Aurelia Blassingame Fitzpatrick.
[2] James Fitzpatrick.

Washington

20th Jany, 1849

My Beloved,

This morning, I went to church, and intend to go again this evening at 7 o clk. I write now my dear, to tell you that I received from Mr Samson, the mementos, which I hope will reach you by this mail. I folded them in a map, and you will find them in it, if it goes safe. The beads have on them, descriptive notes, and they are in, or with a note from Mr Samson to you. Love, I need not say of what they are, as you will, I hope soon see. He gave me also, two small vials, one containing the water of the dead Sea, and the other, the water of Jourdan [sic]. I will not trust them by mail lest they might be broken. I try, and do every thing as you would wish, or desire, that it should be done. Not only in important matters, but in the least. I wrote to you so long a letter last night, that you would be weary reading my bad hand writing, were I to make this a long letter. I will make you a confession, which you may not think, of the most agreeable character, but before you condemn me, I desire you to reflect well upon it!!! If I loved you less, than I do, I would be better <u>contented</u>, than what I am! I do not say, my Dearest <u>that I would be happier than I am</u>! You know, my dear, that love is an agreeable torment. It is rendered agreeable, because the hope of fruition springs from it, and our trust reflects such joys, as the future will possess. One peaceful sabbath day at home, would soothe, & give my troubled affections, and hopes, a delightful calm. Your smiles my Love, beside me the childrens contention for my knees, and Sams surrender to his little sisters, of his rights of primogeniture, would afford me more pleasures in one thrill of manly pride, than all the toys, joys, & pageants of this mighty metropolis ever can. More than one half my time is employed in thinking of home, or attending to subjects connected with it, or my family. I must soon start to church.

Thy devoted husband,
Sam Houston

Senate Chambers
25th Jany, 1849

My Dearest,

I have so long been without letters from you that, I am almost in despair. I can not sleep, at night, nor in the day times, can I be happy. I know not what to apprehend. I am fearful, of sickness, or death, at home. I have no one to whom I can express my distresses. I must bear my situation, as well as I can, until I can receive some news from home. One thing gives me hope, and that is I receive no letters from any one in Huntsville, or north, or west of there.

I sent you to night, an old newspaper, and a piece clipped, from some other paper, and sent to me. The "remarks" were made, on some foolish publication intended well for me, but written by an ignoramus. These things give me neither pleasure, nor pain, only as I believe, they are calculated to effect you, through your feelings.

I assure you my Love, I would be very happy, if I could only be with you to explain my feelings, and pass my days with you, and our children uninterrupted, by all public cases. Late events, which have been passing, go far to explain your dream of the "map." It is so regarded by all who are not <u>mesmerized</u> by Mr Calhoun, and they are few, but will make some fuss, for a while. I will send you, what is said so far as it comes in my way, on this subject. I see your friends, and mine frequently, I mean the Preachers. They call on me, as often as they can. I will say Adieu, in the hopes that I will soon hear from you.

My love, and kisses to all.

Thy devoted husband,
Houston

Washington
30th Jany, 1849

My Dearest,

Not a word has reached me of later date, than the 20th of last month. Three letters are now due, and I have felt the most painful anxiety. For five days, I have not written, hoping every day that letters would arrive. As they have not, I will write again, in the hopes, that ire I go to repose, I will have the inexpressible happiness of hearing from you, that all are well, and happy. I did not assure you, how painful my situation has been. Nor has it added any thing to my comfort, that I have labored under the influence of a bad cold, or influenza. It proves to a greater extent, than I have ever known it before. This morning, I was washed with whiskey. As I do not take anything that contains alcohol inwardly, I can afford to use it outwardly. I have become more pleased, with temperance than I have ever been previously. I witness so many souls, sinking to perdition from the vice of intemperance alone, that it teaches a fearful lesson, to the wise, or reflecting. My influenza up to this time has prevented me from giving a temperance Lecture, tho, I am under promise to do so, at some early day if my <u>pipes</u> will stay open long enough. There is some stir here about the Inauguration Ball, to which I do not intend to go. If I do so, it will be from the fact, that I may think it due, from me, as a devotion to the Chief of the Republic. I do not think, even this will persuade upon me to attend! The <u>Convention</u> of Mr Calhoun[1] has verified the fable, of the "Mountain, and the Molehill." I will either make a popular speech, or write a letter in reply to it. Our representatives have united by signing the address. Their names have not yet appeared but will do so. Genl Rusk, & myself have not, nor will we sign any thing but which we write—or believe.[2] Those who have signed it will regret the deed. It will be compared to the "Hartford convention." It was concocted in "<u>the</u> <u>Dark</u>." I will hope my Love, to receive from you a letter, ire I sleep to night. My Love, present me to our Dear Mother, & Sam. Howda to all.

Thy faithful and devoted,
Houston

[1]Calhoun had prepared a draft of "An Address of the Southern Delegates in Congress to their Constituents," commonly known as the "Southern Address." In January 1849, he held a secret caucus of Southern legislators, where he hoped to persuade the congressmen to adopt his views. M. K. Wisehart, *Sam Houston, American Giant* (Washington: Robert B. Luce, Inc.,1962), 525. New York Congressman Timothy Jenkins reported that the Southern Senators and Representatives held a private caucus on January 9, 1849, to send "the address and resolutions to the committee for revisal" and "It is said that Gen. Sam Houston attended and made a strong speech against the plan, calling the meeting a second Hartford convention." Timothy Jenkins to Charles Jenkins, Congressman Timothy Jenkins Collection, Hamilton College, Colgate, New York. The Southern Address was described as full of exaggerated complaints of Northern aggression, and predictions of an eventual race war. Elbert B. Smith, *Magnificent Missourian: The Life of Thomas Hart Benton* (New York: J. B.

Lippincott Company, 1958), 245.
[2]For Rusk's beliefs on the convention see Mary Whatley Clarke, *Thomas J. Rusk: Soldier, Statesman, Jurist* (Austin: The Pemberton Press, 1971), 174.

The following letter is misdated.

Huntsville
Jan 30th 1848 [1849]

My beloved husband,

By last mail, I recd six letters from you from the 25th of Dec, to the 3rd of Jan. The high waters have been a great hindrance to our mails, but when I get an arm full at once from you, it is such a pleasure to arrange all the dates and begin at the earliest. Oh I am almost repaid for the hours of suspense which I have endured. Yes I may say quite repaid, for while I am feasting on the words of him I love so fondly, I am happy, but it is a short lived happiness for when I calculate the days and weeks that have passed since the last was written, I fancy many things that may have happened, and my heart sinks within me. For the last few days I have had great unhappiness on account of the cholera. I tried to comfort myself with the assurance which you gave me, that you would use the botanic medicine, but my love, you know what trifles will upset our fortitude, and after reading the recipe which you sent me, knowing your enthusiasm about opium, I saw at once, that would be your re[torn] and since that, my anxiety at times renders me perfectly miserable. I can hardly take any comfort in my children, for the idea of your danger unfits me for everything. It would surprise you to know the childlike reflections that sometimes impart to my sad spirit something almost like joy. Today I have felt happy to think that after tomorrow but one month will intervene between this and your departure from Washington. Oh that I could exercise more of that faith in my Heavenly Father, which is our only support in times of trouble. And yet my trust in him is all that sustains me. But for that my soul would sink in deep waters.

61 : NOVEMBER 9, 1848—NOVEMBER 4, 1849

The health of our family is rather better than common. Maggie seems to grow more rapidly than either of the others, but they are all rosy and sprightly. I am sorry you are not gratified at Sam's learning to read.[1] He is making such grand preparations to astonish you when you return. Could not <u>manage</u> to <u>be</u> gratified? I can not as yet tell you much about the farm, as the farming season has not yet set in. Mr Gott is a kind hearted good man, but stands much in awe of Prince and Joshua.[2] He has tried to whip Joshua once, but did not succeed, and I presume he will not attempt such a thing with any of the grown ones again.

My trunk has not yet been received, but I recd a letter from Mr Cordova in Galveston informing me that it was deposited with Mr. Ruthven,[3] and would be sent up by the first opportunity.

I leave it to your own taste to select a present for S. H. Wilson.[4] I will merely say, that I do not think it need be very expensive. I promised before you left home to remind [you] of a set ring for "Missy" Goodall.[5] I was delighted by Young's letter, but I fear the cholera will detain them. Mother's health is rather feeble. She sends love to you.

Thy devoted wife
M. L. Houston

---

[1] See Houston to Margaret, December 29, 1848.
[2] Two Houston slaves.
[3] Archibald St. Clair Ruthven.
[4] Sam Houston Wilson, the son of Jane and B. S. Wilson of Huntsville.
[5] Anne Eliza Goodall, the daughter of Katherine Goodall Lea.

Washington
1st Feby, 1849

My Dearest,

Although, I have but a moment to write I can not deny myself the pleasure of saying to you, that last evening I had the pleasure to receive your letters of the 3rd & 9th ult. They had been well soaked by rain on the way here.

The contents, were not through Providence obliterated. I read with inexpressible delight, their contents. I like Sam's notions, poor fellow, and to hear of our "leetle" ones did me much good. Another letter, to which you refer that I read to Mr Lehr,[1] I feel that I only performed a duty to humanity. If I live to return, I think there will be a padlock placed on the lips of some people, who may now, be somewhat busy.

As to Mr Creath, I think he will keep rather close. He is a poor dog, and deserves contempt. He has, so far as a poor creature could do, brot shame, upon the Christian character. I cannot hate him, but I can not respect him. As for my pretty niece, Mrs [Mary Moore] Lehr I am glad that she proves herself, worthy of her mother. I have only time, my dearest to write this much. I would not have written, until I had more time, but my last letters were so sad, that I feel it due to let you know, that I have rec'd your letters. There is I hope another on the way, which will reach me tonight.

To day I wrote to Mr Gott, but did not let him know, that you had mentioned the servants to me, but gave to him orders for the servants. I hope you will write to me at Memphis Tennessee. You may write weekly to me. I have written to Col Yoakum on some law business.[2] I am more attentive to business, as concerns <u>money</u> than heretofore.

My Love, and howda to all. I sent word by Gov Fitzpatrick to Aurelia, what you wrote, and he was pleased!

Thy devoted husband,
Houston

[1] John Lehr, who married Houston's niece, Mary Moore.
[2] See Houston to Henderson Yoakum, *Writings,* vol. 5, 70–72.

Washington
2nd Feby 1849

My Dear

Now, to day, I write again as I promised you, in my last. To day I have the pleasure to receive a long letter from Bro. Henry, of the 25th ult. This is very recent of date. He writes very affectionately, and announces the health of all the kindred in Alabama. Among other things he invites me, if I can do so, consistently to call by, on my way home. This I suppose you would demur to, if you were consulted. I will write to him, and assign as a reason, your objections, for not going by Marion. This will be a small reason compared to others, which I will suggest. Can you guess the most potent, and prevailing reason? It is simply that I wish to see (anxious as I am to greet the kin) Maggy, my own dear Maggy, and the weans as Burns, would have said.

Yes, if I could make California in my route home, by prolonging my stay, for a short time, I would not take a look, at the Golden region. I would not of choice, take the trip! No, indeed my Love, I am particularly anxious to get home. I will write a long & loud letter to Bro. Henry, and send much love to all the relations. I send Documents to our kindred there, & to our nieces. He did not say anything about Teen, & Robert's[1] journey to Texas. I hope they are on the way as, the cholera has disappeared. I hope it did not get north of Houston. It has so far as we learn here, disappeared from the U. States. It was a fearful scourge, to the earth, and its sinful inhabitants. This season was favorable to its spread, if it had visited here. We have had but little fair weather, this season, and but one fall of snow, tho, we have had a good deal [of] rain. I regret, my Love that you have had so cold a winter, as you described. Had I anticipated such a thing, I would have tried, to secure you at least from the wet, if not from the cold. I am glad that you intend to be pleased with the Cloak, which I had prepared for you. It was only seen by one Lady here, and she said it was pretty, or beautiful.

If all went safe, you would find several small articles with the cloak. The Box—aye, the Box!!! That my Love, I hope would please you. The purse etc etc.

Present my love, and proper salutation to all!

Thy ever devoted husband
Sam Houston

[1] Margaret's niece and nephew, Serena and Robert Royston.

3rd feby 1849

My Dearest,

I send you some Malaga Grape seed. It is now after midnight, and I know you would not have me to write if you knew how much I have done to day.

My love, and howda to all. Salute our friends. To day I got for Teen & Lucy Ann, each a Gold ring (plain) to present in your name. I will send them by mail. Thy ever devoted

Houston

Washington
4th feby 1849

My Dearest,

To day I was present at church, and heard Bro. Samson preach a fine sermon this morning. In the evening, another man preached, but he talked about keeping sabbath, and stopping railroad cars etc. It was in bad taste, I think.

I wrote to Bro Henry a long letter of eight pages, and a note to Lucy Ann, with the plain gold ring, as a wedding gift from both of us.[1]

Since I came home to night I received the enclosed address on myself, in a letter. I send it to you for your amusement more than edification. Read it to Sam, and Mother, if you shou'd not get weary in so doing. This author meant all that was kind, and I thank him for his good intentions.

I would be more happy, if I had received a letter from you to day, than I am now. You would write on the 16th ult, and that was nineteen days. The mails are in wretched condition. Your last letter had been soaked in rain, but not obliterated. When I am in despair, I have the comfort of reading your letters, over, and over again. From this I derive pleasure, but so soon as I have finished, my distress is removed, and anxiety succeeds, to pleasure. You will not care, to receive a long letter from me as I have written, so much to the Lea family to day. In speaking to Lucy Ann to day, about Mrs Fitzpatrick I told her that she showed well, and I was gratified, for there was a lady from Alabama, that I loved far above all others, but she happened not to be in the city, this season. And if she did not visit here next session, I wou'd assuredly stay at home myself. Now if you are half as smart, at guessing, as the Yankees, you can guess the Lady. Try Sam, and see if he can? Tho' I dont think that he will be a conundrum maker. I trust you will be satisfied, my Dear, that I do love you very much, or I wou'd not write so late at night. The town clock has struck 12 M.

My Love, commend me to Mother & Sam, and kiss the dear little Girls. I importuned you my dear, to answer me a question in several letters. You did not heed me. If we live to meet I can guess it. I reckon!!

Thy ever devoted Husband,
Sam Houston

---

[1]Lucy Ann Lea was planning to marry John M. Langhorne. Madge W. Hearne Papers, "The Lea Family."

My dear Love,

Tuesday is come again, my regular day for writing to you, but I find myself a perfect insolvent in the epistolary business, for the two last mails (friday and monday,) brought me such a quantity of letters and papers, that I feel myself entirely unable to discharge the debt, but I will pay as much as I can.

The books I have not had time to read, but if they are your selection, I know they are good. I grieve to say that the beads and letter from Mr Sampson did not come with the other packages, but I do trust they are not lost.[1] Please render him my grateful acknowledgments. The flower and cedar accompanying Miss [Elizabeth] Watson's letter were received last week. I am greatly her debtor and hope soon to reply to her. I can not describe to you my feelings at first sight of the flowers from Jerusalem. Indeed I feel that my enthusiasm invested it with more holiness than it deserved. What a blind papist I would have made, had the Lord placed me in Romish darkness.

I received a letter last week from Charles Power. He wrote from Galveston, and had expected Antoinette to join him there, on thier way to Huntsville, but the cholera in Houston induced him to postpone the visit. Charles writes with much seriousness, and from his language, I am led to hope that he is realy concerned about his soul. The destroying angel is around in the land, and well may the stoic heart faint and the strong arm quake with fear! Oh my love, when we parted last, how little did we know that ere we met again, the "shadows of the pestilence that walketh abroad at noonday" would pass between us! Often as I gather my little lambs to my bosom, whilst a dark presentiment like an adder is creeping though my heart, that ere long some one of our little band or all may mingle with the dust. But it is not thus that I should write to him who needs as much comfort as myself, and indeed dearest it is only now and then that this gloom overcomes me, for I have a sweet source of consolation. You will see it in the 46th psalm. There dearest in that sure refuge, let us rest our souls until we meet again.

I have felt strongly ever since I read your remarks about clairvoyance. Although I am no new convert, yet I have believed from what I have heard and read, but your evidence to me is like the evidence of my own senses, and it is realy awful to think of an influence so spirit-like. Unless you have some objections which I do not understand, I wish you would send and look after us. Mother gives you a very cordial invitation, thinking you can come yourself, but I suppose that would not be possible, unless you could be mesmerized by some one familliar [sic] with the place. Am I mistaken? If so dearest, do pray, come to us. It would be sweet to know that you might be near although invisible.

I did not get my trunk until yesterday. I am delighted with the cloak. It is realy beautiful. Sam's books please him greatly. As to his reading, my love, you may comfort yourself in the same way that old Mr. Henderson[2] did about his son's knowledge of the law.

I enclose a slip for your amusement, from which you will see that he has taken up writing. He has not had the least instruction I assure you. Just as he finished the last letter, he exclaimed, "Oh Ma I was making a good 'Y' the pencil slipped and made a man's nose!" The figure below he says is a king with a crown. The other day he was playing alone, and without his knowledge, I watched him for a length of time. He created a throne of dominoes and set one of his nine pins upon it for a king, and amused himself by throwing at the king and knocking him off. "Sam" said I, "would you like to have a king over our country?" He answered promptly, "If the king were my Father and the queen my Mother." I was perfectly astounded, for I had expected any thing as soon as such a sentiment from Sam.

I send you Sam's measurement. Do not get them too small. I pray you. It is the exact length of his foot without allowing anything. My no. is fours. I am much pleased with the box and soles.

[The letter is not signed.]

---

[1]There is no record of Margaret's ever receiving the beads.
[2]Margaret may possibly be referring to Lawson Henderson, the father of lawyer James Pickney Henderson. Identified in *New Handbook of Texas,* vol. 3, 554.

Washington
8th Feby 1849

My Dearest,

I am in the deserts with the mail Post masters etc.

Every thing here is pretty quiet, and will remain so, I find until the President elect[1] arrives. Then it is fair to suppose that there will be bustling, & fuss, and hopes, & fears, and disappointments. I pity those who have hopes resting upon the firmness, or sagacity, of Gen'l Taylor. Poor Gentleman, he will be in deep water, and I apprehend those who followed him will find themselves in the same Predicament, that Pharaoh's boat did in the red sea. They will find two shores, but can reach neither.

Last night there was a Drawing Room. I attended but found Madam Kirkpatrick, but did not ask her to take my arm at the moment, and lost her, but did not see her again during the night. So I have this to account for, when we meet. I made some display by asking Mrs President Polk to take my arm, and we walked around the "East Room."[2] There are a vast crowd of people there, and they were gratified as it seemed, that I was so gallant a man! I only regretted, that you were not upon my arm, in lieu of the Madam. I would rather have you there, if we were private folks, than any one on earth, and if we had to assume other relations to the public than those which we now do, I would infinitely prefer to have you, than any one on earth. I suppose that not less, than one hundred persons of both sexes, spoke to me on the subject of bringing you to the White House, & living there! It may be so!!

My love, & compliments to all! Thy ever devoted,

Houston

I have not time to read this as the mail will be off forthwith. H.

---

[1]Zachary Taylor.

[2]President Polk was busy escorting Dolly Madison. For a description of the evening see Nevins, 373–74. For a picture of the Polks with Dolly Madison made at the White House

see Margaret C. S. Christman, *1846 Portrait of the Nation* (Washington, D. C.: Smithsonian Institution Press, 1996), 28.

A copy of a letter written by Houston to Margaret on February 9, 1849 may be found in Writings, *vol. 5, pages 74–75. The following letter is from the Burch-Remick-Roberts Collection of Houston letters:*

Washington
11th Feby 1849

Dearest,

I have been to church today, and intend to return to the exercises of the sunday school after dinner.

Your letter, and enclosures gave me a great deal of happiness, for I had been depressed, for some days. I handed Sam's letter to his young cousin,[1] and made a whole family, & Buck perfectly so. He says he will keep up the correspondence, until he persuades Sam, and his ma to visit Washington. I think Buck, would prefer to see Sam's improvements at home, and take some Texas lessons, as he has to go to school, and has not a great liking for it. I will not finish this letter until I return from church this evening. To write about worldly matters on Sunday, I do not like, but I feel that it is [a] matter of necessity on this occasion, for my mind would dwell more upon it, were I not to do it, than if I were to dispose of it once.

Col Wilson wrote to me a letter which I will enclose, and now can <u>take care of it</u>, and comparing what he says about the slaves with what he said to you at times, will at least convince you, that he ought to <u>have</u> a <u>good</u> memory, or that he <u>needs</u> one! He writes to me that Albert has been guilty, of bad conduct, & has been sent home. I regret this. Hire him to anyone that you can. Esquire Hanks[2] may want him. Get Wilson to attend to it for you. You will have to do what you think best, in these matters!

Since writing the foregoing I have been to witness the sunday school exercises at the Baptist Church. This is the anniversary, of all the Evangelical churches. On that all the congregations unite in this matter. There are no less that 3000 scholars in the city. It was a very interesting spectacle and the exercises were agreeable. The speakers on the occasion, were so so. They lacked taste, in the selection of the topics, and their application, to the objects of the institution. They did not interest the children, which should have been their main object. I thought of you, of Sam, and all, My Love! The time seems <u>so long</u>, as Sam would say, that tho' the days pass by, and are gone <u>forever</u>, yet, it does does [sic] seem to me, tho' I know they can never return, I do not wish them to linger, until I am present with you, & our treasures. I need not tell you my Love, how devotedly, I do love you. I feel all the frenzy, of other days, for last night, as I came home from Jack Houstons, I saw our "star."[3] If you can fancy what my thoughts once were, and hopes, and then add to them the realities, which we have since enjoyed, with the addition of our circle, you can partially determine my anxiety, to be with you again, my Love! I do hope that nothing will cause my detention, beyond this day a month! I only regret that I can not be home on that day. The buds are swelling, & spring approaches in Texas. To day has been pretty above head but the snow has not all disappeared, and from the mountains, I do not suppose, it will disappear, before I cross them on my way home!

If we live to meet again, I hope that the little bickerings which originate, in the malice of my kindred will cease.[4] They have builded [sic] a wall, between them, & mine, & me, which never can be pulled down. As to what they say my Dearest, I advise you not to pay any heed. As for me, I, from regretting, what I have done about the letter,[5] I rejoice at it!!! It is only a pretext, used by them, to conceal their terrible malignity. When you reflect that Mrs Moore caused the derangement of her own child,[6] and rendered her own sister[7] (who had been to her children a mother) a confirmed maniac, by assailing her virtue, and employing her children, to slander, or (at least by her own shaming) betray a sister, is too much to bear.

71 : November 9, 1848—November 4, 1849

As an honorable man, I was bound to tell Lehr, all that I did. But when we meet, I will tell you something, that I did not think to tell you, of Lehr. I hope he may never have cause to repent what he has done. If he has to create such a <u>ward-robe</u>, as you you [sic] did for <u>them</u>, he will feel it, and bear it badly. This will lead to a rupture, and that to crimination, and recrimination, between branches of the family. In the contest it is very uncertain which side <u>miss Mary</u>[8] will take. She can't be like the woman was when her husband, and the Bear were fighting. She did not care, which got the best of it! I regret this silly business. If I live to return, I will treat it as a <u>business matter</u>.

Thy husband in faith
Houston

N.B. You may my dearest, if think proper show this to Mrs. Birdwell, as she is confidential.* *[In the margin: *or read it to her]* The fact is, that Mr Lehr, <u>received my</u> <u>communication in strict and inviolable confidence. As much so, as man can do.</u> It is for him, to account to his great Creator, for his broken pledge. I will give him a copy of the letter when I return!

Tell our friends not to be mixed up, with the bickering. I need no help, but truth, and that will confute all their slanders. I have seen a gentleman who was a classmate of Bro. Creath. I have some amusing matters to tell of him. The Gentleman was not sure that he was the same man, and to be assured that he was, he asked me <u>if he</u> <u>had not, a kind of sing song</u> <u>voice</u> <u>tone and manner</u>—Can you guess what I said in reply? "Yes sir-e." That was it my Dearest. I can't tell you all, but it is amusing!

Commend me to our dearly beloved friends,—To Mother, and Sam, present my love, and kisses to Nannie, & Maggie. Howda to Mr Gott, & Virginia. Tell all the servants, that I expect them to act faithfully, & be obedient.

Thy ever devoted husband
Sam Houston

[1]James "Buck" Houston.
[2]Houston may be referring to B. L. Hanks, who owned property in Washington County. Lucille Krisch, *1850 Census and First Taxpayers of Angelina County, Texas* (St. Louis,

Missouri: Frances Terry Ingmire, 1981), 15.

[3] For an explanation of the "star" see Madge Thornall Roberts, *Star of Destiny: The Private Life of Sam and Margaret Houston* (Denton: University of North Texas Press, 1993), 19.

[4] Houston is referring to the family's estrangement from his sister Eliza Moore and her family.

[5] Margaret referred to this situation in her letter to Houston on January 3, 1849.

[6] Pheobe Jane Moore Penland was an heir to the estate of Mary Houston's first husband, Matthew Wallace, in a will dated February, 1839. Ray, 303.

[7] Mary Houston Wallace. On January 13, 1846, Mary married William Wallace, the nephew of Matthew. Ray, 303. No documentation can be found, but family legend is that Eliza Moore was opposed to this marriage and became estranged from both Mary and Phoebe. In later years the Houston family shared a close relationship with Phoebe's son Sam Penland. A collection of his Houston papers is in the Rosenberg Library, Galveston, Texas. No other descendants of the Moore family have been located.

[8] Mary Moore Lehr.

Huntsville

Feb 13 1849

My dear Love,

I have just recd yours of the 26 ult. How pained I am to learn that you do not receive my letters regularly. I am sure that I never suffer a tuesday to pass without writing to you, but it is all in the mails. A few weeks more, and the dreary period will have past. My heart is filled with joy at the thought. Last night, I sat up until quite late, reading the work by Dr Chalmers,[1] which you brought me. It was a heavenly feast to my soul. In his "sabbath exercises," I saw my own heart laid open before me, and I was astonished and delighted to see that, that holy man had passed through that same clouds and doubts that so often darkened my spirit. And my happiness was increased by the hope that those holy effusions contained a remedy for your case. Some of his expressions describe your situation exactly, and gave me great comfort about you. After feasting thus for hours, I fell asleep in a calm sweet frame of mind and arose this morning at dawn. At an early moment, I prayed on my knees, and never have I prayed for you with such a lively faith. Oh my God, how long shall my soul wait for the blessing and hang upon thy promise! Help me Lord, help me to be still and know that thou art God.

It gratifies me my dear husband, to know that you are often with the ministers of God. I do hope you will find time to converse freely, with some one in whom you have confidence, for such conversation may be great blessings. If the Lord in his mercy should unite us again on earth, I believe there are happy days for us. I can not enter into the schemes of worldly greatness, which your friends are planning for you. Should the Lord have work for you to do, I know he will direct you, but the praise of man is an empty thing, and one year of domestic quiet is worth all the laurels of earthly heroes fame.

The family are all well and the children growing finely. Our crop will be planted late, owing to the quantity of rain that has fallen. The tobacco sent from New Orleans arrived today, and Mr Gott seems quite delighted to get them. Please bring me all the yard grass you can git [sic], and some of the sweet scented grass or perfume grass if you can find any.

My beads from Mr Sampson have not come yet. What can have become of them. I recd a letter from Antoinette today. Their visit to us is post-poned on account of the cholera. I trust when they come you will be at home. Sis tells me that her boy is said to be singularly like yourself. Your image seems to be quite the ton. Well I am willing that all the handsome children should be like you. Mother sends love to you, and Sam says "Ma tell pa to come home."

Thine devotedly,
M. L. Houston

P.S.

Love to A. Fitzpatrick and tell her they must certainly make us a visit.

---

[1]Dr. Thomas Chalmers, a Scottish theologian. Margaret may be referring to Chalmers's book *Application of Christianity to the Commercial and Ordinary Affairs of Life*. Winthrop S. Hudson, *Religion in America* (New York: Charles Scribner's Sons, 1981), 312.

The next letter is from the Burch-Remick-Roberts Collection of Houston letters.

Washington
15 Feby 1849

My Dearest,

You may try to imagine my happiness this morning when your dear letter, of the 30th ult reached me. I had resolved, not to look for one, so my disappointment was of the most agreeable character! To hear the welfare of all, you know my Love, would make me very happy, but to learn that the children are rosey, & cheerful delights my heart. By the way my dear, you need be in no dilemma about Sam's reading, since you will have it so. I presume his proficiency will not alarm me much, but at all events, I will not let him know but what it affords me the most agreeable surprise, that he is capable to read. "He was not to go to school, until he was eight years old." So as he has learned at home, I cannot complain of disobedience of orders. He is so active, that he must have employment. In fancy, Sam has often been seated on my knee, as well as other members of the family. I need not tell you my Love, if you even weighed two hundred averdupois, that I would be willing that you should sit on my knees for six successive hours, if I could only hear your sweet voice! My Dear, you will never know how much I love you, and how dearly, and deeply, I feel for you. I could tell you an anecdote, but it would require too much writing, and you know how much, I dislike the employment of using the pen. I will give you the gist of it, by telling you that a poor blind Phrenologist was here, and several of us, obtained charts from him of our heads. He did not hear my voice, and had no idea who I was, but from my reverence, he thought, I might be a Preacher. About this time some one spoke of me, as tho I was not present. He let go my head, and said "I will tell you what I think of that man Houston. I think him one of the most perfect reprobates, and rowdies, that I ever heard of of [sic]" and other remarks of a similar character. He then went on and finished, giving me all the high moral points, and concluded by saying that I had great <u>adhe-siveness</u>, meaning <u>constancy</u>! Well, this was all true! He then re-marked, that if it were the head of Danl Webster or Horace Greely, he could tell whose head it was, but he did not know any character, that would fit the head. A gentleman, then asked him, what he would think if [it] was Genl Houston. Oh! said he, that is impossible, and then ran over many of the best points repeating it is impossible, and appealed to me, when I assured him, that I was Sam Houston. You have [never] seen any one so plagued as he was. But I soon relieved the poor fellow, by joining in the general laugh. The upshot of the matter was, that he fell quite in love with me, and sought my society whenever he could obtain it. So my Love, I am happy to learn, that I improve upon acquaintance. Do you really think so? If you do my Dear, perhaps it is because, you are blind too, as the poor phrenolo-gist, only yours is the blindness of partiality, while his was the blind-ness of prejudice, added to his physical infirmity.

Yesterday I received an invitation to deliver a speech (Temper-ance of course) in New York, at the Tabernacle, by the "Daughters of Temperance."[1] I can not accept my Love, but intend soon to deliver one, to the people here, on the same subject! Except N. Orleans, I know of no place, which needs such influence more than does this metropolis. From some cause my dear, of late, I dislike speaking, but I cant particularize it. My mind is troubled about getting home, and I have come to the conclusion, that it is the last time that I will come alone, or remain here without my Dear Wife, and family. I have at least a thousand reasons, but if I live, and assign you but one, you would say, I am sensible, and rational. It pains me, that that [sic] I have no one, here with whom, I can interchange affection, or in other words, that I have no one here, that I can, or would love. This you will say alludes to your absence! Well, My Dear, rather than quarrel, you may have it so! Sam, I suppose, would contend, that his pres-ence is implyed [sic], if you will impart it to his understanding.

I hope my Love, that all things, will go well until we meet again. I have sent the Phials containing the water from the Dead Sea, and the red Sea by Judge [Daniel] Toler, and also a piece of the mosaic, from the floor of the Temple of Jerusalem.[2] The Judge assured me, that they should go safe if he did!

It is within 10 minutes of two oclock A.M. I will not have time to read this letter, so if any mistakes exist you must correct them. My love to all! and howda.

Faithfully thine own husband,
Houston

[1]See Mrs. John L. Norton to Sam Houston, February 12, 1849. Original letter in Andrew Jackson Houston Collection, Catholic Diocese, Austin, Texas.
[2]These relics have not been located.

The following letter to Sam Houston, Jr., is from the Sam Houston Hearne Collection at the Barker History Center.

Washington
16th Febry 1849

My Dear Son,

Your letter made me very happy. You are a dear Boy to send your Pa a pretty letter. You tell me you are a good boy, and this is so pretty. I know you would not tell me any thing but the truth, so I know you try to make your Ma, Grand Ma, and little sisters happy.

Many people talk to me every day about your Ma, and yourself. They all want to see you both, and say that they hear your Pa has the best wife, and best son, that any husband, and father has in Texas. This makes me anxious to see my dear wife, and son, and to be always with them, and not leave them again, while I live. I, too, think much about Nannie and Maggy. You say Maggy looks very smart. You did not tell me who little Maggy looks like. I am glad to hear that the hogs do well, and that matters are all in a fair way. I suppose, my son, that you will do a good deal of gardening this year. You, I suppose, are not too small to drop corn for, a hand in planting. I think I was seven years old, when I began to work. I hope my son, I will be with you, to show you how to work when you have to learn. You must kiss your Ma, Grand ma, and little sisters for me.

Affectionately
thy Father
Sam Houston

I did not see this scroll [sic] until I had written three pages.[1]

[1]Someone had written Houston's name at the bottom of this page. He drew a line through it and wrote the post script below.

The next five letters are from the Burch-Remick-Roberts Collection, San Antonio, Texas.

Washington
16th Feby 1849

My dear Wife,

About eleven hours since, I concluded a letter to you dated 15 Inst. To day in my place in Senate, I have found time to write Sam a letter, that his little heart may be made light, as his lump of approbativeness is very large. He would think if he received no letter, that I did not care so much about him, as he would wish me to do. You may have him ready to "surprise" me, with his learning, and I will accord to him the gratification, which he will hope for. I hope that he will make the best of men, if not the greatest. He is of peculiar disposition, and must be studied, & cherished. He has nothing vicious, or mean in his nature, but he must be employed, and conversation, with those for whom he understands to be his friends, and from whom he entertains affection, or respect, will be best for him. There is such a noise my dearest, that I can't write more. My love to mother & kisses to the children.

Thy devoted husband
Sam Houston

Washington
18th Feby 1849

My Dearly Beloved,

As usual, I was at church to day, and would have gone this evening again, only that it is so cold. This is said to be the coldest winter, for many years. I must confess, that I have many calls to day, that I would have been happy to have dispensed with. Tho' I had some which I was happy to see. Ben McCulloch & Col. [William] Palmer of Livingston, Texas. The Col, as well as Ben, are the same old two, and six-penses. I learn that my friend Hugh B. Johnson has paid the debt to nature. In the phrase of this world, he was a good man. As to his religious opinions, I never had any information, but I hope he did not depart without some full assurance, of a happy immortality. It is the only solace, for a dying creature! I pray my Love, that we may be enabled to prepare in time, for eternity! I do not neglect, the means appointed, but I fear, that I have not that renewed heart, necessary to the claims, upon Divine Mercy. I trust by the grace of God, I will never cease to exert, all my powers, of mind to be good, and to restrain, all evil propensities, from transgression. At all events I will strive, to obtain eternal rest, with the righteous of God!

You will find a letter from an old friend, in company with this, and will see that my gallantry to your friends, tho they are distant, does not desert me. It will tell you about a stranger, whose visit was caused, by "reading her bible." I have not written to her, but may do so, if I have time. If I should, I will tell her all about our young folks.

I send you a chart of my head,[1] and expect you to laugh at some of the blunders, which the <u>blind man</u> made! I send you some scraps, which may be amusing to you, & mother, as well as Sam, if you will take the trouble, of translating them to him, but it may be well, not to puff him, as I do not know how he will bear such things. You can judge best, my Love!

I do not know of any thing which I can tell, that will please you

79 : November 9, 1848—November 4, 1849

better, than that I love you, if possible, more, & more, every day, as the time passes by. It may be that you are absent from my mind, a portion of the time, but if so, I do not realise, that you are not present to me, for one hour in the day. And the little ones, clustered around your person. Oh! if I could only be with you all, my Love!

Present me appropriately to all.

Truly thy husband
Sam Houston

P. S. I will send you many Garden seeds, if I live tomorrow.

Houston

[1]This chart has not been located.

Washington
19th Feby 1849

My Love,

By to days mail, I send you Documents, which contain seeds. You can make such use of them as you may deem best. You can distribute such as you chuse to our friends. The wheat can remain, with other grains, except corn & Rice until next season. You may divide the corn with Col Birdwell. The seeds of trees, you can plant in several beds in the Garden, or Nurserys. Never fail to soak the seeds, or they will not come up! I send you no less than eight large packages of seeds.

To day I have nothing else to send by [sic] my love, and that, or a part of it, I am sure you will plant in the [heart] of our children! Won't you my Love? The balance you can lay by, in the casket of your affections.

Ever thine
Houston

My beloved husband,

As it would be impossible to get a letter to Washington, before you leave, I have determined to meet you with a few lines at Memphis. I have nothing interesting to tell you, except that we are all well. I recd no letter from you by the last mail, but by the one previous,[1] I learn from you, that you have been ill of the influenza. Oh my Love, how shall I describe my anxiety and uneasiness! and in addition to this you do not receive my letters regularly. I am unhappy indeed, but I trust the Lord will sustain us through the few dreary weeks to come. With the opening of spring my beloved, I sincerely hope, that we who live only in each other will be happy once more. Mother recd a letter from bro. Henry, by last mail in which he mentioned the reception of yours, and seemed greatly gratified.

Mr Gott commenced ploughing today. He could not begin sooner, as the ground has been perfect mud during the winter. The cholera has subsided in Houston, and I trust for good. Do my Love, have a plenty of red pepper about you, while you are travelling, lest you might be attacked unexpectedly. Sam is almost crazy to see you, and I dare not tell him, that I am writing to you, for I should be compelled to stop and talk to him about "pa." Nannie seems to me to grow more beautiful, and yet months ago, I thought she was perfect. I suppose you will see bro. William's[2] family. You must give them a great deal of love for me, and tell them I should rejoice to see our little ones romping together.

Mother is busy in the garden, but always sends love to you. Maggie smiles when I say "papa" and means a great deal, I have no doubt. I trust you will be with me so soon, that I will reserve the rest for your own private ear. It is much safer to whisper things than write them. If I were to tell you here, how much I love you, and the letter should be opened by some other person, there would be an awful disclosure!

Thine forever
M. L. Houston

81 : November 9, 1848—November 4, 1849

[1]See Houston to Margaret, January 30, 1849.
[2]William Houston, who lived in Memphis.

Washington
25th Febry 1849

My Dear,

Having spoiled you so badly, by always writing, it will not do now to cease, tho' I hope soon to leave this vast, but disagreeable city, and be with you, so soon as steam, and diligence can take me. I must write whenever I can!

As my custom has been, I have been twice at church to day, and heard bro Samson preach, able and interesting sermons. In the morning I was accompanied, by bro. William, who is on business, as far as New York. He will spend some days with me, and then proceed on business. He left all well at home, and brought much love, from the family, a portion of which, I transfer to you, and the children. He made very particular enquiries for all, and sends his best love to you, & Sam as old acquaintances, and to the baby part of the family, as new cousins. He sends respects to Mother, and would be delighted to see all the family. He is doing a good business, or at least, he is making something, and says his youngest son Eugene, is now three years old—and sister [Mary] is becoming much more fleshy, than she used to be!!! This I think he regards, as staf [sic] of <u>contingent</u> <u>expenses</u>.— The Mrs Gray <u>Bills</u>, of which a <u>friend of ours</u>, stands in such dread of. Now about this matter, I am fully persuaded, that Mrs Gray, and <u>our</u> <u>friend</u>, would differ, if each were to express their wishes, which might devolve upon us, of responsibility, which we might not be able to meet!

My Love, as I was not explicit, on the subject of <u>mesmerism</u>, I will tell you, that had I, at any time, discovered, that it was at war, with a belief of christianity I would have abandoned it, as an enemy to my peace. But on the contrary, it increases, the wonders, of the power of an Almighty God. It is indeed wonderful, and its curative powers great. The crowd here, increases, and the Eagles, are gathering to the carcass.

I have not seen any thing like the press of company, and the curious are anxious, to see the Lions first, and then amuse themselves, with the smaller animals of the show. I will write again, so soon as I can. Commend me to all. I must soon attend to Sams boots.

Good night my Love.

Thine ever

Houston

Washington
27th Feby 1849

My Dear Love,

We, as the adjournment approaches, hold our sessions as well by night, as by day. We meet at 12 N. and sit until 4 P.M.—Then adjourn until six, and meeting at six, we sit until midnight or day, as the case may be. We have but a few days to act as law makers, but as advisers of the President we will have to stay longer. I hope not a great while. Genl Taylor is here, but I have not yet been to see him. On tomorrow, I intend to pay my respects to him, as the elect chief Magistrate, of the Union. I have not yet had a chance at Mr Calhoun, but intend to come out in a letter, and pay him in part for the notice which he was pleased to take of me at Charleston.[1] It will not be violent, but it will not flatter him by any means. I will not use, all my ammunition at once, but reserve a charge, or two, for him, if he should come back at me! He had no justification for his conduct, and the only underline excuse, which he can now urge, is that he had looked on the south, as so many political plantations, belonging to him, and its Representatives as so many slaves to his silly abstractions.

Tomorrow I learn there will be the last drawing room of the present President.[2] I learn that the President elect[3] will attend the Levee. I may or may not go. The Inauguration Ball will come off on the 5th Proximo. I am not a subscriber, and did not intend to go, nevertheless I may do so, to rescue myself, from the charge of mean-ness. I have been at no Ball, nor did I intend if Cass had been elected to have attended. My situation now is different which I hope to ex-plain to you.

I am bored nearly to fits by prosing speakers—They are going on, so I must cease!

I have only time, my Dear, to assure you that I will not attempt to tell you how devotedly I do love you, and the little chicks, for I could not essay to tell you one thousandth part of my affection!

Thy husband affectionately

Sam Houston

[1]Calhoun had spoken in Charleston in August, 1848, justifying his opposition on the Oregon Bill, and criticizing Houston. For more information see Friend, 193–94.
[2]For a description of Polk's levee of February 28, 1849, see Nevins, 380–81.
[3]Zachary Taylor.

Washington

2nd March, 1849

My Dearest,

As this is my birthday, I must write to you, but I will not prom-ise, to write you any thing interesting. I send you scraps, papers, and Garden Seeds, that you may see, and know, that you are always present, to my cares, my thoughts, & my affections. Last night I sent you a package of seeds from [blurred] Burke, Commissioner of Pat-ents.[1] I hope they will reach you safely. You will not forget, in any case, I hope, when you plant them, to let them be well soaked. If they are not, they will not come up. And I presume, you will find some of them very rare, and acceptable to you.

I did not look at the various kinds, for really I do not know as much about flowers, as I did when <u>first in Mobile</u>.[2] I hope to be able at home soon, to renew my acquaintances with such associations. I have not, my love, received a letter from you since yours of the 6th Feby. I am fearful that you, supposed no letter after that day cou'd reach me here, and have declined writing. I hope this is not the case, but if it should be I will hope to meet letters at Memphis.

I sent you last night a program of the ceremony of Inauguration. The weather at this time is unfavorable, & I fear the day will not be fair.

The auguries, thus far have been inauspicious, to the propriety of his [Taylor's] administration. I am prepared to give him, a fair trial, and if he pursues the true interest of the country, I will support him with pleasure.

I am fearful, that he will fall, or has already fallen into the hands of the Philistines. You will see, that he is a nose of wax, to the Whig Party. He on all occasions, acknowledges his "ignorance, and incompetency."

My Dear, I have been <u>angry</u> for twenty four hours, but am recovering.[3] My love to all.

Ever thine

Houston

[In the margin:] I wrote at my Desk, in great haste, & compulsion.

[1]Edmund Burke of New Hampshire. For a biography see *Biographical Directory of the United States Congress, 1774–1989* (Washington, D. C.: United States Government Printing Office, 1989), 704.

[2]Houston is referring to his first meeting with Margaret and their walks in the garden at Martin Lea's home.

[3]On this date Houston prepared an address to his constituents to explain his action on the Oregon vote and to give his opposition to the Southern Address. In it he questioned Calhoun's position as "guardian of the whole south." Friend, 195. For a complete text see *Writings*, vol. 5, 78–88.

Senate Chamber

2nd March, 1849

My Dear Wife,

To night I had to write Sam a letter,[1] and for that reason, I write to you again. Two letters a day, is rather intense, and it will afford me reason to complain of arrogance! You will see, that I have changed my pen. I have at last, tried to write with a metal pen. It is a dreadful alternative, for me to write with any thing but a wild goose quill. I never wrote love letters with steel pens. They were too hard, to describe the tender passion, and for the same reason I would now object, to the same instrument, if I were to consult my feelings. I will not write more to you, as I am sure, I can not write any thing interesting, while such a "blithering" as [Robert] Burns would say, is going on in the chambers.

It is customary, as the Session draws to a close, for some of the members, to get pretty full of John Barleycorn, and so consume the time of the Senate.[2] I hope you will commend me to our friends, and expect me at the first moment, in my power, to reach you. My love to Mother, & Sam & kisses to the little ones. Howda to the rest.

Thy faithful husband
Sam Houston

[1]This letter has not been located.
[2]Several senators were so intoxicated and the disorderliness became so shocking that on the next night Houston rose to say that although he was familiar with the license and turbulence of the frontier, the present spectacle filled him with shame. Nevins, 226–27.

Washington
3rd March, 1849

My Love,

I wrote you <u>only</u> <u>two</u> letters on yesterday. I am again in the Senate at a late hour, & a prospect of remaining until tomorrow morning.[1] It will be the sabbath and thus, will include a part of it, in legislative sense. This day as counted is the last day of the session. On monday, as you will see, the Inauguration[2] will take place, and the call session of the Senate commences. I hope a few days will terminate the term of our present probation. I will use all my efforts, to be at home by the first of april. I will not brag, or banter, about what I intend to do. If we live to meet, I will tell you that I do not intend, unless I go to hunt Gold again, to be absent from my family longer than a few days, with my own consent. I can not forgo, voluntarily, the happiness of your society, or the noise of the children. For really, I would not consider it perplexing, if they were with me, or I with them. The noise which I endure here from the grown children, is ten times more annoying to me, than all that I know you hear at home, from the children.

Bro. William is still here, and may remain until the call session adjourns, and travel with me, as far as Memphis. I do not intend to make any stay at any point on my way home! He is anxious for us to call & spend a few days with him, but we cant consent.

I may write to you, from day to day, but I do not promise, as I will not tell any stories, no matter how trifling the consequences may be. Indeed if I do not write you will lose much by my silence, for indeed matters here to me, are very uninteresting to me, and were I to take them to you, I can not believe that they would be very charming to you. My love, & howda to all.

Thy ever devoted
Sam Houston

[1]Congress adjourned at half past six the following morning. Nevins, 227.
[2]For a description of the inauguration see James K. Polk, *Polk: The Diary of a President 1845–1849,* 388–90.

The following two letters are from the Sam Houston Collection in the Barker History Center, the University of Texas at Austin.

Washington
7th March 1849

My Dear Love,

I have had the pleasure to receive your letter of the 11th ult. It always creates, in my heart, the greatest pleasure to read your epistles. It is as agreeable to me, when I receive a letter from you, as the reception of a Boquet, by a Lady, from her devoted lover, and such a feeling, as once existed, in a old ladies garden near Mobile![1] Or rather, it existed in the breast of a young Lady, who was in the Garden, at the time. My Love, do you recollect anything about the incident? I do! Ah late my Love, I have reflected, much upon <u>those</u> happy days, as well as others, which have intervened. Every hour, which passes increases my anxiety to reach my home, that I may embrace my all on earth.

I feel, that if I were at home, I could be eloquent, in the expression of my affections, if you were my auditor. By the bye, speaking of eloquence, I can tell you that on the last night of the Session, I made a speech which was said to be one of much merit.[2] I can only say that I cast oil on the troubled waters. It bro't to my mind your dreams of Maps. You will hear of it through the papers. I am fearful my Dear that there would have been no appropriation, for the current year but for me. The wheels of Gov't would have been stopped and anarchy would to some extent, at least, have succeeded and the government been endangered! As it now is, we can look forward to years of prosperity for our Country.

Tomorrow, I design that a publication of mine, in answer to Mr. Calhoun's charge against me shall appear in the papers.[3] I waited patiently for an opportunity in the Senate to scourge him, but as none occurred, I felt bound not to let him pass by without a scathing.[4] You will see my task!

I hope we will adjourn this week and hasten home.

My Love, and howda
Thy ever devoted & faithful husband
Sam Houston

[1]Houston is referring to the evening when he first met Margaret. For a description of this meeting see Roberts, 18–19.
[2]For the text of Houston's speech of March 3, 1849, on the proposition to extend the laws of the U. S. over California, see *Writings,* vol. 5, 89–90.
[3]It was published in *The Northern Standard*, May 12, 1849. Ibid., 88.
[4]In his speech Houston said "My motto is, 'In time,' not 'in haste.'" Ibid., 78.

Washington
11th Mar 1849

My Beloved,

I have just received the enclosed letters, and in return wrote to Mr Royston,[1] and urged him to send out our niece!

My intention my Love, is to leave here for home on the 13th, I hope. The Senate will not adjourn so soon, but I must, if possible be at San Augustine by the 3rd proximo, and from there home, so soon as possible.

Genl Rusk will remain, until the close of the session. The Senate may sit some ten days longer. I may write to you, again ire I leave here.

To day my Love, I heard two interesting sermons, from our friend Mr. Samson. A few days since, he spent part of an evening, with me. I presented him your grateful regard, and esteem, for the presents, which his kindness had presented to you. He is an excellent, & intelligent Gentleman. I hope he may do much good in this place, and add to the fold of the Lord. Some Holy influence is needed. I inquired, and was told of the Bar, of this Hotel, there was, expended for liquor alone, no less than two hundred and fifty dollars. How many wretched, human beings might have been rendered comfortable, and happy, by this sum, wisely laid out. The cause here, of Temperance, is not in the right hands, but I hope it will go on, & prosper.

I only started to write a word, & say that I sent a letter.

Present my love to all the family & howda. Commend me to our friends.

Thy devoted Husband
Houston

[In margin:] In great haste!!

[1]Robertus Royston, Houston's brother-in-law.

To Gen'l Sam Houston
San Augustine Texas

Huntsville March 29th 1849

My beloved husband,

By last mail, I recd your dates of the 7th, 8th,[1] and 11th all of which gave me great comfort, and as you expect to be detained a short time in San Augustine, I have determined if possible to meet you there with assurances of our well-being. My hope of seeing you on the first of April had almost amounted to certainty, so that I had measured my fortitude to that length of time. I know not how to endure a longer separation. To Sam's yet expected question, "Ma when will pa come?", I have generally replied "when the flowers are in full bloom," but the flowers have anticipated me a little, and now he says "Ma the flowers are in full bloom, but pa is not here!" That expression of Sam's embodies my own feelings. The sweet spring is indeed here, and the air is redolent with the breath of flowers, but he is far way without whom the brightest and sweetest objects of nature lose thier charms. Do not fear dearest, that I am forgetting myself, and writing from other days. Indeed no! What time should be sweeter than the present!

While I think of it my Love, I must guard you against the fascinations of a certain person in Huntsville. I hope you will take it kindly, remembering my old infirmity. Her name is Maggie Lea Houston, and she reigns as a queen in our family. The grave and philosophic Sam, the sprightly and self-willed Nannie and even Mother herself all bow to her gentle sway, and unless you guard yourself carefully, I fear you will soon think more of her than any of us. Beware her bright eyes, rosy lips, and merry laugh.

Sister Kate has presented our brother [Vernal] with a fine daughter[2] whom they call for your wife. They are now living in her father's neighborhood[3] and I am told are pleasantly situated. My friend Amanda Smith and Mr. Branch[4] are married and I hope they will do well.

You will probably hear of the death of Edwin Banton, who was killed by Davis the deguereotyper [sic].[5] I dare say you will hear

Davis represented as a monster, for he is poor and obscure, but do not form any opinion until you come home. On his side, there is a history of wrong and oppression, that could plead for him, if there were ears to hear but there is scarcely a listening ear or a pitying eye for him or his poor little wife and child. My lips are closed on the subject, and although I often hear Banton almost canonized, I let it pass.

If you come through Nacogdoches thank Mr [Charles] Chevallier for the shrubbery which he was kind enough to start to me. Unfortunately I did not receive it until it had been four weeks on the way and of course it was all bad. Dr Keenan[6] received a fine collection of shrubs from Judge Sterne's,[7] but none came to me. Did you not speak to him for me? Well it is of no very great consequence.

The garden seeds, which you sent have almost all come up finely, and I hope we will have an abundance of vegetables. The corn is doing well, but is considerably washed by a very hard rain, which has recently fallen. The tobacco did not come up very well, but Mr Gott thinks he will have plants enough.

And now my beloved—beware of Henderson. Lose every thing at stake rather than encounter that bad man. I do believe he would like to get a pretext for killing you. I would rather you should run from him, than have any thing to do with him. It is no cowardice to run from a hyena, and I have more respect for that abhored [sic] animal, than for him. For the sake of them you love and them who love you, do not encounter him.

With the hope that we shall soon meet, I bid you adieu.

Thy devoted wife,
M. L. Houston

[1]No letter written March 8, 1849, has been located.
[2]Margaret Houston Lea.
[3]General James K. Davis had purchased land near Cold Spring, Polk County, in 1848. Camilla Davis Trammell, *Seven Pines: Its Occupants and Their Letters, 1825–1872* (Houston: Published Privately, 1986), 95.
[4]Anthony M. Branch.
[5]Houston would later serve as a defense attorney for George A. Davis. For information on this incident and the later trial see Bowen C. Tatum, Jr., "Henderson King Yoakum," *Texas*

Bar Journal 33 (September 1970): 721–22.
[6]Dr. Charles G. Keenan.
[7]Judge Adolphus Sterne.

San Augustine

11th April, 1849

My Dear,

I had a safe, but not a pleasant trip here.[1] The suit in which I was summoned, has been disposed of. All the vaunting has passed off, and there is but one opinion in society. My old friends are here, and glad to see me. As I will be detained for a few days on business, I have agreed to make a speech, to this Division of Temperance, on saturday next.

The people are all anxious to hear me, and will come from a great distance, as they say, who pretend to know. I will try, and make a clever speech.

From some cause my hand cramps so, that I must cease writing, or I could write to you a dozen of pages, if my hand could serve my heart faithfully. It has been to me a most painful absence from home, and more so since I received your letter.

I intended to be prudent, and to keep any position, which it might be proper for me to assume.

I may return home, on horseback and if so, I may sit but on saturday, or monday, but not on Sunday, which [I] do not wish to do.

It is probable my dearest, that I may buy you a horse for riding, and the Buggy. He would suit you, as I think, or I would [not] purchase him. If I get the one, that I proposed, he will carry you, and the weans, at once, if you can get room to sit on him.

I think <u>so long</u>, to be at home again, and to stay there. You must give, my love to mother, and tell Sam, poor fellow, that I am <u>so anxious</u> to see him. Hug him, and the dear wee girls, and you may say to my dear Wife, that I am crazy to see her! Tho I may spend a day, or so in Nacogdoches, on the way home to sell some land. But rely upon this, that I will go home, just so soon as I can, and stay so long as you wish. Your friends here, all desire to hear from you, and to be presented to you.

Very truly thy ever devoted husband,
Sam Houston

[1]Polk reported that on March 25, 1849, Houston had stopped briefly at Memphis and had then sailed downriver. Polk, *Diary of a President,* 400–401.

San Augustine
14th Apl, 1849

This evening I made the cleverest Temperance speech, that I ever did in my life to my notion. It was well received, and caused one Grocerykeeper to declare that he would close his Grocery.[1] So much for this.

You know, my Dearest, that I do not like to travel on the sabbath, but I intend to set out on tomorrow. I intend to travel in company with an old friend, Doct Sharp[2] from Tennessee. I may stay a day in Nacogdoches, to sell some land, as I have a prospect to do so. Anxious as I am to see you, my Love, I think you will be willing that I should pospone my return, one day on business. All matters has [sic] passed here quietly, and my friends cling to me as brothers.

It will be best that I should go home on horse back. The roads are washed, so badly that it is unsafe, for a stage, and therefore I prefer horse back. I purchased another Poney [sic] for you. You see my Love, I am still trying to suit you in hackneys. I hope to get one that you can ride, or drive, as you may think best.

Please dont think that I wish to stay away from home. No My Love! For I declare that I am almost stupid, with anxiety. I hope to be home, on thursday night unless the weather, or some other cause should detain me.

My love to mother, and the children. Howda to all. Mrs Sublette[3] and many others send a great deal of love to you!

Thy ever truly and devoted husband,
Sam Houston

[1]Establishments which sold liquor were called groceries.
[2]Dr. B. F. Sharp. Identified in Carpenter, 1708.
[3]Ester Jane Roberts (Mrs. Phillip Sublett).

During the summer of 1849, Houston made two business trips to East Texas. While there he wrote the following letters.

Nacogdoches
7th May 1849

My Dearest,

I am here safe. I had a fatiguing trip. I am hoarse and can't speak at all. I have no suffering. I am mute! Genl Rusk & myself will go to Henderson on tomorrow if possible. It is only 31 miles from here. I intend to try, and be home on the 26th. I will return this way, & spend a day or two at court, & then take the stage.

The mail will leave in a few minutes, and I can only write this much. Don't take the [blurred]. My love to all. I hope all will go on well until my return. Let the weeds be hoed out of the corn.

Thy ever devoted Husband,
Houston

Nacogdoches
14th June 1849

My Dear,

On the 11th, I reached here, and found one suit had been tried. It went against my client. I can get a new trial. I traded the Poney [sic], on my way here and got a good horse. On thursday a week Genl Rusk, [David] Kaufman, and my self intend to set out for Marshall. I hope to reach home by the 1st of July. I am very anxious to be at, and stay, there, if I can always. My anxiety increases when I am from home to get back. But there is no end of cases in this life. There is no news in this place. I have not been to see any of our friends, but Rusk, Sterne, & Chevallier. I have been busy, and will be so, until I leave. I tried to send you a letter the day of my arrival, but could not. I will try, and send Peas, by the Stage. Let them be planted about ten on a place. I intend to write every mail, until I leave here, as there will be two departures. I will send all the Peas, that I can get, so as to eke out the group. I find in this country, that my presence aids my business. Genl Davis has gone to Henderson, where I hope to meet him. He was well, when we parted, and in good spirits. I heard there is a Huntsville paper, but I have not seen it in town.

I will call at the office, and may get a letter from you. You may write to me at this place, and if I do not get it, before I leave, I may get it on my way back.

Tell Mr Gott to watch the crop!

Give my regards to Mother, Howda to Virginia, and kisses to all. Poor Sam. I feel concern when walking about town, for want of his agreeable prattle, and on other occasions, for his Dear Ma, & Sisters.

Thy ever devoted husband
Houston

P. S. People are disappointed that you did not come with me. I regret you did not.

Thine
Houston

Very few of the letters written by Houston to members of Margaret's family have been located. The following one to Antoinette Lea Power is in the collection of Houston letters in the Sam Houston Regional Library & Research Center, Liberty, Texas.

Huntsville
4th Nov 1849

My Dear Sister,

    I have not written to you, as I should have done, or as I wished to do. Through my dear Margaret I could always hear from you, and the family. In a letter, which you recently wrote to Margaret, you had the carelessness, to manifest some bad temper, as I call it. However, that may be mere matter of taste.

    I did not write letters introductory for Mr W. Power. The reason I did not, I imparted to your Sister, and requested her to state it to you. I hope she did not, or you would have had no cause of displeasure. Previous to my leaving Washington, I wrote letters to Genl Smith,[1] & Col [John C.] Fremont, that they were the last letters, that I would ever write to them of the kind. I did not personally know either of the Gentlemen, and was daily called upon for letters to them. Had a brother called upon me, I could not under these circumstances have written to either of those gentlemen. This was my only reason, and it does seem to me, although I had not the pleasure of Mr Power's acquaintance, that I merited neither, [blurred] nor reproach! No matter, how well we may think of ourselves or our relatives, it can not furnish a reason, for other persons, to disregard all rules, or promises to gratify us, or ours, and if for any reason they should decline it, it can not or ought not to be cause of offence [sic] to any one, and therefore I can make no fashionable apology, and profess contrition, when I feel none for my course!

    Now having disposed of this matter, I will attend to matters of more importance. I let brother Vernal have five hundred acres of land, of certain dimensions of length & width, commencing on my upper rise—then to you[r] six hundred & forty aces, laying below his lower line, & adjoining to his tract. It has appeared since his tract was run off, that he ran his line too high, and above my line.[2] This will throw him lower down for his compli[blurred], and of course your land will also have to drop down in proportion. This will require the tracts both to be run off again. The Field notes were never furnished me, to make title, and Mr Bledsoe[3] told me that he had eight hundred acres run off instead of 640. Now so soon as, the tracts are run off, it will afford me much pleasure to make title, and if I die, my representatives will do as tho' I were living.

Mr. Hollimans[4] son in law, Deblane, wrote to me a few days proposing terms to me, to get the place, as a renter. I referred him to Vernal, or yourself, for information. Vernal could see to your interest when [he] is attending to his own. He is a noble man, and is kitchened at home, by a clever wife, and two fine brats. His son "Temple," is much like him, "only more so."

I hope you will all make "Bermuda Spring"[5] a visit, and spend the christmas. I will not be here to greet you, but would be truly happy to greet all the Powers, old and young, and make them as comfortable as we are able to do.

Your land will be valuable, and I doubt not, but Mr Power would succeed better there, in producing cane, than he ever can do "Caney" [sic]. It is favorable to the culture of sugar, as Mr Holliman, and others have proved. But I will not pretend to advise. I do not myself aspire to become a Planter. If I can live plentifully, and decently, as the people of the country, and leave my family, an independency, it is all that I desire, or crave of this worlds goods.

Mother enjoys good health, and is pretty well satisfied I think. She is busy, as usual, and at this time her more favorite is a pet Pig. Nannie is rather a rival to it, at times. Margaret is in better health than she has been since my return. The children are now all well, and quite pretty, as their Ma says. We were all disappointed, in not receiving a visit from you all this summer. Many were the exclamations, "That is Sister." "Look Mistress yonder is Miss Anns carriage." Thus we had it, and often disappointed and sorrowful. On the 9th inst I intend to set out for the City.[6] I will be very happy to hear from you, at the city, and I will pay for your letters in Public Documents. I sent a Patent Office Report, to brother Charles for him & Tom.

We all invite in affectionate regards to all the Powers and to Mart.[7]

Truly thy Brother
Sam Houston

[1]Houston is probably referring to General Percifor Frazer Smith. For a biography see *Dictionary of American Biography*, vol. 9, 2, 331.

[2]Houston is probably referring to land owned by the Lea, Bledsoe, and Houston families in Grand Cane, Liberty County.

[3]William Bledsoe, Antoinette's first husband.

[4]Harmon Holliman, Vernal's neighbor in Liberty County.

[5]The original name of the Houstons' Woodland Home.

[6]Washington, D. C.

[7]Martin Royston, the nephew of Margaret and Antoinette.

Chapter II

November 24, 1849—February 24, 1850

January 28, 1850: Margaret Houston to Sam Houston
January 29, 1850: Sam Houston to Margaret Houston
February 3, 1850: Sam Houston to Margaret Houston
February 5, 1850: Sam Houston to Margaret Houston
February 6, 1850: Margaret Houston to Sam Houston
February 12, 1850: Margaret Houston to Sam Houston
February 14, 1850: Narcissa B. Hamilton to Sam Houston
February 18, 1850: Margaret Houston to Sam Houston
February 24, 1850: Margaret Houston to Sam Houston

Houston left Texas in the latter part of November and traveled to Washington by way of the Red River, continuing by the southern route. His first known letter to Margaret on this trip was written on November 18, 1849, from Douglas, Texas, about fourteen miles east of Nacogdoches. For the text of this letter see Writings, *vol. 5, 108– 109.*

Grand Ecore [Louisiana]
24th Nov. 1849

My Dear,

This is the third day that I have been detained at this place. There was a boat, which descended the river since I came, but it was a miserable little thing, and crowded with passengers, being very slow, so that I did not wish to go on board of her.

To day we expect the Caddo, a fine boat, and expect to get off from this place, which, by the bye, is by no means desirable. It is a place of some business—principally from Eastern Texas.[1]

Since my arrival I have become so well rested, that I am now tired of resting. You will see in the New Orleans paper, which I sent you, that one of the most fearful explosions has taken place in Orleans that has ever been recorded, in the history of steam disasters.[2] The scene must have been awful, in the entrance. The ways of Providence are mysterious, & must remain concealed from mortal knowledge. Such occurrences should admonish us to be prepared, for we know not when the messenger death will arrive, and call us to account. Hence it is but fitting, that we should remember, the admonition—"Be ye always ready etc."

For the first time in my life, I have neither felt, nor manifested impatience, from detention, & I will try in all good faith not to allow myself, to manifest, and if possible, not feel impatience, when it is not in my power to remedy, a temporary inconvenience.

There were [many] little matters which I omitted to have done. One was to have glass put in the windows. Will you please to request Captain Hatch[3] to have it done right off hand. I did not have a lathe, put on the crack in ascending the stairs, at the end of the loft plank.

Let it be done. I told Albert[4] of it, but he may have forgotten it, or may not have understood me. I want my "big Book," or "journal,"[5] laid under the head of Mothers bed, and the slat, so that it may be safe. Those papers that were lost, I can only account for as one principle. You recollect how your Tennessee Bible was used. The same persons are with us, that were then. Do not by any means allude to this matter, but think of it my Dearest.

You will wish to now [sic] how I pass my time here. Well I will tell you. I read, I think, and I whittle. Then I walk to the river, and look for a Boat, see none, and return to reading and whittling, and thinking of home, my own dear home. If I could only be transported to my home, for one brief hour, it would be worth all the time which I have passed, since I impressed <u>adieu</u>, on your dear lips. I need not say how anxious I am again, to greet you, and reclaim the pledge of enduring affection! Say to the little ones, that their precious rose pledges, I wear near my heart. My mind should I live, is to call at the Cane brake,[6] notwithstanding my detention thus far. Nothing important I presume, will be done, until the Holy-days are over. I have written to you so often, and so much, that I will have to continue the habit, or you will be disposed to complain of negligence. Well, as it draws me near to you in thought, I do not shrink from the duty which, I owe to you, as well, as to my own feeling. You have written to me, before this, I have no doubt. If all our pigs were lost, you are not to suppose, that I will say, or feel any thing about the matter. On my way, I procured two pigs from Col. Long[7] of a fine breed—not so large as mine, but they will suit the south better, than mine. He is to send them down to Captain Hatch, and I will write or send a male pig to Col Long. This is the understanding, if they were not all lost. I have not seen a better breed of Hogs than these of Col Long's. They are white as snow, and no kin, to the former present. It was my fault, that I did not get white pigs before. My hogs are too large, and I am fearful that I will not have luck, with them, but by crossing, I will be able to have the finest stock in Texas. You need not suppose me discouraged, but it is prudent to amend, any thing that is not perfect. My object is to render every thing useful, and therefore profitable, to comfort, & plenty.

About our home matters, I will not trouble myself as it would be in vain, if it would do no good. I hope our Dear Mother will confine her action to the house, and leave all matters out of doors to Captain Hatch, as I feel assured he would do the best that he can, or that can be done for us. Whatever you may need, or wish for the farm, all that you need do will be to send an order, to Gibbs[8] or Smith.[9] Utensils will have to be procured, and Captain Hatch will tell you what is needful. I do hope, my Love, you will endeavour to be satisfied, as relates to our matters, and be assured, that my prayers, however unworthy they may be, are for your health, and happiness. You will at all times write to me, and let me know your feelings, & troubles, so that I can at least sympathize with you, as you do, and will profess, the full measure of my affections.

There is nothing in addition, My Love, that I can write to you. If I stay in Orleans, one hour, I will write to you, and may contrive to [send] you some trifle from that point, as a trifling memento. I do not at this time recollect, that I promised to send any thing, because it could be needed!

You will I hope, receive letters from me directly, from the points, at which they may be written. I will only promise, to write, when I have any thing worth writing to you.

Present my love to Mother, & kisses to Sam, & the rosebuds. To Virginia & Capt Hatch, commend me. Say to her, that I will send her the "copy book," which I promised. Write to me at all times about the several improvements made, making, and projected!!!

Most truly and devotedly thy husband
Sam Houston

[1]For a description of the town of Grand Ecore and its history see William Physick Zuber, *My Eighty Years in Texas* (Austin: University of Texas Press, 1971), 203.

[2]Houston is referring to the explosion of the *Louisiana*, in which eighty-six people were killed and two other ships were leveled. R. Conrad Stein, *The Story of Mississippi Steamboats* (Chicago: Childrens Press, 1987), 18.

[3]Anthony Hatch. Identified in Carpenter, 2022. Hatch had taken over managing the farm after the departure of the former overseer, Thomas Gott.

[4]A Houston slave.
[5]Houston is probably referring to his "Private Executive Record, 1841–44" which is now housed in the Sam Houston Regional Library and Research Center, Liberty, Texas.
[6]The Royston-Lea plantation in Alabama.
[7]Houston is probably referring to his friend Colonel John Long of Crockett.
[8]Sanford or Thomas Gibbs, Huntsville merchants. Carpenter, 2019.
[9]Huntsville merchant J. C. Smith.

Huntsville
Nov 27 1849

My Dear husband,

I have some hopes that this letter will anticipate your arrival in Washington, but at the same time have some apprehension that I have delayed writing too long, from the supposition that you would remain a few days with our relations in Ala. If you should not find a letter when you get there, I hope you will have no uneasiness on our account, for we are all doing well. We are in good health and as cheerful as we can be under existing circumstances. Of course our home looked desolate enough after your departure, but I have endeavored by constant occupation, to keep myself from indulging in useless regrets. I remained at Mr. [James] Maxy's, with the exception of one night at home, until the death of thier little boy,[1] which occurred on the morning of the 22nd inst. In thier deep grief, I selected many appropriate passages of scripture, and was enabled through the blessing of God, to impart much comfort to thier stricken spirits. You would have been astonished and delighted to see with what childlike simplicity they recieved the word of God. It proved to me that the bible contained a rich store for the afflicted, unpercieved [sic] by others. On the sabbath you left, our bible class was organized, and last sabbath met for thier first recitation. We began with more than 20 scholars, and the exercises were truly edifying. Your friend Gen'l Hatch[2] is our leader and you would be perfectly delighted to hear his explanations of the bible. Oh what talents he has withheld from his master's service! But there seems to be a great increase of zeal amongst our christian friends, and I hope it will continue to increase. Our sabbath school is now in a flourishing condition. Oh how my heart is cheered by it! My beloved husband, I write to you about these great subjects, so dear to my heart, because I know you are not indifferent to thier importance. Would that I could feel assured that you loved them for the sake of the blessed Saviour, whose cause they are assigned to promote. I hope you will never forget the admonition of our afflicted friend Mrs Evans. Dearest I know you would love to possess the hope that could diffuse such lustre throughout a sick room. Oh then strive for it! "Strive to enter in through the straight gate!"

I have not yet acknowledged the reception of your letter from Douglas. It was truly cheering to me, to hear that you were well and getting on so finely. Mr. Baker[3] brought me your letter from Cincinatti [sic][4] and made his home with us as you desired. The college is located on Hanchet's hill on "the old gin hill" (by the bye, not quite so classic a name as "college hill.") Mr. Hanchet[5] has given them 10 acres for their grounds. I was anxious for them to accept your offer, but I rather suspect they will have more causes in the end to regret that they did not, than we will have, for I can hardly believe that the mud and impure water of that vicinity will contribute much to the progress of science.[6] It is expected at our next meeting that Mary Lehr will unite with our church. What will your puritanic [sic] blood say to it? I am told she has given the subject a thorough investigation, and is now very decided.

My Love, do not overlook our baptist friends in Washington. I do hope you will see them whenever you can. You have no idea of the consolation it gives me, to know that you have the privilege of such society. And now, will you be so kind as to settle my debt with the "New York recorder"? Remember I paid for the year 1845, and once had the receipt, but lost it. I have only recd the paper regularly about 3 years, but in that time it has been well worth the price of it. If you say so, we will continue it. Our little ones are very rosy and cheerful and very beautiful (so thinks your humble servant!) If you were near, you would often hear Maggy's plaintive voice calling "pa oh pa!"

Sam and Nannie talk a great deal about you. Mother is well, but much within doors. I know of nothing else, that would interest you just now. I will add that our stores came to hand, with the exception of the hams, and as no bill accompanied them I am at a loss to account for thier not coming. I have written with a wretched pen, but hope you will be able to read my scrawl.

Ever thine own

M. L. Houston

[1]James Maxey, Jr., died of a "brain ulcer." Roland Vern Jackson, *Mortality Schedule, Texas, 1850* (Bountiful, Utah: Accelerated Indexing Systems, 1979), 15.

[2]Margaret is probably referring to F. L. Hatch. Identified in *Writings,* vol. 5, 19.

[3]Daniel Baker, who later taught at Austin College.

[4]Cincinnati, Texas, fourteen miles from Huntsville.

[5]L. B. Hanchet, a Huntsville lawyer. Identified in Tatum, "Henderson King Yoakum," 719.

[6]This site is now part of the campus of Sam Houston State University.

New Orleans

28th Nov. 1849

Dearest,

Robert Royston[1] is in my room and reports all well at home, and very anxious to remove to Texas. In an hour, I have to set out to the Boat. My intention is to spend two or three days in Alabama. Lucy Ann [Lea] is with her Pa[2] at Montgomery. I intend to pass as much time as I can on my way, as it is not important, that I should be in the city immediately. If I have time, I will go out and send you some things by the Boat.

Other letters will accompany this that my distraction at leaving home caused me to forget, until I was cleaning out my pockets, when I found them.[3] I hope no evil will arise from the neglect.

I will have to close this letter, as my room is full. I will try, and write to you from Montgomery. I will fail in nothing which can contribute to your happiness.

You will as usual present me to the family. As I have been detained here on my route, I hope, you will have anticipated me by letter at the city.

I have seen Mrs. [William] Christy, who has been very ill. I fear that she is not long for this world. She was kind in her inquiries, for your health, and the children. Col. Christy was glad to see me, and is the same man, that he always was. I hope to be very composed, when I write to you next.

Commend to all friends,
Thy Devoted Husband
Sam Houston

Make Sam send me his autograph in your first letter after this is received.

Thine
Houston

[In margin:] I arrived last night & start at 2:00 P.M. Now 30 minutes past our [sic].

[1]The son of Margaret's sister Varilla.
[2]Henry Clinton Lea was serving in the Alabama Legislature.
[3]One of these is the following letter to Margaret from Albert Goodall, the half-brother of Virginia Thorn, which Houston had apparently picked up by mistake.

The following letter was addressed to Margaret in Huntsville. It has this notation on the outside in Houston's handwriting, which is dated 28th [Nov] 1849: I opened this by mistake. I got it at Huntsville with the other letters. I will answer it so soon as I reach the City.[1]

Philadelphia
Oct 20 1849

Mrs Houston
Dear Madam

It was not untill [sic] about three weeks since that I knew of your residence or I should have written to you long since. Mr. Crawford[2] from Galveston came in here to purchase goods and from him I got the first information from your family since I left Texas[3] and also of my sister Virginia. Perhaps you are not aware of what my movements have been since I left Texas. From Galveston I went to the West Indies where I was very unfortunate with the person I went with, loosing [sic] by him all I had. I then took up my residence in Havana where I have been residing for the last five years, and where I learnt my trade Engraver and Copper Plate Printer. Last March I left Havana to return to the United States. I landed at Boston and came by land to this City, visiting the principal places and Cities of the Eastern States. I have now been here some five months. It was my intention of setling [sic] down here in business, but through changes of business and other occurance [sic] it is very probable that I shall return to Texas next Spring.

While in Havana I wrote to Mr. Vernal Lee [sic] twice but got no answer, neither could I hear from Mr. Crawford although I wrote to him often, and the only person I could get answers from was the family of Mrs. Morriss[4] on Galveston Bay with whom I have corresponded regular. I have often requested them to give me information of my sister but they have not been able to do so untill their last letters which I received a few days since by which they informed me that directly from her by a lady that had seen her a few days previous and that she (Virginia) requested them to write to me and Mrs. Morriss has very earnestly requested that [I] will allow Virginia to come and reside some time with her family and as her family are old and intimate friends of mine, of cours [sic] I have willingly consented for Virginia to go. She has three large daughters with whom Virginia will have good companions as they are well Educated besides they have a good school near their house whare [sic] I have made arrangements for Virginia to go as I have heard that she as yet has no Education of any account, cannot write nor read writing. I presume that you have not had the advantage of a school in your neighborhood. I informed Mrs. M. to send for her whenever she wished and I would write to you & your Mother thinking of course that you would have no objection to such a request from me. I have also heard that your

Mother said she had only recd thirty $30 dollars from the wages of the negro woman Rachel. If this is true it is very strange for Mr. Crawford told me here that he had regular paid over the wages to the order of Mr. Lee, therefore I think it must be a mistake, for C. informed me that he paid over an average of from seven to ten dollars per month.[5] This in over five years would amount to a considerable more than thirty dollars, therefore please inform me correct about it, and if the income of the negro has not been sufficient to pay the expenses of Virginia, I will make up the difference as I know the care you must have taken of her has been of some expence [sic] to you and your Mother.

Should I return in the spring of this winter to Texas I shall come up and see you and Mrs. Lee and in person return the many thanks that I am indebted to you and your Mother for the care you have taken of Virginia, for the long lapse of time and hope that in the course of time I shall in some way be able to have an opportunity of returning some of the many obligations I feel myself under at [present]. I am working at my business as a journeyman doing tolerable well. I am much pleased with this city and [wou]ld like to remain permanently in it. I have the pleasure of much good society and any quantity of all kinds of amusements. There is nearly as much enjoyment of the gaieties of high life as there is in Havana. I hope you will favor me by answering this soon. Please give my remembrance and respects to Mrs. Lee, Gen'l Houston and to Mr. Lee. It was only by Mr. Crawford that I heard of the death of Mr. Bledsoe and of her [Antoinette's] second marriage. Any information I can give you from here I will be happy to do. There is no gen'l news at present worth writing. Hoping this may find you and all the family in good health & that I may hear from you soon I am yrs

With much Respect and Yr Obt Servt
A. G. Goodall

By a letter I have just recd from my brother,[6] he has in company with a party of Texas Ranger[s] that was with him in the Mexican war departed for California. He said he had written several times to Mrs. Lee but had never had any answer.[7]

[1] The original letter, which is believed to have been destroyed in a fire, was part of the collection of Virginia Thorn's granddaughter, Ruth Linda Sneed. A copy of the letter was furnished the editor by Joe Weldon Sneed, San Antonio, Texas. For more information about Albert Goodall see his obituary in the *New York Daily Tribune,* Monday, February 21, 1887, p. 3, col. 5.

[2] A. C. Crawford ran the oldest mercantile business in Galveston. Charles W. Hayes, *Galveston: History of the Island and the City* (Austin: Jenkins Garret Press, 1974), vol. 2, 880–81.

[3] Albert Goodall had lived in Texas in 1844 and served in the Texas Navy. Information furnished by Joe Weldon Sneed.

[4] Goodall is probably referring to Elizabeth Morris, who lived near the Crawford family. Carpenter, 771.

[5] In a sworn accounting of the estate of Virginia's mother, Mrs. Elizabeth R. Worcester, Vernal Lea stated that the amount of hire of Rachel from 1842 to 1848 was $500, which was appropriated to the support of Virginia. Worcester Estate File, Galveston County Courthouse. Copies furnished to the editor by Virgie Looney, Virginia Thorn descendant, Gonzales, Texas.

[6] James P. Goodall. He had visited Vernal and Nancy Lea in Grand Cane in the summer of 1842. James P. Goodall to Robert Johnson, August 8, 1842, Worchester Estate File, Galveston County Courthouse. James and Albert Goodall were sons of Virginia's mother, Mrs. Elizabeth Lucas Goodall Thorn Worcester. Thorn-Gott papers, Gonzales, Texas.

[7] No letters from the Goodall brothers to Vernal or Nancy Lea have been located.

Montgomery
6th Dec 1849

My Dear Margaret

I am now in brother Henry's room. I came here this morning, and so soon as he heard that I had arrived he called upon me at the exchange, and pressed me kindly to call so soon as I cou'd, as I was then sitting down to breakfast. After I was done, I called to see Lucy Ann, & to my surprize [sic] I found that she was a large young Lady, but not so tall as represented. She is very glad to hear of all the family, and to see me. Enquiries were various, and agreeable, and such as made me feel very pleasant. Bro. Henry is well, and all that you could wish him to be—amiable, respectable, and kind.

Well, I came by the "cane Brake" and spent three nights at bro Roystons, and one with Columbus.[1] I found all well, and delighted to see me, as they thought I had passed by another route.

I arrived there (at Roystons) on saturday, and remained there until monday. I then went over with Teen and Young to dine with Columbus, and Aunt Lea[2] was there to meet me, so we all stayed all night. Many and kind were the enquiries about Mother, you, and all the weans. His children, and good cousin Bettys[3] were well, except Knox, the youngest. He was puny, but recovering. I would not swap Sam for Emmet. We might well exchange Nancy for Mag. She is the age of Nannie, and you have never seen two cousins so much alike as they are. Her forehead and eyes are not so fine as Nannies, but except for that, the likeness is perfect. Aunt looks just as she did five years ago, and quite as well.

I saw the Goats, and told to all the jest about your fears, & Mothers of naming the matter to Columbus. Someday, I am [to] have the Goats, so we all said! I made a good jest of it. Teen is crazy to get out to see you all. She may go out this winter, but I fear not. All are as anxious to get out as you cou'd suppose them to be, but intend to make another crop, or try it, at least. In a short time, I have to deliver a speech, by request of many friends. A resolution was passed, by the House of Representatives, (or Hall) for me to make a speech there, without my knowledge, or consent, for I did not even think of speaking, I was so busy.

I am anxious to get to the city, to meet letters from home, and where I can write to you at leisure. Then I will have many things to write, which a want of time will not now allow me to do.

Present my love to Mother. Hug Sam & kiss the Girls for me. All the kindred send a thousand . . . *[The bottom is cut off]*
[In margin:] . . . Brother Henry says Sam is a wonderful lad. He has not seen any . . . *[cut off]*

[1]Margaret's cousin Columbus Lea.
[2]Margaret Moffit (Mrs. Green) Lea.
[3]Elizabeth Parker (Mrs. Columbus) Lea.

Washington City
15th Dec. 1849

My Dear Wife,

On last night I arrived after a journey not the most pleasant, but safe. I found many letters, but none from you My Love. I hope the mails have been delayed, and to that cause, I am willing, and anxious to attribute the fact, that [none] has come to me. To day I was at the Senate, which met, only to adjourn. The House has not as yet elected a speaker, nor is there much probability, that it will for some days.[1] There is much excitement and the Ultras have hope of mischief, but I have no fear for the country.

I have hardly begun to read my mail, that I found on my arrival. I suppose I have at least fifty letters yet to read.

I only write before I retire to rest to say that I am here, & to say, how much happier, I would be, were I with you, and our dear children, at home.

Tomorrow is the sabbath, and I will attend the Batist [sic] Church (if spared) and write you a long letter. Don't be angry that this is so short. I have only a steel pen. Kiss the children, & give my love to Mother, & commend me to all.

Thy ever devoted Husband
Houston

[1] It would take fourteen days and sixty ballots to elect Howell Cobb by a margin of two votes. Friend, 200.

Huntsville
Dec. 17th 1849

My dear husband,

Tomorrow is my regular letter day, but as I expect Mrs [Tirza] Birdwell and Mrs [Virginia] Maxy in to dine with me, I thought it best to begin my letter today, lest I should be deprived of the pleasure of writing to you as I was on last tuesday. My health was quite feeble at that time, and the weather so intensely cold, that I was compelled to sit as near the fire as possible all the day. Last week, I recd two letters from you, one from Grand Ecore, and the other from New Orleans. They gave me great comfort I assure you. At present, we are all enjoying good health. The dear little ones seem to grow more rapidly, than I have ever known them. Maggie has several little words, and her intellect is developing wonderfully. She has the most affectionate disposition of all, and a single sad tone from one of the family will make her spread her little arms and put up her rosy lips, and she seems to think that one of her kisses is certain remedy for all sorrow. Nannie's beauty and vivacity seem to increase every day. She is a rare girl I assure you. Last, not least, our boy, our noble boy still gives evidences of great genius. What should I do without him! I tremble when I think of my devotion to him. Indeed my little circle seems beautifully fitted to cheer the widowed home that falls to my lot. Whenever a feeling of despondency steals over me, it is checked by a bright smile or a musical laugh.

Before you left home, you asked me a question which I did not then answer. I will now reply to it—a la yankee. What do you think of "Temple Lea" as a name?[1] It may be that you will object to the latter part of the name on account of its being the "appendage" to Maggie's name. You must remember my love, that you once professed to look upon it as a great obstacle in the way of your happiness, and if you say too much, I shall think that some of your old prejudice remains. But I rather suppose I shall see some of the magnanimity which you generally show to fallen foes. My design is not to exploit my own wishes, but to ascertain yours.
Sunday 18

It was my design to arise early this morning, and write you a long letter, before my company arrived, but I had an uncomfortable night, and feel quite languid this morning. The day is raw and chilly, and I must sit close to the fire.

Every thing seems to be doing well at home. Mr Hatch is doing well, and is a great help to me. He is pretty much a porcupine to all but myself and the children, but is kind and good humoured to us. I am sorry to tell you that Charlotte's[2] conduct was such that I was compelled to sell her. I fear you will not be pleased at the price I received for her, but I assure you, I was compelled to dispose of her. I sold her to Col Gilespie[3] for five hundred dollars. I bore with every kind of insolence until a mixture of some kind was discovered [in] one of our dishes, and circumstances fixed it on her as the guilty one. If others are implicated, it will no doubt prevent further mischief.

I will now speak of something more pleasant. Sam sends you his autograph and a portrait which he has taken of Nash.[4] He commenced one of his Grandma's Lucy Neal,[5] for which he was to receive one dime, but unfortunately, he painted her face black, and could find no place for her nose.

I expect you will soon hear that Col [John W.] Wade has broken the temperance pledge. There was universal lamentation over his fall, but I trust his case is not hopeless. The society has forgiven his first offence [sic], and I am told his mortification is intense. It all originated from his taking bitters after exposure to the weather. I am sure my beloved husband needs no admonition. I will therefore drop this painful theme. I hope soon to hear from you, and to know that you have arrived safely in Washington.

Thy devoted wife
M. L. Houston

P. S.
Remember the "New York Recorder."

[1]This was Margaret's way of letting Houston know she was expecting a baby in the spring.
[2]A Houston slave.
[3]James Gillispie. Identified in Carpenter, 2023.
[4]A Houston slave.
[5]Nancy Lea's slave.

Senate Chamber
18th Dec. 1849

My Dearest,
I did not write as I proposed, in hopes that I should have the

pleasure of responding to a letter from you. It was only last night, that I got thro' with opening, & reading my letter mail. The hour at which I finished was half past 12 oclock. You can now, my Dearest Love, have some idea of the press of business which I must undergo.

I am, my Love, if possible, a thousand times more anxious to see, and be with you, and our dear children, than I have been before. You are always present to me, and really I am miserable that I can not see you, and be with you. Politicks [sic] have not any charm for me. I find that my letter to Genl Gadsden[1] has been published through-out the Union. It has been, and is lauded by all parties except the Calhoun men, and they are squabbling at me! Genl Hunts[2] letter has been sent here by David Yoakum Portis.[3] It has met with ridicule or contempt, and some returned with remarks, which will not be rel-ished either by Hunt or Portis. I have received letters from members of our Legislature which speak of Hunt and the letter, in any thing but flattering terms. I do assure you, my Love, that I feel nothing unkind toward those who assail me. I might not like it so well, if they could injure me. They have a fine effect, and I like them!!!![4]

This will be an excited, and exciting Session. The House has not yet elected a speaker, nor is it probable, that the members will make an election before the 25th, or last of the month. It may turn out for good, but there has been very angry expressions used, by both par-ties as I learn, for I have not been in the House since I arrived. I will not take much part in the matter. I desire Howell Cobbs election. I have seen our friends, the Houstons, and Watsons. They are all well, and made as many enquiries, as you can imagine.

I showed Sams likeness,* which was very gratifying to all, [*In the margin: *all say he is much like me. Tell him so.] and I gave to the Houstons the pretty Roses, and rose buds, which our dear little ones gave me, before I left home. I had pressed them very neatly, and they really looked very pretty. They were received as quite a trea-sure. When I was exhibiting Sam, and distributing the flowers, it was less pleasurable to me than painful. I thought of you, a world to me, in which every other thought is absorbed, and would, could I have been with you, proudly, and gladly have foresworn, all honors &

stations on earth, that could separate me from home, the place where my hearts core abides. The long, the painful absence which I contemplate is sorrowful to me. Painful [beyond] all that I can express to you my Love. I feel a rush of cares, and anxieties, upon my mind, and seek to find an excuse in the fact that it was necessary, for my reputation, that I should come this session. I now think it was more a matter of feeling, (as I had been chafed by those who were enemies to the union) than of necessity. But I am here, and must hope that all will be well, as my conduct arose from a sense of duty. You may rely upon it, my Love, that I am and will ever be for <u>the Union</u>. Yes, and for <u>our</u> <u>Union</u>!

I know, my Love, that you will have much trouble, but I sincerely hope you will find time to write me a long letter at least once a week. Sam, I hope will soon be able to add a Post Script of his name, if it is only in print, for Sam can print. Nannie can add one, in rays of light from her bright eyes, while little Mag can add hers in a frown! Try her, and see if she has forgotten me. She prattles prettily I suppose. Do tell me how she chats, and what she says. My bosom is full of home, and joys of home, but I am alas, far distant from all I love.

I will look dayly [sic] for letters until they come. Were it not for the bad character of the mail, I would be more unhappy than what I am! I will soon write to Capt Hatch. Give my love to mother, & kisses to the children. Remember me to all.

Thy ever devoted Husband
Sam Houston

[1]General James Gadsden, an ally of Calhoun, had taunted Houston with having a defective education. Wisehart, 531. For a copy of Houston's letter see *Writings,* vol. 5, 95–106.
[2]Memucan Hunt had written a thirty-page letter attacking Houston to the *Texas State Gazette* (Austin) which filled five columns of the issue of November 10, 1849. For more information about this see Friend, 198–99. For a copy of the letter dated September 27, 1849, see the *Galveston Weekly News,* February 11, 1850.
[3]Portis was a former member of the Republic of Texas House of Representatives.
[4]Hunt's letter, of September 27, 1849, was a circular addressed to creditors who had claims against the Republic of Texas, and proposed that they should finance him in an effort to induce the legislature to assume the payment of the debt. Houston sent a copy of Hunt's

letter to the editors of the *Union. Writings,* vol. 5, 113n. For a copy of Houston's letter see Ibid., 112–13.

Washington City,
23rd Dec. 1849

My Dearest,

I was made very happy last night by the receipt of your letter of the 27th ult. I did not wish to write to you again, until I could hear from you, as I felt assured that it wou'd soon be the case. Had I written, it would have been in a melancholy strain, & partook of the cast of my feelings. Although your letter imparted a melancholy piece of information,[1] I was prepared to hear it, as the little creature had suffered so long—there could only remain cherished hopes of his recovering. The religion which his parents profess, is all that can afford consolation, to the wounded spirit, under such afflictive bereavement. I am happy that you found it in your power to point them, to the only balm, that can cure wounded hearts, & soothe them, into resignation, & tranquility [sic]. I feel sad, and sorrowful, on their account, but why may not the Saviour like the good shepherd, take the tender lambs to his bosom, and protect them, from the rude storms which assail his creatures in lifes journey.

I am very happy to learn that you were able to undergo so much fatigue, without injury to your health. I suppose Mrs Birdwell was with you, tho. you do not say she was.

You make me very happy by telling me about the children. I usually look at my Dear Boys likeness, before I retire, and that recalls all the past. I almost fancy that I can hear dear Mag, say "Pa, oh pa," and indeed my heart is responsive to every thought, and act of affection. If spared by a kind Providence, I feel more, and more resolved not to remain a part [sic] from my family. In all the truth of tender, & devoted affections, I assure, that I do not enjoy one thought, happy in itself, with which you are not associated, and your happiness involved. It is fit that I am here, not withstanding that I now wish to the contrary. There has been, and will be much excitement, as you will see on the Resolution to admit Father Matthew[2] on the floor of the Senate, tho, it was nothing but a mere compliment due to a Philanthropist. My speech[3] is miserably reported, not only in words, but in sense. It was esteemed, by those who heard it, as very clever, and for which I have been much complimented. I only intended to say, that my presence is wanted here as a southern man, to meet, and to rebuke southern fanaticks [sic]. The Union will be preserved, and I must act out your dream about the "Map." You need be under no apprehension, about the result, of what I may undertake. The Gadsden correspondence[4] has done as much for my reputation as the battle of San Jacinto. The manner, and the temper of it, are rightly appreciated, and well commended. As I have sent you my remarks, on Fr Matthews case, you will see that I can not now "back out," for I have acknowledged my pledge before the Senate, and the world. And pledged too for the Union! These are two important matters, and I have to stand by them. You will, I hope, my Love, explain them to our dear son, and Mother, as he will take care of the paper.

To day I was at church, and met our friends Mr Samson, Mr Cushman[5] & his lady, also Col [David] Kaufmans sister in law.[6] She is at school at Mr Cushmans caused by my letter to Kaufman, as you will recall my Dear. I hope on tomorrow Mr Cushman will be elected chaplain of Congress. If I live, I intend to set out early in the morning, and electioneer for him as such, all that I can. You will thank me, my dear, will you not? My wish, and intention is to do every thing, that can afford you pleasure, were you to know it, and nothing that could give you pain.

I send by this mail for Sam, & Nannie, Books, and you, my Love, must show, the pictures, to dear little Maggy Lea. I told Aunt Lea, all about her namesake. She was pleased. I have spoken for a Copy Book for Virginia, and will send it to you by mail, so soon, as I get it. I intend to write to her brother[7] tomorrow. It is now late at night. I have passed two hours of precious time by company, to night. I am resolved to lock my door hereafter, and shut all persons from my room but such as I tell, how to get in.

I will try my Love, and write, or send you something, every day.

My health has never been so good, as at this time, and I pray, that you are able to make the same assurances.

Write to me everything. Let me know, if I can leave, and go home, at which time you wou'd most wish to see me!

Give my love to mother, & kiss the weans. Howda to all

Thine own
Houston

[1]The death of the Maxey child.

[2]Reverend Theobald Mathew. Southern Senators objected to admitting the Irish Temperance leader within the bar of the Senate on the grounds that Mathew would compare poverty in Ireland with slavery. Houston refused to be guilty of making a philanthropist a victim of party bickering, and urged the senators to extend courtesy to a foreign visitor. Friend, 201.

[3]For a copy of the speech see *Writings,* vol. 5, 109–12.

[4]For a copy of Houston to James Gadsden, September 20, 1849, see *Writings,* vol. 5, 95–106. This letter was in reply to correspondence in which Gadsden berated Houston for opposing Calhoun. For more information see Ibid., 107n and Friend, 197.

[5]Houston is probably referring referring to Reverend George L. Cushman. Identified in Flora D. England, *Alabama Notes* (Baltimore: Genealogical Publishing Co., Inc., 1978), vol. 3, 42.

[6]Eliza Richardson, the sister of Jane Kaufman. Carpenter, 1685.

[7]Albert Goodall, of Philadelphia. Identified in the Thorn-Gott family papers.

Senate Chamber
27th Dec. 1849

My Beloved,

In my room, I am really so oppressed with company, that it is rarely in my power to write, as I would wish to do. My greatest pleasure, next to reading your letters, is in writing to you. It is a sort, (imperfect tho') of communion with you, and our little ones. I regret that there was a failure, by [George A.] Davis in taking your likeness, for I assure you, even Sam's is a great consolation to me. Every night I look at it, and feel "goodnight dear Boy." I indulge every thought, and hope attached to you, and to home. When I look forward to the future, and the time of my absence, my heart is pained, almost to agony. To day I propose to send to you by Mr. Rose[1] a Book, a "Christmas Gift." Also two presents which my cousin Narcissa Houston has sent to you. They are wrought ottoman covers. I will send her letter, so as soon as I answer it. You will be pleased with them. I can not comply with her request, in going to Richmond to make a speech. The subject would not suit me for display. I will if I live have enough to do this session, in my place in Senate. You will see that I send you the earliest notice of every thing which can interest you. Do not ascribe my attentions to vanity, for really I have not so much, as some people around me have. I have reason to fear the [blurred] which may await us this session, but you know my motto is "integrity," therefore I distrust nothing, which I undertake. The Union shall be preserved. To this effect, trust me.

I omitted, I think to tell you that Col Long, was to send two pigs to Capt Hatch, and he is to let the Col have a male pig, in return. You did not say to me whether the pigs survived the bad night, after I left you. I hope you will get on well, and be quite happy in my absence. I could tell you some things, which would be agreeable to you, but I will defer it for a while. I hope mother has become satisfied, with the House, and yard, and that she does not expose herself to the damp, and out of doors. She will be happier, and I doubt not healthier, if she will remain, with dry feet, and in doors. I am sincerely anxious, that she should be happy, for many reasons, and one is, that you would be very happy to what you [blurred]. You may buy her filly and "Omagan," at any price if it will content her. I am glad that a selection was made off, or from my land for the College. The land, which would have been selected, on our place will some day sell at any price, if Huntsville prospers. When I was in Alabama, I could not get Young Royston to realise the importance, of removing to Texas, or to make an effort to pay off their debts in land. I wish you wou'd commence a correspondence with him, over the subject, and get his reasons, for not entering upon the experiment. I do not think that he takes the best view of matters. I gave him my candid opinion, & it was adverse to his notions. You can perhaps, get him to assign better reasons than he did to me.

Mr Rose has started, and did not call as he promised to do, for the articles. I will try, and send them by the first safe opportunity, and hope you will be pleased with them. This is thursday, and congress has adjourned until monday. If spared, I will have much to do, of business, and will try, and write to you, as <u>usual</u>. Major Donelson has returned, with an addition of two fine boys, and Madam is quite <u>lusty</u> again. They keep even with us. They made most affectionate enquiries for you, and Sam, and bade me present them in terms of kind, and sincere regard to you. They all look very well, and Mary [Donelson] is the same gay Mary, and with all, as unsofisticated [sic], as when you saw her. She says she will write for Sam, and claims him as her own, but took care to ask kindly for Miller and spoke humorously of it Frog-digy [sic]!

Present my duty, and love to Mother. Kisses to the weans, and howda to all. Salute our dear friends for me.

Thy ever devoted Husband
Sam Houston

P.S. I take no Christmas, but hope you have a cheerful one.

[In margin:] My dear, I have lost a slip of paper which I intended to send you from Alabama. I may not find it!

[1]Robert Rose of Galveston.

Senate Chamber
31st Dec. 1849

My Love,

I had just written a pretty long letter to you, and intended to cast sand on it, when by mistake I took the ink-stand [things?] having been changed in there [sic] places, and covered it with ink. I had told why I did not write to you yesterday (sunday) and that I had purchased two pretty Canary Birds and called them "Sam" & "Nannie." They sing sweetly, and I keep them in my room. I hope to have many more to take home. They are becoming acquainted with me, and with Sam's likeness, and the songsters, you will suppose that I have quite a family circle. They afford me some pleasure, but my Love, there can be none real, where you do not preside. I say none. I mean by that, none which can perfect my happiness. I do confess, that the hope that they are at [home?] some day, to sing to you adds some what to my happiness.

You will see my dearest, be [sic] the sketches of land, for the college be where it may, I care not, but if it fall to Hanchett's lot, so much the better. I am glad that the avenue is completed, and until I can write to Captain Hatch, I wish you to express my satisfaction to him.

I trust my Love, that ire this reaches you, our dear little rose-bud will be able to frame more than one sentence. If I could only hear her say "Pa," I would be truly happy, for it would bring around me, all that I love. As Mr Rose went off without sending by him the pretty things, I intend to send them by the first chance.

I write, as you will perceive, in the confusion of the Senates noise. You wish my Love, for me to say whether I intend to see you in the spring! It is not only my intention, but it is my ardent desire, as well as my hope! It will depend upon the pressing of business, in which my presence will be imperatively required. The hope that I will be able to be with you cheers me, at this time and, I hope to realize a greater pleasure in fruition. I wrote to you in my last, requesting you to say as near the time as possible, when you most desire to see me. You can guess, but with no great certainty.[1]

Hereafter my Love, I will write to you more constantly, than I have done thus far. I would venture to write oftener, but I think if I were to write a short letter, you would think that I did not love you, as I ought to do, or I "would have written a longer letter." Now and for all, never think this I pray you, for you engross my whole heart.

Tomorrow the people are to visit poor old Zac,[2] but no "Washington." I send you a scrap, from an Alabama paper,[3] and a "Gold dollar," for Master Sam. Commend me to Mother, and all.

Thy devoted Husband
Houston

P.S.

Like all post scripts, this will allude to the most important fact of your letter. Your indisposition has been upon my mind, day and night. You did not tell me, the nature of your attack. I will be unhappy, until you write to me the cause & the character, of your ilness [sic]. Do I pray you, my Love write to me, and let me know.

Thy husband
Sam Houston

[1]Houston is referring to the expected date of the birth of their fourth child.
[2]President Zachary Taylor.
[3]*State Guard* (Wetumpka, Alabama), November 10, 1849, p. 2, col. 2. This clipping is in the Sam Houston Collection, vol. 5, in the Barker History Center, University of Texas, Austin, Texas.

Huntsville
Jan 1st, 1850

My Love,

Another year has commenced. May it be the last, that shall find us this far a part. It is a joyful day in Huntsville. The sons of temperance are making quite a display. They have one or two other divisions with them, and the ladies have prepared a basket dinner for them. I have determined to spend the day quietly at home, though I am sure there is not a being on earth who feels more deeply concerned for the prosperity of the order. Sam has just set off with Mr Hatch, and wears his regalia most gracefully I assure you. Your little ones were up before dawn this morning, and even little Maggie, though only her second new year, danced and chirped more merrily than usual.

On friday, I read your letter and bro. Henry's from Montgomery. I was truly gratified to learn that you were getting along so pleasantly, and read with delight the account of your visit to the canebrake and your meeting with bro. Henry in Montgomery.

I have almost lost the last hope of seeing our relations settled in Texas, but you know I am not in favor of urging them very much. It is best I think to let them take thier own time for it. Mother seems a few years younger since she heard from them, and I hope she will be comfortable for a long while. I am more attracted to our home and neighbors than ever. If I could only get you to love this place as I do, I would be perfectly satisfied.

I recd a letter from Antoinette not long ago. When she wrote they expected to make us a visit very soon. I can not tell, why they have again declined coming, but I suppose it is owing to the condition of the roads. I heard from bro. Vernal's family a few days ago. They were all well again. Mrs Reily and the Maj.[1] are in Houston again, and she has written me a very affectionate letter. She says the Maj. is with you on the Oregon question, and is astonished that every one is not. I fear it will be late in the session before these two questions, I mean those of Oregon and the "Texas boundary line" will be settled. I am selfish enough to hope that they will make the boundary line of your sabbatical life.

Would it be possible to obtain the office of marshal of the state of Texas for Col Birdwell? I know that he desires it very much, and I have therefore determined to mention it. While I think of it, I will inform you that your friend Col [John] Wade is reinstated by the sons of temperance. His penitence I am told was deep and very touching.

I shall soon be looking for one of your long letters, and tell me dearest when may I look for you. I will not suffer myself to think for a moment of your staying till the close of the session, for I do not think I can possibly be reconciled to it.

If you can think of it please send me a copy book for Sam and one for Virginia. He seems so determined to write, that I fear if we do not furnish him with letters he will make some of his own. Shall I jog your memory about the New York recorder, until you tell me whether or not you have attended to it? I have declined taking it longer, unless you have already ordered it.

I do hope soon to hear from you, and to hear that I may hope to see you soon. It is a cold disagreeable day, and I can hardly write at all. When the weather becomes pleasant, I hope to write longer letters.

Ever thy devoted wife,
M. L. Houston

P.S. Martha Ransom is just come in, and says I must send her love to you.

[1]Ellen Hart and Major James Reily.

Washington City
2nd Jany 1850

My Beloved,

From the date of this letter you will perceive, that a new Year has commenced. Yesterday was, as you will suppose, a day of display and show. I went to the Presidents as is the custom, and paid my respects to the chief magistrate of the Nation. I was accompanied by several friends, and among them two Texians. I found it a great squeeze, and particularly for the Ladies. I had no responsibility for I went with none. Had I done so, I wou'd have been vexed, for they were treated by the crowd without any apparent regard for their finery. Mrs Bliss,[1] the wife of Col Bliss,[2] and Daughter to the President [Taylor], is a genteel lady, and is quite popular. She is rather plain, & her modesty, and I think purity, makes her the most acceptable personage of all the inmates, of the White House![3] The General makes a woeful figure, and "I sink him, will be very sorrie, before him shall leave zat wite ouse." He is not in good ardour with the people of this nation. Indeed, so far as I can judge, his own party, are sick of him. But the[y] have to stand him.

Now my dear, I am about to present a matter, to your attention. Many persons and those in high position in the democratic Party, are anxious that I should yield my attention to the succession, and they honestly think my chance is quite as good, if not better than that of any one who can be brought forward by either party! It has been, and is now my intention, to defer to your wishes, if you are opposed to my remaining, in public life, or really believe, that it wou'd be safer, for our happiness, that I spend the balance of my life in private station. I declare to you, if I know my self, that my heart is not set on the Presidency, and I will hear your suggestions, and wishes, with paramount consideration. If you do not approve this, condemn it, or let it remain, if we should live, until we meet again. It is not necessary that you should answer this suggestion, until you look at it, in all its bearings. I assure you, it would not be the splendour of the station, that would induce me, if it were at my disposition, to accept it, nor any other consideration short of a conviction, that I cou'd benefit my country, more than another, upon whom, it wou'd otherwise fall, to act for the country.

You can ponder all the pros, & cons, of the matter. The mass of the people of this nation, are in favor of the <u>Union</u>!!! before this rock my feet are placed,—with Gods help I will stand upon it, and I feel well assured that truth, & patriotism will uphold my hands, while the battle rages!

My mind has never been more composed, when from home, on general Subjects, than what is, at this time. And my Love, I beg you to be assured, that all the turmoil in which I am situated, has not prevented me, from reading my Testament, one single night, before I retire to rest since I came here! I say this only because it will satisfy you, that I omit no means of trying to be good, if I even am unworthy of peculiar Grace, from our Heavenly Father! In reading, I commenced at the first of the new Testament, with the intention to read it thro' regularly, and attentively, if spared, this session. It may be, and I will pray, that the means used may be sanctified to the salvation of my soul. I feel that there is a void which nothing but true, and evangelical Religion can ever fill, in my heart and mind!

My care and anxiety for your comfort, & happiness, is constrained, and at times, I feel as tho' you wou'd be well contented, if our "little ones," & Mother are in health. You may say to our son, that every day I show his likeness to some one, or another. Ask him, if he don't think me "very kind," to treat his likeness, with so much affection, and if he does not pity me, because, I have not his Dear Ma's, and little sisters likenesses, also to keep me company, when I am so far away from all of them.

You wrote about Nannies smartness, touching her likeness. You can if you wish it, have Sam's, and her likeness taken, on separate canvass if you wish to do so, but by no means fail to have Mothers taken for us. I want our Mag, to have it, to look at when she becomes old, if she shou'd live. She will surely see a likeness. I do not wish, by this, to make her a rival to Nannie, in Mothers affection.

In affection present me to all!

Thy ever devoted
Houston

[1]Mary Elizabeth Taylor. Identified in Elbert B. Smith, *The Presidencies of Zachary Taylor and Millard Fillmore* (Lawrence, Kansas: The University Press of Kansas, 1988), 67.
[2]William W. W. Bliss. Ibid., 66.
[3]Mrs. Bliss substituted as official White House hostess for her mother, who was in ill health. Ibid., 67.

Washington City
6th of Jany 1850

My Dearest,

This is sunday, and I passed the forenoon at church, where I heard our friend, Mr Sampson preach one of his best sermons. I met there also our friend Mr Cushman. I have omitted this far to call upon either at their home, but I must try, and do so.

The mails have for some days disappointed me, in not bringing a letter from you, which you know I anticipate weekly! Dont understand me as complaining, for indeed, I have no such intention. I doubt not, but what you will, at times, suppose that I have failed to write, as I have done heretofore. You will find that my constancy does not flag, but keep [sic] pace with your wishes, if not with your expectations, or the delinquencies of the mails. I do not know how, to fill up the many letters, which I write to you, as you do not expect me to tell you tales of love. I feel an inexpressible amount of affection my dear for you, but as my absence is prospectively to be so protracted even should I be able to visit you in april, (I suppose that is the time you will designate) that I am fearful my heart wou'd be so set upon, giving you all verity of my devotion, that I would <u>desert</u> <u>my</u> <u>post</u>, & bring imputation, upon my name, & fame, which Mr Calhoun, has tried to affix there. In this tho' he will most signally fail. He is in dread of retribution, as I think. If I live he shall have it, freely & fully. Do not suppose my dearest, that I will provoke any unkindness of feeling from [any one] but cultivate good feelings with all, when I can do so with honor to you, and to myself! Again my Dear, when talking of love letters, I can assure you, that the harshness of political discussion, and the direction of the mind to such subjects, is not favorable to the expression of the tender passion.

I feel, and cherish it with all the enthusiasm, that I did before wedlocks silken cords had bound us! And as a proof in point, I assure you, that I lay down to rest last night, after looking at Master Sams likeness as usual,—and my mind seizing upon you, and home. I was not able to sleep until the Town Clock told me, it was after three oclock A.M. You will now, my Love, (I guess) be satisfied that if I can not write love to you, it is not because I do not feel it, as much, if not more than I have done in life. Fancy all my professions of former times, and multiply them by the days of our union, and they will not amount to a sum greater, than my present love for you. While my mind is so intensely engaged about you, I do not forget our dear little cherubs, and our fine Cub boy. He will hardly appreciate the kindness which I design to express, unless you assure him that it is a term of affection!

I will not describe to you the fashions here for many reasons which I could state. One would be sufficient, and that I may state. I pay little, or no attention to them! I have seen, sometimes dresses, that I fancied I would like to have such for you, and no doubt, but I cou'd easily obtain them. You will not make any requisitions upon me, for finery, so if I get any, it must be upon my own responsibility.

If spared, I will try and incur a reasonable amount—enough to make a selection to suit my fancy, unless, you will enlighten me with some intimation, as to what you would fancy, & prefer!

Sam's hat and drawing show to me considerable improvement in <u>his art</u>.[1] I have shown them. You may say to him, and with much pride. Let him send to me every fine specimen, that he may make, and I will be gratified with it. My heart bounds with pleasure, when I receive anything from home! even a Rose leaf from your hand, I would kiss, with delight. Learn Sam to turn his S thus. He will make it left handed thus [Here Houston drew a backward S.]!!! I hope this week to send Virginia's Copy Book to you. The political elements, at this time, are rather calm, but I think are not long to remain so. Genl Cass introduced a Resolution to stop all further intercourse with Austria, owning to her cruelties, towards the poor Hungarians.[2] This is well enough, and I expect to speak upon the subject before the Resolution is disposed of! Dont be anxious about the result, my Dear. I will try, and sustain myself. I never was more calm, than at present, and regard my situation, as a "looker on in Vienna!" My love to all!!

Thy devoted
Houston

[1]In his letter of November 18, 1849, Houston had written Margaret, "I hope Sam will be industrious so as to earn his 'hat.' What hat? Ask him to draw it on a piece of paper and enclose it to me." *Writings*, vol. 5, 108.
[2]For more information about this situation see Smith, *The Presidencies of Zachary Taylor and Millard Filmore*, 86.

Washington
6th Jany 1850

My Dearest,

I wrote to you last night, and as I have a few minutes to day, I write again, but will not vouch for the length of my letter. Enclosed you will see a note from Mrs Cushman, handed to me by the Gentleman himself, who added his influence, so I promised to spend an hour, this evening.

As I have the floor for tomorrow, I have no time to loose [sic], but must employ every hour. Mr Clay concluded after a speech of five hours, in the two days. It was creditable to him, or to any one, but did not reach the expectation, of his friends. His opinions, on various subjects, will meet opposition, by the south. He is currying favor with the north, and would like to have it with the south. If I should be fortunate, my intention is to direct my course to reconciliation, of sectional difficulties, and promoting the general prosperity of the Union, as a <u>Union</u>. Sectional policy must destroy the harmony of the country, if persisted in, by either Party.

The great object of the south or its <u>leader,</u> is to create a sectional Division of <u>parties,</u> and in that way to create disunion, by general feeling, in the two sections. This I sincerely hope may never take place, during my life time, or in that of my latest posterity!

I advise you my dear, to entertain no apprehensions, of such evils, as <u>Disunion</u>. I trust that a kind Providence, will so order all things, as to retain the American people, subjects of His peculiar care!

I may write to you again, before I leave here (if spared), & I hope, unless the letter is in haste, that I will arrive before it. I am not yet resolved which route, I will go home. If there is no snow on the mountains, I may go by that route. Not that it is the speediest, but I might find it so, if fortunate in meeting Boats, at the several points of my journey.

My love & regard to all.

Thy devoted Husband
Sam Houston

Tell Sam to be a good Boy, that I love him!

Washington
7th Jany 1850

My Dearest,

A few moments after I sealed my long letter to you last night, the mail was handed to me, and I had the pleasure by it, to learn many interesting facts. The welfare of all was to me truly gratifying. All that you state to me about the children, I need not assure you, is truly pleasing to me. Bless the little ones, my heart is often with them, and their dear Ma! Were it not that I am acting for you all, I would deem myself truant, to happiness, as well as home. Indeed, I have not been happy, if I know my own heart, since my arrival here, nor do I expect one until we meet again,—Then I anticipate joys which absence can never afford!

In your letter, you allude to a very interesting subject, and one that derives peculiar interest from the fact that it presupposes the accession of a play-fellow to our Boy Master Sam. Well you on more than one occasion alluded to the subject of a name, and tho' I may not have expressed my assent to your suggestions, but I assure you, that they met them, and now meet my most cordial approval. Maggy Lea, will not interfere, with the name of "Temple Lea Houston." I would not have the lad, if such it should be, to bear any other name, and my prayers will be that he may, in all things worthily bear, so worthy a name! Be it boy or girl, I am willing to call it Temple Lea— But if not a boy, I may, (if you do not exercise the privilege given) consult about what the name shall be! This is so pleasing a subject, that I may say too much, therefore I will change the subject, to one less agreeable!

I am distressed at the conduct of Charlotte. I do not know to which Col Gillispie you sold her to, Col Barry, or Col James. If Col James, I fear she will be too near to our premises! Wou'd not Vernal have given you Bob, or I mean Sams friend for her! Indeed I thought you would hire her out until my return. I do not in the least blame you my dear, for the sale, and hope it will be for the best! I ought to have attended it before I left home. You I know did what you thought best, and therefore, I am satisfied! If you sold her to Barry Gillispie, and he did not swindle you, it will be a wonder. Now dont think of this matter again! Nor, I pray you do not let it cast you a single reflection!

I learned with painful emotions the defection of our friend Wade, to the principles of Temperance. I pray that he may be restored! It will not do for an old delinquent to take bitters, or any stimulant whatever. Beer tho' not inhibited by the pledge, is as much against the spirit of the pledge, as if it were embraced in it. For my part, & as I have expressed to you, I will never touch any thing that ever can be <u>drugged</u>, or that can stimulate more than Coffee or Tea! Until reason shall desert me, or I cease to be a man, with the help of God, I will never indulge in any thing that can violate my pledge to the society, or a higher and holier pledge, which I made at the altar when you became my wife! I know men are frail, and they are so, because they wish to be vicious. Virtue is absolute, & admits of neither compromise, in its purity, nor excuse for its violation. I shall with the blessing of Heaven, cling to these principles as the sheet anchor of Happiness on earth, & constituting a part of my hope of Heaven!

Mr Clay is speaking, and I want to close. I had paid and send you Vernals Draft for $1,500. Keep it! I thank Sam for his drawings.

I have not time to read this letter. Salute all.

Thy devoted Husband
Houston

A holographic copy of the following letter from Houston to his cousin Narcissa B. Hamilton is in the Sam Houston Collection of documents at the Daughters of the Republic of Texas Library, San Antonio, Texas. The location of the original is unknown. Parts of it are too faded to read.

Washington City
8th Jany 1850

My Dear Cousin

I know that you suppose your letter has not reached me or that I am a scamp, and do not intend to answer it. In both conclusions you would be wrong, for I assure you my Dear Cousin, your letter afforded me the highest [blurred] gratification. Being, as you know, it pertains to our blood, purely clannish, it delights me to know, that others, as well as myself, feel all the kind emotions of regard and kindness. You will percieve from my hand writing, that the wound in my shoulder, has affected my nerves. I thank kind Heaven it is not the effect of age, for in your recollection, you have not seen me in so fine health at this time. My habits being of the Father [blurred] order for years past, have restored me all that less care, and less prudence at one time had deprived me of. Since my union with my Dear Margaret, my disposition, as well as my habits have changed, and new cares, with new pleasures, have excluded, all that was useless, and I am proud to say, some things which were esteemed vicious. You would like your cousin, for she is intelligent, amiable, affectionate, and pious. You will of course suppose [blurred] loves, and the "weans" & myself a great deal! In the next place, you will desire to know how many there are? We have Master Sam, a lad in his seventh year, and his mother says "he is all, and just such as she would wish him to be." From this, you will suppose he resembles me. I think he does, in mind & person. Well then we have Nancy in her fourth year, pretty much Houston, only that she is esteemed beautiful. Next comes Margaret Lea, now in her second year, said to be pretty, but resembles Sam, very much! In short, we are greatly blessed in our children!—I wish you could see them. You could see them as [blurred]

You see my dear Cousin, I have given you the particulars, as far as we can count, and I can only say, that my dear Wife wrote to me a long paragraph in her last letter on the subject to family names! How would you like this, or this, and this, or so, and so, on certain contingencies? If you are [blurred] you can "guess" the rest—and if not you are a Virginian, and I am sure you understand reckoning. Now my Dear Cousin the presents were duly received, and announced to my wife, and by next mail, your letter will go to her, and tho she will be pleased greatly with the presents, she will be <u>charmed</u> with your letter. I was in hopes that I could so arrange matters, as to see you, at Richmond, with the Bairnes, and in deed all the family. I will send to our wee Nannie, the beautiful present which [blurred] to me. She will be delighted with the conceit that a cousin has sent her a present, that never saw her. But this was not always the case. Can not you Cousin, extend your travels to Texas? We will all be rejoiced to see you there, and render you welcome to our rude, or rustic hospitality.

I was rendered gloomy by your allusion to declining health, and your anticipation of no[t] returning spring on earth. I hope it is no more, than mere depression of spirits, which at times, comes over us all. I pray, that [blurred] long lives, and be happy, and that you may reap a rich reward, of past, and future usefulness. I know we can not elude destiny, but must submit to its stern mandate. I nevertheless hope, that your anticipations are not evidences that the [blurred].

Could I have seen you, my Dear Cousin, when here last, I would have been gratified, and would have rejoiced, again, in your society. I have seen ardent friends of yours here, and they sympathise in my regret.

You will not loose [sic] much by not joining in the [blurred] of the city, this season, as I suppose, tho I am not a competent judge, for I do not go to Theatres, or Balls. I have attended a few Levees, and have found them extremly [sic] crowded. Indeed they are more crowded, than I have seen them, since the days of Genl Jackson! The demeanor of Mr Fillmore & his family is very becoming, and makes the Levees agreeable. I see (as the saying in Texas) "the Ladies dress to <u>kill</u>." It does seem to me, that they dress badly to <u>live</u>! Mrs Houston dont wear <u>corsetts</u> [sic]!!!

Cousin present my affectionate regards, to all our dear relations.

Thy affectionate Cousin
Sam Houston

Huntsville
Jan 8 1850

My ever dear husband,

Two mails have passed since I recd a letter from you, and I am quite concerned about it, I assure you, for I had expected long before this, to hear of your safe arrival in Washington. Great allowance I know must be made for the irregularity of many of the post-offices, but no consideration will satisfy me, until I can hear from you again.

Our dear little ones are all enjoying good health, and nothing would make them so happy as to have dear papa at home again. Little Maggie continues her plaintive calls for "pa" and often raises her voice to the highest pitch, with the vain hope of being heard. Nannie is a stout rosy girl, and as beautiful and sprightly as ever.

Sam improves rapidly in spelling and reading. He retains his extraordinary fondness for the scriptures. He can repeat without a moment's reflection, any one of the ten commandments which you may call for, without any regard to the order in which they stand, for instance the 3rd, 5th, 9th etc. I am so accustomed to thinking of him as a labourer in the Lord's vineyard, that I know not how I could endure to see his toil employed in any worldly pursuit.

In the night before last, our vicinity was visited by one of the most terrible hurricanes, I ever heard of. It swept along between Huntsville and Col. Birdwell's, and carried every thing in its path. Capt. [T. H.] Simms's hill on yesterday was a scene of desolation. Not a house was left standing, and a portion of the dwelling house was found on the other side of his gin. None of the family were killed, but some of them considerably bruised. The neighbors have all united to repair the injuries, and I hope the family will soon be comfortable again. Your own little flock were quiet at home, and never dreamed that the fearful visitant was so near them. Oh how merciful is God to the desolate and defenceless [sic]!

I recd a letter on yesterday from Antoinette. She writes me that they would have been with us before, but were waiting for the arrival of Charles' son, who had been several weeks on the way [from England]. They had just heard of his arrival in Galveston, and thought they would then set off very soon. Sis [blurred] she recd the letter, in which you lectured her about her temper. I hope she received it kindly, but it is difficult to ascertain, for I think few people like to be told of thier faults.

Mr [Anthony] Hatch is still in expectation of a fine crop. We get along very well, but I have long since found out why he must have a house to himself. His ungovernable temper would destroy the peace of the happiest household. You need have no apprehension about his leaving, for I have determined to take no offence [sic] at any thing he says or does, for I will endure almost any thing rather than he should leave in your absence. Mother runs from the old man like a frightened hare, and has not interfered with any thing on the place for a long time, but still he pursues her with the most cruel and merciless hatred, and I should insist on her leaving the place immediately, but for my approaching trial. I think the old man is under a misapprehension about your feelings towards Mother, but I know not how to correct it, but will do the best I can. Thus far I have never given him a harsh word or look, and I seem not to hear his language in the yard. I will seek direction from a throne of grace, and I believe I shall be sustained. I entreat you not to write any thing to him about his conduct, for I have every reason to believe he will always be polite to me, and I think we will agree, though after a rough fashion. As to Mother's interference you need have no fears, for she is perfectly dear to the farm and every thing in which he is concerned. Mother and Sam send thier love, and Sam begs me to enclose one of his paintings. I hope you will not show it.

Thine ever,

M. L. Houston

Washington
13th Jany 1850

My Dear,

I write this note, only to say to you, that endless, and annoying company has, for the last week, prevented my writing to you. I did hope on yesterday sunday to hear from you, but had not the happiness to receive a letter. I doubt not but what it is on the way, and that I will soon hear from you.

There is little here that would interest you, unless I were to write about myself. This I know you do not approve, as it savors of egotism, or vanity, and either I know you condemn. To day I presented a Resolution proposing terms of compromise between the North & South, or rather I wish to take the wind out of the sails of Nullification, and abolition![1] Tomorrow I will send you a copy. I hope, and you are statesman enough to see, that it is the only feasible plan, by which such matters can be reconciled! I think you will perhaps, recur to the "dream of the map." It is not I assure my Love, either vanity, or ambition, or the love of fame, which have induced me to take the course that I have, but mostly a sincere desire to serve the best interests of my country, and to leave to my posterity all the blessings of Freedom, which I have enjoyed in life. Another mail has this moment arrived and no letter from you, but "plenty" from those whose letters I care less about, than my dear wifes.

You may say to Sam, if his Ma says so, I will send him, or take him a sword if I live, provided he is a good Boy, and has good, and kind feelings to all the family. My intention, is to have the sword made better to my liking, than his "red" shoes were. Ask him if he would like to have his name upon it, or ask him if he wou'd rather have my San Jacinto sword, than a new one?

To day I wrote to Albert Goodall, and told him about his sister [Virginia Thorn], and said many clever things about her. Commend to all! I will write oftener, than I have done in the last six days.

Thy ever devoted
Houston

Give my compliments to captain Hatch.

[1]For a summary of this resolution see *Galveston Weekly News*, February 11, 1850, p.1, col. 3.

Washington
15th Jany 1850

Dearest,

I wrote to you yesterday, and take pleasure in replying to your letter of the 26th Ult just received.[1] It is late at night, but I can not sleep without saying to you, <u>that is my intention to see you in the Spring if I live</u>. I can get some one of the whigs to pair off with me, on important Party questions, and that will enable me to return and see you, and my absence, will neither incur censure, nor render me, obnoxious to the charge of neglecting my duty, either to the country, or to my Party.

Since I have made up my mind to go, and see you, I am quite happy, and would not have been displeased if you had sent me Master Sams tooth.

You will see my Dear, that I have written to you, to tell me, at what time you will expect your confinement. You can guess pretty well when it will be. I need not advise you why, but if a boy, the lively symptoms usually occur, at 3 1/2 months, and if a girl at a later period. If a son, the aurola [sic] becomes darker, than if it was a girl.

You may laugh at my learning, as much as you will, for I have told you about all that I know, on the subject. I hope soon to hear from you, in reply to my letter attending to this matter. I am sure my Love, that I have made—greater sacrifices, for my country than I will ever be able to make for you, and if it required me to neglect its interests, to some extent, that I might render my duty, and delight my inclination to you, I would not hesitate, as to the course, which I would pursue!! I am very happy, to hear that all are well, and that mother has become satisfied, to drop all outdoor matters, in the hand of Capt Hatch! It is pleasing to me, and, so say to him, to learn that matters are going on, so well. I think I wrote to you, that two pigs were to be sent from Col Longs, in which the Captain, and myself were to be partners, in the stock! He will take care of them, and they will be large enough to save in our climate!

My Love, I am quite rejoiced, that a Preacher has located at Huntsville, and I pray to our God, that he may be a powerful instrument in the "ingathering of souls." I am not disappointed at the conduct of Sam's friend & brother, Mr Creath. I have long had my mind made up, as to his being a bad man. I do not think that I wrote to you that I travelled with a Gentleman in the <u>Cars</u>, a preacher from Virginia, who told me that he was blamed for his arbitrary conduct with his churches in Virginia. I never could believe, that he left his pastorage [sic] in the old Dominion, for the love of the Gospel, but to be a great man, and to get rid of something, which he did not like, as well, as he thought he could get something, that he would like, better <u>than something else</u>.

On his ladys account, I wish him all luck, only in mischievous designs, upon the church, or any thing that has good connected with it. Tell Sam I will try, and take the sword & Hat, and expect him to be my own dear, good boy to every body, and his Dear Ma, particularly.

Thy Devoted
Houston

¹This letter has not been located.

Washington
19th January 1850

Dearest,

All the day, have I intended to write to you, but as usual I have been prevented by useless company. I would be happy if I could transmit to you, each affectionate thought which I entertain of you. I am sure if I could you would be contented, and gratified, so far as my devotion, and affection can make you happy. My mind is much at ease, and I am comparatively happy since I have determined to return in the spring, & be with you (God willing it) in your time, of intense interest, and anguish. I am only waiting to hear from you, so as to fix the time of my departure. My impression is, that you will be confined sometime about the middle of April. I think the 13th of October, as well as I recollect, was the time that a memorable symptom occurred, as when you called my attention to it. Ere now, I suppose you have answered my letter, which bore the inquiry to you, as to the time.

My whole heart is absorbed in solicitude, for your health & happiness. Your peculiar situation, and consequent depression of spirits,[1] renders me more anxious, if possible than I would otherwise feel, tho' under no circumstances, could I exist without a vast portion of feeling, and regard for your composure, and safety! I hope, my Love, that your fears, are only those which all Ladies feel, who are in your situation, more than once! But whether your solicitude arises from the cause only, or from others, my instructions would be the same, as well as my determination to contribute to your happiness by all means in my power.

You will have seen by my letter, written soon after my arrival here, that I intended if possible, and you required it, to return. So your letter fixed my resolve, and I only wait for the time to arrive to put my resolve in execution.

I send a house to Sam which, I doubt not, will cause him some hours of laborious study, so as to imitate its design. I send you also a card of Genl Ujhaza, the Hungarian Chief, & Exile.[2] I also send you a letter from a man whom I do not know, but who seems, to know that I have a capital wife, as he thinks me so clever, and she is my "better half."

All, and ever thine

Houston

---

[1]Margaret was having problems with Virginia Thorn.

[2]László Újházi was the leader of the Hungarian exiles who fled to America. He would later emigrate to Texas and settle in San Antonio. For more information see James Patrick McGuire,

The Hungarian Texans (San Antonio: The University of Texas Institute of Texan Cultures at San Antonio, 1993), 35–77.

Washington,
20th Jany., 1850

My Dearest,

Although, I wrote to you last night, I am satisfied, you will excuse me for writing again. Not that I can write any thing new to you. I attended church to day as usual, and as I intend to do every sunday if spared, that I am in the city. Since I came here, I have not lain down, a single night, tho' frequently, 2 oclock A.M. that I have not read a portion in the new Testament. This I am resolved to continue, with the help of God! I know it is a duty, and you are aware that I have so regarded it. I feel more pleasure, and instruction in reading the scriptures, than I once did, as I think, but I assure you, My Love, that I do not feel that holy, and grateful devotion, that I ought, and wish to do. The time, I pray for, when you, (with many other pious persons) will find in my conversion an answer to your prayers. I avoid all the paths of Sin, and do not in any instance, go into society which ever you wou'd condemn, or censure! I intend to purchase for you a Book which I have recently heard of, for the first time. It is "Butler's analogy on natural, and revealed religion"! I will try, and send it to you, when I see it, if it is worth sending. It was written, I think about the beginning of the 17th century. I do not as you know fancy many Books, but if I find any worth your notion, I will not fail to obtain them.

To night, for it is now late, I expected a mail from Texas, and a dear letter from you, but have been disappointed. I hope the laziness of the Post Master, is the cause of its not arriving, and that I will receive it tomorrow morning. If I do, I will drop you a line to say so. I have been so busy that, I only write to you, & have not time to write to my friend Captain Hatch, and must rely upon you to make my apology, to him, for my silence. I am half sorry, that Doct, and Mrs

Evans are going farther from us, but not that "Aquilla," shou'd leave the vicinity. Salute all our dear friends, and congratulate Mrs Birdwell upon her happiness.[1] Love to all.

Thy devoted Husband,
Sam Houston

[1]Houston is probably referring to the engagement of the Birdwells' daughter Elizabeth.

Senate Chamber
24th Jany, 1850

My Dearest,

The mail is in among two letter with me [sic]. I am sure you have written but they have not come to hand. I will look for them daily, until they come.

I intend to write you a long letter soon. I would now but a speech, is making by Mr Butler[1] of S. C. in which my feelings are enlisted, tho' I will not speak on the subject. I send you my resolution as it is presented.

[Although the original letter is intact, it appears that a loose sheet may be missing between this page and the one that continues:] . . . and another copy of a House. Nannie may have it. I will send such things, as will amuse the children, as they come to my hand. I will not designate to whom they are to be given. That will be left to you.

I can only repeat how much I love you, as it can only confirm your own conviction of the lasting truth, that my love for you is boundless.

My love to all. I am waiting for notice from you, when to start home.

Thy devoted Husband,
Sam Houston

P.S. I don't intend to trifle with your feelings, but my Love, I am in hopes, your apprehensions are groundless. So far as I can with delicacy, I have inquired, and I find, that Ladies are more distressed with the fourth child, than at any previous birth, and that the longer they have children, or the more they have, the more they are distressed in spirits. It is nevertheless my duty to see you, and be with you. I would be almost crazy, if I did not expect to be with you, in your hour of trial. I intend so soon, as I am ready to start, to telegraph my friend [William] Christy in Orleans to advise you, of my departure, from here. It will be providing you, some eight days, earlier than than [sic] a letter could reach you. Eight—but it may be fifteen! My great desire is to be with you, my Love! I hope you will take as much exercise as you can about the house, avoiding going up, and down stairs. If the weather is fine, you may take exercise out of doors, but don't stoop any more than you can help. You may direct setting out flowers, but not do it yourself.

Thy devoted Husband
Houston

[1]Andrew P. Butler. *Biographical Directory of Congress*, 149.

Washington
27th Jany 1850

Dearest,

Another sabbath day has passed, and as usual, I have passed a portion of it a[t] church. No mail has reached me from you, for more than two weeks, and you will readily imagine my distress. It arises from that fact, that I am sure you have written to me <u>if you are well</u>, and as no letters arrive, I am left to the painful conjecture that you are ill. Or if you are not, and have written, and your letters do not arrive, I am left to the conclusion that my letters do not reach you, and then I am truly miserable. I hope, ire I sleep to night, that letters will come from you. I have not heard from you since you received any letters from me at this place. I can only hope that my letters have, and will safely reach you! You will not find much, beyond the fact, that they are my letters, to you, that will interest you! Since I wrote last, I happened in a store, and was tempted, greatly, to buy a dress for you, but posponed the matter for consideration, which will soon be out, and I must determine, what I will do, as I have no expectation, that I can receive any advice from you, on the subject, before I hope to leave here. Every day, I have looked for a letter from you, to say to me, when you most desire to see me at home.

My letters as you see in them, will give you my <u>speculations</u>, and my <u>intentions</u>, on the subject of being with you. It absorbs much of my thoughts, & affords me boundless anxiety. I hope my dearest, that you will have as much of Mrs Birdwells cheerful company as you can, and such other company, as will conduce to your cheerfulness, and I pray you not to yield yourself up to depression, or low spirits. I have said to you, what I intend to do when I leave here for home, so that you will be apprised of the probable time of my arrival, supposing my trip over twenty days from this home. If you have serious apprehensions, and your time should come before I can reach home, do <u>or any how</u>, <u>in advance of the time</u>, do you get Col Yoakum, thro Mrs Yoakum, or apply to him yourself, to write to Doct B. F. Sharpe, or do it, (write to Dr Sharpe) yourself to go, and attend upon you. I do not know where he resides, but Col. Yoakum does, and if either he, or you should write to him, let there be a note on the outside of the letter to the Post Master, requesting him to send it immediately, as it is important. Now in this matter, do not <u>I pray you</u>, calculate the dimes, or dollars, for if I live to go home in time (as I hope to do) to take him with me. Now my Love, I do hope you will let no minor consideration, prevent this course. Do not by this suppose, that I think your situation more dangerous than Ladies in your situation usually are. I wish to act, upon the principle, that if you should be ill, all possible assistance will be at home. I have unbounded confidence in the skill of Doct Sharpe, and should you be in danger, he can be of great assistance to you. In these things usually, I rely much upon <u>nature</u>, with fair play, & little assistance <u>unless</u> skillful. I am writing too much on this subject, for it may have a tendency, to cause too much meditation, and you are now afflicted by it, I fear. Dont, my Love suppose that I intend to reflect upon you, for I declare, that in my heart, there is no other feeling, than the feelings, of sympathetic affection.

My suggestions arise from the confident hope, that all will be well with you, and that your forebodings have arisen from some physical cause, of which now will be entirely relieved, before your time may arrive. I will look hourly for letters from you, until they do come & if I could I would punish all delinquent Post Masters and Contractors in advance. In a few days, I hope to speak on my resolutions,[1] and then I will have nothing to do but to start for home! W. D. Miller[2] arrived here two days since, and travelled up the river from Mobile, to Parks Landing, with Columbus & Young.—all were well with them! My love to Mother, and many kisses to the dear children. Howda to all, and regards to all friends.

Thy ever devoted Husband
Houston

You will find confusion in this letter. It written with several persons in my Room.

[1]Houston made resolution speeches to the Senate on January 14, and January 30, 1850. *Writings,* vol. 5, 113–19.
[2]Washington D. Miller was Houston's secretary.

The following letter written by Margaret is from the Temple Houston Morrow collection in the Barker History Center of the University of Texas, Austin.

Huntsville
Jan 28, 1850

My beloved husband,

I have just recd quite a package from you. I need not attempt a description of my great delight, for my fortitude had been sorely tried by the failure of the mails for the last three weeks, so that I was quite overjoyed this evening at the reception of your several dates of the 27th and 31st of Dec. and the 2nd, 6th, and 7th of Jan. Tomorrow is my usual letter day, but as I feel quite well tonight, and the children are all asleep, except Sam, who as usual is at my elbow, I have thought it best to begin my letter, lest I might be interrupted tomorrow. We are all enjoying good health, and although my spirits may be somewhat deprest from the confinement with my sprained ancle [sic], and from being deprived of your letters by the failure of the mails, I have yet many mercies for which to thank my Heavenly Father. I have had some severe trials, but the Lord sustains me through them. You may prepare yourself for an astounding peice [sic] of news. On last night Virginia eloped with Gott, as I supposed to marry him, but today I learn he has taken her to Cincinatti [Texas] to go to school to Miss Rankin[1] one session and then they are to marry. You may form some idea of my astonishment by your own, for I was totally unprepared for it. Indeed she had seemed happier and more cheerful for the last few weeks than I ever saw her, and I thought we were getting along finely, but I can now find from various sources that I was nursing a viper and am quite confident that she was the person who rendered Mr. Hatch so dissatisfied for a while, as he has repeated some of her tatling [sic] to me since she left. You will remember dearest that in my great perplexity, I told you I would carry it to a throne of grace, well truly the Lord has delivered me out of my great troubles but in a way which I looked not for.[2] It is all right, and though she may have rushed upon her own ruin, I have the sweet assurance, that I have been faithful to my trust.

I think I can percieve [sic], notwithstanding all your cares, that you are making advances in the divine life. Go on my beloved "from strength to strength, from grace to grace," and the Lord will give you more and more light. Will you read before you retire, the 3rd ch. of Phillipians? Read it carefully and prayerfully, and meditate particularly upon the 14th, 15th, and 16th verses, as I think they are peculiarly applicable to your case.

Tuesday 29th. Well I have taken up my letter again. It is a bright cheerful day. Every thing looks happy, and even I am not sad. I am so mercifully sustained, that I am truly a wonder to myself. Oh what should I do in my lonely and widowed condition amid all my trials and cares, without that hidden manna, on which my soul feasts daily!

I sold Charlotte to Col. James Gilespie who paid me one hundred dollars down and gave me a judgment for four hundred dollars in Maj. Smither's[3] hands, which I have since transferred to Mr James Maxey and taken a mortgage on the place which he now occupies. He gives me 10 pr ct interest and has made me quite sure. You speak of my selling her to bro. Vernal, but the truth is, I did not want to keep her in the family. Col Gilespie knew her faults, and as he was willing to risk them, I felt myself clear. You would be delighted to see how pleasantly the servants get along, since she has been removed from them. I thought I had told you about the pigs. They are all dead except one, and that was given to Thomas Palmer, in accordance with your directions. I think you will find that Mr Hatch does not know much about hogs, but never mind we shall have a plenty, and I merely mention this to prepare you for a dissappointment [sic], when you get home. The old man does the very best he can I assure you, and I hope we will have a fine crop. Mother never interferes in any thing at all appertaining to the farm, but reads and meditates a great deal. I told her a short time ago, that I believed the Lord sent old Mr. Hatch, that she might be forced to give up her earthly cares and prepare for another world. Sam was delighted with his gold dollar and insists earnestly on keeping it in his waistcoat pocket. You recollect that waist-coat. Nannie and Maggie increase daily in loveliness. They are very fond of each other, and I hope they will always be so. I had Mother's picture taken[4] but declined having Sam's and Nannie's for the reason that it was so uncertain whether or not I could get a good likeness, that I did not like to risk so much money. Very few persons consider mine a likeness. Mother's is thought by some persons to resemble her very much, but I do not think it is a perfect likeness. Please ask some of your female friends to make a selection of sacred music for me, adapted to the piano. I may have an opportunity now and then of practising [sic] a little. I think Sam will sing well, as he improves rapidly. I would be glad to have some good pens, if you can send them by mail. You may calculate certainly on my writing once every week, unless providentially hindered.

Thine ever,

M. L. Houston

Mr. Hatch expects to plant two or three acres in corn this month by way of experiment. I think I will write to some of bro. Royston's people soon, but I can not promise you that I will urge them to come out, for I think my love, we will let them use their own pleasure about it. I have told Sam that for his first report which has all gs and no cross marks you will get him a pretty reading book. He says "ma please tell pa to let it have pictures in it and not to let the men have black mouths and noses!" By that I suppose he means that he wants painted pictures and not wood cuts.

[1]Malinda Rankin, a teacher. For a biography see *New Handbook of Texas,* vol. 5, 445.
[2]Margaret was mistaken. Gott would bring charges that Margaret had abused Virginia. Margaret was indicted by the Grand Jury of Walker County and forced to stand trial.
[3]Huntsville merchant Robert Goodloe Smither. Identified in Carpenter, 2027.
[4]No photograph of Nancy Lea has ever been located.

Washington

29th Jany. 1850

My Dearest,

Last night I wrote to Bro Henry at Montgomery, as the Legislature has not yet adjourned,[1] and as I wrote to him, "may not until I pass thru, on my way home, if I should go that route."

I write to you now, as I have a little while without company, and can not so well dispose of my time in any other way, or at least so much to my liking, as in writing to you, tho' I should say nothing interesting to you.

I have a slip, from an Ohio whig paper, which I will send you, that you may see that the whigs, in the free states, are less abusive of me, than they are in the south. <u>Nullification</u>, and I, are at outs, and can not be reconciled, by any means. I will do all in my power to save the Union, and my efforts with others, must succeed!

For two days past we have enjoyed fine weather—, a rare thing in Washington. I think it is the first time since I arrived here, that such a thing has taken place, nor do we expect pleasant days until March. Then I hope to be in the sunny south, and enjoy your smiles, and the children's which are far <u>brighter</u> to me, than all the glare of fashion, or the splendour of place! I know that you will feel, and realise the fact. I would not give one day at home, for all the pleasures, that I can ever enjoy from home, or in this place.

My love of the dear objects, of home have brought me here, and are all that can ever induce me, to leave my home! To be a good man, an affectionate husband, a kind Parent, a generous master, a true patriot, and to leave to my family, and the world a spotless reputation, comprise all the objects of my earthly ambition! No one of these objects, will be disserved, by my being here, while others will be advanced, and my country's good promoted, as I fervently hope!

You will see my dear, that they call me "old" who do not know me, and Mr Miller (who does not flatter as you know) says, that I look younger, than he ever saw me before! Tis true my health is fine, and if I were with you, I would be happy. My love to all.

Thy devoted,
Houston

[1]Henry Clinton Lea was serving in the Alabama Legislature. Brewer, 499.

Washington
3rd Feby 1850

My Dearest,

I have just returned from Mr Sampsons church, where he gave a fine sermon, & took a subscription, and a collection was raised for foreign missions. I gave only one dollar, because at the time, I was short of change. I will get, and send you some very interesting statistics of the mission cause so soon as I can. I saw Mrs Cushman there, who sends her love to you, and says she would be delighted to see you. I told her, that I intended in a few days to set out to see you. She was rather surprised, and spoke to the "great distance," making enquires, and I delicately answered them, in such sort, as to rid her of surprise!

On tomorrow, I intend to speak, on my resolutions,[1] and if I can give cement to the Union, and stability to our Government, I will be happy. I hope to be able to do some good, and make a fair effort. To day I feel well, and as if I would be in order. If I live, I will correct it, before it goes out to the world. [William Henry] Dangerfield has been to see me, and made for you, and Master Sam (as an old friend) many kind enquiries. You know he was married last session.[2] He is now "looking out," and has been here, to consult me about sundry matters, connected therewith. Such as suppose so, and so were the case, what will be the result? To all which, I replied, according to my limited knowledge! You can not my dear, fancy how anxious I am to be with you, and hope to see you, between the first and tenth of March, or earlier, as I wish to leave on the 10th or 12th instant.

I am fearful, that the mails do not reach you regularly. On to night I hope to get letters from you, as several are now, due me. You will excuse me, for not writing as much as usual, & believe my heart wholly with you, and belonging to you. I intend to write so soon as I get thro' with my speech.

My love, and regards to all. Kiss the little fellows.

Ever thy
Houston

The reason why, I can not say more precisely when I hope to be home is, that I am told the stages have stopped, on the Texas routes.

[1]On January 14, 1850, Houston had presented a resolution concerning slavery and on January 30, 1850, one concerning public domain. *Writings,* vol. 5, 113–44.
[2]William Henry Daingerfield married Mary Dunlap on December 12, 1848. Wesley Pippenger, comp., *District of Columbia Marriage Licenses Register 1811–1858* (Westminister, Md.: Family Line Publishers, 1994), 146.

Washington
5th Feby 1850

Dearest,

No letters have yet reached me, and of course I am very unhappy, and must become more so, until I can hear from you. I did not
speak on yesterday, as I expected, when I wrote to you. Yesterday
was my day to speak, and I gave way to another Senator (Mr. Berrien[1]
of Geo.) To day was Mr. Clay's day of course, on his Resolutions,
and he accordingly spoke for two hours, when the Senate adjourned
for him to continue on tomorrow.[2] Then, I intend to get the floor and
speak on thursday.[3] Mr. Clay is not in good health, and age, as well
as free living, together have made irupairable [sic] inroads upon his
health. He is yet an able man, but I do not think he can take the same
vigorous and clear views, of subjects, that he cou'd once have done!

To day there was the greatest concourse of Ladies that I have
ever seen in the Senate! They almost crowded the senators out of
their seats. This, I was not particularly charmed with, as I do not go
among the Ladies as I once did—for instance, I do not know, (as I
have never seen them, the Ladies of our house) as I have not seen
them, tho, two are members daughters (as I hear) and Mr King[4] of
Alabama, has two nieces here! You will blame me, doubtless for being so remiss! The truth is, my Love, I can tell you, there is but one
young Lady on earth, that I care one fig for, and tho' I give you leave
to blame me as much as you please for my attachment, I feel, that it
is for me impossible, not to <u>love her</u>. Or in other words, it has not
been in my power to avoid loving her! It began before our marriage,
and since that, I have never ceased to love her, with pure, and unsullied devotion. I believe, it is laid down, by authors of the past ages,
that we do not know ourselves! Upon this principle my dear, you do
not know the Lady! When I first knew her, she was Miss Margaret
M. Lea, and now is Mrs. Maggy Lea Houston. Now, my Love, be

generous, and say, that you dont care how much I love her. If you will, I agree, that I will never love another while I live, but her! Have you been provoked, my dear? If you have, I only did it, to cause a smile, while you breathe forgiveness. Well, I hope to see her soon, as I wish to get off from here, by the 10th or 15th inst, and will embrace you, God willing, the first moment in my power. Tho' I expected a letter telling me when to be at home, as it has not arrived, I am left to make my own calculation, as to when I ought to be at home, I pray that I may be at home previous to your hour of trial. Do not, my Love, suppose for a moment, that I regard my leaving here, as an unjust extraction by you upon me! I go with great pleasure, uniting a sense of duty, with unbounded affection!

I am in affection constantly with you, and if I were to retire the balance of my life, (tho it might be long) I would rather do it than that my absence, should cost you pain, or by chance afflict you.

My love, and regards to all. Salute all friends.

Thy devoted Husband,
Houston

[1]J. Macpherson Berrien. *Biographical Directory of Congress,* 147.

[2]For information about Clay's speech see Robert V. Remini, *Henry Clay: Statesman for the Union* (New York: W. W. Norton & Company, 1991), 735–36.

[3]Houston spoke on February 8, 1850. For a text of the speech see *Writings,* vol. 5, 119–44. The galleries were packed, and as Houston began to speak the rules were suspended so that the overflow crowd could be admitted to the floor. Ladies sat on stools between the senators' desks. Wisehart, 533. This was the speech where, in an effort to reconcile the North and South, Houston said, "a nation divided against itself cannot stand." Abraham Lincoln would later paraphrase this in one of his speeches.

[4]This was probably Porter King, but Houston may have been referring to his father, Edwin Davis King. For biographies see Thomas McAdory Owen, *History of Alabama and Dictionary of the Alabama Biography* (Chicago: S. J. Clarke Publishing Company, 1921), vol. III, 982.

Huntsville
Feb. 6th 1850

My beloved husband,

It is so cold today that I can not do much else than nurse myself over the fire, but as it is my regular day, I must write to you though I may only make out a few lines. We all feel the cold spell very sensibly, as we have had several days of fine spring weather and the system was much relaxed by it. On last friday, I recd your favours of the 13th and 15th ult. for which I thank you sincerely. The stage has stopped on account of the high waters and the embarrassment of the contractor. I have therefore recd none of your speeches, and I know nothing of what is going on in congress, except as your letters inform me. But I have no great anxiety, for I am sure you will do nothing that is not bound on sound judgment and integrity.

I am delighted to learn that you expect to make us a visit in the spring. I wrote to you, that I would rather you should not come, unless you resigned your seat in the senate, and at that time, I realy [sic] felt as if I could not endure to have you with me through a scene of anguish and then part with you immediately, but if you will postpone your visit until may, I can think of it differently. I would have no objection to the 9th of may[1] if it would suit your convenience to arrive here about that time. You know it is a pretty time of the year. The woods and garden will look cheery, and if I should survive, I hope I should be quite cheerful myself. Besides all this, there is another consideration. The remainder of your absence would be somewhat shortened, and even a day thrown off that dreary waste seems to me, a day less of sadness and loneliness. As to the time of trial, I can tell you no more, than when you left. I am uncommonly helpless, but it arises principally from my lameness. My ancles [sic] were both twisted, but one much worse than the other, and I fear it will be a great while before I recover entirely from the accident.

In one of your recent letters, I was reminded of a fact which I have omitted to mention to you. I gave Mother the price which you set on her pony and filly soon after you wrote to me on the subject. She keeps within doors and interferes with nothing and no one beyond her limits, but it does not seem to lessen old Mr Hatch's dislike to her, which I expect he imbibed before he came here. If he would only refrain from calling her names and talking about her to the servants within my hearing, I could have more fortitude, but as it is, I am compelled to run away out of hearing in order to keep up my politeness to him. I account for it in this way. The old man is naturally obscene and illnatured [sic] and must have an object on which to vent his spleen. He has never been accustomed to being with ladies, and I can see that he is very tired of the restraint imposed on him. I intend to keep up my politeness, and will give him no possible chance to fall out with me.

Our family and neighborhood are quite healthy. I have heretofore omitted to tell you that Mrs Simons[2] was no more. She died about three weeks ago, within a short period of her confinement. I hope I shall get your letters regularly, and that will sustain me greatly.

Thy affectionate wife
M. L. Houston

[1]The Houstons' tenth wedding anniversary.
[2]Ana Simons died of congestion. Roland Vern Jackson, *Mortality Schedule, Texas 1850*, 21.

Huntsville
Feb. 12, 1850

My ever dear love,

There was a failure yesterday of the mail, and as usual after such a dissappointment [sic], I am rather out of spirits, but I will try to be cheerful, for after a dark cloud there is generally a gleam of sunshine for me, and I will hope that when your letters come, they will bring me cheering news of you. We had quite a storm last night. The hail, thunder and lightning were terrific, and today is bleak and cheerless and we have had a tempestuous season, and it is rare that the sun looks out upon us with his cheering beams.

Mrs. Birdwell and Mrs. Wilson[1] came to see me yesterday, and had much to say about you. The former in particular was very anxious to know if I had urged you to come home in the spring. I told her the substance of what I had said to you on the subject, and I believe she thinks I have done wrong in asking you to leave your post. If I have, I am sorry for it, but I am perplexed and know not what to say about it. She says I must tell you to have no uneasiness on my account, for I shall have every consolation that friendship can supply, and on no account to leave your post at this unfortunate crisis. Remember that her words are not my own, and that I merely repeat them that you may know how much consideration your friends feel for your reputation. All that I can say upon that subject is that I wish you to do just what you think is right and proper.

We are enjoying good health, and the children improve rapidly. Sam still persists in his writing and drawing, and I have had a neat little desk made for him with which he is greatly delighted. I was amused this morning at the scene between him and Nannie. He was using the most persuasive language to induce her to sit for her portrait, which the young lady refused very peremptorily. I am satisfied that her reason was that she had apprehended from Sam's specimens hers would not be a very pretty picture. Poor Sam never suspected the truth, but seemed to think his sister extremely obstinate. I enclose two of his drawings for your amusement. The house, he says, is the one in which Nebuchanezzer's heart was lifted up with pride. The other is in imitation of one my own sketches when a little girl, an old field on which I used often to look out on my chamber window. The scene was certainly not very picturesque, but it is associated with remembrances of childhood. I do not know if Sam's is an improvement upon the original for I never was a very distinguished artist.

You will see that I am teaching Sam economy, requiring him to preserve the envelopes for his drawing. He is teaching Nannie her alphabet and is delighted with the employment. Oh I wish you could see our little Maggie! She is the most bewitching little creature I ever saw. She has the manners of a polished lady, and her rosy cheeks and bright eyes would charm you completely. Whenever Sam or Nannie hurt themselves, her little arms are spread in an attempt to embrace them and her pretty mouth put up to kiss them, and she never fails to soothe them immediately. Mother is at length compelled to say that she never saw such a child in her life.

I recd a letter from Antoinette by last mail relating, that they expected to set off for Huntsville the 25th ult. I can not tell why they have not arrived, and I trust nothing serious has detained them. If you can find time to write to Charles, it would be very satisfying to them I know.

Have you heard any thing of sister Polly [Mary Wallace] lately? If you hear any news of her do write me about it. I do not know that I have any news that would interest you particularly unless you can rejoice with our church in hearing that bro [James] Maxy has at length consecrated himself entirely to the Lord. I expect he will be ordained at our convention in May. He seems to be a different man since his earlier dedication. His conversations with bro. Bains[2] were greatly blessed to him. We expect bro B. and his family at our March meeting. I think you will be pleased with him. He is a meek and humble Christian, and seems entirely devoted to the cause of Christ.

Mother is well and sends her love to you. Sam sends his love and says to "tell pa I have read through lessons for little readers, and now I am reading in my peep of day."[3]

Thy devoted wife,
M. L. Houston

[1]Jane Wilson. The two women were sisters. Ruth Grant to Madge Roberts, March 4, 1996.
[2]George Washington Baines, pastor of the Huntsville Baptist Church. *New Handbook of Texas,* vol. 1, 340.
[3]This book is in the collection at the Sam Houston Memorial Museum, Huntsville, Texas.

The following letter was written to Houston by his cousin Narcissa B. Hamilton. The original is in the Madge W. Hearne Collection of Houston materials in the Barker History Center, Austin, Texas.

Richmond
Feb. 14th [18]50

My dear Cousin,

Your kind favour was duly received before my first visit to Richmond, and on my return to the College,[1] I received your paper; for both I must sincerely thank you. I know not how long I shall have to remain in this place; if I can accomplish my business to my satisfaction, I shall certainly visit your City, and remain under your protection whilst Mr Blackwell[2] goes on to New-York. I do not wish to go so far north in such cold wether [sic]. Ex Gov. McDowell[3] proffered me his courtesy, but I should prefer yours, even if Miss Sallie should be with her father. Could you steal any possible chance [to] slip away from the City, and spend a few hours with us. Ah! it would be such a pleasure to see you. The enclosed communication is a reply or whatever you may call it, to a most unwanton assault upon you, in his Richmond speech. Mr Blackwell thought I had better not publish it, but send it to you. You must give me your opinion. I hope to hear from your dear wife soon. All our friends are well. In great hast [sic].

Your affectionate Cousin
N. B. Hamilton

[1]The Buckingham Female Seminary, also called the Female Collegiate Institute. Samuel Rutherford Houston, 52.

[2]Thomas Blackwell is identified as a resident of Richmond living in Jackson. Roland Vern, Gary Ronald Teeples, and David Schaefermeyer, *Virginia 1850 Census Index* (Bountiful, Utah: Accelerated Indexing Systems, Inc., 1976), 46. However, she may have been referring to her cousin, John Blackwell, who was principal of the Buckingham Seminary. Madge W. Hearne Family Papers.

[3]James McDowell was an advocate of education. Virginius Dabney, *Virginia: The New Dominion* (Garden City, New York: Doubleday & Company, Inc., 1971), 279.

Huntsville
Feb. 18, 1850

My ever dear husband,

On yesterday I recd your several ones of the 9th, 20th, 24th, and 27th ult.[1] From the number which came together, you can form the idea of the days that have passed since I recd a letter from you. I find that you suffer the same inconvenience from the irregularity of the mails, and I am sorry that it is so, as it may cause you much unnecessary anxiety. I can not but hope from your letters, that you will be with me in the course of a few weeks. It may be that I have done wrong to insist on your coming, but I trust that it will be for the best. When I did so, it was under the melancholy impression that I should not survive the spring, and even now I am not free from apprehensions, but my health is much improved, and my cough has almost left me altogether. I am beginning to think that you were right about the 13th of April. If Dr. [B. F.] Sharpe were in reach of us, I would have him here, because you request it, but as it would be presumptuous in me to incur the trouble and expense of getting him, as it would seem like trusting to an arm of flesh, and how easily can the Lord define the skills of man! My great concern is, that I should be entirely resigned to his will. When I think of my husband and little ones, my heart clings to them so fondly, that I can not feel that resignation to death, which I desire. The Lord grant that the hour of trial may find me prepared for any dispensation of his will.

Our poor friends Thomas Palmer and his wife are in the deep waters of affliction. On last saturday night, the messenger of death bore from thier humble home its brightest ornament, the noble little Othaniel. Mrs [Rachel] Palmer about a week before he was taken, had given birth to a daughter,[2] but when she found the dear boy was dangerous, every other feeling was lost in that of the mother, and seven long days she watched him incessantly through that terrible disease, the "black tongue" or "putrid sore throat." The rest of the children have all had it, and it is now raging through that neighborhood in its most malignant form. Dear little Othaniel's throat was swollen to such a size, that he was speechless toward the last, but he was able by signs to make his parents understand, that he was not afraid to die, and that his trust was in the blessed Jesus. Oh how often I have told Sam, that he might live to be a man, and have many friends, but I feared he would never know another such a friend as Othaniel Palmer. Dear boy, his grave gentle face was always a welcome one to me, and how will his parents endure the loss! The Lord "tempereth the wind to the shorn lamb," and he will sustain them.

Esq Keenan[3] is no more. He died calmly and peaceable, but I fear his trust was in the universal salvation of mankind. Oh how many precious souls have been wrecked on that deceitful shore! I have heard recently of a little book called "Principalities and powers," which I would like for you to get and read. My greatest uneasiness on your account arises from your views on the subject of universalism, although you do not suspect it yourself. God forbid that you should ever fall into that delusion. From what I hear of this work, I humbly trust that you may find it useful to you.

Sam says that I must tell you that he was much pleased with the horse you sent him, and that he will draw it with pleasure. He and Nannie did not receive thier picture books until a few days ago, but there was quiet [sic] a sensation when they once arrived I assure you. The whole house was called upon by Miss Nannie to lament the sad death of cock robin, and to listen to the exciting adventures of Mother Hubbard and her dog. It has put her quite in the notion of reading, and she has learned her alphabet in half the time that children usually require. She still insists on my sending efforts by her to you like Sam's. Poor Sam has been so ill with a cold through the last week, that I have not kept a regular effort of him. Little Maggie's charms seem to increase. She is so bewitching that old Mr Hatch with all his roughness and repulsiveness can not look at her without a smile.

I have not yet read your temperance speech, but Bro Maxey tells me that he has it, and I hope that he will send it to me soon. He gives me a glowing account of it. I would like to write more, but I am busily engaged in preparing medicines for the black tongue, as in all probability we will be visited by it. With the blessing of God, I hope I will be able to manage it.

Mother sends her love to you. I read a note on yesterday from Mr [L. B.] Hanchet, stating that he had brought me a bundle from you, and sent it to the care of Mr [Ebenezer B.] Nichol[s]. It has not come to hand, but I thank you in advance.

Thy devoted wife,
M. L. Houston

1No letter for January 9, 1850, has been located.
2Mary. Carpenter, 1538.

[3]John Keenan. Lucy Alice Bruce Stewart, Verna Baker Banes, and Anthony V. Banes, comps., *Walker County, Texas, Cemetery Records* (Huntsville, Texas: Walker County, Texas, Genealogical Society, 1992), 155.

Houston had reached the decision that Margaret needed him at home. Telling his colleagues in Washington that he must make a short trip at home because of family illnesses, Houston left Washington sometime in mid-February. Margaret continued to write, not knowing that Houston was on his way for a short visit.

Huntsville
Feb. 24th, 1850

My dear husband,

It is late at night, but Gen. [George T.] Wood has just sent me word that he expects to set off early tomorrow morning for Washington. I will therefore try to write you a few lines, though I feel quite dull from sitting up last night until past midnight. Sister Antoinette arrived on yesterday, and we had so much to talk about that sleep was almost forgotten. She came up the river to Cincinatti [Texas] on the steamboat, and had rather a tedious and tiresome journey. Bro. Charles did not accompany her, but I hope he will be up by the next trip of the boat. His son Charles now about fifteen years old came with her. Her dear little Thomas is a fine looking boy and very sensible.

I am living in great hopes of seeing you shortly. I rather think the trying time with me, will be near the middle of April. We are all well except Sam who still suffers from his cold, but he is about so noisy as usual, and seems extremely anxious for you to come home. He says I must tell you, that whenever I send you a weekly report of him, all good marks and no cross marks or blanks, that he wants you to get him a box of magnetized fish. Nannie knows her alphabet perfectly and is becoming quite familiar with portions of bible history. Little

Maggie is as lovely as ever. Cousin John Moffitt is with us, and I think is quite pleased with my young friend Laura Hatch,[1] and as I rather think it is mutual, there is no telling what will follow! All send their love to you. I hope to write you a long letter on teusday [sic], my regular letter day. Good night dearest

Thy devoted wife
M. L. Houston

[1] The niece of Tirzia Birdwell. D. Anne Crews, ed., *Huntsville and Walker County, Texas: A Bicentennial History* (Huntsville: Sam Houston State University Press, 1976), 61.

Chapter III

March 18, 1850–October 1, 1850

June 6, 1850: Sam Houston to Margaret Houston
June 9, 1850: Sam Houston to Margaret Houston
June 12, 1850: Sam Houston to Margaret Houston
June 15, 1850: Sam Houston to Dr. Alva Woods
June 15, 1850: Sam Houston to Margaret Houston
June 16, 1850: Sam Houston to Margaret Houston
June 17, 1850: Sam Houston to Margaret Houston
June 18, 1850: Sam Houston to Margaret Houston
June 18, 1850: Margaret Houston to Sam Houston
June 23, 1850: Sam Houston to Margaret Houston
June 26, 1850: Sam Houston to Margaret Houston
June 30, 1850: Sam Houston to Margaret Houston
July 3, 1850: Sam Houston to Margaret Houston
July 5, 1850: Sam Houston to Margaret Houston
July 7, 1850: Sam Houston to Margaret Houston
July 14, 1850: Sam Houston to Margaret Houston
July 18, 1850: Sam Houston to Margaret Houston
July 21, 1850: Sam Houston to Margaret Houston
July 23, 1850: Margaret Houston to Sam Houston
July 29, 1850: Margaret Houston to Sam Houston
July 29, 1850: Sam Houston to Margaret Houston
August 1, 1850: Sam Houston to Margaret Houston
August 4, 1850: Sam Houston to Margaret Houston
August 8, 1850: Sam Houston to Margaret Houston
August 10, 1850: Sam Houston to Margaret Houston
August 11, 1850: Sam Houston to Margaret Houston
August 14, 1850: Sam Houston to Margaret Houston
[undated]: Sam Houston to Margaret Houston
[ca. August 18, 1850]: Sam Houston to Margaret Houston
August 19, 1850: Sam Houston to Margaret Houston
August 22, 1850: Sam Houston to Margaret Houston
August 23, 1850: Sam Houston to Margaret Houston
August 25, 1850: Sam Houston to Margaret Houston
August 26, 1850: Sam Houston to Sam Houston, Jr.
August 28, 1850: Sam Houston to Margaret Houston

September 2, 1850: Sam Houston to Margaret Houston
September 4, 1850: Sam Houston to Margaret Houston
September 5, 1850: Sam Houston to Margaret Houston
September 6, 1850: Sam Houston to Margaret Houston
September 8, 1850: Sam Houston to Margaret Houston
September 9, 1850: Sam Houston to Margaret Houston
September 11, 1850: Sam Houston to Margaret Houston
September 12, 1850: Sam Houston to Margaret Houston
September 12, 1850: Sam Houston to Margaret Houston
September 15, 1850: Sam Houston to Margaret Houston
September 18, 1850: Sam Houston to Margaret Houston
September 19, 1850: Sam Houston to Margaret Houston
September 20, 1850: Sam Houston to Margaret Houston
September 21, 1850: Sam Houston to Margaret Houston
September 22, 1850: Sam Houston to Margaret Houston
October 1, 1850: Sam Houston to Margaret Houston

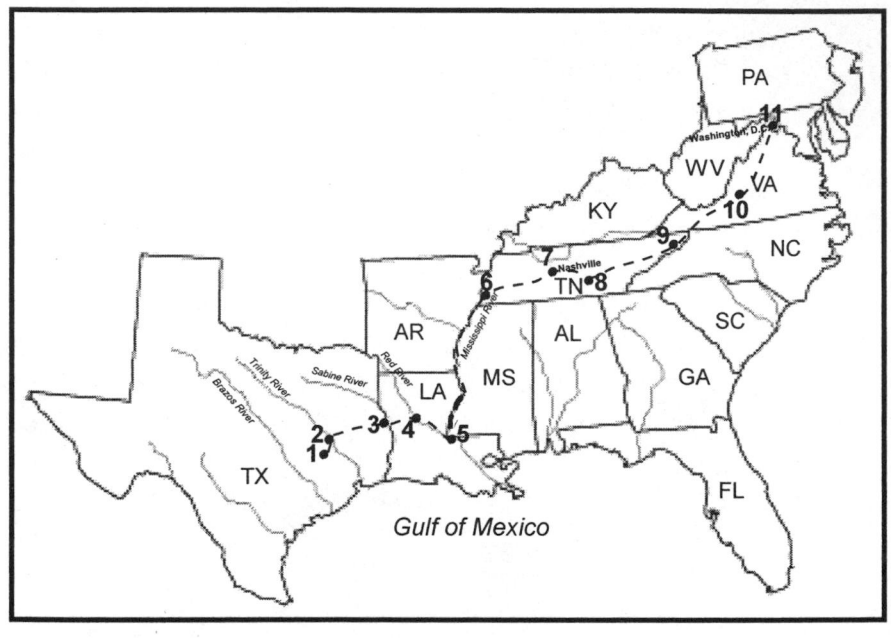

Houston's Northern Route to Washington, D.C.
March—April, 1850

1. Huntsville, Texas
2. Cincinnati, Texas
3. Sabinetown, Texas
4. Grand Ecore, Louisiana
5. Mouth of the Red River
6. Memphis, Tennessee
7. Nashville, Tennessee
8. Sparta, Tennessee
9. Blountsville, Tennessee
10. Rockbridge County, Virginia
11. Washington, D. C.

Houston remained at home for a few weeks and attempted to help Margaret solve some of the family's problems. He was on the road back to Washington in late March of 1850. The following letter does not have the year, but it is believed to have been written from Cincinnati, Texas, as he began his return trip.

11 oclock P.M.

18th March [1850]

My ever dearest,

I hope you are at this moment, blest with sweet repose, and pray that you will awake in the morning refreshed, & cheerful. Bless you all, my heart is with you, tho' I am absent. I had no one with me on my way, and my recollections, were of you, and for you, and the little flock. You need not my Dear One, suppose that I will fail to cherish unceasing love, & devotion for you. If you could only read the emotions, of my heart, you would behold yourself impressed, the vivid object of all my affection. I left you, with a confident hope you will do well, and have a good time of it, and a prospect of more peace, and happiness, in my absence, than you have before enjoyed in my absence. I called at Mr Mersfelders,[1] and if you at any time, want money, he will let you have it, & you can draw on me for the amount. I want it understood, that you do not keep money about you, or any about the House, so far as can be. I said nothing about my journal,[2] Let it be put under your head, so that no one, but Mother, & Eliza,[3] and Sister [Antoinette Power] will know it.

You will hear, that the "Galveston News" has come out with some slanders against me. Something about my writing to Bryan[4] for stores for my use, and to "charge them to the Government when I was President." I have not seen the piece, but will soon. You know I got no stores, nor did I ever do a dishonest act. All that I wish is for you to be assured, whatever, it is false, & slanderous. As Sam said, "Pa will fix it!!!"

I like such things now and then!

Present my love, and kisses to all. I will write as often as I can my Love!

Thy devoted Husband

Houston

P.S. You will recollect that I never had any thing to do with Bryan, in any way of <u>private matters</u>, but the purchase of my carriage, or yours, and that was a loosing [sic] business.

Thine

Houston

[1]Huntsville merchant Paul Mersfelder. Identified in Carpenter, 2012.
[2]Houston is probably referring to his *Private Executive Record, 1841–44* which is now housed in the Sam Houston Regional Library and Research Center, Liberty, Texas.
[3]Margaret's personal servant.
[4]William Bryan operated a mercantile firm which provided financial assistance, supplies, and services to the Republic of Texas. He also served as Texas consul to New Orleans. *New Handbook of Texas,* vol. 1, 792. See also *Writings,* vol. 3, 449–50.

Sabine Town

22nd Mar 1850

My Dear Margaret,

This is another point, from which a mail returns. I have nothing of note to inform you, unless you deem it of importance that I rode to day for several hours, (in a stage without cover) under a heavy rain, and that the balance of the day, I rode in a cold Norther. On my arrival, I found a pretty good fire, and soon became warm, and comfortable. I now feel well, and hope to get off in the morning, on my way to the East. I feel much disposed, to go by way of Tennessee. I am anxious to see Sister Wallace,[1] if I can. I hope it may have some effect upon her mind, for the better. Should it be so, I will feel more happy, than I cou'd be, were I in possession of all the wealth, of California. Her situation is a cause of great sorrow to me, & the cause of it, (as <u>I believe,</u>)[2] adds poignantly, to my grief. I hope I be mistaken! I think it would not detain me more than two, or three days, were I to pass thro Tennessee on my way.

Since my arrival here, I have learned that Mrs Kaufman[3] had a fine son,[4] on the 10st instant, and is about, and doing well. Of course,

I will not call on her. She has sent me a package for her Husband,[5] and among other items, I presume, there is a lock of the <u>Baby's</u> <u>hair</u>! I hope my Love, that you will not be more than a month behind, her, and that you will have, as good a time, as she has had! I have learned some of the particulars, and they are these. Some friends had dined with her, that day, and they left the house to walk into the town about three hundred yards, and a runner came after them. By the time they had reached town, and told them, that all was over, and Mrs had "a fine son." How natural this was! The next day, she was up, and about the house! In this my Dearest, I do not wish you to imitate her! Do my Love, I beseech you, be greatly prudent, as to the matter, of too early exposure! You cant be too careful. My believe is, that your general health, is greatly dependent, upon the care which you take of yourself after confinement. If you are very well, you have only to take the more care of yourself, to keep so.

You see my Love, that I write to you, as often as I can send letters! It is near 12 (midnight,) and the stage from the East has not come in yet. If it does not I will get a horse, and go on tomorrow, or next day, if I live. The wind is now howling, around the cabbin [sic], in which I am located for the night![6] Tis really a Norther, and a first rate one too. My Dear, if I were you, I would have my Trunk placed, under the bed, and not let it stand in the floor. I did think of it, but forgot to suggest the change!

My Dearest present me affectionately to our Mother, Sister,[7] Sam, Charles [Power], and all the dear little ones a kiss, and dont forget <u>Tom</u>,[8] for he is a noble child.

I am thy ever devoted Husband
Sam Houston

Beg of our mother not to think about Miss <u>Thorn</u> & Mr Gott, [blurred] any more for my sake![9]

Thine H.

P.S. If Beck[10] sends down Powhatan.[11] let Mr Johnson[12] send, or take him to Col Rogers[13] at Cincinnati, as I made the arrangement with him, if Beck should send him back. I hope Beck will keep him!

H.

[1]Mary Houston Wallace.

[2]Houston is referring to his belief that their sister Isabella Houston Moore contributed to Mary's mental breakdown. See footnote 7, p. 73, Chapter I.

[3]Jane Richardson (Mrs. David Spangler) Kaufman.

[4]Sam Houston Kaufman. Edna McDaniel White and Blanche Findley Toole. *Sabine County Historical Sketches & Genealogical Records* (Beaumont, Texas: LaBelle Printing Company, 1970), 20.

[5]David Kaufman was a Congressman representing Texas.

[6]Houston was probably staying at the stagecoach inn of E. P. Beddoe. His son Dr. A. F. Beddoe later told how he sat on Houston's knee as a child, when the Senator spent the night at the inn. Virgie Speights. *Old Timers of Sabine County* (Nacogdoches, Texas: Ericson Books, 1983), 35.

[7]Antoinette Power.

[8]Thomas R. Power, the two year-old son of Antoinette and Charles.

[9]In 1842, Virginia's stepfather Dr. Charles F. Worcester had placed Virginia "in the hands of Mrs. Nancy Lea" and retained Virginia's property. James P. Goodall to Judge Robert Johnson, August 8, 1852, Worcester Estate Files, Galveston County Courthouse. Thomas Gott filed a suit against Nancy Lea to recover money he thought was due to Virginia's estate. It would be dismissed on March 29, 1851. Walker County Court Records furnished by James Patton, County Clerk, Walker County.

[10]Alexander Beck.

[11]Houston's horse.

[12]Daniel Johnson, the new overseer hired by Houston during his trip home. Identified by Carpenter, 2028.

[13]Col. George W. Rogers. Carpenter, 1999.

Mouth Red River

26th Mar 1850

My Dear Margaret,

I left Sabine Town, by horse, as the stage did not arrive, on the day after I wrote to you. I reached Grand Ecore, late at night, and left there yesterday morning. I came here this morning, and a Boat is now in sight. I hope it is for Nashville, as I intend to pass thro Tennessee, and see my poor unfortunate Sister (if, I live) and she yet lives. I could not write to you from Grand Ecore, as the house was so mean, that they had nothing convenient. My friend Col Clapp[1] loaned me his horse to ride. While I think of it my Love, if Col Long, of Crockett, calls upon, or sends to you, for two pigs of the white sow, give, or send them to him! This is all the business that I have to write about, only if you want any money call on Mr Mersfelder, and draw upon me, for as much as you want. The first of June Mr Danl Johnson will want will want [sic] to get $20, or $30 dollars. I hope he will do well, and if so, you will let him have the money. Dont stand in need of any thing, but get <u>what you want</u>!

I can express nothing of what I feel. I would fain to do so, if I could, but I can not essay to tell, my solicitude, for your safety, and happiness. To be absent is too painful, and my desire to be at home, is inexpressible! I can only pray for you, and our dear Pledges, and commend you all to the care of our Father, and our God!

I hope my Love, you will have some one, to write to me the moment that you are thro, with your trial! But this is useless, as a request, for it will be over, before this can reach you. I calculate that your time will be over, by the 7th Proximo, at the furthest. This, I fear, will not reach you so soon. When the stage did not come to Sabine Town, Mrs Kaufman sent down for me, and Col Clapp, and myself went up to see her, and the Boy. They were well. She said he was "a nine pounder." Her other children, (or the Boys) are monsters for size. Anna[2] is quite pretty, but I dont like her beauty as much, as I do that of our "gals." Indeed, I see none that I do admire, so much as them.

Do my Love, if you can, write to me once a week, and as much oftener as you please!

Commend me kindly to mother, & Sister, and kisses to the weans all. Regards to <u>our</u> <u>friends</u>, and to Mr Johnson. I do hope he will please you.

Ever thy devoted husband
Sam Houston

P.S. I hope Sam, & Nannie, will have many good marks, and see if our Miss Mag understands them.

Thine H.

---

[1]Elisha Clapp. Identified in Carolyn Reeves Ericson, *Nacogdoches—Gateway to Texas: A Biographical Directory, 1773–1849.* (Nacogdoches: Ericson Books, 1991), 30.
[2]The Kaufmans' six year-old daughter. Carpenter, 1685.

Huntsville
March 26th 1850

My ever dear love,

I write to you today, in the deepest gloom, as a painful duty devolves upon me. That duty is to inform you that sister Mrs Moore[1] departed this life on the 20 inst. Oh what anguish wrings my heart, when I think of all the emotions that will overwhelm your affectionate spirit! But be comforted my own one. "The Lord God omnipotent reigneth!!!" His purposes are hid from us, but we know that he is a merciful Father, and understands all our sorrows and pities our griefs.

I did not know that your sister was ill, until I heard that she was no more. She died very suddenly, and from what I can learn, her disease must have been an inflammation of the brain.[2]

We had a fearful hail storm last night accompanied with terrific thunder and lightning. The affect on my nervous system was very painful, but the Lord sustained me through it. Oh how merciful is my God, thus to uphold me through all my trials! When I first realized that you were gone, oh what a desolation of spirit was mine! But I must not attempt a description of it. I am alive, and a wonder to myself. My cough is much better than when you left, and I hope I shall have strength for my approaching trial. The rest of the family are well except sister A. who is suffering from an affliction of the throat. I feel much anxiety on her account, as she is subject to the affliction, and I fear it will terminate seriously.

Since I commenced writing, several visitors have come in and as they are to stay for dinner, I will conclude my letter and have it sent into the mail. My company consists of Mrs Birdwell, Mrs Evans, your Dutch friends Mr Brok and his wife[3] and Mr [George W.] Bains[4] (our preacher) and his wife.[5] Bro. Bains thinks they met you near Douglas [Texas], on this side. I may be able to write next week. If I am, I will certainly do so. If I am not, you may expect some news from me.

Thy devoted wife,

M. L. Houston

[1] It is believed Eliza Houston Moore died in Polk or Walker County, Texas. Efforts to locate her grave have not been successful.

[2] Eliza Moore died of apoplexy. *Jackson, Mortality Schedule, Texas*, 1850, 17.

[3] H. and Mena Brock of Galveston. Carpenter, 782.

[4] For a biography of George W. Baines, see *New Handbook of Texas,* vol. 1, 340.

[5] Melissa Ann Butler. Ibid.

Nashville, Tenn.

5th of Apr 1850

My beloved,

I came here two days since, and will be off this evening, and precede the Stage to Maj [Andrew] Donelsons about two hours, and will stay long enough to say howda. The Maj is here, and will take me up in his Buggy. I have seen all our kinsfolk here, and the[y] have been delighted by my coming. The most kind, and affectionate expressions, and enquiries about you are made by all persons—kindred and all. I called at Memphis, and saw all our kindred. I told William about the "name"[1] and requested him to tell sister,[2] that "Mary" was a fancy name. This leads me to the fact, that Sister [Mary] Wallace is said to be much better than she has been. I have some hopes, that my seeing her may have a good influence, and possibly restore her reason entirely. I hope to see her in four days.

I will write to you, so soon as I can see her, and give you particulars. My trip here from the mouth of Red river was tedious. The cholera was much in Orleans. The river was all over its banks. I have seen most of our friends here Shelbys[3] etc. Again my Love, I must say to you, how vast my anxiety is, and must be until I hear from you. You will be present in my thoughts, my hopes, and my prayers. It has not been in my power to write as often, as I wished to do.

You must not my dear, complain of this short letter. I will if I live to get to the City write you many long letters. I suppose Sister will have left before this will reach you. To day, I send you a Hogshead of Bacon, hams, sides, shoulders, & it will be sent to Rice and Nichols, Houston. Get Gibbs to have all our hauling done. I hope the Bacon will reach you in a month. My Love to Mother, and the children.

Thy devoted,
Houston

[1]The name "Mary William" had been chosen if the baby was a girl.
[2]William's wife, Mary Ball Houston.
[3]Dr. John and Mariah Shelby. Byron and Barbara Sistler, *1850 Census, Tennessee* (Evanston, Illinois: Byron Sistler & Associates, 1976), vol. 6, 52.

Sparta Tenn.
6th Apl 1850

My Dearest!

You will see that I have thus far come safe. You will recollect this place. It is one hundred miles east of Nashville. I have not slept since I wrote to you yesterday, at Nashville. I came out with Major Donelson, saw the Lady, and a part of the family. Mary went to Nashville and I did not meet her. The Madam has presented the Maj with a fair daughter now six weeks old.[1] I saw the baby—it was clever and pretty I think, as young babys are. When it was born her youngest son was about thirteen months old, and couldn't walk, tho a pretty child. This is what you will be authorized to call quick work! I say nothing, which reflects upon what <u>might</u> have taken place with others. The Madam & Major both were most kind, and solicitous in their enquiries, for you, and Sam, as well as the Gals. I was pleased with the way their baby was fixed, and I requested a pattern of it from Mrs D, which she gave me, and directions how to have it made. If I live to reach the city, I will have it done, and send it to you by mail, if there is no other way for you to get it. It is German, and the baby is lain upon it like placing it on a pillow, only it is a dress, as well as an arm couch. I am sure you will be delighted with it, and amused at it. Dearest, I feel less distressed about Sister Wallace, than

I did before I reached Nashville. It was Cousin Robb McEwen who informed me, that she was improving, and he heard it from Mr. Bricknell,[2] Gen. Wallace's son in law. I hope for the best, and pray our God, that it is so ordered, that my hopes will be fully realised.

I promised all our kindred in Nashville, and Memphis, as well, as our friends, & particularly Mrs Kingsley,[3] Mrs Donelson, and the Major, to present their love, and affection to you. They were disposed to reproach me for not bringing you with me, until I intimated that you were not in a situation to travel, nor would you <u>be</u>, for sometime to c<u>ome</u>. They were kind enough to excuse me!

I will send you some prime apple seeds to plant in drill, or to sow as you please. Soak them twelve hours before they go in the ground.

My feelings, and my affections, translate me to you, and our little ones, tho I am far far distant, in person! Feel, my Love, that you are always with me. Your impress will remain upon my heart, so long as love or one hallowed emotion can exist in my bosom!

My Love, present my duty, & affection to Mother,—Kiss all the little ones, as well as Sister, and her grand boy, "that child," if they are with you, and if not, send them. Commend to our friends, also, and to Mr Johnson, & speak a kind for me to the servants.

I saw Kittys[4] poor old Father. They are all well, he told me, and send word, and love to Kitty. The old man said, "Tell her to remember her poor old Father." My Love, we must see to Kitty. On seeing the poor old man, I felt the force of our obligation! We must see to her. I hope it is not too late. She is an "orphan" in our charge! Dearest! I would rather than the state of Tennessee, that I could be with you, and remain so, while we live on earth.

Thy devoted Husband,
Houston

[1]Catherine Donelson. Identified in Sistler and Sistler, vol. 2, 164.
[2]William Bricknell, Justice of the Peace in Blount County, Tennessee. Identified in Worth Ray. *Tennessee Cousins* (Baltimore: Genealogical Publishing Company, Inc., 1994), 321.
[3]Mrs. Felix Kingsley. Identified in Roland Vern Jackson, *Tennessee 1850 Census Index* (Bountiful, Utah: Accelerated Indexing Systems, Inc., 1977), 229.
[4]Kitty Hoffman was a ward of the Houstons.

Blountsville Tenn
13th Apl 1850

My Dear Love,

As I intended, I visited my poor afflicted Sister. She knew me, and was very glad to see me. She embraced me just as she had always done. For hours in general conversation, she was as rational, and her style, and language, as good as ever. You would suppose that it could not be possible, that she was insane.

Again she would manifest, a fearful desolation of mind, and reason, for a few minutes. She conversed about her visit to the assylum [sic], and detention there. For Genl Wallace, and his family, she manifests the greatest affection, & of their unceasing kindness to her. She asked about you, and Sam, & particularly about Mary Lehr. She wants her, & Mr Lehr to make her a visit this summer. You have never seen a memory, more perfect than hers, not only of scenes previous, to her derangement, but up to the present hour. She wished to know all about our family, and she says, that I made Moore no especial promises, and seemed to understand the relations, of our family, and Mr Moores. She is even yet charitable to Eliza, & Isabella. She speaks of Phebe Jane [Penland], and Mary with great affection. She speaks of no being, with the least unkindness. She sent love to you, and the children, and says she will write. She thinks so, but she will not unless she should improve. She is treated with all the kindness, that her situation will permit. She has not been confined for a long time, and sits in the parlour, but has a dislike to sit on a chair. She desires to sit on the floor. They have great trouble to keep shoes, & stockings on her, and she will not wear any thing on her head. The day that I spent there, she wore her clothes without trouble, and consented to go, and sit at table, but we could not prevail upon her to eat. She sat, and conversed, and told about my <u>stealing</u> cream, from the spring house, as she called it, and mentioned many amusing incidents, of my early life, and seemed disposed to plague me! in kindness. She never smiles, but looked pleasant, but never cheerful![1]

Her affliction has arisen from varied causes, combined. An abscess, in the head affecting the membrane of the inner part of the skull. The <u>change</u> of life, with her, and matters connected with the Moores, as I think, and their violent opposition to her marriage. She never uses any expression, in company that is misproper, but is perfectly delicate, in every thing.

These facts will gratify you, tho' the subject is the most melancholy, that I have ever contemplated. The deep reverses of my own past life, never, so much called into action my sympathies, & melancholy as, has that of my poor Sisters afflictions. I apologized for my conduct to her, that night that I spent with her. She is now a wreck of a noble mind, and the most foully [sic], & cruelly [sic] slandered female, on earth, in my opinion. I further, my Love believe, that she was a converted christian. To this I will add my most fervent prayers, that God when he calls her home, may restore her, to reason, and her heart to his Divine favor. We only stopped here for a few hours, at midnight waiting for an eastern stage. I employed the time in writing to you, as I have not had any time, since I left sister. I hope to reach Washington in six days from this. If I live, I will write to you, so soon, as I reach the city.

This country looks dreary. The oaks have not yet cast their old leaves, and there is, but little appearance of verdure. Present my love to Mother, & kisses to the children. Our kindred in Kingston with whom I spent an hour, have a thousand things to ask about you, and the children, and a world of love to send you! I might allude to <u>another matter</u>, but I will wait for a report as it has <u>transpired</u>.

Thy ever devoted

Houston

Sister had made a pair of pantaloons the day before, I saw her. It helps her mind to be employed, and sometimes, she demands work!

[1]In the Sam Houston Memorial Museum, Huntsville, Texas, is Isabella Moore's copy of a book on Houston genalogy. In the section pertaining to Mary Wallace, Isabella wrote that Mary was "the handsomest woman I ever saw." Rev. Samuel Rutherford Houston, comp. *Brief Biographical Accounts of Many Members of the Houston Family* (Cincinnati: Elm Street Printing Company, 1882), 35.

The following letter, written by Henderson Yoakum to Houston, is from the Madge W. Hearne Collection of Houston Correspondence in the Barker History Center, Austin, Texas.

Livingston, Texas
April 15, 1850

Dear Sir

Being here at court, I recd a note from home yesterday giving the news that you had another daughter. You will doubtless have heard it ere this.

On the 6th inst. the Trustees met in Huntsville & located Austin College on the Hill east of your residence. G. W. Rogers gave us eight acres of land on the hill.

I recd the other day from Gen Rusk a copy of his speech on the Texas Boundary. It is decidedly the best speech I ever saw on the subject. Indeed it cannot be answered. Rusk has covered himself with honor by that speech. We have heard of the death of Calhoun.[1] A rumor has also reached here that Foote has killed Benton in a duel.[2] It is hoped that nothing so barbarous has occurred.

The frost has nearly used up the farmers in this country.

Wishing you much happiness
I am sincerely yours
H. Yoakum

[1] For information about Calhoun's funeral and Rusk's memorial to him see Nevins, *Ordeal of the Union.* Volume I: *Fruits of Manifest Destiny 1847–1852*, 314.
[2] This was incorrect. For information about the altercation which occurred on the Senate Floor when Foote aimed a pistol at Benton see Nevins, Ibid., 309–11.

Senate Chamber
22nd April 1850

My Dear Wife,

I am here again, and with the exception of a bad cold, in fine health. My trip from Blountsville was terrible. I had rain & snow, and wading in the mud "plenty." The stage travelled day, and night, and I only had my clothes, off but one night from Blountsville to this place. As I passed by my native place,[1] there was a snow storm. This you will think was a cool reception, for a son, of the old Dominion. Well the weather was cold, but the hearts of those who could see me from [when] I reached Tennessee, until I left Virginia, were as warm, and cordial to me, as you can imagine. I thought to have passed in cog [incognito], but I did not succeed. Had I used a fictitious name, or no name on the way Bill, I might have got along, without trouble. I will write no more about this, but take pleasure it telling you when we meet. I am anxious, beyond all things to hear from you, and to hear that you are well, and the Boy, or Gal, as the case may be is well. I have from some cause felt confident, that you wou'd do well, and soon recover. Why this is, I cant say. My anxiety has been as great, as you can imagine, but my fears have been less, than before I went home. My prayers tho' unworthy, have been sincere, for your health, & happiness, and a helping to your Babe. I will tear many letters open, with painful anxiety, until I can know the result! I will close this, for to pursue the subject, remote as I am from you and the impossibility, of doing any thing by writing, but to burthen you with my feelings.

I will hope, and pray that you, and our dear little flock may enjoy the smiles of Heaven. Write to me! I send you a letter from my friend Major Jo. Daniels[2] by which I received a humorous present, a chain[3] made from the crude lumps of Gold! You can tell Sam it is "California Gold." My love to all & kisses.

Thy devoted and affectionate husband,
Sam Houston

[1] Rockbridge County, Virginia.

179 : MARCH 18, 1850–OCTOBER 1, 1850

[2]For a biography of Joseph Daniels see *New Handbook of Texas*, vol. 5, 508.

[3]This chain was listed in the inventory of Margaret's estate after her death. Roberts, *Star of Destiny*, 371. It is not known what became of it after that.

On April 9, 1850, the Houston's fourth child, Mary Willie Houston, was born. In a letter to Margaret on April 30, 1850, Houston mentions he had received the news in a letter from Margaret's sister Antoinette, and he expresses his joy. For the text of this letter see Writings, *vol. 5, 145–47.*[1]

[1]Antoinette's letter has not been located.

Washington
5th May 1850

My Dear Margaret,

I owe you a thousand apologies, for not haven written to you, every day, for the last week. This is the sabbath, and the morning I passed at church. I heard a good sermon, and saw our friends. They were all most kind in their inquiries for you, and the little flock. They congratulated both of us, upon the advent of the babe! The mail, by which I expected a letter from you has not come to night. I am very solicitous about letters from you, for I anticipate no other source of pleasure while I am doomed to be absent from you. I may always have placed too loud an estimate upon you, but I am sure if you could look into my heart at this moment, you would not desire, that I should love you, more, than what I do! You are as you say a little "jealous" in disposition, and think that you are not loved enough by those whom you love! I think you ought to be satisfied, with the affection of all your relations, and most particularly with the devotion of Sam, & myself. If you are not, you must be a great <u>skeptic</u>. Now my only anxiety, is to be with you, and <u>those of you</u>. You may say to Sam, that a sword has been procured for him, that I will take home, if I live, and in return for it, I want him to be a good boy, and attend to what his dear Ma says to him, for this will embrace every thing. My Love, tho' I have not written to you every day, as I should have done, I will try, and write every day. The reason that I have not, was the constant flow, of company until after midnight, and then my repose did not begin, until 2 A.M. When I could eat my breakfast, and return to my room it wou'd commence again, (company) and when-ever I could be in my room, company would begin again, and as before continue. Dr Moorman,[1] of Va, who, married a cousin of mine[2] is here, and wishes me to present the love of himself, and family to you. He is a wealthy, & a clever fellow. His wife is a fine woman. He was not at home as I came on, and I called for five minutes, and saw his family. All our relations in Virginia, are anxious to see you, and the children. They all appear to think, that they must be something, past common, and so do we, my Dear!

I may have told you that I passed near to my native place, as I came on, and that it was in the night, and snowing. I saw a cousin of Mothers, who was 83 years old, who was delighted to see me! She was residing with a son, and in comfortable circumstances. I saw several of my kindred, but only for a moment.

They are all very solicitous, that I should spend the 4th of July in my native county, but as yet, I have not made up my mind, if I should live! The duties, which devolve upon me here, are important, and I do not intend to neglect them! My absence was of no detri-ment, to any business, and the unbounded pleasure of seeing, and being with you, and the joys of home, would have compensated me, for much chagrin, tho' I had none to commute! Previous to the mel-ancholy of Sister Eliza's death, I had purchased some dresses, and other things for you, two summer silk dresses, and two of linnen [sic], as I thought, but I fear they are part cotton. Well, I did not know but what you would wish to give one of each to some friend. To Mrs Birdwell, or some lady, who was most kind to you, in your late con-finement. I also, will send two parasols, for you to keep, or do as you please with. Do with every thing, as you please, my Love, and you will meet my wishes! My friend Senator Brashear[3] of Houston, will send them to you, by some safe person. Gov [George] Wood is here, but I do not like him very much, and will send nothing by him. Brashear is my true friend! I send you, a Draft my Love, for $50. that Mr Mersfelder will be glad to give you the Gold for, as he will make a <u>dollar</u> in Exchange. I hope you will have a pleasant spring my Love, and enjoy health. The Bacon has, I hope been sent ire this to you. I have the Bill, of it, and will send it to you, that you can see it. I <u>may</u> send you, some additional articles. My Love, I have not told you, that I presented my watch to Bro. Will, as I came on. I had never made him a present, and he was extremely gratified.

My love to Mother and all!

Thy devoted

Houston

P. S. I intend to send Sister Mary Houston some present for you!

[1]Dr. John J. Moorman. Identified in Rev. Samuel Rutherford Houston, 149–50.
[2]Elvira Margret Walker Houston. Ibid.
[3]Isaac Brashear. Identified in Carpenter, 933.

The following letter written by Margaret is in the collection of Mrs. R. E. McDonald, Dallas, Texas.

Huntsville

May 8, 1850

My ever dear Love,

I have had a long and wearisome confinement, and although the baby is five weeks old today I am just able to walk about my room. I have not exposed myself at all, but it seems impossible for me to recover my strength. I recd your letter from Blountsville on yesterday. I felt sad on reading the account of your visit to sister Polly but rejoice to learn that she is so calm. The Lord grant that she may yet be restored to her reason. What about the little girl's name? Shall we call her "Mary" or "Mary Wallace"?

I have thought of "Mary Paxton" as a means of keeping up the old family name, but do just as you please about it. Antoinette left me about two weeks ago and went down to Br. Vernal's. Since she left Bro. Charley has been here for her. He was quite disappointed on finding that she was not here, but followed after her with great speed, I assure you. The family are all well except little Nannie, who is still very delicate. I have had great anxiety about her. The children all talk a great deal about you and try to be good that you may love them.

We have a poor prospect for a farm, but I trust we will make something. The rains have injured the corn very much, and Mr Johnson says the servants are wandering about all night, so that they are so stupid next day that they are really not able to work. He is too good natured to manage negroes. We have one servant that has been kind and faithful to me during my sufferings—that is Eliza, and I would be glad if you would sell all the rest when you get home, but my dearest, I will not weary you with my annoyances, though they are unceasing with me. If you will only give me a simple assurance that I shall be released from this mockery of a farm, after this year, I think it will keep me cheerful until you get home. I am so unwell today, that I can not write more, but my love, I hope to write you a long letter next week.

P. S. I think sister A's health was better when she left. She was a precious sister and kind nurse during my illness. I miss her more than I can tell you.

M.

8th May 1850

My Beloved,

The last letter contained a promise, that I would write every day. I meant if <u>possible</u>. Yesterday I could not write, from the usual cause—company!

To day I have an opportunity of sending to mother & yourself mourning dresses, vails [sic] & collars. I also send one to each of our nieces, Isabella & Betty. They are alpaca, and the finest, that I have ever seen. I hope you will be pleased with all that I send, my Love.

Least you might feel somewhat dissatisfied, if I were not to send the Babe something, I have sent her two dresses. I am not a first rate judge of baby finery, but hope it may please the young Lady, and I wish you to write to me what she says, upon their presentation. My friend Brashear will send them all by some safe opportunity. I may send you also, some trifles. You can judge of their value. I will now commence looking for your letters. I suppose my dear sister Antoinette has left you. I will be anxious to hear from her. The next letter that I intend to write, is to her, and bro. Charles.

Mr. Clay has to day made his compromise report,[1] and in the main I approve it. I would write more, but it is discussing, and interrupts me. I have written to Col Yoakum, to use my Books, The Laws of the U. States.[2] They are in my office, or in the Boxes, I think. Can you my Love, after a while send to me a copy of my letter to Flacco,[3] with the date, place etc. Don't trouble yourself, but if perfectly convenient send it.

Dont you complain of me for extravagance, in buying articles for you. I can only say "strike but hear me." I hope when I may have the happiness, of telling you my means, and reasons that you will excuse, if you do not justify me. My little canaries are hatching, and Sam sings sweetly. My love to mother, and the family.

Thy devoted husband,
Sam Houston

Tell Kitty that if she is a good Girl I will take her the Ring. Tell Mr Johnson howda and say kind things to the servants.

[1]For information on this report see Remini, 747.
[2]For Houston's letter to Yoakum, May 6, 1850, see *Writings,* vol. 5, 147–48.
[3]The Lipan-Apache Indian chief. Houston may be referring to the letter he wrote to Flacco, the younger, after the death of Flacco, the elder, March 27, 1843. Houston's copy of this letter is in the Madge W. Hearne Collection in the Barker History Center, University of Texas, Austin.

Washington
11th May 1850

My Dear Wife,

I have been greatly provoked by the importunity with which I have been beset. Were it only in the day time, I might submit, but my nights until long after midnight, are consumed, and by those who will not profit me to the extent, that I am troubled.

The contracts to carry the mails, have been letting, for some-time, and I have been a pack horse for many persons interested, in the various bids. Lance has got the contract from Huntsville to Washington, and from Huntsville to Houston. In this matter I have had no hand. My only wish is to have the mails expeditiously conveyed, and safely. I fear our Post Master at Huntsville, will not do. I am sorry that I can not confide in him. He recommended Grant,[1] & Lance, and Madox,[2] with two others as able to carry the mail three times a week, in fine coaches, and four horses. Now they cant do it, and the years salary would not if it were paid in advance, enable them to more, than start the lines. They have no means, and the advance will not be less than $5,000. They will have to send north for coaches, and harness. Yet I hope the mails will be well carried, for if they cant do it others will get the contract.

You care but little, my Love, about these matters, and I will write of matters more interesting to us both. The compromise has been reported, as you will see by the paper I send you. I think, and hope, that it may pass congress, with some modifications, slight in importance. Public sentiment will fully sustain me, in the course, which I have pursued for years. The people are now satisfied that others intended Disunion, and that my course was to prevent it. I, as you know, have been honest in my course, and I have at times, felt for you, fearful that you would doubt my judgment, because I was so much opposed, and abused. It will be all right, and honest!

You may have seen my Dear, that some one wrote to Austin (from Huntsville), & stated that my "visit home was not to see my family, as they knew to the contrary." I fear it was poor [A. P.] Wyly,[3] If so I pity him! I will have no quarrel with him, but I will smoke him in my own way, if I live.

You can tell our dear little ones, that my little Cannairy [sic] Birds hatched on the 9th of May. This my dear is a great day, you know for us.[4] Yes, the 9th of May!!!

Three was the increase. Sam, and Nannie will have a thousand questions to ask about them. Do my Love, write to me, a great deal that they say, and I am very proud to get good reports, of Sam. It makes my heart joyful, and happy! You know my Love, that about the compromise, I will do all in my power to accomplish it for various reasons. One is that I can retire after this session, having done my work, as a true man, and another is that my country will be happy.

There is much anxiety among the people of the U. States to have rest, and peace. All good men wish to see the compromise, and those who wish Disunion, will be disappointed! I will send you from time to time such papers marked, as will show you what I say, on subjects.

I will look with great interest for letters from you, that I may hear from our little pet. Do you call her Mary? Mrs Graham protests, that she is to be named after her, but I told her, that I dare not say a word, on that subject. I told both our sisters, that Mary was to be the name, and so I suppose it is. If you had not so determined you would have wished to call the babe for Sister Antoinette, or I am mistaken, and to this suggestion I can only say, you may do as you think proper. As I have not been with you, in your affliction, I will usurp nothing.

I can tell you an incident. You would have been amused at my Sam Canary while his mate was hatching. He would select nice pieces of food, and take up to the nest, and give to her. He is a most gallant, and interesting little fellow. You must tell Sam all about him. He is the finest songster in the city, as I am informed!

Now, my Love I will assure you, that I did not let the "9th of May" pass, with out fit pleasure, and many considerations of happiness. You can see that I want to say some thing very civil, and indeed, rather to make love! Well, I do feel quite disposed to make love, only that my sheet is so nearly run out. I could tell you, very truthfully, that each passing day, only increases my affection for you, and my anxiety to see you, and to be so situated, that we will not part again. I consider my absence an exile of the most painful character! Not one moment am I, nor can I be happy, where you are not. Where you are, I am altogether happy. For you, and our children, are all there!

My Love to Mother, & the children. Howda to all.

Thy devoted husband
Sam Houston

[1]George W. Grant. Identified as the mail contractor in Carpenter, 2029.
[2]T. W. Maddox. Carpenter, 2011.
[3]Wyley did not write the letter. He would later assist Henderson Yoakum with Margaret's defense.
[4]The Houstons were married on May 9, 1840.

Washington
13th May 1850

Dearest,

To day Mr. Clay spoke on the compromise, and made quite an able speech.[1] Tomorrow I expect an abolition speech, from the notorious Jno. P. Hale. The debate will then proceed, & I look for a good deal of excitement. I intend to speak, but not for several days, or perhaps weeks. I am, as you know always very cool, and so I intend to be on this occasion. The Ultras of the south, will endeavour to make mischief, as they have lost their head, and as yet, no one can tell, on whom the mantle is to fall. I think the Bill will pass, and all excitement be allayed. This will frustrate the advocates, of a Southern Convention, and <u>Disunion</u>. Some have been for a Convention, who were not for Disunion, but all who were for Disunion, were in favor of the Convention as preparatory to Disunion. The Union will be preserved, and its friends sustained. Some modifications will be made in the Bill, and so ought to be. You need not fear my Love, that I will not do all in my power, to have the matter settled. My Love, the wish to be with you, and to be with you, under the Stars & Stripes, of the underline double union, will cause me to exert all my energies, in the settlement of all discord, that I may retire, and be at rest if a kind Providence should spare me, longer days. Surely a wise man should not desire to waste all his days, in turmoil and anxiety. For my own part, I am meany [sic], but it always is well doing!

I did not write to you yesterday, tho' it was sunday. I was as usual at church, and heard a good sermon. I also witnessed a Baptizing. It was a young man of college, recently converted. The text was Titus 2nd C. & 14 v. They have an organ, & I told brother Anderson, one of the pillars of the church, that <u>whenever it struck up</u>, <u>I involuntarily looked out for the monkeys</u>. If you were ever at a menagerie, you can guess the bit. It is a small organ, and but little solemnity in the sound of it. My love to all.

Thy ever devoted
Houston

[1]For information about Clay's speech see Remini, 747–49.

Washington
15th May 1850

Dearest,

As I have a moment to write, I do so, mainly to let you know that if I cant write a long letter, I will send a short one by way of apology.

As you do not, my Love, care about Politics, I will not write about them, and only turn my attention to home matters. I have not advised about our Pigs as yet. Let Mr Johnson sell all the white sows, but one pair at $10 each Pig. Col Long was to have a pair as a present. I want a pair of the McGoffin sows kept, and if they can be kept in a pen, a part from each other, also a pair of the white sows—the males to be kept in one pen, and the sows in another, if the corn will hold out, I will be gratified. But of all these matters after you have suggested them Mr Johnson will be the best judge. I want my colt well <u>regarded</u>, and taken care of. I <u>don't</u> <u>mean</u> to keep it up, & feed it, but to have it and all the stock salted. If you want any stores, send to Rice & Nichols for them, and don't buy by mail. Let Mr Johnson request Mr. Gibbs to have all things hauled for you, that may go to Houston.

Now these are the matters that I recollect in the way of business.

I told you my Love, that I would render a reason for "apparent extravagance." Since I left home I collected a fee of $500, so that I have not drawn upon our estate. My intention is, if I live, I intend to get you some handsome plates, or spoons at all events.

Now my Love, you will see that as this is a business letter, you would not wish me to dress it off, with the character of a love letter. I could assure you, that I only love your dear self, more & more and that I prefer home to all the fooleries, fancies, and vices, of this great metropolis. I yet have hope of a compromise, on that before long.

<u>On dits</u> [sic]. Joe Eldridge is here—all well at home—a son[1]— Dangerfield, a daughter not larger than a <u>kitten</u>, so he says, badly disappointed in size, and sex! Don't say that I am in part like him— I am <u>used to it</u> my dear, but I really would like to know, how you are pleased. Talk much to Sam, for me and tell Nannie, of the little birds.

Give my affection to mother, & the children.

Thy devoted,
Houston

[1]For a biography of Joseph P. Eldridge see *New Handbook of Texas,* vol. 2, 813.

Washington
20th May 1850

My Dear,

For two weeks, I have not heard from you, or rather Sisters letter dated on the 17th of last month. I know you will do me the justice to believe me very unhappy, in not hearing from you, and our dear little flock. So confident was I, that I would hear from, or of you, that for some days past, I have not written to you, in hopes that I might say that a letter had reached me, from home. I account in this way for one not coming. I see that a Boat has been up the Trinity, and I suppose that Sister went off on Board, so that you were left without an amanuensis, and that you have taken my advice, and have not exposed yourself, as Sister was fearful you would! In this way, I divine solace, and for the present, I am reconciled.

You have but little idea of my varied feelings since I left you my Love, and at this very moment, I feel, not only all the affection, that is possible, for you, and our dear little ones, but I feel for my country, a painful interest. It does seem to me since the compromise has been reported, that some men are either mad, or that they are false to the true interests of the country. I mean those who are opposed, to the compromise. My belief is that if they could, they would dissolve the Union tomorrow. This thank Heaven they can't do. The Union is too strong, to be destroyed by Fanatics! Honest men, and good patriots, are misled by them, in many instances, by the specious professions, of designing demagogues, who are a great curse to any people! You know my Dear, that I am so much pleased, with our union, that I abhor disunion. I mean my Love our matrimonial union. I do not love the union only, but I love the dear fruits of it.

I am very anxious to hear more about our new comer, and to know whether her head is black, or red?[1] The lock of hair sent to me, was red, or auburn, when it came to me. I have not heard from the cane brake since I sent it there. I look for a letter soon! To day I sent many old Valentines to Sam, and there were so many, that I intended he might be literal [sic] with his sisters, his playmates, and little servants in making presents.

Present my love to mother, and the children, to our dear friends. Howda to Kitty, and to Mr Johnson!

Thy affectionate
Houston

[1]For a first hand account of Houston's fascination with red hair see "Old Timers Recall Sam Houston as Admirer of Red Hair—Whittler—Grand Speaker," *Houston Press*, April 21, 1936.

The following letter from Houston to Margaret is missing the first four pages. It is placed here because it was written some time in the spring of 1850 before the bust of Houston was completed.[1]

. . . but to let you know, that I think, I love my wife, and children, more than other men. This I infer from the fact, that I am always thinking, or talking about them! They are among the first things when I wake which command my thoughts, and surely, they are the last subjects of my thought when I drop to sleep! I feel that every day, and hour, which I pass from home, is lost to happiness, and contentment. The spring has just opened, and is now about as warm as when I left home! It is not the climate, that I object to, nor the soil, tho. poor, but the society (tho. no doubt, for some, very good,) that I am not pleased with. Here it is, that I feel, that I am a stranger in a strange land, and, feel the want of a heart and speech, responsive to my own! And then, if I see a pretty child, it reminds me of ours, and a hearty lad recalls, our master Sam. As for you, my dear, I do not compare any one to you, so that your image remains upon my heart, and uneffaced, and unrivalled [sic].

Speaking of images, my Dear, I can tell you that an artist, here wishes to take a bust of me, which I have consented, that he shall so. He has commenced the work, and expects to finish it, in a fortnight. It is for himself, and will cost me nothing, tho. I may get a <u>cast</u> of it, when they are produced! I wish my Dear, that you were here, for then, I could have at least, a perfect Deguaretype [sic] likeness of you! I wish you were here for a thousand reasons, and one that you will admit I am sure to be, all prevailing, (i e) I love you, most truly, and devotedly, and another is if you were here, I could see the Babe, about which I feel a restless curiosity. I will look for a very "long letter" until it arrives.

Present my love to mother & the children.

Thy husband,
Sam Houston

[1]See Houston to Margaret, July 29, 1850.

The following letter is from the collection of Mrs. R. E. McDonald, Dallas, Texas.

Huntsville
May 21, 1850

My dear husband,

By last Friday's mail I rec'd yours of the 25th[1] and 30th of April. They gave me a great pleasure, I assure you, and I will now acknowledge that I was not without anxiety until I received your assurance, that you were gratified by the birth of a daughter. A lovely creature is our little Mary, more lovely than I can describe to you. My health has been so feeble, that I afford little nourishment to her and we are compelled to feed her on milk (the sugar teat I have discarded) and yet she grows more rapidly than any infant I have ever seen. Sam has not complained to me yet, but said to Kitty a few days ago, that "he believed he was never to have a little brother." But he is so charmed with her, that I think he has forgotten his disappointment and Nannie and Maggie are perfectly eloquent over her. Mag seems to be particularly pleased with her little ears and goes into rapture at the sight of them.

Kitty was delighted to hear from her father. She seems to improve in every respect, as she grows older. I am sending her to school to Mr Edwards[2] who is an excellent teacher, and she seems much interested in her studies.

Mr Johnson says I must tell you that the corn is improving a little, but I do not think he knows much about it, as he does not seem to take any control of the servants and I can see myself that they are doing little work. But enough of this. I will console myself with the hope, that after this year, I shall be done with these annoyances.

I did not receive the letter from Nashville, to which you allude in yours from Sparta. I regret that it has not come to hand, for in that, I suppose you said something about bro. William and his family, and I was very anxious to hear from them. When you write again tell me something about them. Some strange things have happened since you left home. One of them is that [Benjamin] Wilson has taken up the cause of Gott and Virginia. She is boarding at his house and going to school, and seems quite a fit in the family. I begin to suspect that he is the grand instigator of the whole plot,[3] but God forbid that I should judge too harshly. The World is busy with the affair, but from my quiet home, I try to look calmly on the storm as it passes by, and await with humility whatever my Heavenly Father designs for me. Of one thing I am certain, it could not have happened without his permission, and if I can only be resigned to his blessed will, it will all be for my good. Mrs Birdwell seems more devoted to me than ever but I can see that she is in trouble.[4]

Huntsville has lately been visited by another hurricane. I have not heard of any houses being blown down, except two of Capt. [T. S.] Simm's negro cabins, but the crops were much injured by trees and fences being blown down. The wind was very severe with us, and I had serious apprehensions of the house going over. The storm passed through bro. Vernal's neighborhood,[5] and I'm told his crop is almost ruined.

I have been giving Nannie a kind of vermifuge for worms, and her cough is much better, but if it should return, I will try your remedy. Mother is well and always wishes to be remembered to you. I believe that I have not yet told you that Dr. Ransom[6] has a fine son,[7] born a few days ago after our girl. I enclose a letter to Kitty's father, thinking that you can send it more directly than I can from this place. Of course you will read it.

Thy affectionate wife

M. L. Houston

P.S. Sister Katherine, it was expected, could be baptized last week.

[1] No letter from Houston dated April 25, 1850 has been located.
[2] Thomas G. Edwards, a teacher residing with Benjamin and Jane Wilson. Carpenter, 2011.
[3] Thomas Gott had accused Margaret of abusing Virginia.
[4] Margaret is referring to the fact that Tirzia Birdwell and Jane Wilson were sisters.
[5] Vernal Lea now resided near Cold Spring in neighboring Polk County.
[6] Dr. Devereau. J. Ransom. Identified in Carpenter, 2011.
[7] John Ransom, Ibid.

Washington
26th May 1850

My Dear Love,

Your sweet little letter has just reached me of the 8th Inst. I have not heard from you since the 17th of April, and of course was very unhappy, but by my last letter, you will see how I accounted for your apparent silence. It was your weak state of health, and the absence of our dear Sister.

Happy as I am to hear from you, I am not without pain, that you should be in any way perplexed, in my absence by any of my affairs. I realise all that you say about Mr Johnson, but if he is kind and attentive my Dear, it is all that I care for. I mean careful, of the animals, as well as the family. I wish you to say my Dear, to the servants, that a <u>friend</u> has written to me, that they do not stay at home, and go without leave of Mr Johnson, and assure them that in case they, or any of them goes off the place again without his leave, or yours, that I will punish them. They will get into scrapes, and I will not be there to protect them! Have they no pride, or shame? I am kind to them, & why do they not try to obey me, & make me happy? Read this to them my Dear!

Do not my Love have any concern about the Farm, if it does produce nothing, I have made up my mind not to fret, or to be disappointed, should I live again to reach home, and find you all in health, & happy. You may rely upon it my Love, that should I ever leave you again of which I have no intention, you shall not be left with any cares of business I assure you of this my Love, so now you must bear up until I return. Your letter bears too many evidences of your feebleness not to make me unhappy. You forgot to sign your name, and you say nothing about Mother, or the children, except the Babe, & that they talk of me, and try to be good, that they may please me. These facts are evidence to me that you are depressed, and low-spirited. So sensitive of this am I that my heart is sad, & sorrowful. My Love, do try and be cheerful. You say all are well, but Nannie. Bless her little heart, do try the cold bath, & every wet, or damp day, let there be some fire in the room.

To day as usual on the sabbath, I was at church, and heard a fine sermon. I attended more to it, I believe, than I ever did to one before! It was the scene of Nicodemus, & the Savior. The views taken were somewhat new to me, & quite proper. If I could be at home my Love, and attend church with you, I would be happy, indeed—Until then I never can be!

You may say to Sam, and Nannie that there are two little young canaries due. I call for each of them, (of the two old ones) The young ones are now nearly fledged. You would be amused to witness their domestic economy. So soon as the mother ceased to sit on them, to keep them warm, Sam took charge of them, and fed them altogether. Moreover, while Nannie was hatching, Sam would select the most delicate morsels of food, and give them to her, while on the nest. Was not this connubial tenderness, my Love. They afford me some pleasure, but it is small, and soon my thoughts recur to home, where my whole heart is. I have nothing else to feel tenderness for, in this waste of feeling, but the poor Birds. I do my Love intend, if I live, soon to get a Newfoundland dog, and take him home, to guard our little ones.

About the name of our Babe, you wish me to say something! Well, my Dearest, I thought you had settled that, and it was to be Mary. If any thing else, let it be Paxton, but Mary will do yet! Is it really black <u>eyed</u> & black haired, or not? I doubt from the little lock, which Sister sent me. Bless the little one. I am sure, I will love it, be its hair Black, or Red, or <u>white</u>, as I presume it will be if it lives, ire it is as old as little Mag. In writing about them my own one, I feel, or almost fancy, that I am with you, and the little flock!

195 : MARCH 18, 1850–OCTOBER 1, 1850

Instead my Dear, of my visit home injuring me, I learn that it has raised me much, in the estimation [of] all persons of correct feelings. It added to my own happiness, and I trust, to yours, and this is all the requital that I desire, or care for! I will tell you of an incident which has taken place. You are understood to be a tall lady. Many Texians have been here this winter & spring, and they wish me to go to the reception evenings to introduce them to the President. About two weeks since, I went there, and a member of Congress, from a frontier state had his Lady there—he introduced me to her, and I asked her to take my arm. She did so, and we walked round the East room among the crowd, and some of the letter writers supposing, that you had accompanied me to the city, wrote to the "Herald" that "Genl Houston and his Lady, were at the reception." The Lady was very tall, and as <u>plain</u> a looking lady as was in the room. She, I suppose was, or is, about <u>forty</u>. Her husband is one of the best Houston men in his state.

Now my Love, do not think that I was trying to palm her off for you. I am satisfied with you, and would not* exchange you for all the <u>fair</u> daughters of Grand ma Eve! *[In this sentence Houston had originally omitted the word "not." He later inserted it and wrote in the margin:* * what a mistake this would have been had I omited [sic] "not," would it <u>not</u>?]

You will wish to hear something of the Compromise. Well, I hope it will be passed, and matters put to rest forever. In a few days, I intend to speak on the subject. It may be two weeks yet ire I speak.

Will you please to tell me your <u>number</u> for shoes. I intend to send you Marys <u>palate</u>, [sic] so soon as I can. Present affection to all, and say to the children, that I am happy to hear of their goodness.

Thine Ever
Houston

The following letter was written to Houston from his cousin Narcissa B. Hamilton. The original is in the Franklin Weston Williams Collection of family letters at the Woodson Research Center, Rice University, Houston, Texas. Several words are missing due to a hole torn out of the side of the letter.

F. C. Institute
May 27 [18]50

My Dear Cousin,

Your visit to Texas deprived me of the pleasure of see you; had you remained I should certainly have paid you a flying visit. But this is not the object of my present writing. I wish to invite you to our commencement, which will come off on the 10th of July. It would cause you an absence of work from the city. You could leave Washington on Saturday morning reaching Richmond that evening; Monday morning take the Lynchburg and reach New Canton that night. Our carriage would be there, and bring you to the Institute, Tuesday evening. [Torn] is our commencement day, we will have four graduates [torn] will be Mistress of English literature, and [blurred] We will have a discussion from the most eloquent young men in Va. But [torn] I wish you to be here. I want you to be present when the first female collegiate alumni in Va. presents it. Your presence would stamp it with a golden [blurred] that would give it attention throughout all coming time. [blurred] your coming refreshed me like a breeze in fragrance [blurred] would not ask you to make a speech. I only wish to see you once more [blurred] of the grave, which may not be long, for I am threatened with congestion of the brain, at least, I think so. I have so little physical strength and that was surely taxed during my stay in Richmond, five weeks farther attendance upon the Legislature. I had quite a time with in the lower house only 29 votes against me, but I had a hard battle to fight to first obtain the voting. Circumstances prevented me from remaining longer, and during my absence, the ungenerous [blurred] on the senate defeated all.

Cousin, I presume Mr Jones of Richmond has made your acquaintance (he was my guardian during part of my stay in that place), if so I hope you will, for my sake, render him all the assistance you can (without prejudicing yourself) in the production of his business, and by so doing you will transfer the obligations I am under from him, to yourself, which will be quite a relief.

Cousin I have still a higher object than a purely selfish one, in pressing you to come to Va. You are more misunderstood here than in any [other] state in the union, and the principle reason is, that you are less [torn] people here than in any other state. A visit to us at that [torn] the year would not render you obnoxious to the charge of elec[tioneering] [torn] and the great crown you would encounter here, might be of [torn] to you in the future.

Tell me how your dear wife and children are. My most affectionate regards to them. Cousin John and Mary Blackwell[3] unite with me in most earnestly requesting you to honor us with your presence, and also send their [blurred] regards to you. Many thanks for your beautiful speech. It is indelibly stamped with the character of your alumni. [blurred]

I must finally command you by saying come to us and cheer us with your presence. You will have plenty of friends when I am gone, but none who will esteem you, in the value that I do. I shall await you [blurred] with the utmost impatience and anxiety.

Your affectionate Coz
N. B. Hamilton

---

[1]An unidentified member of the Virginia Legislature from Rockbridge County described Hamilton: "She is to a great degree a self-made woman, having a strong mind, firm in her purposes, ardent in her attachment to her friends; and for a lady, quite well versed in politics, having embraced, early the Jeffersonian system of government. With her limited educational advantages, it is remarkable with what freedom and ease she is able to converse." Samuel Rutherford Houston, 52.

[2]This may refer to her successful efforts to secure "chemical and philosophical apparatus, telescope, and library" for the school. Ibid., 51.

[3]Mary Letcher Blackwell was the sister of John Letcher. Rev. John Blackwell was the principal of the Buckingham Female Seminary. Madge W. Hearne family papers.

Huntsville
May 28th, 1850

My Love,

By last mail, I recd your dates of the 6th[1] and 8th of May. I was truly gratified to find that you were well and that you still remembered me with affection, but I have not been happy since I read those letters, and I will here give you the reasons. I discover from their tenor that you have taken it for granted, I would put on mourning for your departed sister. I have not done so my love, and I fear you will be hurt with me, but hear my reasons before you blame me too severely. My Father was opposed to the custom, and in consequence I have had scruples about it myself, and for that reason I did not wear mourning for brother Martin who was as dear to me, as a father. When bro. V. and sister A. lost their companions,[2] out of respect to the living, I would have worn black, if I could have reasoned myself into the belief that is was right. We had a conversation about that time, in which I expressed my opinions on the subject, but I suppose it has escaped your memory. And now dearest, let me assure you, if I had supposed that you would have expected me to wear mourning, my scruples would have been a ready sacrifice to the desire of pleasing you, for I consider that paramount to every duty, except the desire to please my Heavenly Father.

We are all enjoying good health, and the children grow finely. Sam improves in reading and writing, perceptibly, but slowly from the fact that he is not confined very closely to them. I perceive my love, from the purchase of the sword, that your inclination prompts you to foster a military spirit in our boy. Well I will not censure you for it, and yet I wish we felt alike on that subject. I gave him your message about the sword and it elicited more pleasure, than I liked to see.

I can not account for the fit of extravagance which has come upon you, but trust it has passed off before this. I will not quarrel with my dear husband, but just think of four costly dresses for the mother of three daughters, and those daughters yet to be reared, fed, clothed and educated. Do not think me harsh dearest, but remember we live in a <u>harsh world</u>, and if we do not take care of our little ones, who will do it for us!

The hams which you sent me have not been received yet, but I hope we will get them soon. However we have not suffered for them, or any thing else. Bro. V. paid me 30 dollars last month, which was the interest on the money in his hands. That would have been more than I needed, but for the expense of finishing our house. I paid Mr Thornton[3] 40 dollars for completing the shed, and Mr Smith[4] about 28 dollars for lumber. Mr Thornton offered me a dollar and a quarter per day for Albert, but they would have him in the farm until lately, and now we can only get 20 dollars per month for him. If our affairs are managed so that you will be pleased, I shall be happy indeed.

I am sorry that I wrote to you about Wilson taking Virginia to board with them. Mrs Wilson seems so distrest lest I should be hurt with them, that I now wish I had not told you about it.

Kitty learns well at school. Her greatest fault is to tell things which are not true, and she does it without any malicious motive whatever and in such a harmless way, that all my arguments fail to convince her that it is sinful and that she will thereby lose the confidence of her friends. How shall I correct this unfortunate habit?

Sister A. and Mr Power are still at Bro. V.'s awaiting the boat. The Baptists have had a great meeting in that neighborhood. Many have professed conversion and several have been baptized. Among the latter your old acquaintance Grubbs,[5] Did you not rejoice to hear of a desolate wanderer being brought into the fold? Oh what a sweet thought that the Lord Jesus will love and cherish a soul uncared for and unnoticed by the world! When you write tell me how you feel about these things. Send my love to my Baptist brothers and sisters and tell them I hope they will love you and pray for you.

Thine ever,
M. L. Houston

[1]No letter of May 6, 1850 has been located. It is possible Margaret is referring to Houston's letter of May 5, 1850.
[2]Mary Lea and William Bledsoe, who both died in 1845.
[3]F. G. Thornton, a Huntsville carpenter, identified in Carpenter, 2022.

[4]E. G. Smith. Identified in Carpenter, 2022.
[5]Thomas Grubbs, Polk County neighbor of Vernal Lea. Ibid., 1543.

Washington
29th May 1850

Dearest,

I wrote to you two days since, expressive of my anxiety, on account of your health. I hope, before this time, that you have found your health, as well as your spirits are much improved. I feel constant, and deep solicitude about your situation, and little Nannie's. I hope you will try the bath, for her as I have suggested, in my former letters. I know my dear, that my letters are far from being interesting, but I know, that you will suppose it reasonable that I should write about such things, as I think, and feel. I do not forget Sam, and Maggy, nor the Babe, but really, I do not feel about them, as I do about you, and Nannie. The Babe is a stranger, and curious as I may be, to see the dear little thing, I am left to hope that she is doing well! and is as beautiful as Sister said she was. It is not reasonable, that she should be more beautiful, than our daughters. As for Sam, I am like you. I am satisfied with his appearance! And I am well satisfied with his intellect, and I hope, his moral qualities will surpass both!

I have sent two scales, of Virus, or vaccine matter to Huntsville. One to Col Yoakum and one to Dr Ransom, I think, or to Dr Keenan. I hope they will prove good, and I requested to have our family vaccinated.

Your friends here are much concerned about your health. You have many friends tho' you are only known to them by the hearing of the ear.

I suppose that my fine conduct renders, them quite as curious to see you, as every person in America. From the carefully exaggerated slanders, against me formerly, persons were prepared to see me any thing but, a decent man. Since I am a genteel, and well behaved man, the minds of the inquisitive must account for it, upon some principle, and the most plausible is, that "my wife has reformed me." Since I am the beneficiary my Dear, I am perfectly willing, that <u>you</u> should have the credit, of my management. Dont you think that I may afford to "<u>be generous, when it costs me nothing</u>."

My Dear, I have been invited to Boston, to unite in a Temperance celebration, on the 11th of June. If at that time, the Senate should adjourn to have the carpets taken up, as is usual, I intend to join in the Celebration, for I know it will <u>gratify you</u> that I should do so. If I unite with the brethren, I will have to speak. It is supposed that there will be present at least <u>thirty</u> thousand strangers, & sons. It is to be an <u>anniversary celebration</u>!

My love to Mother, and the dear children! Salute all our friends. Tel Mr Johnson & Kitty Howda!

Thy devoted Husband
Houston

Tell Eliza that I will bring a present for <u>you</u>, to give her for her good conduct. I am glad to hear of it!

The following letter is from the Franklin Weston Williams Collection at the Woodson Research Center, Rice University, Houston, Texas. It was sent along with the one written by Narcissa B. Hamilton on May 27, 1850.

30th May 1850

My Love,

I wrote you a letter yesterday and send you this to dày, from my cousin. I cant visit them, and I regret the fact. I have not seen her for sixteen years. She must now be some thirty one years old!

Last night Mr Ellmore[1]—the successor of Mr Calhoun in the Senate deceased of pnumia [sic]. He was an amible [sic], & worthy Gentleman. The Sen. will have to adjourn for two days.

Thy devoted
Houston

[1]Franklin H. Elmore died May 29, 1850, after serving only 23 days. *Biographical Directory of the U. S. Congress*, 149

The following letter from Henderson Yoakum is from the Madge W. Hearne Collection in the Barker History Center, Austin, Texas.

Huntsville
May 31/1850

Dear Gen

Yours of the 14 inst recd.[1] Thank you kindly & I the more value it, because of the inconveniences under which you write.

We are perfectly quiet here. Public opinion is getting right here. Nobody voted for the Convention!

We are murdered here in cold blood—Pray look into the mail contracts for this state. How long—oh how long are we to be killed with mail contractors! If they will take the contractor off of the Houston Line we will take it in charge ourselves!!! I receive no papers—but one from you in three or four months, but two Galveston papers since Christmas. We know you are doing for the best, but we never learn what it is.

Your family is well. Your corn looks well. The town is growing, so is the penitentiary. There are ten convicts already.[2]

I hope you will not forget to write a short line of clever words to your friend Col O. Evans[3] of San Antonio. You know him. He is brother of Lemuel Evans the judge.[4]

Sincerely yours
H. Yoakum

[1]See Houston to Yoakum, *Writings,* vol. 5, 153–54.
[2]The *1850 Census* lists 11 convicts. Carpenter, 2022–23.

[3]Oresumus Evans was a San Antonio dry goods merchant. Ibid, 122.
[4]A district judge in Harrison County. *New Handbook of Texas,* vol. 2, 906.

Washington

2nd June 1850

My Dear,

This evening I hope to receive from you a long letter, but I will write now, and if I get one, I can write again without taxing myself greatly.

This morning I went to church as usual, and heard a sermon, from a very aged Divine, the Father of Mr Samson. The old gentleman was blind, & all his earthly feelings afforded him [blurred] while his mind was clear, and unclouded. I heard him with much pleasure, and I hope not altogether without edification. This evening at four oclock, I attended the administration of the sacrament of the Lords Supper, by Mr Cushman in the temporary absence of Mr Samson, the Pastor. I did not know, that the custom here was for only members of the church to attend the ordinance, but I found that they almost exclusively, were there. It appeared strange to me, and I once remarked to you, that <u>leavened bread </u>should be used, on the occasion like this, as though, it was but an ordinary meal, & had no other association, than that which arises from the every day business of life, and the vanishment of our natural, and perishable bodies. Do not misunderstand me, my Dear, on casting any reflection, or censure, upon any one, & above all, the most solemn, of mans associations, with the memory of a Saviour!

My Dear, on my way home from church, I found a Temperance Lecturer [torn] who was holding forth, in loud, and impressive strains, against the vice of Drunkenness! For a while, I listened to him, but thought you would prefer that I should write you a pretty long epistle! You will suppose my Dear, (I am fearful,) as singular, if I am sane, when I tell you, that I, as usual, steped [sic] in with my friend, Mr. Lewis, whose cousin, or sister, sent you the "Bible mark," to see my little Birds! Really, they seem to me, to associate my feelings with home, and family. The young ones are now flying about, in the cage, and are very pretty. I have not brought them home, since my return, but intend to do so soon. I know you [torn] and that I must have something, which I love, that is present. Now my Dear, I am sure you would rather that I would love twenty Birds, or dogs, than one person, for you know my Dear, that you were a little mad at me, or were fearful that I would love Sam, when a babe, more than I would you. It is not this so my dear? If you chuse to deny it, I will not insist upon its correctness. If it was so, I am sure that you have now gotten over it, for we have now a goodly number to divide our affection with, or to bestow them upon. It is strange, how we can love so many objects, and yet, not abate our affection for the first. Love must be indivisible, or derivative. That I love you as much, or twenty times more than I ever did, (as it seems to me, if I were to measure it, by my desire to see you) I feel quite assured you will not distrust me. Notwithstanding this my Dear, I do really love our dear children a great deal, as Sam would say. In my anxiety to see them, I am unable to determine, which I am most desirous to see. The young one, or the Babe, I am as you wou'd have me to be, very curious to see her. It may be my Dear, that you are desirous to call her for Sister Antoinette. Now if this is the case my Dearest, do it. I know how dearly you love her, and if you will be more happy, do so! You will have my free consent. It may be my Love, that you have an understanding with Sister, if you [blurred]. This may be the case, and if so I cant advise. Consult Sam (if you have any further calculations) on this subject? I hope my Love you will be able to make out my meaning, and that you will excuse me, if you are disposed, to take umbrage, at trifles. This may not be well expressed, for you may not be disposed to regard such things, as trifles!!

The spring has hardly come yet. On the mountain a days travel, from here, there was frost, on night before last! I would not my Love, exchange our sunny clime, for any, or all that lye [sic] North of us! It may be owing to the association of the South, that I love it so well!

It is now 10 P.M. and the mail of to day has not yet arrived, but I hope it will before I retire!

Mr [Robert D.] Johnson is here from Galveston, and says he will leave in about ten days. I will try, and send some trifles by him, and it may be a "play ball" for our son, as it will cause him to exercise, and amuse him. I have procured some pretty engravings for you, as well as the children. To give you an idea of those sketches for you, I will tell you of one—it is the two Marys at the Sepulcher, of the risen Saviour. Others are equally interesting. The childrens will convey fine moral sentiments.

Give my love to mother, and embrace all the children for me!

Thy faithful Husband
Houston

Washington
3rd June 1850

My dear,

No mail arrived last night, owing to a failure, as I suppose. To day we are again engaged, in the discussion of the Compromise Bill. What is to be its fate, no one can tell. The wise, as well as the <u>unwise</u>, are at fault, as to the result. I yet hope some plan will be adopted, so as put to rest, the present agitations, and give tranquility [sic] to the people at large, who are entitled to peace, & rest from useless troubles. As for those who seek to advance themselves, at the expense of the good order, and good sense, they do not deserve peace, nor could they enjoy it, for they are radically mischievous, and would well fit Milton's description of unenviable characters! I was always right, about the design of the "Southern address." <u>Treason</u> <u>was the object</u> of its originators, and many who were honest, and patriotic, now find themselves committed. They are not willing to retrace their steps, put persist in error.

To the last my Dear, you may rely upon my fidelity to the <u>Union</u>,—always for the <u>federal union</u>, and the <u>union</u> domestic!!!! I hold, that I am much better, by the existence, and maintenance of both. From union the country,—the people, have every thing to realise, and hope, and from disunion, nothing but anarchy to expect. I feel that an over ruling Providence will in his wise design, will preserve us, as a people, who have yet a great mission to accomplish—connected with the civil, political, & religious reformation of the world, and I think that it already has its commencement. This is the first political letter that I have written to you, or any one this session. My love to all.

Thy devoted,
Houston

Huntsville
June 4th 1850

My dear Love,

It is my letter day, but so late in the evening, that I can only write you a few lines. I intended to have written you a long letter today, but have had company sincerely this morning. Gen'l Hatch.[1] They came recently, and Mrs Hatch[2] spent the day with us. They have recently lost their little girl,[3] and of course I endeavoured to make the day as cheerful to them as possible. He is much enlivened on the subject of religion, and I rejoice to see it, for he can be an ornament to our church.

We are all enjoying our usual health. You have not yet told me our little Mary's double name, or if she is to have one. If you would like to call her Mary William I should have no objection, for our bro. Will you know is a dear brother to me. As to what you say about naming the baby for sister A., I would have rejoiced to do so under different circumstances, and it would have gratified her, but she thought with myself, that it was our duty to call her Mary. My dear kind sis seemed perfectly willing to await her turn, and I really believe she looks upon it as a mere postponement of courtesy.

Kitty [Hoffman] is doing well. As to the ring, she says I must tell you please to get her a pair of plain gold ear-rings instead of it.

Not my fancy you know. I humbly trust she will yet turn out well.

I hope my dear husband will excuse this little scrawl. Next week, I think I will begin my letter on Monday, lest I should be again interrupted.

Thine ever.
M. L. Houston

[1]Frank L. Hatch. Carpenter, 2012.
[2]Eliza Hatch. Ibid.
[3]Blanche Hatch died of dysentery in February. Jackson, *Mortality Schedule, Texas 1850,* 11.

Senate Chamber
6th June 1850

Dearest,

When I can snatch a moment, I take the greatest pleasure in writing to you. Business matters, of the Senate, are much as they have been. On yesterday some votes were taken, on amendments to the Compromise Bill. There are hopes, that the Bill, with some amendments I think will pass. If it should be defeated, it will be by the ultras of the north & south who are the extremes, and on this matter act <u>with</u> each other. Their object manifestly is, to defeat all measures, that propose to restore harmony to the community. They can only maintain their standing by keeping up agitation, so as to create a morbid feeling against the Union. You will learn that I have not yet spoken, as I expected. I do not now propose to speak until, all the amendments to the Bill have been proposed. I assure you my Love, that I hear so much nonsense, that I fear to speak, lest I speak, as others do, and charm my friends. I feel ten times the hesitancy, in speaking, that I did when I first came to the Senate! This tho' is not so interesting to you, that I will prose about it. I know you care more about the Union, (I mean the <u>Federal Union</u>,) than any minor matter. I will therefore tell you that it can not be destroyed, by all the machinations of of [sic] those, who have all to gain, and nothing to loose!!! Such men, as the "Wiglacts," the Hendersons, etc., etc.[1]

Now my Dear, do not, because, I write somewhat on politics to you, think that I am more in love with them, than I have heretofore been. No, the contrary is the fact, My love of home increases, and in the same ratio of that increase, does my fondness, for public life decrease. Should we live to meet, I assure you that you will find me, the most kind, constant, and affectionate husband, & tender Parent in Texas. This is not to disparage other husbands, I have but little doubt.

I do not care much about Sams learning very fast and my Love, if I were to advise, I would say never whip him. It will do him no good. I do not enjoin this, and He does not know my opinion on this subject. His sense, and feelings will be the best medium of correction.

My Dear, you say we have three daughters to rear, clothe, and educate.[2] This I have felt my Dear, and I have felt it in all its force. I have denied myself many things, which I would not have done, but for you, and the children. You, and them, are objects of my constant care, and unslumbering solicitude. I have not talked to you about money matters, so much as I would have done, had it not been, that I do not recollect that I ever alluded to any expense, but what I thought you became some what excited, and at last, I resolved never to name it again. I determined to make all that I could fairly, and honorably, and thus discharge my duty to you, and the children! I hope my Love, you will not think that I intend any charge, or complaint against you. No, indeed my Love, I have much to reproach myself with, but nothing against you. When I look back on the days, which I have spent in vain, and viciously, I can condemn myself, more than the world is disposed to condemn me! When you wrote to me, your mind was not even, but excited, from some cause, was it not? The only effect, which the notice of Wilsons conduct had upon me, was to send him more papers than before. I have not written to Mrs Birdwell yet, but will soon! I never intend to know any thing about what Wilson has done, until he tells me himself, and then not notice it! I do not know what to say about Kitty. You can tell her, that I hope she will be a good girl, and do nothing, that would mortify me, or distress her poor old Father, and if she is clever, and should marry to please me, she shall have a fine start to begin the world with!

My Dear I read a part of your letter to a Baptist Brother, & he was much gratified with it. You wish my Dearest, to know how my feelings are on the subject of Religion. I can only say, that I know, I am a sinner, but fear, that I do not feel the need of a Saviour, to the extent which I ought to do. I use the means of Grace, but I feel that the Grace of God is necessary to render the means, efficacious. Not one night passes over my head, that I do not read, and invoke the blessing of our Heavenly Father upon us, and ours!

My love to mother, and kisses to all.

Thy Devoted,
Houston

P. S. My Dear, have you ever noticed particularly the VI chap. and 4th verse of Paul to the Romans? What a beautiful allusion it is to Baptism!!!

[1]Houston is referring to Louis T. Wigfall and James P. Henderson.
[2]See Margaret to Houston, May 28, 1850.

W. City
9th June 1850

Dearest,

After dinner to day, I lay down to sleep, or to take a nap, and when I woke up, I found my mail on my table, and to my great delight a letter from you. I assure you it made me very happy as, Sam wou'd say. To learn that your health was good, or improving, & little Nannie was better, imparted joy to my heart. I feel for you, my Love, since Miss Thorn has come to your village to reside, and with our friend Mr Wilson. My Dear just act as tho' you did not know the fact. That matter will cure itself in time. Patience will work wonders! In a few days I will write to Mrs Birdwell a letter of kindness, and thanks for her affections to you, but not allude to any thing of which you have written. Treat her as a sister always. This other matter with Gott, & Wilson will blow up. Gott has neither influences, nor money enough to satisfy Wilsons avarice, and you will recollect, what the Phrenologist said of him! Be calm, and trust in God. He is wise and all goodness, & mercy!

Ere this you will have received my advice to the negroes, and I hope told them what I expect of them! I will send your letter to Mr Hoffman, & I am happy to hear, that Kitty [Hoffman] is a good girl. I will be happy to take you some present for her. I would advise you, if you can, to keep her from Virginia [Thorn], or you may find another Thorn "in your side." I hope my Love, you will be able to sustain yourself, until by the care of Heaven we meet again. I was not myself when I was last at home! The impression was so constantly on my mind that I had so soon to leave, that I could not feel cheerful, and only partially happy! I was all the time constrained by my feelings. Should we ever meet again, I hope it will be different.

So far my as affection, will delight you my Love, you ought to be happy, for I am sure, no one was ever so much delighted, with, or devoted to a wife, as I am to you. I grant you, that it is not the fashion altogether, but I am willing to have it thought that I am peculiar, or excentric [sic] in this. You will excuse me, I am sure for there is nothing my Dear, that I can write of further interest to you, that occurs to me, at this time, only that Bro Samson announced from the Pulpit to day, that revivals are progressing every where.

He has just returned from Charleston, where I am informed he was on last sabbath, and told me to day he had been much pleased with the trip. I did not ask him where the Convention wou'd next meet. I hope we will live to see the day when it will meet in Texas.

To day has been cool, and cloudy, and I am apprehensive, if spared, that about the time I start home, the weather will be quite warm!

My friend Mr. Williams, and I expect to be busy until the time comes for me to leave.

To night several Galvestonians have been to see me. For instance, Col Louis Cleveland, and Thom. League.[1]

My love to all
Thy Devoted Houston

[1]Thomas League had served as a municipal judge in Harrisburg. *Writings,* vol. 1, 464n.

Washington
12th June 1850

My Dear,

It is so uncertain for me, to command time to write to you, that I am obliged, to write at intervals. Sunday is a day that I will not attend to business matters, and as I hold, that it is a religious duty, for a man to attend to family, I feel that I am not neglecting entirely, my Sabbath duties in writing to you, on that day. I always fear or am fearful, that I can not interest you by writing farther, than merely letting you know, that you are an object of great interest to me, and that our little fellows are dear creatures, and that you, and them constitute my whole capital of earthly happiness. It is the only capital, which pays <u>interest</u>! I mean that it is every day prised [sic] more, and more, highly by me.

You can say to our son, that I have more pictures for him. They were presented to him by my friend Mr Jo[seph] Lewis. They are pretty, but I cant send them by mail. I will have to take them with me, if I live to reach home. The pretty engraving, & paintings, which I wrote to you about are, by this time I supposed [blurred]. They will delight you I am sure. There is a speech making by Dayton[1] of New Jersey, against the title of Texas to Santa Fe. I must close and attend to what he says.

I have no news to write, but would write much more, if I had time. I am as badly tortured, by company at night, I assure you, that I never get to read my chapter (which I do every night before I retire) until midnight. Then I reflect upon home, or business, and never sink to repose until hours have passed. Sometimes I see daylight around my bed before I can sleep. I see, that I have written more, so far as <u>space</u> is concerned, than I anticipated.

You will please to present my respects to all our friends, and tell

Sam, Nannie, & Maggie, always to send me some word, when you write to me. Dont you fail my Dear, to tell me, the colour of the Babes hair & eyes. I suppose, you are right when you say the Babe is beautiful, but I imagine she is not prettier than our other girls. Poor Sam. I suppose, by the aid of his characteristic magnanimity, he will be reconciled, to the advent of his little Sister. You know, he was willing, "to eat bread." I have not been able to procure, the <u>pallet</u> for the babe. I hope to do it soon, and send it home, by the middle of July. If I fail, it will be a disappointment to me! I told you in my letters I think my Dear, to send word, to let Mr Gibbs to have all your hauling done from Houston (Rice & Nichols) to Huntsville. Mr Johnson can say so to Mr Gibbs, and he will attend to it.

Tell the servants my Dear, that I expect them to behave, as I have told them before.

Give my love to mother, & the children.

Thy devoted husband
Sam Houston

[1]William L. Dayton. *Biographical Directory of Congress*, 148.

The following letter was addressed to Dr. Alva Woods. It is from the Woods Collection of the Rhode Island Historical Society.

Washington
June 15, 1850

My Dear Sir,

In a few days, I hope to have time to thank you for your very welcome letter. In the meantime, permit me to convey to Mrs Woods, your self, and family, Mrs Houstons and [my] own very affectionate respects. Since my visit home Mrs H. has presented me with a third daughter. She says by far, the most beautiful of all! How natural? Sam, hopes "yet to see the Doctor, & Mrs Woods." He is clever, and his Dear Ma is trying to train him for the ministry. I, for my own part, pray that he may be worthy, of the station!

Truly thy Friend
Sam Houston

Washington,
15th June, 1850

My Love,

I wrote you a short letter on yesterday,[1] at a time when an important vote was pending, upon striking that part of the Bill out, which relates to Texas. It did not succeed, and I yet have hopes of its passage, and final success. My hope is not sanguine, because we have some men, who would prefer <u>disunion</u>, to their countrys Glory, and the happiness of millions! For some days, we have had much excitement. Mr Clay & Mr Benton were much excited, and used personalities, which sounded very unpleasantly, in the Senate.[2] For my part, I keep very cool, and as yet, I have only spoken, on some minor points. The time has not yet come, when I intend to say what I feel, think, and desire in relation to compromises.

With few modifications, the Bill should pass. Gen Rusk has sustained himself extremely well, and as I have assured you, he is a very able man![3] But you dont care about politics, and I wont trouble you with them, further, but will send mother, the newspapers.

You may say to Sam, & Nannie, that to day I intend to move my Birds home, as they are called Sam & Nannie, but the young ones, I find are both Sams. The little fellows will be company to me. My Newfoundlands, I have not seen, since I sent them out to board! They are of the most faithful, & sagacious strain of dogs, that can be, & are perfect guards to children!

Now I am through with my business part of my letter, and I hope you will not think, that I might have reserved more of it, for the purposes of saying how much I love you! As I intend to write again tomorrow (Sunday,) and wrote on yesterday, I will only say that my devotion to you, & home, increase every hour!

Thy devoted
Houston

[1] No letter has been found for June 14, 1850.
[2] For information about the Clay-Benton feud see Robert V. Remini, 744–45, 748–49.
[3] For Rusk's comments on the subject see Clarke, 176–78.

Washington
16th June 1850

Dearest,

This is sunday night, and [as] I proposed in my letter yesterday, I will write to you. To day as usual I went to church, and heard a missionary, from the Island Madeira, but the precise object of his mission, I did not learn. The usual hour has passed for your letters to come, and none has arrived. I am sad at the failure of the mail, as I hope that is the cause, of my receiving none. While in my room to day my little bird <u>Sam</u>, has warbled sweetly for me, and I was much amused, at the <u>lad</u>, to see how much he was excited, at the song of his father. He can not sing, and was fidgeting, & hopping all the time, the old bird was chanting him smart notes! He reminded me one <u>some one</u>, that I have seen <u>somewhere</u>, that imitated feats, which he cou'd not achieve. You may read this to our dear Boy, & see if he will discover the allusion.

Indeed, they are company to me, and it is an innocent whim, that I am secure you will not censure, if you do not commend! My object in buying them was to have something, of <u>home</u>, with me, and as they were dedicated to our little ones, and intended to be taken to them, I regard them as tho' they had already been there. I fancy how melodious they will be, and how kind, and joyous, a reception awaits them, if I live to take them with me.

I have talked about "love letters," in my former epistles, but I think you will imagine, that I have written a <u>Bird letter</u>, and will hold me responsible for the love letter, still. Indeed my dear, every letter, which I have written, has been a "love letter," because love was the inducement to my writing! However, I will say in conclusion, that I see no one, nor do I hear of any one, that I would go half so far to see, nor with whom I could be one thousandth part so happy with, as my own dear Margaret. One thing I will say, and you must not pout about it, is this. I have no doubt but what you require more <u>petting</u>, than any dear wife in the land, and yet, you dont know, or believe the fact! Well now, do you know that I like this? I assure that I do, and would not wish you to dispense with the quality! So long as, I am the <u>petter</u>, I am willing that you should be the <u>petee</u>! I love to make you happy, because, then I must [blurred] be happy. I think so much about you, that I fear, I am not so smart, as I would be if you were with me! You will say, <u>stay at home then, and you will be smarter</u>!!! This is just what I intend to do my Love! Give my love to mother, and the children.

Thy Faithful
Houston

In the margin: The first part of this letter was written with a steel pen!

Senate Chamber
17th June 1850

My Love,

I am again in my seat, and find the same humdrum routine of business. There is a constant, & endless, discussion on matters, upon which we should vote. I was in hopes that we wou'd be able to vote, upon several amendments, to day. From the manner in which the business, of the day, has begun, I hope for little success, in getting on with the compromise Bill soon. Appearances are not more bright than they have been. Great efforts will be made to defeat any compromise. The abolitionists of the north, and the Disunionists of the south, rely upon <u>agitation</u>, for thier future success, and political thinking. Hence, they will use all their efforts, to defeat all objects of harmony, and peace.

As I have written every day for sometime, I think you will have too many letters, to read and in view of that calamity, I have concluded to write upon note paper.

From the size of this letter, I think Sam, will be for claiming it, as his own!

When the subject of adjourning the present session, is moved, you may rely upon my voting for the earliest day, as I am half crazy to get home. I look to the event, as one of perfect happiness, if I should live to get home, and embrace my family, in health!

Thy devoted
Houston

The following letter is incomplete.

Washington
18th June 1850

My Dearest,

Greatly was I gratified last night to receive your letter of the 28th ult. I was gratified, to learn that all were well, but distressed at your state of feeling. My Love, I never once thought, about a matter which has given you so much infelicity. I had not reflected for a single moment on the subject of mourning, but regarded it without reflection. I now recollect something, of our conversation, in relation to the subject, when br. Martin[1] deceased. It passed from my mind, and when Sister [Eliza Moore] deceased, I supposed, as a matter of course, and without adverting to the fact, that you would wear mourning. It was not intended, my Dearest, as any requirement, upon you, nor do I feel, at all displeased, because you could not, conform ably, to your opinions wear mourning. I know, these are mere matters of form, & are an outward show, often, and have become custom, without any sensible reason. Black does not affect those who wear it, but it has an association for those who look upon the mourn-ers, and causes, with the world, a more reserved demeanor, towards those persons. It may, in some instances, prevent levity, and the use of expressions, which might be ill timed, and unpleasant. If there are any reasons for the custom, these suggestions may embrace some of them.

You have done right in this matter, because, we ought never, to sacrifice a principle, to any power or custom, no matter what it may be, or who its advocates are!

I regret my Love that you think I am anxious to cherish in our boy, a martial spirit. I declare to you, it is not so, and I think by letting him become tired of these things, he will throw them by, or neglect them. If he more desired them, his mind, active as it is, woud never cease to imagine, the happiness that he would have enjoyed, & his mind, thus became more, and more a slave to fancy, & desire. It cost nothing, and I think he will soon fancy, that it is worth but little! You did not my Dear, understand the subject of the dresses, which I sent. I hope they have reached you, with the letter which I wrote, & sent saying, what was to be done, with part of these. Since I left home last fall, I hope I have made $5000 in fees. $500 I have re-ceived, and I hope to get $500 more in next month. The $4000 re-maining, is contingent, and I think I will get that, when certain suits in Texas, are recovered, of which . . .

[1]Martin Lea had been killed in a duel with Napoleon Lockett on March 26, 1843.

Huntsville
June 18th, 1850

My ever dear husband,

There was a failure of the mail last week, so that I did not re-ceive letters until yesterday, but now I am happy in the possession of your dates of the 26th, 29, and 30th of May. The latter it is true was but a little note, but a single sentence from you my love is of more value to me, than I can tell you. Whenever there is a failure of the mail, my spirits sink, but when your letters come, I am comforted again. Indeed since our little Mary's birth, I have been so feeble, that the least excitement overcomes me, and this will account to you my love, for the gloom of my letters. My cough is not worse than usual, but my general health is bad. I often think I shall never survive, but if anything can restore me, it will be your presence. I suffer more from want of appetite and indigestion, than any thing else, and this convinces me that it arises from my continual anxiety of mind. I try to be composed and patient, but I see no possibility of it until you are with me again. I have heretofore been guarded on the subject of your return, lest I might say something that would make you unhappy, but I begin to think that "honesty is the best policy," and I will now tell you, that if you knew how anxious I am to see you, I think you would <u>almost</u> come home right away. Ah no, I can not hope to accomplish that much, but I do really hope, that the remembrance of our present distress will have some bearing on your future course.

While I am writing, our lovely babe is near me on a little pallet. Her bright blue eyes are looking up very meaningly in my face, and she waves her lyly [sic] arms towards me and warbles something very like a message for dear papa far far away. The little angel was nearly gone once, with the bold hives, before I knew her disease, but the Lord in mercy prolonged her life. Mother says you must come home and take care of your red-headed girl. I do not think dearest it will be <u>very red</u>, but it is a <u>little inclined</u> that way. I think our girls will be very beautiful, (I may say this to you,) and they all seem very sensible. Nannie begins to show a great penchant for merriment and fun. I would sometimes be annoyed by her, if I could help being amused. I will give you a specimen. On Sam's birth-day[1] he had two little boys[2] to dine with him, sons of our minister Mr Baines. One of them, a beautiful black-eyed lad very nearly Sam's age was so charmed with Miss Nannie's rosy cheeks, that he crept up slyly and stole a kiss from her. The young lady walked out in silent indignation, in a few minutes returned with a double handful of flour, and very soon Master Baines' pretty black coat presented a perfect spectacle. Maggie's features have not changed since you left us, but she grows very rapidly. Our boy still evinces his great fondness for metaphysics. He would astonish some of your learned ministers in Washington. And yet at times he is way-ward and heedless as other boys. What is to grow out of it all, I know not. May the Lord grant the desires of my heart concerning him!

Kitty is doing pretty well. She does not learn much at school, but I wish her to attend until she acquires some ideas of writing. After that I expect to teach her at home. She is still very wild, but so kind-hearted that I have great hopes of her.

Betty Birdwell was married to Mr. Simons[3] on sabbath afternoon and came home the same evening. Her family seems to be delighted.

Mr [Daniel] Johnson says I must tell you that he is about laying by his crop. Contrary to all expectations, we have now a prospect of a heavy crop of corn. He says the pumpkin vines are very promising, and the peas are doing well, but we did not succeed in getting as many to plant as you wished. Lewis Lance has recently had a letter from Beck, stating that he expected to leave that vicinity immediately, and advising you to send for Powhatan,[4] Mr Johnson thinks he will go for him himself, that he may have the rest of your horses taken care of. He says I must tell you, that he will do his best to please you, and indeed I believe he will. I have not yet told you my opinion of the subject of the letter which was written from this place to Austin.[5] I refer to the one you mentioned to me. I do not think Wiley wrote it my love, but I think the Hon. William D. Leigh (pronounced lie or leff) was the writer.[6]

The children are delighted to hear of the canaries. You would be amused to hear Nannie talking to little Mary about them. "Papa doin to bring it some ittle nary birds when he tom home!" She excels any one at baby talk, that I ever heard. The presents have not come yet. I am growing anxious about them.

Thine with true affection,
M. L. Houston

[1]May 25.

[2]Thomas and William Baines. Identified in Carpenter, 2010.

[3]Paul Simons. Vick-Rainey, 8.

[4]Houston's horse.

[5]The *Texas State Gazette* on March 16, 1850, stated that the people of Texas had the right to know the reason that Houston had left Washington during this time. Friend, 203.

[6]See Houston to Margaret, May 11, 1850.

23rd June 1850

My dear Margaret,

Another sabbath day has passed, and another opportunity has been afforded of Sunday improvements. I heard Mr Samson, preach to day, a sermon from 2nd Peter III chapter and 11th verse. My habitual reading in the New Testament has reached to the XI C. of Pauls epistle to the Romans. Though I had often read this epistle, it never struck me with so much force, and in the same light, which it now does. No one, who will read Pauls writings, can for one moment to my mind, doubt their inspired character, or that he was a "chosen vessel," in the hand of God, to advance his work, on earth!

I always read his writings with pleasure, and much edification of mind, but not with the influence, upon my spirit, which is useful, and desirable to my eternal peace. If spared my Dearest, it is my fixed purpose to retire from the scenes of public life, and return to the bosom of my family. For if meditation, and religion, can not be found, and enjoyed, in the domestic circle, I know not where to hope for them. I know the Power of God is not limited, as many power is [sic], to place, or to circumstances, but that it is every where present, and that his creatures are the work of His hands, and that he can mould [sic] them, or change them, as he pleases. At all times, and in all places, it is the duty of the creatures, to seek, by the appointed means, the mercy, and pardon of the Creators! I know how very imperfect all my efforts must be to accomplish any good work. Yet I will endeavor, to do as little harm, and as much good with Gods helping, as may be in the compass of my power.

Each day, but renders me more dissatisfied here, & more anxious to be with you, but I feel that there is a crisis, in our natural affairs, that demands of me, as a Patriot, to stand by our country, and if in my power, to aid her, in her struggles. I hope we will leave posterity, on the earth, when we shall descend to the tomb. It is for them that I am now acting. The stake <u>now</u> is <u>five</u> fold greater, for which I am acting, than what it was, when I perilled [sic] all that I had, (my life) in other days. The subject involved is too vast for me to indulge, in any attempt, to impress my feelings. I yet hope, that the storm will pass by, and leave us, more happy, and prosperous (if possible,) than we have ever been. Yet certain, [if] it is, that there are men, who only seek, to destroy the Union, with the desperate hope, that something better may turn up for them! The people, if the matter can be brought to them, are sound, upon all subjects, if they are in possession of the Truth. They are intelligent, and will find out the foundation, of this threatened mischief, I hope, before they will yield up their rich inheritance, of Liberty. Our present troubles are owing, much to the instability of The President, who wields himself up to a miserable cabal—to men who only care for themselves and the creatures who sustain them, in places obtained by fraud! The President, is opposed to the plan, proposed, by the committee of thirteen of the first men of our country! He speaks of <u>his plan</u>, when in fact, what he proposes for a plan, is no remedy, for the present evil state of things![1]

Having stated this much, was because, I have to say it, as I presumed, you would wish some general idea of the condition of affairs, here. My mind is constantly upon them, and home, for if they were arranged, I would hope soon to have you to my heart, and in the embrace, of the most devoted husband living on earth!

My affection draws you so near to me, that I almost fancy, that I hear your voice, or see your sweet smile. Yes my Love, these are the fancies, which chide me, and leave me again, a prey to anxieties, which almost madden me. I can see as fancy, aroused, by memory flys [sic] to our home, you seated, and our little group, around each one, emulous of notice, or if any one is unfortunate, that Mag is ready to apply her Panacea (a kiss) & cure any malady. I have not been able, making the picture complete, unless I were to find a place for the Babe, and then, I would have to introduce myself. Where do you think I would be situated, in the fancy canvass? To have it to the life, I would have to be seated, and you on my knees, with babe on your lap! Then you see my Love, what fancies are before me, and haunt me, by day, and by night! How can I be happy while absent from home? from "wife, children & friends"? It is not possible my Love, and if I write to you about politics, you can excuse me, for indeed, it arises from, my desire to be at home, and to stay there!

Do give my love to mother, and the children. Salute our friends, and tell Kitty to be a good Girl.

Thy devoted
Houston

[1]For more information on this subject see Friend, 207.

Senate Chamber
26 June 1850

My Love,

I was very happy last night, because of the receipt of a letter, of the 4th inst. It should have arrived two days earlier, if the mail had been regular. Important matters first. As to the name of our dear little stranger, I have left that to you my Dear, to make the disposition, that may please you most. Mary William would be a pretty name enough and, it would be made prettier by contracting it to "Mary Willie," which I doubt not would be the case. Anything would be agreeable to me. Agreeably to your arrangement with Sister Ann, am I to conclude that you are about to gratify Sam, by complying with his request. Do not suppose me my Dear opposed, to Sam's <u>number</u>. If it should be the case, I will have to make a <u>short</u> trip to California, and bring home a bag of Gold, to lay in a store of bread, and meat. Poor Sam must not be confined to "bread alone." His generosity must be requited! I am willing to undergo, all the duties of making provision, if you are reconciled to incur your part of the domestic responsibilities, incident to such an arrangement with our dear boy!!!!!

I am sorry to hear of the distress of our friends Genl & Mrs Hatch. They have been peculiarly unfortunate.

You may say to Kitty, that I will with pleasure take her pretty "ear rings," and all that I ask in return, is, that she may be a good girl. As I intend to write often, I will close this letter.

Thy devoted Houston

Washington
30th June 1850

My Dear Love,

To day has passed, and no letter from you. This is my letter day, and I feel that the mail is entitled to the blame. I heard Mr Samson preach to day from the 25th C. and 41st V. of Matthew. A Baptism was to take place to day, but owing to some cause posponed [sic] until next sunday. I think four persons are to be immersed. It is done in the church, and the font is under the pulpit.

The last letters which I wrote to you, were on note paper. You learned me, but really when we have not much to write, it is very convenient! We condense our thoughts, and the letter is full. I could write all day, or all night, if I thought that, it would add to your happiness. There is no contribution that I would not cheerfully make to render you, more happy, than what you are. I am pained that a sense of duty to our country compels me to remain for the present in position. I believe that our country is in no real danger of <u>Disunion</u>, but if we avoid great <u>confusion</u>, we will be fortunate. Nothing but the crisis, could keep me from you My Love, and our children.

On yesterday I spoke on the subject of Texas wrongs, inflicted by Genl Taylor, during war, as well as recently.[1] Tomorrow, I expect, if spared, to finish my speech, as I did not conclude, on Saturday. You will see by it, when it reaches you, that I have not spared the adversary of Texas. I have sent to him, some shafts of ridicule, and have not withheld impressive truths which, will tell upon the public mind! I am on amiable terms with the members of the Senate generally. Mr [Henry] Clay, and Mr [Daniel] Webster, are very kind to Gen'l Rusk, and myself! I will not write more than four pages to night, as I intend to write to you again, so soon as I conclude my speech. My love to Mother, and the children.

Thy devoted Husband
Sam Houston

[1]For a text of this speech (June 29 and July 3, 1850) see *Writings,* vol. 5, 167–92.

Washington
3rd July 1850

My Dear Love,

On yesterday I had the pleasure to receive yours of the 10th of June.[1] It was detained two days by the delay of the mail. It was nevertheless welcome, when it did come. I read it over, and over again. I was not mistaken it seems in the colour of Miss Marys hair, if it actually turns out to be <u>red</u>. But no matter, whether her hair is red, or black, or her eyes black, or blue, I am prepared to fall in love with her, at first sight, as I did with her dear Mother before her!!!!. So I pray you, not to despond, until I have failed to <u>fall in love with her,</u> or until I have <u>fallen</u> out <u>of</u> <u>love,</u> <u>with</u> <u>you</u>!!!

I am sorry, that you have had any perplexities, as I know you have. Gibbs is a petulant man, but as I thought him honest, I was disposed to bear with him. I will not let him know, what I think. [Paul] Mersfelder, is I believe the element since he married our fair friend "Mary."[2] How would it do, to call our daughter "Mary Mensfelder," instead of Mary William? (a laugh) as they say in a speech! Suppose you wrote to bro Will, about his part of the name, as I told Sister[3] of hers, agreeably to your order! I heard from William, the other day, and they all send much love to you, and the children. I have been able to lay my hand on his letter, and will enclose it to you.[4]

In a letter, which I wrote to you, I told you, that I would write to Mrs Birdwell. I have not yet done so, but intend to do that very thing. You will not, I hope, be jealous of her. If I were of that disposition, I might be jealous of her, taking my place in your affections!!! To this I must submit, and therefore do so! I mark the prospect of our fair friend Miss Betty![5] I wish her joy, and happiness. Mr Simons, I regard as a clever man. Ere this you will have had messages plenty to Col & Mrs. B. Col Yoakum writes to me, and tells me of your welfare![6] I will send papers to our Baptist Brother, Mr Baines.

To day I finished my speech, on the subject of the late aggressions, by Gen'l Taylor upon the rights of Texas, at Santa Fe.[7] It was caustic, and so soon as it is out, I will send you a copy of it. I hope, my Love, that you will bear with my absence this time. I have no intentions, ever to put, either of us, to such a trial again! My love to all.—I must write on tomorrow as it is the 4th of July Congress has adjourned, until the 5th, so I am to make a Temperance speech at Baltimore by special request. You see, my Love, that I try to do all the good that I can.

Devotedly thy Husband
Houston

[1]This letter has not been located.
[2]Mary Calhoun. Vick-Rainey, 4.
[3]Mary Houston Wallace.
[4]This letter has not been located.
[5]Betty Birdwell.
[6]See Yoakum to Houston, May 31, 1850.
[7]Houston had begun the speech on June 19, 1850. See *Writings,* vol. 5, 167–92.

Washington
5th July 1850

My Dearest,

I informed you, that I intended on yesterday, to visit Baltimore, and make a Temperance address. At 6 oclock A.M. I set out in the cars.—reached there at 1/2 past 8, went to the Grove at 11 A.M., heard a 4th of July address, and at 2 oclock P.M. I commenced my address. I spoke for an hour to the members of the Marian temperance society. There was a numerous assembly of Ladies and Gentlemen, Preachers, & others of high moral standing, and positions in society. I wish you could have been there, for I made one of the best speeches, that I have made on any subject for years past. I had not before seen any one present. I left the Grove at 4 ocl P.M. when three <u>cheers</u> were given to me, and made my way back to this place, by 8 oclock P.M. having travelled, in the day <u>ninety miles</u>!! I slept soundly, and to day feel well!

I was much pressed with business, in getting out my speech, and preparing an address to my constituents, upon the irritating subjects of the day. So soon as they are prepared, and published I will send them to you. Not to incite you, or awaken solicitude but that you may judge for yourself. I do not expect, nor exact any <u>compliment</u>, for I have said, that <u>I could never extract a direct compliment from you</u>!

Now dont suppose that I am disposed to censure this quality in you. No indeed, my Dear, but I approve it, and laugh at it, and if we live to meet I will tell you why, if you wish to know. Present my love to Mother & the children. Salute our friends.

Thy devoted Husband,
Houston

Washington
7th July 1850

My Dear Love,

I have been prevented writing to you this evening, by the usual annoyance of company. I have been anxious to tell you of to day. It is sunday, and was a most interesting time at church. I have written to you, that the ordinance of Baptism, was posponed until to day which was to have taken place, on last Sunday. To day it was administered, at the font in the church. The subjects were a young man about eighteen years old, and six females, from thirteen to sixteen. They were all genteel, and apparently very intellectual, & of respectable families. They were all dressed in white, and most of them, with little bows of white ribbon, in their hair. While the preparatory arrangements were making they were all arranged in a row, near the font, with their faces to the audience. The scene was one of solemn interest, and was quite imposing. I have not witnessed any thing more so. When the service ended, I spoke to Howell, & Mrs. Cobb,[1] and was introduced to Miss Jackson, and I think a Mrs Cobb. I have never visited them, but intend to do so soon, for they inquire most kindly about you, and the children, and all send much love to you. At four oclock this evening I attended the administration of the Sacrament of the Lords Supper. Many partook of the sacrament. I think more than one hundred & twenty. Could you have been there, you would have been gratified beyond measure. The morning discourse was from preached by Mr Cushman, from the <u>first</u> Epistle of John, 1st c. & 1st v. It was a beautiful sermon, and very forcible! He relied mainly upon the last clause, the "word of life". I know my dearest, that you will not deem my description, of the services of the day, as either useless, or tedious. I can assure you, that the interest of the scene, very far surpassed any description which I can give of it. Mr. Cushman impliedly charged me, with not visiting him, as often as he wished me. They all inquire very kindly, for you, and the children, & send affectionate greetings to you. The gnats, & little flies, flock so to the candle, and on my paper, that I can not write, or I would undertake another sheet of paper. I will write as often as I can. Tomorrow, if I live, I intend to get out my last speech. Give my love to Mother, and the children.

Thy devoted husband
Sam Houston

[1]Mary Ann Lamar Cobb.

My Love,

This is sunday, and I heard a funeral sermon, from our friend Mr Samson. His text was from Ecclesiastics 7th c & 2nd v. I found from some cause, that I was unable to give more attention than usual. I endeavor, to direct my mind, to Holy things, but fear, that I came poor spred [sic], in the way of duty, when I reflect, how much I receive, and that I am unable to make the least return, for the infinite goodness, and mercies, of my Creator! I will try, and do all that I can, and in His abundant Grace, he may open my eyes, to see with an eye of faith, the beauties, and glories, and wonders, of His plan of mans salvation. I am willing in my heart to forego, all the honors of this world, if I thought for one moment, that their pursuit, stood in the way of my eternal salvation, or that by giving them up, I could be instrumental, in serving my God with a perfect heart! I have so lately witnessed the worthiness of all sublunary things, that I am not anxious to pursue the vain illusion, which I see thousands, chasing at the hazard, of their eternal souls salvation! It is no present, or accidental circumstance which has led me to this conclusion, but my mind has been for some time, been gradually inclining to the resolution. Of time, and time things I have seen much, and all that I have seen, or Known, must perish with the using, and leaves the soul bankrupt, at death, and no provision made for eternity!

I am not my Love, intending to read you, a lecture, or to preach you a sermon. The one is not needed I trust, and the other I am not capable of doing. My thoughts have intentionally taken this direction, and I have indulged them! My prayer, has been, and is, that <u>we</u> may yet be able to unite as christians, at a throne of Grace, in this world, with an assured hope, of a happy immortality. My love to mother, and our dear little ones.

Thy devoted husband.
Sam Houston

My Dearest,

For several days past, I have not written to you, in hopes that I could announce to you, the passage of the compromise Bill, in some acceptable shape. It has not yet been disposed of, and I am not certain, that it will be, in the present week, of which there are two days yet remaining. I apprehend that some new expedient must be tried, to settle the difficulties, as it does not seem, that the present Bill will pass, in any agreeable form for Texas. We have had every disposition to yield, a full share, towards an amicable adjustment, & beyond that we can not go. The cliques of abolition, and southern Ultraism, have come to a mutual understanding, to do all the mischief in their power. Thus far in my opinion, they are coworkers, and confederates, without looking to the consequences. We have some very bad men, and those who are guided by ambition, alone, without one feeling of Patriotism, or nobleness of soul. Thus far, I have avoided collision with any one, but it seems to me a duty to not stand back much longer. There is as yet, no tangible point sufficiently prominent at which to strike, so as to affect any great good. I will not preach politics to you, but cease by saying, that the measure, which will soonest dispose of the subject,—to give peace, and enable me to get home to you My Love, is the one, that will meet with my ready concurrence!

To day I had the pleasure to see one of the pillars, of the Baptist church here, and told him, that I had written you a description of the last Baptism. He remarked to me, that another would soon take place of six, or seven persons, and asked me if I ever remembered them to you. I replied affirmatively. They always, inquire for you most kindly, and send Greetings! To day has been one the most rainy, that I remember to have seen, and the wind blows, as fiercely as winter. I have fire in my room, and took a good nap this evening—not being in the habit, it makes me feel stupid, so if this letter does not interest you, impute part of the fault, to that cause. Phrases, and composition, I do not study, for they can not express my affection for you, and our dear children! Nor do I hope, if we should live to meet, to express in language, one thousandth part, of what I cherish. I do not know, how much other men love their wives, but I do think, if you cou'd compare mine, with others, you would feel abundantly gratified by the portion of affection, which I cherish for my dear Wife!

Thy devoted husband
Sam Houston

Washington
21st July 1850

My Love,

This is sunday night, & to day I have heard bro. Samson preach, an abler sermon than usual. I spoke to several members of the church, and they all made many enquiries, and sent much love to you. They regretted much, that you were not in good health, as I told them what you wrote in your last letter. It was detained from sunday until friday. Sunday is the day, on which the Texas mail ought to reach here when regular!

I thank you for the "flower, from Marys eyes." Of course I kissed it for two reasons, and one you will not guess, until you read it. Tis this. It came from <u>your hand</u>. You did not tell me to kiss it, but I tell you of its reception, that you may hereafter, know how much I value any memento, from you My Dear. You will suppose that I feel great interest about your health, as it absorbs, to a great extent, all other thoughts, & cares! I will not urge my last prescription, of the Blue Mass, knowing as I do, your great aversion to it, but if I were at home, I would promise myself more influence, and shou'd hope to achieve it, with benefit to your health. All that I can do, at this distance, is to pray, & hope for your restoration to health.

My anxiety to be with you, is most painful, and to leave here at this time, or until Congress adjourns, or while the rights, of Texas, and the preservation of the Union, are questions, or subjects of discussion, would be a desertion of the highest duty, of a man, and a

Patriot. Such subjects only, could detain me from you, and our dear pledges. You have very little idea of my curiosity to see Mary, and decide for myself, whether her hair is red, or her eyes blue. Sister[1] wrote, that they were all black. You say that Mother says, I must go home and attend to my "red headed daughter." What does Mrs Birdwell say on this subject? My Love, I do not recollect to have conversed with Sam, about Gen'l Jackson at any time, but if I did, he can tell you. You can find out, how he received his impressions, of high character! I am truly gratified, to think, that Sam bids fair, to be religious in early life. You may rest assured my dear, that I will never place, let, nor hindrance in his way to piety, nor holiness, but if it should ever be in my power, I will be happy to aid in all things connected with his souls salvation, as well as his earthly good!

I am often musing, and fancying how you all look at home, and I imagine that I can hear little Maggie's "bird note" saying "Pa Oh Pa" and hear Nannie's occasional hearty, and thrilling laugh. If I could only be at home and find you, and the dear ones, with mother in health, and happy, I would be more than blessed. It is indeed, a painful exile for me to be absent from you! No earthly honors, apart from stern duty, could detain me, for a day, nor an hour from home.

I have not one ray of happiness, before me here, for I declare to you my Love, that I would not forego your society, as I have done, for years, not for the Presidency of the U. S. States, if that would secure it. My Wife, my children, and my home, are more dear to me with my friends, than all the honors of this world! For happiness here, as well as hereafter, we must look to One, who stands, far above all earthy honors, or powers.

I hope my Love, that I will never cease, to revere my Creator, & if reason lasts, I never can!

I hope my Love you will try, and not despond, as much as you have done, but try, and be cheerful, and take as much exercise, as you can. I must answer my sons question. The Ball is a bluish white, and as large, or larger than his fist. It is Indian Rubber, filled with air, and he can make it bounce, half as high as the House![1] Salute Mother, and the children with my love. Regards to Col & Madam Birdwell,

Mr Baines & Lady, and all friends!!!

Thy devoted,

Houston

[100]Antoinette Power's letter has not been located.

[2]On July 29, 1850, Houston wrote a letter to Sam describing the Ball. For a copy of this letter see *Writings*, vol. 5, 204.

Huntsville

July 23rd, 1850

My beloved,

Two successive mails have brought letters from you, so that I esteem myself highly favoured. Indeed I can not describe to you how much I was delighted with those dear letters. Your latest date was the 2nd of July, more than three weeks on the way, and yet to my anxious spirit, it seemed fresh from your hand. I must acknowledge to you, that I am gratified to see that you are homesick and weary of public life. I exact no promise from you, but oh my love do not leave me again. You say my letters evince great excitement. Well dearest I fear they have been sad effusions, but I will tell you no more of my troubles, if I can possibly avoid it, and merely say, Oh never never leave me again.

The last mail brought the intelligence of Gen'l Taylor's death.[1] How wonderful are the ways of Providence! And oh how elusive ambition's fondest dreams! May this solemn warning not be lost on you my love, but may it be the means of awakening you to a greater sense of your danger! I rode into town yesterday evening soon after the news had arrived. As usual on such occasions, the village was all alive. Each shop-door had its crowd. Wise looks were exchanged on every hand, and many were the speculations with regard to the future. Ah none seemed to care whence the immortal spirit had fled!

The world is busy with your name, but I can not yet sanction the ambitious schemes of your friends. If fully satisfied that the Lord had work for you to do at the helm of government, I should feel that you were honoured indeed, but let me beseech you not to be precipitated in allowing your name to be used. Were my own feelings alone to be consulted, I would say let our home be amid the quiet shades of rural life, but I need not tell you this, for on this subject, I know that we think and feel alike.

My health is improving and I hope soon to regain my usual strength. The children are all well. I give them all a cold bath in the morning, and the only thing that reconciles them to it is that it is pa's wish. Nannie says I must tell you to bring her some magnetized swans, and Sam says he would be glad to have a box of magnetized fish. I suppose you can get them at any of the toy-shops. Of course Miss Maggie will expect something of the same kind if the others are remembered.

I have tried very hard to get along without using the draft which you sent me, but yesterday, I was compelled to use it in order to get 30 dollars for Mr Johnson. I have economized as much as lay in my power, but after all our expenses are heavier than I like to have them. My love you must not think hard of me for jogging your memory now and then, about the New York recorder. If you have not paid up, please sit down just now and arrange it will you not my love. It is an excellent paper and editors are a much neglected people.

Mother enjoys her usual health. She and Nannie are gone to see Dr Keenan's second son[2]—a newcomer.

I thank you for bro. William's letter, and hope sincerely we shall see him in the fall. I must try to write them about our "Mary Willie." I dare not mention her in the beginning, it is so difficult to quit the subject. She is lovely beyond all description.

Ever thy devoted wife
M. L. Houston

[1]Zachary Taylor died July 9, 1850.
[2]Apparently this child did not survive, as it is not listed on the census taken two weeks later.

My dear love,

By the last mail I read your welcome favours of the 5th and 7th inst. Many many thanks for those precious letters. For some weeks your letters have come to me regularly, and the dreariness of separation is much relieved by them. I humbly trust that our period of trial is drawing to a close, and that when another month is passed we shall be happy again. Our little ones are looking forward with eager joy, to the time of your return, and when told that we hope in a few weeks, dear papa will be at home, their sweet faces are radiant with delight. I had an interesting scene with them this evening. After the sun had gone down and the stillness of evening was around us, I drew the little girls to me, one on each side, and gave them a little talk. Nannie seemed to be much moved and promised that she would try to be a good girl, so that when papa should come, he would love her and call her his little rose. During our conversation, little Maggie looked up earnestly in my face until I turned to her and said "well Maggie do you want to be a good girl like sister Nannie, and be papa's rose too?" The little creature immediately closed her large blue eyes, and dropping on her knees exclaimed, "I want to say my prayers." The innocent lamb thus unconsciously asked goodness, where alone it could be found. It was a thrilling incident to me, and I do not think I can ever forget my feelings at the time.

Sam is making some improvement in reading and writing, but he is more fond of oral instruction, than of reading for himself. He is rather irritable and self-willed, and it is a great grief to me, but I will try to carry it to a throne of grace, and in due time, may the Lord soften his heart, bring down his proud spirit, and give him the meek and lowly spirit that was in the Blessed Jesus. Our little violet seems more lovely each day. She is a sweet warbler and seems to be practising some rare tones for your return. It is difficult to decide upon the colour of her hair, but I think it will be a rich auburn.

Mrs Birdwell and the Col. came to see me on saturday and brought your letter with them, for which I thank you most affectionately. I was delighted with its contents, and the evident pleasure which it gave them was an additional source of happiness to me. His health is better than for months past, but hers I fear is not good. Mrs [Jane] Wilson was out to see us yesterday, and seems more attached to me than ever. I trust the storm is past.[1]

Mary Mersfelder was out this evening. I told her that we wished her to take a share in the name of "Mary" but said nothing about the "Mersfelder." She was greatly delighted at the compliment from you, but she had anticipated you a little, having claimed it from the first. Mr M.[2] is in bad health. He has a cough, which I think if not arrested, will go into consumption. He is following my prescription at this time, and I hope it may cure him.

We are all enjoying our usual health except Mother who has been for several days a severe sufferer from Neuralgia. I think she is better tonight and hope soon to see her relieved.

But for Mrs Birdwell's messages which you say I must give you verbatim. She says, "Tell Gen'l Houston I think he would be wasting himself very much to stay at home and help you nurse the children!" I do not subscribe to her opinion my love. I might do so if they were not <u>such</u> <u>children</u>! Mrs B. says you sent her a paper not long since, with nothing in it but the description of a baby jumper. How could you do such a thing! Present me affectionately to our relations the Houston family and to Mrs [Elizabeth] and Miss [Elizabeth] Watson and Mrs [Jane] Graham. If my health would permit me, I would write to them all, but writing is so painful to me that I have dropped all my correspondents except yourself, and a little note to Antoinette and Sarah Ann now and then.

Thy devoted wife

M. L. Houston

This is written late at night. I put off writing until the children were asleep, that I might not be disturbed, but I fear that you will find it a rough scrawl

[1]Margaret is referring to the fact that Virginia Thorn had been living with the Wilsons.
[2]Paul Mersfelder.

Washington
29th July 1850

Dearest,

Yesterday was sunday, and I passed it as usual, only that I did not write you, as I have always done. I had nothing to write my Love, but the oft, very often told tale of my devotion to you, and the children, and how sweet the word <u>home</u>, sounds to my ear, and to my heart. To day, I will send you some remarks, which I made the other day in debate.[1] They were impromptu, and you can judge of them. On yesterday, the mail deceived me, so I expect it will be two or three days before I will get your letter. I have not received any later dates, than the 26th June. The compromise Bill it is said will neither pass, or be defeated today. I have but an opinion, and that is that whether it passes, or not, Texas is not to be made a scape Goat, for the sins of other people, than her own.[2]

I merely write you this hasty note this morning, to let you know, that I intend to write to you a letter. I write to you at least every three days, and that is not as often, as I wish to write, If I had time. But I guess it is twice as often, as any other lord, writes to his Lady. This I know will be no reason for you, that other wives are "treated badly," that you should be neglected.

This morning Rusk, and myself have important matters to transact with Mr [Daniel] Webster at the State Department.[3]

My love to Mother, and our dear flock.

Thy devoted Husband
Houston

P. S. Tell our dear Boy, that I have purchased for him, and his little Sisters, some pretty casts in Plaster, of various characters. Amongst them a little boy picking a briar out of his foot. The bust taken of me has been cast, and is very perfect. If I live, I will take one home!

Thy ever devoted
Houston

[1]Houston is likely referring to his speech concerning the Texas-New Mexico boundary which he made in the Senate on July 25, 1850. *Writings,* vol. 5, 197–203.
[2]The bill finally passed in parts. The Texas Boundary Bill passed the Senate on August 9, 1850, by a vote of 30 to 20. Friend, 209.
[3]Houston is probably referring to the problems of the Texas Boundary line and the payment of Texas's debts

Senate Chamber
1st Aug. 1850

My Dearest,

Indeed I thank you, for your letter of the 8th of July. Last night it reached me, being detained two days. I was delighted, with the letter, because it informed me that you were in pretty good spirits, and rather cheerful. I was very happy too, to hear of our Marys welfare, and auburn hair. I can hardly realise that her hair is red. If it is really so, I will be gratified. I am happy to hear, of Sam and our little Girls. Poor fellow. I did not know that his sword had been sent. I thought it was yet in the drawer of my side board. Mr Brashear must have made it up, with the other articles, and took it with him, I suppose, thinking it was necessary to Sams welfare. You did right my dear, but pray don't whip him. He is not of that disposition. He has pride, & affection, and as far as he can understand he Will be governed, by those feelings. He is a noble boy, and I hope, will be a great blessing to us, and if God pleases, a helping to mankind.

Yesterday, the compromise Bill was defeated. I hope the several parts, will now be taken up, and passed in some acceptable shape. I am very impatient, truly so, to get home. I need not tell you <u>why</u>, I wish to get home. I can tell you, I want to see you, and our weans, and kiss you all, very warmly. I am fearful our Marys mouth will be spoiled, if she is half as pretty, as you think she is. I reckon my Love, there is some allowance, to be made for a mothers love! I doubt not but she is pretty, and if you had told me, that she resembled you, I would have believed any thing, that you would have asserted, in relation to her beauty. Really my dear, I would like to see how she does look.

There is a Judge Rogers here from Mississippi, whose mother[1] was a Lea. He is a very intelligent gentleman, good looking, and clever. His mother was a cousin to your Father—Yes, and he went to school at your Fathers.[2] He recollects you! and sends love to you & mother! He is on his way to the North, to spend the summer.

My dear, I do not know what to say about Kitty. You can tell her for me, my Dear, that if she will attend to what you wish, that I will take you some pretty presents for her! Tell her, that I wish her to be neat, and not use naughty language. I will not be pleased, or like her, if she does not behave prettily. Do my dear, urge her pride kindly, in gentle tones of advice. Get Mrs Birdwell to talk to her. She will have weight!!!

My Dear, I cant say, when we will adjourn, but I can say when I hope to get home. I pray it will be by the 10th day of September! It is a long, long time my Dear, but you can bear it, I hope, in comparative happiness, to what I must endure, while seperated from you. There is great, very great excitement, here in consequences of the defeat of the compromise Bill. Rusk, & myself, voted against it, for the reason, that Texas was placed by an amendment in a most humiliating condition. When this was done, we were compelled to oppose the Bill. We had no doubt as to the course which we shoud pursue. I do not wish you, my Dear, to have any fears for me. You know I am honest, and an honest man can always justify himself,— at least with his own conscience. The course taken by my Nieces does not surprise me! I intended you to give one of the check silks, to your friend Mrs Birdwell. Did I not say so? Do with all of them, as you please my Love. Do write often, and love me, as I do you, if you can!

My affection [to] our Mother & children.

Ever thine
Houston

---

[1]Houston may be confused. Euincy Lea [Mrs. Nathaniel] Deane had a granddaughter, Polly Miles, who married Timothy Rogers. Hearne Papers, "The Lea Family," San Antonio, Texas, in the possession of the editor.

239 : March 18, 1850–October 1, 1850

[2]Temple Lea at one time held a school in Henry Lea's house. Interview with Elizabeth Hall, a descendant of Temple and Henry Lea, Tuscaloosa, Alabama, March 22, 1998.

Washington
4th Aug. 1850

My Dearest,

    This is again sunday night, and I suppose you will wish to know how I have passed the day. As my custom is, I went to church, and heard Mr Samson preach a very good sermon. It was from the 28th C. & 9th verse of Matthew. So soon, as the sermon was ended, the ordinance of Baptism was administered to a young man, and three young ladies, hardly grown. I also attended the ordinance of the Lords Supper, in the afternoon at 4 oclock. While I was in church, and they were singing, my eye fell upon a beautiful Hymn, or Psalm. You will find it in the Baptist collection, No 46. "How sweet etc." is its beginning. It brought to my feelings, the calm of a sabbath evening, at home. I pray that I may yet be so happy, as to pass (if spared) the remains of my sabbaths, as thus described. In my last letter, I did not respond to your mention of your friends, Mrs [Theodorah] Baker, Miss [Rouwanah] Crawford, and others. I am happy my Dear, that you have such society, & would be more happy, if I could only make one of the circle, of which <u>you</u> form a part. My heart is with you, if I am not !!! You asked me, <u>if I</u> <u>really</u> <u>loved you,</u> <u>as much as I professed to do</u>! Indeed I do, and a great deal more, than I can confess, to love any one, or I am much more eloquent, than I fancy myself to be. Eloquence reminds me, that I have sent you lately, several short speeches made upon the spur of the moment, in debate. Run your eye over all the stories in the papers, which I send you, as I may not mark, at all times, the items intended for your notice. You tell me, to say if Mrs Graham is handsome. Well, she is good looking, but you must know that she has two grand children, and must have faded much, from other days. You need not be uneasy my Dear, for I assure you, even in our young days, I never made love to her. I went yesterday, and presented her, your love, as you told me, and she showed me a small mattress, which she said she had made for you, and if it should be too small, for our Mary, it would be large enough for "Jenny Graham," for she declared before her Mother, that she never would be contented, until you give her a namesake. Note that my dear, and think of the claims our dear Sister Ann, has made!

My Dear, I do not know that I have anything else to write. Yes, on yesterday, I was called on by four ladies begging for brother Samson, and I gave them five dollars. I felt mean, that I had not more to give, but if you order me to give more to him, I will do so. Every Sunday I give 25 cents to some fund at church, but I do not know what fund it is. I suppose it is the mission fund.

If Kitty will be a good Girl, I will bring her a new dress, and the ear Rings.

Thy Husband,
Houston

Washington
8th Aug. 1850

Dearest,

I truly thank you, for your letter of the 17th[1] of last month. It reached me last night and made me very happy. It was long on the way, as you will see. I was distressed to hear that you had suffered, & been in danger. My prayer is, that you may not have a relapse, but enjoy good health, & happiness.

I was happy to hear of our dear "weans" all, and take with all due submission, the compliments, which you pay me, on our Marys account. If she is like me, & auburn hair to boot, I am fearful that some jealousy will be created, with her little sisters. Is she really red headed? for I am crazy to know the fact. Poor Sam. Tell him my Love, that if he reads prettily, when I get home, I will surprise him agreeably! I am pleased that Kitty seemed moved, when you told her of my message to her. I do hope that she will be a good girl. If she will be clever it will make me happy indeed.

You must not my Dear, for one moment suppose that I will ever be in love with public life, for I declare to you, that so soon as I can I will retire,—preferring as I do, my home, to palaces. I hope you will rely upon this pledge. I am truthful. We are yet going on slowly, but I have hopes that we will get off, by the 4th, or 10th of Sept. I am pained to the heart to contemplate such delay. It arises from the perverseness of members, who care only for their own selfish ends. I will try my dear, and write as often as possible. My love to all. Your Baptist friends send love to you.

Thy devoted
Houston

[1]No letter of July 17, 1850, from Margaret has been located.

Washington
10th Aug. 1850

My Dearest,

On yesterday the Senate passed a Bill proposing to Texas, to purchase a portion of her vacant Territory, & to pay her Ten Million of [sic] dollars. Genl Rusk, & myself voted for it. It is probable that it will become a law. I would tell you of the boundaries of the land sold, but I am sure, you feel no concern about bargains, nor politics. To day we are on a Bill to admit California. It will pass the Senate, but how it will fare in the House I do not pretend to say.[1] I begin, or at least I hope, to see matters nearing the appearance of getting home to my Dear Wife and Children. I confess that I am ever anxious to see our Mary, since you have given me such a glowing, or at least elegant description. If she is as pretty as you say, others say, she is, she must be something charming. Is she prettier than Nannie or Maggy was at her age? They, you thought, were very pretty, nay beautiful. Sam was "good looking," but "not handsome." Is he yet as well satisfied with his looks as ever? I would like to fathom his feelings, when he hears his little sister praised, as she must be, extravagantly. Does he look upon her with pride, and as family property? If he does, all will be well, and he will feel rich, & happy. How are his manners, & feelings towards his sisters, & Ma, & Grandma. To you my Dear, I know he is devoted, but I am fearful, that he was too long in the family, without any rival. I hope he will forgit [sic] the influences, then imposed upon his mind. I do hope he will be a noble Boy. I feel only anxious to be with you, and to cherish, in our dear children, such sentiments of a social, and religious character, as will contribute, to their happiness in time, and in eternity. My nightly prayer is, that they may "be reared in the nurture, & admonition, and admiration of the Lord." You may suppose my Love, that because I send you notices of myself, that my mind is addled by such things. I grant you my Dear, that they are not disagreeable to me. I regard them only, as a small compromise, of good actions. I assure you my Dear, that they do not change my pulse, nor my purpose. I think if fair, to send them to you, that you may see something of what is said of me, in commendation as you have seen so much in derogation of me. This, and this only, is my object, a part from the fact, that I think you will be gratified, to see that I am improving in morals, and manners. I sent you my Dear, a paper inviting me to the state of Maine to address "a democratic mass meeting." I did not contrive it I assure you, nor do I think, it will be in my power, to attend the meeting. If it is, my intention is to come home by Providence, and see our friends Doct [Alva] & Lady Woods. If I should, I will at least have the pleasure of seeing, and talking, with those whom you love. I have not written to them since I parted with you. Every week I send the Doctor southern papers. My intention is to go to Maine if there is no business of importance pending in the Senate, when the time arises. If I go, I must set out in two days, and may be absent seven, eight. It will cost me no more, than to stay here. It will take me two days, & a half to make the distance, by cars. If I can go, it will not injure Texas.

We have arrivals here from Texas—two Ex Governors.[2] Neither of which will disturb, or change me from the "even tenor of my way." It is ridiculous to imitate, the vices, of any man, who is not superior to myself in genius, or in character. So my Love you can judge of my danger! You know them, and you know me also!

243 : MARCH 18, 1850–OCTOBER 1, 1850

I do wish my Love, that I was at your elbow, that I might say enough of pretty things to make a Book, and that I can not write. I can not write a <u>kiss</u>, but if I were with you I could whisper it!!!

Thy devoted Houston

My love, & kisses to mother, & all.

---

[1]The California Bill passed the Senate on August 13, 1850. Friend, 209. For Houston's explanation of his motives in voting for the bill see a copy of his speech, *Writings,* vol. 5, 214–30.
[2]James Pinckney Henderson and George W. Wood.

Washington
11th Aug 1850

Dearest,

It was my intention to have written you, a long letter, but several persons have come this evening from Galveston, & have kept me employed, in talking, and listening to them talk. To day I went to church, and heard Mr Cushman, as he supplied the place of Mr Samson. He read preparatory to his sermon the 62nd Psalm & addressed some ideas, new to me. He is an able divine! On Sunday, I always write to you, and but for that, I need not have written, as I wrote yesterday. There is of course no news, which wou'd be interesting to you, since then. If I should go to the East, I will have to start, as I wrote to you, on tomorrow evening, or the next day morning. Yes, I have news for you. If I did not tell you, you would not know, that I have read your last letter four times, and each time, with pleasure.

Tell Sam that I have taken a look at his likeness, and kissed it before writing this letter, and would rather that I could kiss him, as I hope he is a good Boy, and then I could kiss all the dear family.

Give my love to Mother, & kisses to our wee ones.

I am faithfully thine ever
Sam Houston

Washington

14th Aug. 1850

Dearest,

I wrote you a letter, but found it so badly done that I tore it up. So soon as I was seated, after making a speech, I commenced writing. I had been much excited, for the Union was my subject. I made a speech, that you would have thought pretty well of.[1] So soon as it is published, I will send you a copy. Indeed my vanity is not concerned in the matter, for I do believe that no human being was ever more anxious to retire from public cares than I am. So long as I am compelled to remain, I must do my duty. I am sure my Love, you can never appreciate my anxiety, to retire, if you were to reflect upon the anxiety of some persons, to attain honors, of inferior stations to the one which I occupy! Honorable as it is, I would resign it with more pleasure, than [I] accepted it. My situation, tho. is one of peculiar delicacy. Texas is not on her legs fairly, and I wish to see (if spared) a good work finished, which I saw commenced. I consider every day lost to happiness, which I spend here, and sacrificed to duty. I feel that what I have done, is done, and I can not now amend it. I was aware when I accepted a seat in the Senate, that my character had been aspersed, and was misunderstood, and misrepresented. These were reasons why, I thought it due to others, as well as to myself, that I should let men of character, in the U States, have an opportunity to judge of my merits. This opportunity has been afforded, and in justice to you my Love, to our children, and to a Fathers memory, I have discharged my trust! I am prepared to spend my days with you, if a kind Providence should lengthen out my span! If you my Dear, are anxious for my return, I think (if possible) I can rival <u>you</u> in anxiety! It is my intention to leave here, so soon as the Bills concerning Texas have passed Congress, whether it should adjourn or not. I have written this letter in the Senate, in the midst of confusion, talking & noise.

My love to mother & all

Thy devoted
Houston

I did not go to Portland, and did not see our friends—the Woods.

[1] For the text of this speech disavowing sympathy for disunion sentiment, see *Writings,* vol. 5, 232–36.

The first part of the following letter is missing. Its content indicates that it possibly was written around this time period.

I said in the commencement of my letter, "to hear that you were all well." No my Love, you are not all well! You tell me that you are feeble, and from that you will not recover. I hope my love that is hippo [sic] in part, & that you will find that your fears are groundless. It pains me, that I can not fly to you, and at least render you all the aid in my power, and render you evidences of my devoted affection. Yes, I cou'd cheer, and solace you to some extent!! This to me, would be a great comfort. It would at least add to my own happiness, by trying to promote yours!

I have not written to you for four days, which is a longer interval than usual! To day I was not well, and took some camphor mixture, which relieved me from the symptoms which I had. There is a general predisposition to Diarrhea, and my affliction was of that character. To night I feel well! My Dearest, if I were at home, I would beg of you, to take two grain pills, of good blue mass, each night, and morning, until you would feel a tooth pinch, or a gland in the throat, or you would feel a taste of copper, in your mouth in the morning, and then cease for a week, and resume it again, for a few days. In this way my Love, you would soon be restored, to perfect health. Do you not my dear, remember an instance on the Trinity, what a decided effect it had upon you? I know your prejudice, is strong, but why indulge it contrary to experience? I can not command you, but I suggest it because I love you!

I am glad my Dear, that you suggested to me, the probable author of the "Huntsville letter."[1] You are right, I have no doubt! I have not heard from the Roystons, since I wrote of them last. I have two relations here from Alabama—Ladies, & a young man. They are from Sumpter. One of them saw you, and Sam, at bro Henry's, & say much about you. They are on their way to the North, and will spend a few days here! My God daughter, Mary Houston, is soon to be married, to a clever fellow. The family, as well as the other Houstons, all send much love to you!

I want you my Dear, if Mr Johnson brings Powhatan down to send him to Col. Rogers at Cincinnati, as I made a bargain with him. If the horse matter turns out bad with Beck, don't be distressed, I will not be! I wrote Mrs. Birdwell a letter, and fear that it will not be very interesting to her, as it was, I believe, pretty nearly, all about you! If she shows it, I must consider it a betrayal of confidence, and I must charge you, & her with conspiracy against me. Give my love to Mother, and the children, and regards to all friends.

Thy devoted husband,
Sam Houston

[1]See Margaret to Houston, June 18, 1850.

The first four pages of the following letter are missing. It is believed that Houston wrote it on August 18, 1850.

. . . I do not know what sacrifice I would not make to be with you, unless it were to incur the charge, of <u>deserting my duty</u>.

My desire is to be a free man, and be with my family, and remain with them thro' life! Each smile of yours, or harmless prank of one of our little ones, would impart to my heart more real pleasure, than all the manifestations of renown, or celebraty [sic]. It is for you, and for them, that I toil, and work, that you may be the happy beneficiaries, of my exertions! I know this is vanity, and I would, that I could withdraw my mind from all vain pursuits, and fix all my hopes in Heaven, & upon divine things. As I have not been enabled, by the grace of our Heavenly Father to do this, I ought as a rational being, to exert myself to be of use to those whom God, & nature have ordained dependent, to some extent, upon my exertions.

I thank our Heavenly master, that you have all been saved from the tempests of His power, and that you have all been, preserved by His mercy. To day, as usual, I was at church, but was attacked with dysenteries, and had to leave before the sermon was over. It was the first time in many years, that I have had to do so. I am entirely relieved this evening of all affliction, and pain from the attack!

My Love, I need not now attempt to write you a part of a love letter, as I have said so much, without trying to say pretty things, about you, and "our wee lamkins." If I had your poetic genius my Love, I would say "beautiful things," as Sam would say, of you and them. I would say them, for I am sure my heart is Poetry, and Love! I know, and feel the "local habitation" of my affections, but can not give it "a name."

My Love, you call the Babe Mary. Well as you pleased, in this you will see, that I left it to you, to call her Antoinette if you prefered [sic] it. If you have named her, it may be best, on account of superstition, to let it be, as it is. Poor Sam must be unhappy, I fear. He is a lad, of great reflection, and thought. You will find in my letters many questions to answer about the children. I can not refrain from inquiries.

Thy Devoted
Houston

P.S. I send joy to Martha, and the Doctor [Ransom] on act. of the baby boy![1] My love to all.

[1]John Ransom. Carpenter, 2011.

Washington
19th Aug. 1850

Dearest,

I thank you for your beautiful letter of the 29th of July, in which you write about our dear little Girls. I was delighted with the incidents which you related of little Maggie, as well as of Nannie. I am sorry, that our dear boy is not as amicable as I could wish him to be. If I live to return, I will try, and see if I can not improve his disposition, without any direct effort. I hope he will be noble. I wish you my dear, to tell him when he acts badly, or is selfish, that if I knew it, I could not be happy, but would be miserable!!

I am very happy to learn my Love, that your health is improving. I pray, that, it may be restored perfectly! If I should be detained longer, I shall be partially, if not positively deranged, on account of my anxiety to see you. I will be glad to see our little ones, but you I must confess, are a primary orb in the sphere of my felicity. That I loved you first, you will admit, & they are but consequences, upon my love of you. I ask you, not to become provoked at this, because it is true! Indeed I am more curious to see wee Mary Willie, than all the others. I have seen them, and loved them, but I love, and have not seen her!!!

My Dear, I did not see the "baby jumper," or know, that it was in the paper, which I sent to our dear friend Mrs Birdwell. You can say so, and see if it was not the "Mirror" a Ladies, or Literary Journal? It was funny, tho. accidental. Tell her to hand the paper to you, and after reading the description of it, see if you will order one. I will get one, I think without an order. The Madam's message, I have noted, and agree with you my Love, fully in opinion. I want to help you to nurse, and would be happy to extend the art, even to nursing you! Not only in sickness, but in health! In this you will say, I have some little experience—much less than I desire!!! The first good news that I have about getting off, from here, I will get [William] Christy, to write, so soon as the Telegraph can reach him, from here. Tomorrow my Dear I have to go, & make a Temperance Speech, at Port Deposit. I expect to be absent for one day. I send you a news paper, containing a few remarks of mine, so as I try to keep you posted, on my affairs here. You will see that I have to meet the Disunionists at all points. A violent attack has been made upon me, by a <u>Disunion News paper</u>[1] established here, but I will not send it to you, until I meet it, on the floor of the Senate. I intend to use its authors without Gloves. All persons here of correct feelings, look upon it as malignant and base. It is of a character, not to incite my anger, but my contempt, and it will all esteem to my credit. My enemies will be sick of it. Enough of this! I send you a letter from Bro William, and Sister Mary, by which you will see, that Brother intends to visit Texas with me. I am glad of it, and more so as it is unexpected. I hope he may find it to his advantage to settle in Texas.[2] If he should, I will yet hope to see some happiness from my relations. He is a noble fellow, and in him I have found no meanness, and his children would be such as I would wish mine to associate with in life. They are all fine children [and] are very well behaved. Sister is a first rate woman. In a few days, I intend to write to them!

You may tell Sam, my Dear, if he is a good boy, that a friend of mine, in Texas, has promised to send him a pretty <u>Poney</u> [sic]! Now if he should not be a good boy, and learn to <u>read well</u>, I must not agree to my friend sending the Poney. It is the same Gentleman, who sent me my silver spoons,[3] Col George Thomas Howard of San Antonio! He is now here and intends to set out on tomorrow for home!

The Swans, and the Fish, & such like matters, I do not intend to forget. To day my Dear, I paid the Draft of Fifty Dollars, & send it to you. I hope you will not think that I begrudge it, or any thing else, when I have given my heart, and all my affection to you! If you did not return my affection, I should a very Bankrupt in heart [sic]!

You say to Mrs Birdwell, and the Col, that I send as much love to them, as you are willing to spare, from yourself, & further I will send no more "baby jumpers," until they are <u>ordered</u> <u>specifically</u>. I sent the Madam, and the Ladies, a Lady's Book, and one to my own dear Wife. I thought the Engraving in the work would please you! I sent to your particular friends, except Mrs Wilson, & Mrs Maxcy, & Mrs Doct Evans. Them I will send to soon! Salute all our friends. My affection to Mother, & <u>hugs</u> and <u>kisses</u> to the children!

Thy devoted Husband
Sam Houston

---

[1]Houston is probably referring to the *Southern Press*, August 15, 1850. *Writings,* vol. 5, 231n.
[2]There is no evidence that William and Mary Houston ever visited Texas.
[3]These spoons are believed to be the ones which are now in the Sam Houston Memorial Museum, Huntsville, Texas.

Washington
22nd Aug 1850

Dearest,

The other day, I went on my way to Port Deposit, to make a Temperance Speech, but the day was so unfavorable, that I only went to Haure de Gras, about two miles short of the port. I was met there by Gentlemen, and as the day wou'd not authorize a meeting, I concluded to return, and so, I came back to the city the same day, having travelled in one day, two hundred miles.

The place for meeting was in an arbor, prepared for the purpose, as was sufficient to shelter, eight thousand persons. I have half promised, to attend on some other occasion if I can be absent, from my duties here! I have been invited to Raleigh, in North Carolina, on a like occasion, but it will not be in my power to attend. I will send you the invitation so soon as I have answered it. To day I send you the "Baltimore Sun," which has allusion to a scurrilous piece which has been published against me[1] by a Mr Wallace[2] of South Carolina. So soon as I notice it in my place in the Senate, I will send them both to you. Like <u>all</u> my enemies, he has done me a favor. You need not apprehend that it will lead to any <u>fighting</u>, for you know my rule is "<u>not to fight down hill</u>." He is a disciple of the "Gadsden school." You can now judge of the <u>production</u>. I am truly sorry, that I can't yet say, when we will be able to adjourn! I can't advise you to be <u>patient</u>, for I have none myself, only all that I can say, and hope, is that the longer we are separated, the more we will love each other. I would much rather risk loving you very constantly, and tenderly, than to believe absence necessary to increase my affection & devotion. My heart swells, to embrace you, and our dear little ones!!! I pray our God, to preserve me, to meet soon, and to have us in his Holy Keeping!

My love to Mother, & kisses to the children.

Thine Ever,

Houston

Col [Edmund] King begs me to present his most respectful compliments to you. Your Father was his early friend!

[1]*The Southern Press,* August 15, 1850. Sam Houston Papers, V, Barker History Center, University of Texas, Austin, Texas. For more information see Friend, 210.
[2]Daniel Wallace. Wallace described the difference between Calhoun and Houston as the difference between the eagle and the owl and charged that enmity between the two men dated back to Houston's malfeasance in his office as an Indian agent in 1817. Friend, 210.

Washington
23rd Aug 1850

My Dearest,

Yesterday I wrote you, and as the business, in Senate is not important, and all the talking unnecessary, and not interesting to me, I can derive more pleasure, from writing to you, than from listening to the orators, who fail to command the attention of the Senate.

I send you papers every day, or nearly so. The passage of the boundary Bill for Texas, and adjournment, are the most important matters which interest me. I am so anxious my Love, to see you, that I am not on[ly] reflecting about you daily, but I <u>dream</u> <u>of</u> <u>you</u> <u>by night</u>. Yes my Dear, I dream of you, though I am not a <u>dreamy</u> man. Such things, have <u>such</u> <u>an</u> <u>influence</u> upon me, that I do not intend to remain, to the close of the Session, unless <u>our</u> matters are the last, which may be transacted. I intend to write my next letter to Sam, and by him advise you of anything new, or interesting.[1] Do not I, my Love, trouble you by writing so many letters, and those of so little interest? I am not My Dear, trying to impose a belief upon you, that I am very much in love with you, or any thing of that kind. If I were not so vexed, or perplexed, as I am, I could write you pretty ("comparatively speaking") or beautiful love letters. I must restrain all professions of love, and devotion, until I can suit the action, to the word, and the word, to the action. Then my Dear, I will not have to lose your credulity. I am sure you will never again, (if you ever have doubted,) doubt my affection, and devotion to you.

You will see by a note from my God-Daughter[2] that she is soon to be married, and I must be there to give her away, to her Lord! She is a noble girl, and I hope she will get a noble husband. He is a Lieut Garland,[3] and his Father[4] is a General in the army. Since I received your letter speaking of the Watsons, Houstons, etc I have presented you to them all! They all send love! Give my love to Mother, & kisses to our Weans! Regards to our friends.

Ever thy husband truly
Houston

[1] For a copy of the letter Houston to Sam, Jr., August 23, 1850, see *Writings,* vol. 5, 236–37.
[2] Mary T. Houston.
[3] John S. Garland. They were married August 24, 1850. Pippenger, 292.
[4] John Garland. Identified in Francis B. Heitman, *Historical Register and Dictionary of the United States Army, from Its Organization, September 29, 1789, to March 2, 1903* (Baltimore: Genealogical Publishing Company, Inc., 1994), 447.

Washington
25th Aug 1850

My Dearest,

Another sabbath day has passed, and the pleasure of writing to you has recurred. I heard a sermon preached to day by Mr Robb. It was quite an able one! I had known him long, & known that he was a preacher, but had not before heard him preach. He was in his early days a soldier of Genl Jackson's, at New Orleans, & bore a gallant part in that conflict.[1] He has been for many years, a soldier of the Cross, and I hope a faithful one. This would interest Sam, I suppose if he were in possession of the fact. You know my Dear, that I allude to his <u>plan</u>, about the sword! Last sabbath, I was at a camp meeting, of which I think, I told you. Mr Peel,[2] Methodist Preacher, of our state was there. I heard two sermons and returned to the city. There was a vast concourse of people there. It was, some ten miles from here, in Virginia. It would be well for the people here, to visit Texas, and learn how to behave at church! For several days past, the weather has been so cool, that we have to resume our thick clothing, and I found it pleasant, to have fire in my room. It is too bad to be detained here, by a parcel of men, whose selfishness, & vanities, blind them, to the interest, and welfare of the country. Men who seek Disunion, as a remedy for imaginary ills, conjured up by ambitious Demagogues—reckless of the countrys Glory, or the happiness of Millions. You will, I hope by this mail receive an extract of a speech of mine, in relation to this subject.[3] You can judge of its merits, and tone, by the remarks of a Whig Editor.

You may, my Dear, say to Col, and Mrs Birdwell, that I would much rather, that you, & myself were paying them a visit for a <u>week</u>, than to stay here one day, or hour. Have they as <u>little</u> <u>company</u>, as <u>usual</u>? If so, and I live to get home, would it not be a good situation to retire to, and be <u>secluded</u>? I wonder if Mr Roark[4] ever visits there with a number of <u>quiet</u> <u>little Girls</u>, when some member of the family is sick? You may assure the madam, that I will send no more papers containing "baby jumpers." Now if I had sent it to Mrs. Ransom,[5] it would have been proper enough!

Well my Dear One, I have nothing else to say, unless it is to tell you, how painfully anxious I am to see you, and how tenderly, and devotedly I do love you! And now my Dear, I pray for the time, soon to come, when you will say, "<u>I not doubt you</u> [sic]!!" My love to Mother, and the dear little ones.

Ever thy Husband truly
Houston

[1] Both Benjamin F. Robb and John Robb are identified in Heitman, vol. I, 834, as having servied in the army during the time of the Battle of New Orleans. It is not clear to which one Houston is referring.

[2] Bryant Lorenzo Peel. Identified in Homer S. Thrall, *A Pictorial History of Texas* (St Louis: N. D. Thompson, 1879), 186.

[3] Houston may be referring to his speech of August 15, 1850. *Writings,* vol. 5, 231–32.

[4] Reed W. Roark. Identified in Carpenter, 2029.

[5] Martha (Mrs. D. J.) Ransom. Ibid., 2011.

Washington
26th Aug 1850

My Dear Son,

I suppose, before you will get this letter, your dear Ma will receive one, which I wrote to her last night. Although you will get your Ma to read to you this letter, you must recollect, that it is yours to put by, and keep it as your own. I was very glad to hear that you were happy to get my last letter to you. Your Ma wrote to me that you were much gratified, that I had written to you! Since my first letter, and hearing that it made you happy, I wrote you again, a few days since. I want you to know, that I love you, and therefore, loving you as I do, I try to make you happy. If your little Sisters, were old as you are, I would write to them, and try, and make them happy. Now, my son, I am far away from them, and you are with them. I want you to make them happy, as well as your Grand Ma, and your own dear Ma! It is by making people happy, by acts of kindness, that they will learn to love us, and then they will try to make us happy. In this way we are made good & kind. God is a kind Father to us all, and all good people will learn to love the almighty. You love your Parents, because when you first knew any thing, you saw, & felt the kindness of your Ma, and knew that she loved you. You saw that I loved you, and was kind to you, and you loved me in return. This will show you, that you ought to be kind to all <u>good</u> people, and not injure bad ones, but let them pass, in peace! If you feed a dog, or any dumb animal, except the Hyena, or the Tiger, they will love you! <u>They</u> are cruel things, and can not love, even one another. The dam may love her young, and they may love her, as her love, is natural, to all creatures, but this is because she feeds them, only. When almost all animals love each other, how much more ought human beings to love each other. Our God has given us reason, and made us like himself; and he tells us to "love one another." Love your kindred. Kiss your Grand Ma, your Ma, & dear little sisters, and tell them it is for Pa!

Thy Father,
Sam Houston

28th Aug 1850

My Dearest,

On the day before yesterday, I wrote to our son Sam, and as you would have the full benefit of it, I counted it, as one for you. I knew you would be gratified at the fact of my writing to him. It will gratify him, and cause his inquiring mind to exercise, in things which I hope will result in advantage to him, and gratification to us! I am inclined to believe, that Sam has a mind of great power, as well a quickness, of perception. Should he be spared, he must be a remarkable man. I do not say so, because he is our son, but because of manifestation already given, of the character of his mind. My Dear, I must exhort you to patience, as I have to submit to so much, and the greatest distress is, that I can not be with you soon! Nothing but that urgent, & critical condition of our country, at this moment cou'd induce me, to remain absent from you. One hour with you, would be more valued by me, than all the pleasures, which could come to me, in years of absence, from you. I am sick of the cares, incident to my place, & position, and once <u>again</u>, <u>I assure you</u>, that my constant care, and wish is to cease, the turmoil here, and retire, to the home of all my earthly treasures, & joys.

This, I am assured, you will admit, nor have I an expectation, that you will disapprove, my desires, or my intention to retire. My resistance is worn out, and my love of home increases every day! Our dear little <u>stranger</u>,[1] you know I have not seen, and as I have said, my curiosity as well as my affection, is greatly taxed! If business woud permit me to leave here, I could have some recreation, for I am sent for, to many places to make Temperance speeches. In some instances, I comply, but not in one, out of many! If the Senate adjourns over saturday next, I am rather under promise, to make one, at the Red Church Maryland. I know you will commend me, for making Temperance Speeches, when in my power to do so. I feel, that I certainly do no harm, and hope that I may do some good!! The autumn, has now set in here, and the rays of the sun, are now growing pale, & its rays remind me of October at home. There is but little hope that we will get away, before the middle of next month! If I should live to reach home, and should return (which is uncertain) I will not leave home, until December! As to my ever returning if I should live, will be refered [sic] to your <u>decision</u>. My choice would be to remain at home, and so far as <u>ulterior</u> matters relating to politicks [sic], are concerned, they do not weigh a feather with me, however much they may affect my friends. Home to me has charms, which office has never had power to impart! The joys of home are pure, and rational, while the excitement of public life, brings no sweet solace. The consciousness, of having done well in the harvest of public life, will afford gratification to the patriot, but it seldom reaches to the tender affection of the heart. "Wife, children & friends," are the green spot, to which memory recurs, from distance, and where the tenderest affections of the heart are blooming, and are rendered more charming by time.

In this view, I regard public, and private life. I will, (shou'd a kind Providence spare, and bless me,) I trust always regard the two positions, in life. With these facts, I hope you will feel pretty well contented, until the time may come, when I can with affection, & truth call you <u>mine</u>, and when you will realise, that I am only yours!

Give my love to Mother, and kisses to the children. Salute our friends.

Thy ever devoted Husband
Houston

[1]Houston's fourth child, Mary Willie Houston.

My Dear Love,

Last evening I was rejoiced, by the arrival of your letter of the 6th ultimo.[1] I had been absent to Churchville, Maryland, to a Temperance Festival, or a Grand Pick Nick [sic], and that is, taking victuals to the ground, and eating them in groups. I rode about eighty miles in the cars, and then rode eight miles to venerable church, where the meeting was held. I arrived at 12 N. when a speech was making by a Reverend Gentleman (a Presbyterian) who was a crack orator! When he concluded, the meeting adjourned, until after dinner. The recess was about an hour, and a half. I then spoke, and I only regret, that you were not there, and simply because, you have heard many indifferent speeches of mine, and you woud, had you been there, heard one of the best speeches, that I have made (to my opinion) in five years! Yes, I may say ten! If you had been there, you woud have thought so, and that wou'd have recompensed you for some not overly fine. The Ladies, (for of them there was a great concourse), requested to pass by me, and shake hands—This was arranged, and many a <u>fair</u> hand was offered to me,—to <u>shake</u>! This I did, & left for the Depot, to take the Cars, to return to the city, on that evening. The people, ladies, and gentlemen plead [sic] with me to stay, and go to church, and spend a week. This I cou'd not comply with, as I hoped to meet a letter from you, on my arrival here, which so happened. While I think of it, I must request mother to bathe her face, with No. 6, and it will cure her face, and I would say use it for her tooth, if she can bear it, in her mouth! Do let her try it? I was pained, and rejoiced, by the news of our dear Mary. Her suffering, and your distress, pained me, while I was happy to hear of the probable recovery soon, of the dear Infant. How did her brother, and sisters seem to feel, of think about her situation? tho. they were too young to reflect about her danger! My absence has prevented me from writing to you as often as was my habit to write. Did I tell you, my Dearest that I gave away my God-Daughter, on thursday last? Yes, I think I did! The "bracelet" was prized above every thing else! I had it neatly, but not costly set, and the color, of your hair, on the Bridal dress, looked very pretty![2]

If we live to meet, I have a good joke to tell you about the wedding. It took place at 12 N, and the <u>Pair</u> set out on their "honeymoon" trip at 5 oclk. Now a matter, which interests me more, than all the weddings (save, and except ours) which I hope will take place soon, is that I hope we will not be much longer detained here! I have told you my Dear, that I will, if I should ever return, suit the time, to that at which I get away from here! I have no more wish, intention, or expectation, to remain longer in Congress than the 4th of March next, if living, than I have to be the great Mogul.[3] To see you, to be with you, to stay with you, and not leave you, to cherish, and instruct our dear pledges, engross all my hopes of earthly happiness. I am weary, truly weary of the world around about me, and much of it <u>beneath</u> me! I assure you my Love, that you are not more anxious, that I should be with you, and stay there, than I am, that it should be so! I was plagued last evening on my return from the East. There was a child in the Car in which I was. I did not see but heard it. Its tones, and growls, reminded of Sams, when an infant, that I was not happy! it was not crying, but half crying, and half scolding. It was precisely like Sams infant tones! I would be so happy to see our dear little <u>wee ones</u>, at their mama's knees, and cheerful. I fancy the conflict, which must arise as to the place and right of each, should I live to return! My Dear, they are now, more numerous, than we <u>bargained for</u>, but I fancy you wou'd not be willing to trade them, or sell out any part of <u>your share</u>! My Love to Mother, & the children.

Thy Faithful
Houston

P.S. I sent Mrs and Mary Houstons notes about the wedding. This is the way people here do things.[4]

---

[1]Margaret's letter of August 6, 1850, has not been located.
[2]In the mid-nineteenth century, jewelry with settings of the human hair of loved ones was popular.

Washington
4th Sept 1850

My Dearest,

I had the pleasure to be surprised, by receiving two letters from you in two days. This was agreeable to me, and would have been very delightful, if they had not informed me, that you were "suffering from a pain in the breast." I am uneasy about it, as I can not tell of what character it is, whether it arises from the operation upon your breast, or from some internal affliction. I will be very unhappy until I can know which is the case.

My Love, do not pospone the use of the blue mas [sic], until my return. Have it prepared in pills of three grains each, —take one each night, and morning, until you feel a tooth ache a little, or a gland get sore about the neck, or a taste in the mouth of copper, or copperas, and when either of these symptoms occur, I would advise to cease, the use for three or four days, and then resume it again for a few days. So soon as you find that your health has improved, you can cease altogether. Try and procure good Mas. Dr Ransom, I presume, can procure good. I do hope my Love, that you will find relief, and that complete restoration of your health will follow!

So James Davis and your pretty Lady are to marry.[1] Well, I wish them great happiness, & joy. I had not for one moment thought of [Daniel] Johnsons amour, or love fit with Kitty. I am sorry that he is such a simpleton! Do ask him my Love, to go up, and see about my hands. Give him four dollars, to bear his expenses. His first day ought to take him to Mr Plasters,[2] and he ought to make the trip in four days. Do ask him My Dear, to have all matters in good order, and all the lots for horses, Hogs, etc, in good order. If you are about to have any trouble with Johnson, about Kitty, please consult with Col, & Mrs Birdwell, and if need be, let the colonel talk to Johnson. The Col can do <u>this</u>! Give my love to mother, and embraces to our children.

Salute our friends all.

Thy Faithful, & devoted,
Houston

[1]James Davis, Jr., and Sarah Finch married August 25, 1850. Imogene Kinard Kennedy, *Polk County Marriage Records, 1845 through 1880* (St. Louis: Frances Terry Ingmire, 1984), 6.
[2]Thomas Phiney Plaster had a plantation near Bedias. For a biography see *The New Handbook of Texas*, vol. 5, 229–30.

Washington
5th Sept 1850

My Dearest,

Although I wrote to you yesterday, finding that I have nothing important to attend to, at my desk, I am happy to write again. If I do trouble you often, to read my letters, I will render you but one apology, and that I hope will suffice. When I am writing to you, I feel as tho, I were enjoying a sort of communion with one, that I love, and one, whom I hope, soon to be with. I must not write, or attempt to write, a down right love letter, but just to say how glad, or happy, I wou'd be, if I were in a situation, when I could dispense with writing, and tell you, how much, I really do love you! Just in the proportion, that I am anxious, to see you, I feel disgusted with every thing, about me. To day it seems, that something will be done with the Texas matters, but I can make no positive calculation, as to what will be done. I have seen so many dark days, in Texas, that I have become inured [sic] to something like patience, if not the thing its-self. I hope my Love, you will take a glance at my change of disposition, and be <u>reconciled</u> until I can be with you. You need not think, my Love, that I have the slightest inclination, to remain absent from you. My heart, my affections, and all that I deem worth caring for on earth are, and will be part of you! And your dear self, embracing all minor matters! So far as my affections can give you happiness, so far you may repose, upon confidence!

This will do for lovers, before marriage, but I fancy it is a very insubstantial comfort afterwards if you can't tell it to each other, in a whisper! My Love, don't you think so? My love to all. Salute our friends.

Thy Faithful
Houston

Washington
6th Sept 1850

My Dear,

Enclosed you will receive, the Draft of your "recorders," in New York. I wrote to him to draw upon me. He has done so, and to day I paid it to Bro. Anderson, the Father in Law of Mr Samson. You see my dear how dutiful I am, to your orders. When I wrote to him, I said some civil things to him, and commended his papers!

Yesterday my Love, I wrote to you, saying that I hoped the Texas Bill wou'd pass the Senate. It did not pass, but was rejected. To day it has been reconsidered, and passed by a majority of 10 (ten) votes.[1] I am glad of it. Send word to Col Yokum that "Pearces Bill giving Texas ten millions has passed by a majority of ten votes." I can now my dear resign at any time that you may wish, after adjournment of this Session—But of this, I hope we will soon speak, and I pray face to face, on all matters in which we are interested! This is the first time that I have felt, since I have been here, as tho. I could breathe freely. We are about to adjourn, and as the mail will close, so must I. Now my Love, I can only say, Indeed I do love you most truly and devotedly. I have not time to read this over.

My love to all!

Thy devoted Husband
Houston

[1]For information on the telegraphic dispatch concerning this bill, which was endorsed by Houston and sent to Texas Governor Peter Bell, see Friend, 211.

Washington

8th Sept 1850

My Dearest,

Yesterday I did not write to you, as I had for several days written each day. To day I passed as I usually do the sunday. Bro. Samson officiated, & many attended the church. I took with me Judge Hemphill[1] with me [sic], as he happened to be at this time, in the city. He will spend some days here. I hope my Love, I can look with pleasure to an early adjournment of Congress. For the time to arrive, I am, as you will suppose, most anxious. In my last letter, I told you that the Texas Bill had passed, and I can now add, that all the delegation voted for it. Since then the California, and Utaw [sic] Bills have passed, and I hope will become laws tomorrow. The fugitive Slave Bill has also passed the Senate, and may pass the House. Thus my Dearest, you see that business is now progressing rapidly. I have told you my Love, (Should I live, and return) it will not be until in the month of December. So you can see how much joy, and happiness, I anticipate on being with you, and the estimate I place upon remaining, at home. I hope this with a thousand other assurances, which I could truthfully and faithfully render to you, will be most satisfactory, when I may have in my power to do so in person! To day I called by the Birds[2] with Judge Hemphill on our return from church, when I fancied that some of them knew me! I fear that I will have trouble, to get them home. The <u>Fish</u>, and Swans, if They are to be had my Love, shall be, and taken to our children.

It is late at night, and as I intend to write often, my Love, I must close my Epistle, by requesting you to present my love to Mother, and the children. Salute our friends.

I am thy devoted, & faithful Husband

Sam Houston

[1]John Hemphill, former Chief Justice of the Republic of Texas. *Writings,* vol. 2, 438.
[2]Houston is referring to the canaries he had been raising.

My Dearest,

To day the Senate passed a joint Resolution from the House of Representatives, to adjourn on the 30th of this month. I will not say whether or not I will stay until the 30th. I am so anxious to get home, that I will not stay, if I can excuse myself, to my sense of duty, to my country!

To day I made a "personal explanation" of a most triumphant character, against a <u>slanderous</u> charge made by a member of Congress from South Carolina.[1] The records of the War Dept proved its utter <u>falsity</u>. It did to give me an opportunity, to not only vindicate myself, and my reputation, but afforded the means of showing myself, a useful citizen, and a faithful soldier.[2]

You know my Dear, that my enemies do more for me by assailing me, and my reputation, than my friends could do by commending my conduct. So it has, in this case, resulted!

So soon as my speech is published, I will send you a copy of it, and a copy of Mr Wallace's letter![3] My friends (and they are many) are all much gratified, at my course, as well as my speech. You will think well enough, of it, but I will not ask you to tell me so! After the receipt of this letter, you need not write to me unless you write to San Augustine, or Nacogdoches. To day I intend to write to Bro. William to be ready, to accompany me!

I wrote to you last night, and I think it probable that this letter will fall in company with several o[f] them on the way. Present affection to Mother, and embraces to the Dear Children!

Thy faithful & devoted Husband
Houston

[1]Daniel Wallace. Identified in *Biographical Directory of the United States Congress*, 149.
[2]For a copy of this speech "Reply to Reflections Upon His Record as Sub-Indian Agent" see *Writings,* vol. 5 , 238–52.
[3]A copy of the Wallace letter was printed in *The Southern Press*, August 23, 1850. Friend, 210.

Washington
11th Sept 1850

My Dearest,

To day, I send by mail two newspapers. One contains a synopsis, of my last speech, and the other an opinion of my vindication. It overwhelmed the author[1] of the calumnies. I pity him, but he deserved it all. The speech is badly reported, and I never saw the notes to correct. I may come out with all my last speeches corrected, and published, in Pamphlet form. If I do I will send you one, & you may lay them by for Sam if he should live, to look at, in after times, for from them he may imbibe some sentiments, which may have an influence, upon his moral, social, & civil character!

The mail is just leaving the Capital for the Post office, and I must close my letter. I intend to write as often as I can. My Love, I can only say that each day adds to my affection for <u>you</u>, and for <u>home</u>.

Faithfully thy most devoted
Houston

[1]Daniel Wallace.

Washington
12th Sep 1850

My Dearest,

On last evening I went to Baltimore,[1] after I had written to you. I made a political speech, and if you had heard the cheering of the great concourse, you would have thought that the speech was very fine! It was a fine speech. I was most kindly treated, and this morning I returned to my duty. I take all the exercise that I can, and if I can unite benefits to others, with recreation to myself, I am gratified. You, I am sure, will approve of my intentions, and sanction the course!

The day of adjournment is fixed. The Senate is dilatory in the transaction of business. It seems to me, that my anxiety is hastened, by delay, and increased. I have already written to bro. William to be ready, but of this, I think I have apprised you of. I am at a loss, on one subject, and I am sure, you will not guess until I inform you of its character. I have ordered according to my taste, a beautiful set of Table, Desert, & Tea spoons. I mean a Dozen of each, of the first, and of teaspoons a half dozen. Well, I wanted to mark them, and I did think, of having them marked, for Mary Willie, and in that way, we would have them longer perhaps than by having them <u>marked</u> for any other name!!! But I am concluded. They are a present for you my Love, really, and I need not, disguise the fact, so I will have your name engraved upon them! To my fancy they are rare, and very beautiful, as well as snappy. They are not like any (I think) which you [have] seen. The Fish—I, the fish and the Swans! They are to be forthcoming, and other small matters!

I send to my son some pretty poetry. I hope he will memorize it. I would be so happy to hear him recite it, as prettily as he used to recite, the Lords prayer! My love to all, and I send regards to friends!

Thy Faithful and devoted Husband
Sam Houston

[1]Houston spoke in the 20th Ward Democratic Association. See [Blurred] Root, James Lawson, and Nicholas C. Smith to Houston, September 4, 1850. A. J. Houston Collection # 3942, Texas State Archives, Austin, Texas.

Washington
12th Sept 1850

My Dearest,

I send you marked, the notice of "Jenny Lind," and her performances. You may suppose, that I will be curious to see, & hear her. Well, I do not expect to see her, and I am sure I will not hear her! What would you think, if I were to tell you, that the reason, why I will not hear her is, that I might <u>think</u>, that she can sing as well, as you do. You sing as well, as I wish any one to do, and if she sings better, I do not wish to hear her. This would do, to control me! An other is at hand. If you were here, it is possible that you might wish to hear her, but as you are not here, I will take it for granted, that you would not, and therefore, I will not even <u>wish</u>, to be present, at her concerts.

How silly, and frantic people are in large cities! I do not envy them all their pleasures, my Love, and would infinitely, prefer to be with you, and hear our Marys serenade, (of which you have spoken) or, her dear Mothers lullaby, than to hear all the vocalists in the world.

Thy devoted Houston

Washington
15th Sept 1850

My Dearest,

I am able to write to you, and feel thankful to Providence, that I am. Evening before last, I was quite ill with bilious cholic, and was confined to my bed, until this evening, when I was able to ride out a while. I feel, as tho. I was over it, tho. the attack was pretty severe. I had a physician, of high character, tho., as you know, I am a great quack, I believe, I would have been about as skillful, as he was. If I am cured, I do not begrudge his <u>fees</u>. I was not able to visit church to day, but my room mate, went as is usual with him, did attend [sic].

For several mails, I have received not [sic] letters from you my Love, or from Huntsville. I have been fearful that you have quit writing, with the hope that Congress would adjourn, before your letters would reach here. In that event, I will lose some four, or five, which I wou'd otherwise have been written to. If this has been the case, it will not prevent my writing to you, as often as I can command time. Tomorrow two weeks, I hope will enable us to leave here.

You recollect Major, & Mrs Martin,[1] our friends near Nashville Tenn. He was here on business, and was accidentally shot by a room mate of his, in the thigh, and pretty badly, tho. not dangerously hurt. His Lady, was advised of it by Telegraph, and came on in about seven days. She found him doing well. I was with him when she arrived. The meeting was a tender one indeed! They both unite in sending a thousand, kind recollections to you, and Master Sam.

Your Baptist friends, send many kind wishes to you whenever I see them. All churches I believe, have their troubles. <u>One</u> <u>discontent</u>, in the First Baptist church here, has caused bro. Samson to resolve on leaving here, and going near Boston to a call there. He is a good man, and I doubt if they will not be able to supply his place. I hope they will prosper, in well doing.

My love to all!
Thy devoted Houston

[1]Peter W. and Mary Martin. Identified in Sistler and Sistler, *Tennessee 1850 Census Index,* v. 4, 169.

Washington
18th Sept 1850

My Dear Margaret,

My anxiety to be with you, has been so great, that I dream about you, again, & again! Last night I dreamed about you, & after waking, and reflecting for a time, and again sank to repose. Again, I dreamed of you, and woke to distress. I hope, & pray, that my dreams were not augurries [sic] of truth, for I was unhappy. It seemed to me, that you were under an influence not favorable to your happiness, & mine.[1] The dream was after midnight, and I chose to read it by contraries.

The absence of your letters, renders me less happy, than I would have been, had they continued to come. I was apprehensive, when I received your letter, saying that you hoped, I might be on my way home when your last wou'd arrive, that you would not write again. I do not wish you to think, that I censure you, no indeed my Dear, for you had a right to expect me home, at farthest, by the last of the present month. Instead of this, we are here, and here are we to remain, until the last of the month. You will suppose my Dear (if I am living, and able to travel) that I will not lose a single moment in reaching home.

Yesterday I purchased for you, a pretty silk cape. Dont suppose, that it is extravagant, though, I think it beautiful. The colour is not "flashy," but tasty. I mean according to my fancy. You will be pleased with it, independent of my <u>motives</u>, which would commend it to your especial acceptance. I do not with-hold them, from you my Love, but am willing to assure you, that they are to make you gratified, and happy, by evincing to you, that you are as much present to my thoughts, and heart, when I am absent, as when I am present with you. I am not as happy my Dear, as if I could hear your voice, or enjoy the <u>trouble of nursing</u> you, and recalling days gone by, and expressing hopes of the future, touching the prospects of our little ones.

From my nature, I am sure you will believe me sincere, in all that I say & feel. The assurance my Love, that led, to a conclusion, from my love of you, to resign a situation, in the Senate of the U States, at an early day, would if known to the world, be deemed satisfactory that I am your very devoted husband, and lover! Dont <u>you</u> think so, my Dear? Well, I now hope, it will not be long, until I can render you an earnest, of all that I profess.

Col Paxton, from Penna,[2] called upon me this morning (he is a relation of mine) & told me that, a lady wished to see me on your account, that was his sister in Law. I called to see her, and found that originally, she was a Miss Rupert, and now widow, Mrs Gillispie. She spoke of seeing you, I think at her bros wedding with Miss Jones. She was very kind in her enquiries for you, and the little Houstons. I think she now resides in Penna, & for the purpose of educating her daughters! I do not know how many she has. She stated that her bro. had been at to [sic] Texas this year, and was charmed with the country!

I do not know, that I have any thing interesting to tell you, about matters here.

You may say to Kitty, that I have, a pretty set of Ear rings for her, if she is clever. The fish, and swans, or mice, are sent for, as there was none here!

Sams balls are procured, & they are quite pretty. The spoons are nearly done, and what else I may add, I dont know.

My Love to all, & salute our friends

Thy faithful and devoted
Houston

[1]Indeed Margaret was experiencing a most unpleasant situation. Thomas Gott had brought assault and battery charges against Margaret on behalf of Virginia Thorn. In just a few days after Houston's dream, Margaret would be indicted by the Grand Jury with a trial set for the following April.

[2]It is unclear if Houston is referring to Francis Paxton or Joseph Paxton, both of whom lived in Philadelphia. Ronald Vern Jackson, et al., *Pennsylvania 1850 Census Index* (Bountiful, Utah: Accelerated Indexing Systems, Inc., 1976), vol. 2, 1218.

Washington
19th Sept 1850

My Dearest,

To day it is damp, & raining, and not pleasant. I am now in the Senate, and tho. I wrote to you on yesterday, I nevertheless feel, as tho. my time will be as well employed writing again, as I would be, if I were to listen to some members, who wish to make speeches.

I do my dear, really think, my letters must be barren of interest, so far, as to incident, is estimable, or variety. To be sure, you will be gratified, that I render you, so many evidences of my affection, and devotion, as the frequency of my letter evinces.

You care, but little about politics and I can not expect to gratify you much, by treating of subjects in which, you feel so little interest. If I attempt to write about home, why, I have been so long absent, that I hardly know how to write, or even what to write. I could tell you that I am unhappy, from detention here, and that, I am nearly crazy to see you, and the children, and that my desire to see <u>you</u>, exceeds that, which I feel to see the children. Bless their little hearts. I do feel, at times most intense anxiety to see them, and to see our little Mary. I can say, that I can add curiosity, as well as anxiety, to get a peek at her blue eyes, and red head. By the bye, I can not yet realise, that her hair is red. Sister wrote that her hair was black, and eyes black. You say her hair is auburn, and her eyes blue. Now you will recollect, that the hair was auburn, when it reached here, and I was satisfied that the eyes were blue, altho. I do not recollect, that I wrote to that effect.

Well, I rejoice that the time is fast approaching, when I hope to see the young Lady, and judge for myself of her beauty. But really, I do not expect, to find her more beautiful than Nannie, or Maggy, nor than I once thought her Ma, when I loved her, <u>perhaps less</u>, than I now do, and have done since, she had the <u>temerity</u>, to become my dear Wife, and place herself, in a situation, to become the mother of babies!!!! I do not think you will be angry with me, when I assure you, that I will be satisfied, with the <u>Gal</u>, if she has her Mothers genius, her heart, and her personal charms. To give her a suitable dowry, I would be willing to look beyond, that which I have intended, if I should be spared, by a kind and merciful "Providence." For some time, I have written no letters to Sam. I must resume it, as I do not expect to hear from home, until I may reach there. My love to all!

Thy devoted Husband
Sam Houston

P. S. I am quite recovered, from my indisposition!

Washington
Sept 20th 1850

My Dearest,

We are moving on, as usual pow wowing & speaking for Buncombe, and not attending to business, as we should do! It can not detain us here, but will leave much business of importance unattended to, at the close of the session.

Long was I baffled on the subject of the <u>fish</u>, and the <u>swan</u>, and could not obtain, or hear of any, in the city. I was fearful after promising to get them, I would either forfeit my word, or have to go, or send to New York for them. Yesterday, tho. somewhat feeble, I set out, as I say, <u>almost desperate</u>, in my resolves, and in a little establishment, found every thing that I wished, except the Mice. But in lieu of the Mice, I found a small Boat, or ship, and I bought <u>four</u> Fish, <u>one</u> vessel, and a Swan. Now, the Division will be matter of difficulty. Our little Mag, you know, will claim a partnership, in the concern! Miss Mary, I presume will be content with the playthings, which her dear Ma, can furnish her with. If her amusements are so extravagant, they are not yet, so numerous as those of her sisters. A few yards of flannel, will be worth more to her, than all the toys, that Dutch men could devise.

I am preparing, for my departure, at the first moment, that I can get off for Home! I am fearful, that I will find some trouble in reaching home, by the red river. The <u>stages</u> I learn, are not running, and I fear that they will not be of much help to me. Carroll Smith has acted very badly, and has caused all the derangement in the mails of Texas. He will not do, you may be assured. It will be months yet, before the mail will be regulated.

I may purchase a horse, and Dearbourn, and go from the mouth of red river. I will try, and reach home, by the most speedy route!

You may say to our friends, that I am anxious to see them. Give my love to Mother, and our dear children

Thy Faithful & devoted Husband
Sam Houston

Senate Chamber
21st Sep 1850

My Dear,

I write to you not to provoke you by a short letter, but to say that I am pretty well, and hope on this day week, to set out for home, where I do ardently desire to be.

My love to all! Dont be angry, that I write so short a letter. Wait until I can reach home!!!

Thy Devoted
Houston

Washington
22nd Sept 1850

My Dear Wife,

This is at the close, of another sabbath day, and I can only say that I have passed it by visiting church. I was there this morning, and to night. The text of morning was John 17 c. 20th and 21st verse, and this evening, or night it was 2nd Pauls epistle to Peter, and really I do not recollect what verse, but I know it was about the glorification, of his Saints, whom the Father has chosen, & justified. This evening, I rode out for an hour or two, on the hights [sic] of Georgetown. It is a beautiful view, and the scenery was delightful, tho. I assure you pleasant as the scenery was, I would incomparably rather have been at home, helping you to nurse, or nursing you, than being in the company that I was. It was good enough of the kind. Two gentleman of fine intelligence, were with me. I bored them, as I often do my companions, about you, and the children. Well, this is pleasant to me, and if others do not like it, I can only say, they can easily avoid me! The world is very wide, and if they chuse [sic] to leave me I will not run after them.

This is the last sabbath save one, (if I do not get off on Saturday) that [I] expect to be here for months to come. I dont know what to write, but if I were with you my Love, I would have much to say, and a great deal to tell you. I was very glad that bro. William had your letter sent to me. It was not long, but it told me, of a world of interest. It told me "all were well." This was to me, at this distance, a world of news. But [when] I calculated the time, which had elapsed, since it was written, I was but the more anxious to be with you. The trifling presents, which I have for those at home, seem to render to me, when I think of them, something like society. They seem to create a clairvoyant relation, to you, and the children. I hope to see you, my dear, and the little ones all happy and smiling, when they are displayed at our fireside.

I am like the hound, thirsting and panting for the cooling brook, or like the wounded hind, which seeks protection, where it has once found repose, & safety.

My Dear, salute our friends, & present my love to Mother, and render warm embraces to our children.

Thy ever devoted Husband
Houston

Washington
1st Oct 1850

I wrote to you after midnight, when, I told you I would be disappointed in getting off, this morning at 6 oclk.[1]

I now write to enclose you a memorandum of Deposits made in a Banking house in this place.[2] I retain a Duplicate, if any thing should happen.

I hope to be home in twenty days, but that seems to me a long time to be absent from you my Love, and I may add the little ones. My love to all I hope to be off in four hours.

I am thy devoted husband
Sam Houston

[1]This letter has not been located.
[2]These documents have not been located.

Chapter IV

December 17, 1850–March 10, 1851

December 17, 1850: Sam Houston to Margaret Houston
December 21, 1850: Sam Houston to Margaret Houston
December 22, 1850: Sam Houston to Margaret Houston
[December 25,] 1850: Sam Houston to Margaret Houston
December 28, 1850: Sam Houston to Margaret Houston
January 7, 1851: Sam Houston to Margaret Houston
January 8, 1851: Sam Houston to Margaret Houston
January 10, 1851: Margaret Houston to Sam Houston
January 12, 1851: Sam Houston to Margaret Houston
January 18, 1851: Sam Houston to Margaret Houston
January 24, 1851: Sam Houston to Margaret Houston
January 26, 1851: Sam Houston to Margaret Houston
January 31, 1851: Sam Houston to Margaret Houston
January 31, 1851: Sam Houston to Margaret Houston
February 8, 1851: Sam Houston to Margaret Houston
February 8, 1851: Margaret Houston to Sam Houston
[undated]: Sam Houston to Margaret Houston
February 12, 1851: Sam Houston to Margaret Houston
February 15, 1851: Sam Houston to Margaret Houston
February 18, 1851: Sam Houston to Margaret Houston
February 19, 1851: Sam Houston to Margaret Houston
February 20, 1851: Sam Houston to Margaret Houston
February 28, 1851: Sam Houston to Margaret Houston
March 5, 1851: Sam Houston to Margaret Houston
March 6, 1851: Sam Houston to Margaret Houston
March 10, 1851: Sam Houston to Margaret Houston

Houston began his trip back to Washington in mid-December of 1850. His first letters were written from East Texas.

Crockett
17th Decb 1850

My Love,

I have only time to say a word to you, as we have a distance to travel yet today. If Mr Baines did not take the Buggy, let it be put at the back of the corn crib, and secured, so that the oxen cant injure it, and let the Boys (Prince) stretch the cow hide, that is there, and place over it, so as to secure it. If Thomas Parmer has not yet taken the three oxen, (not the Dun's)[1] and the hogs, all but the little white one in the pen, and the McGoffin, please send for him, and let it be done. Better would it be to pay ten dollars to have them sent, than they should stay two weeks. The corn, if we can save it, will sell well. Col Yoakum, if Mr Smith[2] of the Steam Mill, does not take Joshua as a Teamster (for I dont want him at the mill as a hand) can hire him to any one that he may think fit, at the rate of 150$ per annum, until the month of april.

I told Albert, and the Boys, what I wished them to do first, and so soon as Albert has done what I told him, he can go to work under any arrangement which Col Yoakum may make. My Love, advise with the Col, in all cases where you feel any perplexity.

Please tell Prince to give to each horse a night, and in the morning fifteen ears of corn when they do nothing, with shuck, and fodder, or to give the shucks [to] oxen, and fodder enough to the horses. To give to the mare 8 or more ears night and morning, and to my colt six, or seven ears each night and morning with fodder. In bad weather, I wish them all in the stable, & in good weather the colt may run out in the Priara [prairie?], with his dam, in day light. Whenever she is fed, let her be turned out day, and night. Let the waggon be placed under shelter.

My Love, I dislike to trouble you for a moment about such things, but pardon me.

These are not matters of my thoughts, but I wou'd now and then recur to them, and I resolved to dismiss them. The matters of thought, of interest, and of feeling to me, are your health and happiness, and the welfare of the children, & mother. These are matters, which I could not, and would not if I could, discard from my memory, or my heart. You may imagine that I will write to you as often as possible. The stage is waiting. My love to all, and kisses.

Ever & affectionately thy Husband

Sam Houston

P. S. My Dear the letter to Mr. George Law, of New York!!! Don't think I will commit you. He has a family. Respects to his Lady,[3] and an invitation to call, or visit you in your "Rustic Home."

Thine H.

[In the margin:] This is a miserable scroll. Feel no embarrassments about money. Draw upon me for any you may want. Mersfielder will cash it, or Rogers or Gibbs.

[1]Possibly William S. Dun was the Huntsville tanner. Carpenter, 2008. However, Houston may instead be referring to oxen of a dull grayish-brown color.
[2]E. M. Smith. Identified by Carpenter, 2022.
[3]The former Miss Anderson of Philadelphia. *Dictionary of American Biography,* vol. 6, part 1, 39.

San Augustine

21st Decb 1850

My Dear Love,

You will be surprised to find that I am at this place only, on my way. The disarrangement of the Stages at Nacogdoches kept me one day there, and yesterday on my way down, was the most awful day, and the hardest, & most constant rain, that I ever felt, or saw. I had a violent dysentery, and there was not an inch, on the miserable <u>hack</u>, which was not wet as it could be. The bottom was the only part thro which water would not pass. It was tight, and held water. I had, from Nacogdoches here to get out several times, and exposed in the rain.

The <u>griping</u> [sic] which I experienced was dreadfully exhausting to me. When I arrived here, I was barely able to get into the house. Huston[1] made me as comfortable, as he could, but I was quite ill. I took your composition, and it helped me. I slept well, and by the aid of Dr. I. J. Roberts I now feel well. I was unable to sit up, or go on with the stage, so I lost a trip. To day, I would have reached red river, and when I will be able to do so is uncertain. I will try, and go so soon as I can.

My Love, My horse was sent to me, but was taken on to Austin. If he is sent home, I wish him taken good care of, and do not let any one ride him. Tell the boys to put Powhattans old halter upon him in the stall, and see that he dont rub his tail. You will pay the man (if he should bring him to you) <u>twenty</u> ($20) dollars. I was to pay him ten ($10) for curing the horse, and ten $10 for keeping him is enough. See Col Yoakum if any trouble should arise.

If you should have any trouble, I wish you to send down for Bro. Vernal, and let him come up to you at once, and do not at any time pospone so doing. "Take time by the forelock," I pray you. If Thos Parmer has not taken the hogs and three oxen let it be done at once. You will be more happy. The large Bell, that I sent to you can go on the oxen.

I have repented that I did not resign last fall, but I am now in for a while. You my Love, our children, and our home, are more dear to me, my Dear, than all the Halls of State, or the honors, which this world, can bestow upon me. I have told you often, if I even regard Fame, it is that you may be recipients of it with me. You will claim many thoughts, and prayers of me, when fame, and the world at large will not be remembered by me.

Whatever troubles you may have, let this console you my Love, to some extent. I really feel that I love you more, than I have done before, if possible, and will feel more the want of your society than I have done. This would say, that ambition yields to Love, and my affection for you.

Do not give yourself any concern, about property matters, and if the fellow brings my horse tell Col Yoakum what I say, and rather than have any trouble if the horse is not injured, pay the scamp $30 dollars.

Tell the Col, that I am willing to lease to Proffr McKinney[2] 25 or 30 acres, of the field, on the end next [to] the Priara, or next [to] Mr Leaches.[3] I am still improving in my feelings to day, and hope to get over my exposure entirely. Can you write to me twice a week? Love to all.

Thy ever devoted
Houston

P. S. Write to Toms Power, and tell him that Martin[4] may study any thing that Power may wish.

[1]Almanzon Huston operated an inn in San Augustine and ran the stage line from Huntsville. *The New Handbook of Texas,* vol. 3, 803.
[2]Austin College professor Sam McKinney. Identified in Carpenter, 1999.
[3]William Leach. Ibid., 2005.
[4]Martin Royston, the brother of Sarah Ann Royston Power.

Sabine Town
22nd Decb 1850

My Love,

I left San Augustine to day at 12 M, and arrived here at 8 P.M. The ride was not so bad as the one which brot me to that place. In my life, I never was so much exposed in the same space of time, nor ten times the space, that [sic] I was that dreadful night, & half day. I hope to get on without any further trouble. You will hear that cholera is prevailing on the Boats and in Orleans. I will do all that I can to escape the disease, and by way of prevention I am getting here, some good No. 6. My stay at San Augustine was very proper, for I do really think if I had attempted to come on, and not taken the composition I would never have lived to reach this place!

Many times have I regretted, that I ever left my peaceful home, for I feel as tho. I were again, adventuring upon a stormy ocean! I can only say my Love, that while [I] have to act, I will try, and act worthy of you, and the best portion, of my past life.

This is sunday night, and I am sorry that I am compelled to write to several persons on business, but I have it to do, and a work of necessity. My Love, I will write to you from every point at which I may have a chance. Should I pass the Southern route, I will try, and write to our kindred, and tell them all the news. I hope Martin [Royston] is with you, but if he is not please write to Mr Thomas Power, and tell him that he may study mathematics, & that will be necessary, if he shou'd go to the Military Academy. Ask him where he wishes the application to be made from? Texas or Alabama?

I am fearful my Love, that you have been annoyed by the fellow who took my horse, if he did take him!

My Dear, let my Guns, and shot pouch, be placed up stairs, and Sam's also, and neither to be touched. Let them be sit [sic] in a dry place. My love to all!

Thy devoted Husband
Sam Houston

Christmas 1850

My Dearest,

We are at Alexandria, taking freight, on the "Caddo" Steamer, and may be detained sometime. You will see that I have made but poor speed to what I expected when we parted. My trip to Red river was any thing but pleasant. I feel no bad effects from it.

Since I reached Grand Ecore, I have heard but little of the "cholera." There are no cases on the Boats. At all events, I will do all that I can to avoid it.

I send you some papers, in which, I hope, you will find some amusement, or entertainment. I have seen but few, as no Boats have recently brot papers.

You will see my Love, that I am compelled to write with a steel pen, my abhorrence.

Every day I feel more and more anxiety to be at home, and to remain there, the remainder of life. I need not tell you again how tenderly, <u>I love you</u>, and the affection, which [I] bear to the dear pledges of our mutual love.

I will tell you now my dear, that I think Mary Willie, one of the most beautiful children, that I have ever seen!!! Whether it is, that distance lends enchantment to the view, I will let you determine.

Commend me to Mother in affection, and render my love, and kisses to the children. Write to me long letters.

Thy devoted Husband
Sam Houston

Mobile
28th Decb 1850

My Dear Love,

I am here. I passed thro. N. Orleans, and made no stop as a Boat was ready at the Lake to sail. She got a ground [sic] at Grants pass, and detained us 12 hours. It is 9 P.M. and I am on board the Danl Pratt. We are to sail immediately. None of our folks, the captain tells me, are down from Perry. I have I suppose[d] he meant our Niece, and thought she embraced <u>all</u>!

I intend to write to some one of the family from here, but dont know which. I arrived this evening at 4 P.M. and we are to be off at 8 A.M. tomorrow. I intend to go by Raleigh N. C. I do not expect to write again until I reach the city. We are no[t] stop[ping] an hour at any one place! Christmas has passed without my realising [sic], that it had come! It will if we have luck, be in the city on five days. I fell in with two Virginians, & they were lately in Texas. We travel in company to Raleigh. My love to Mother and the weans.

Thy ever devoted Husband
Houston

If Sam should require a special remembrance, tell him my Dear, if he will be a good Boy, and obey you, he will make me very happy.

P.S. The first letter which you write, tell me the No. of your shoes. 4 I think. Write to me soon for any thing you want. As I cant send you apples, I send you apple seeds. They are good. I have written to Teene,[1] and told her to write to you!

Ever thine
Houston

[1]Margaret's niece, Serena Royston.

Washington
7th Jany [1851]

My Dearest,

Today at 4 P.M. I arrived safe and my friends were delighted. Many have called to see me, and have kept me up until the Town or city clock has struck 12. My trip has been so long, that you may be anxious, so I will not sleep until I write you. Tomorrow if I live, I intend to write you a long letter, but not to tell you how much I love you, for that would be <u>impossible</u>. My friend Tom Shankland[1] is with me, and has quoted no scriptures. He sends his best respects to you, and Sam.

My Love to all

Thy devoted Husband
Sam Houston

[1]Thomas Shankland was a New York judge. Friend, 340.

Washington
8th Jany [1851]

My Dearest,

Last night I wrote to you, to say that I was here, and safe. My trip was any thing but pleasant, and you will see by the dates, that it was tedious also. I rejoice, that my health was not affected by my exposure. I was never in better health, than I am at this moment. I was fearful, while I was wet, and cold, that when the occasion passed off, I wou'd feel the effects remain.

To day I resumed my seat in the chamber of the Senate, where I now write. I was greeted by the Senators, with the greatest cordiality, and apparent good feeling. I have many things to gratify my feelings, in my present situation, which can exist in the absence of my family. With <u>all those things</u>, as Sam said, I cannot be happy tho. in some respects, gratified. The aspects of the political horizon, is as my friends wish it to be. To avoid allusion to it, hereafter, I will send you news-papers, marked, so as to call your attention, to <u>items</u>, without the trouble, of looking over the whole paper. I will not let my feelings enter into any <u>canvass</u>[1] so far, as to involve my happiness in the event of a miscarriage, or failure. My friends are as sanguine, as they can well be!

You may rely upon it, that it is with pleasure, I have counted the days which I am to stay here, if I live. They amount to fifty-five only! These when I look forward with pleasing anxiety, as the time seems short, compared to other sessions. I have lost nothing by my absences, up to this time. The session will pass without much important being transacted. A good state of feeling seems to exist, so far as I can judge. Genl Cass has been, and is yet making strong efforts to arrange matters for a nomination,[2] but only renders his defeat more apparent. Every one inquires particularly, for "Mrs. Houston's welfare."

My love to all.

Thy devoted
Houston

[1]Houston is referring to the presidential election.
[2]For more information see Andrew C. McLaughlin, *Lewis Cass* (New York: Houghton, Mifflin and Company, 1898), 280–81.

Huntsville, Texas
Jan. 10th, 1851

My dear husband,

By last mail I read yours from Alexandria. It was a great source of joy and gratitude to me, to know that you were then in good health, but your detention must have been very tedious and annoying. I shall look with great anxiety for a letter from Washington, and shall be so happy when I know that you are safely over the fatigue and dangers of the journey. If this can make me happy, how much greater will be my happiness, when me meet again with the hope of being together, till death shall part us.

Since I wrote last, I have had a sick family. Our three youngest have suffered from a distressing diarrhea which is prevailing in the vicinity. Nannie and Maggie I feared had strong symptoms of cholera, but they are now nearly well. I am more pleasantly situated, than I have ever been during your absence. In getting rid of our farm and hands, I feel as if I had thrown off a little world. I do hope that you will abandon the idea of cultivating this place at all. If we ever have another farm, let it be at a greater distance from town.[1]

Miss Goree and Miss [Ellen] Kittrell are still with me, and their society is very cheering to me. They are very intelligent girls, and their manners are quite superior to the generality of our Texas girls. We talk a great deal about you, and when you get home, I think we will make a happy little circle.

Mr. [James] Maxey arrived at home, a few days ago, accompanied by Mrs. Mosely, Mrs. [Virginia] Maxey's mother. She is a fine cheerful old lady. Mr. Maxey saw cousin Ovid Eiland during his visit to Macon, Miss. He was quite pleased with him, and says he is highly respected in his neighborhood. He was chairman of a union meeting while he was there and takes an active part in that question. Mr. Maxey gave him a full history of my recent trials,[2] which astonished him very much. He is anxious to come to Texas and so soon as he can sell his property in Miss, he intends to come. Please send him a paper now and then "Judge Ovid Eiland, Macon, Miss." The Gothites are as busy as ever with their machinations. Mrs. [Jane] Wilson went out a few days ago to see Dr. Evans' family and questioned them very closely to ascertain what they know of me in Alabama. I do not think she was very well pleased with the result of her visit. Wilson's store reminds me of the fabled upas tree.

Sam is studying a little at home, but does not improve very fast. I must tell you some of Sam's smartness. I mentioned to you before, that he is smitten with Ellen Kittrell. Her father teases with her some-times about getting rid of her, and says any gentleman that wished to marry her may have her for a cow & a calf. Sam on hearing this proposed that she should marry some other person first, and he could pay the cow & calf and then die, and afterwards he could get her for nothing. This is some of Sam's financeering [sic]. Please do not forget to send me the different volumes of Peter Parley's geography for him.[3] You will see Mr. Sam Smith I presume, and I expect he could bring them to me. I wish you also to get me "Kingley's social chair."

Kitty is about the same that you left her. If I suppose it will encourage her in improving herself for you to bring her any presents, I will tell you of it. At present I do not. If I can possibly do so, I will write to you twice a week, and do you my dearest write as often as you can.

Ever thine own,
M. L. Houston

[1]Houston had transferred part of his farm to Henderson Yoakum on December 11, 1850. Walker County Record Book B-1, 134. "Property Bought and Sold by Sam Houston and Wife, Margaret: Period From 1847–1858." Information from Deed Records, James D. Patton, County Clerk, Walker County, Huntsville, TX. Manuscript dated 1989.

[2]Margaret is referring to the charges of abusing Virginia Thorn. Margaret had been indicted by the Walker County Grand Jury on September 25, 1850. Walker County Court Minutes, Book A, 274.

[3]Samuel J. Goodrich wrote books for children under the name of Peter Parley. Nevins, *Ordeal of the Union*, 34.

Washington

12th Jany [1851]

My Dear Love,

Yours of the 25 ulto,[1] has reached me tonight. I was quite uneasy until it arrived. Col Yoakum also sent me a letter about the horse.
I need say no more about that, as I have already written to you touching the matter. I am quite uneasy for fear the small Pox may have
reached you before the children, and servants were vaccinated. I did
it as I should. As to the affair of Martin [Royston], I will duly express
my regrets. I wrote to Serena [Royston] on my way here, and told her
how matters were, but said nothing angry. I am provoked beyond all
measure, and regard Tom [Power][2] as a poor creature and will not
change my opinion. I hope you wrote again? To day is Sunday and I
have been perplexed with visitors beyond all measure, and if I am
spared, it shall cease for the future. I am sorry that my friend Palmer,
has had trouble, but I must recompense him. As to the hire of the
servants, I can say nothing. If you hired out Joshua for the year, it is
done, and it must remain so. I mentioned to Col Yoakum that Mr [E.
M.] Smith of the Steam mill wou'd hire Joshua for a few months. I
am sorry that you distrust my Pea speculation, for really, I do not in
the least, if any thing is certain, it would be [sic]. Not Peas alone, but
Rice, Rye, and Barley would secure us milk, & Butter thro. the winter, in abundance. The letters sent to me, I will with much pleasure,
give direction to as you desire. Jack Houston, and my friend [Joseph]
Lewis, being present when your letters arrived, fearing that I might
be a too partial Judge, I submitted your letter to Mr [George] Law to
their criticism, and as it "passed muster," admirably, I will send it by
next mail. I will also send Kittys to the care of Cousin Bob McEwen.

You will wish to know something of matters here, and of them I
can tell you that I went on friday to the Levee of the President. I
found Mrs Fillmore,[3] a large matronly, and homely Lady. Clever no
doubt. Her daughter[4] is not handsome but genteel! The scene was
crowded, and a thousand inquires for Mrs Houston, by Ladies &
Gentlemen. And the little Houstons came in for a share also. There is
a great opposition to my resigning, but thus far it has produced no

change upon my determination. Genl Rusk will not hear of it on any terms. I have seen a Lady from the South who was once at Fort Jessup, and she assured me that she suffered as much with asthma as any one could do, until she came North, and that she is now robust & fat. I do not say this to disincline you to resignation, but state it as a fact. If you could have come on with me, it might have been well. I am invited to a Great Temperance celebration at New York on the 24th of Feby, at Tripler Hall, the finest Hall in America, and will contain 5,000 persons. It was built for Jenny Lynds [sic] concerts. It is intended to have [in] it the greatest display, that has ever been in the Union! I have not yet accepted the invitation, but think I will do so. The intention is for me to address the meeting. I feel a little scary, as it will be upon so vast a scale, to what I have been used. You will I hope have notice in time, (as you will not be there,) to wish me good luck.

You mention Wilsons faults. My Dear, dont think of them, if you can avoid it. I am happy to hear of the health of you all, and to know that Sam regrets my absence. I hope it will be so no more! Kiss them all tenderly for me. My love to Mother, & howda to Kitty. I will write whenever I can, and as long as I can.

Salute our friends.

Thy Husband
Houston

[In the margin:] Poor McDonald! he has paid the great debt at last!!

[1]No letter from Margaret for the date December 25, 1850, has been located.
[2]Thomas Power was married to Sarah Ann Royston, the sister of Serena and Martin.
[3]Abigail Powers. "Millard Fillmore," *World Book Encyclopedia*, vol. 7 (Chicago: World Book Incorporated, 1995), 101.
[4]Mary Abigail Fillmore. Ibid.

Washington
18th Jany 1851

My Dear Wife,

Since I last wrote, I have been looking, and hoping for another letter. I am happy that more than half the Session has now passed, and that I may hope to leave here for home, and its joys, in less than six weeks. I need not complain of the pains of absence. Complaint will not lessen them. You see my Dearest, that my mind is made up to stay, and abide at home, tho. very few seem to think (should I live) that I can have that pleasure long, as the canvass seems now to have commenced, by skirmishes and maneuvering, by some of the light troops, of the avowed candidates, in the next election. You may my Dear, feel assured that I will not allow myself, to be troubled, about this matter. To me it seems strange, that men who are much older, than myself, should engage with passion, in the pursuit of Fame, when it seems to me, that they would be more wise, were they to enjoy, the reputation which they have acquired, in the bosom of their families, and the circle of their friends. But for such pleasures, they seem to have no relish, but eschew all rest, and tranquility. I hope, we are soon to be free, from agitation, and the country at peace and rest. We are surely the most glorious people on earth, and if we are wise, we will rival the fame, as well as the happiness of, all the nations, who have gone before us.

This morning I sent you a "Sartain" [sic] from my friend Mr Lewis, and I was amused to see that in choosing a present for you, he should have fitted our son, so well in the Frontice [sic] piece. Some thing throws, symbols of Glory in Sam's path. Well My Dearest, they will not change his destiny, from the ordination of Providence. I wish him a Holy, a useful, and a happy one! You are with him, and can best judge of his character. I know you will do all that you can, [to] mould it in the most perfect shape. At times my love, I think I can hear your voice, and see the smiles, of our little ones. They are worth to me, not only all that I see in the world of happiness, but I esteem them worth all, that I could fancy beside them. I long to see, and be with you again, & say "we will not part again, as we have done." After the 15th of Feby, you need not write to me, unless you write to Memphis, Grand Ecore, or Nacogdoches.

Thine Ever, Houston

[Written across the margin:] When I send you bundles of papers marked, you may if you choose send them to Col Yoakum when mother & yourself have read them!!!

Washington,
24th Jany 1851

My Dearest,

But one letter has reach me from you, up to this date. Tis true, that but one mail from Huntsville has arrived since I reached here. I am willing to charge it, to high waters, or the irregularity of the mails. I hope that is all, but I assure you my Dear Love, that does not satisfy my anxious desire to hear from you, and our dear little chicks. You are all present to my mind, and heart, and cling around me in every scene. On my walks, in my room, at church, in the Halls of Legislation, and the last dreamy thought, as I sink to repose! Yes, my Love, you are indeed, a large portion of my existence. Forty days only remain, for my confinement at this place as I hope!

I have not written to you as often as formerly, because your letters have not as usual reached me, and because my time is consumed with company, to an extent, much greater, than it has ever been. Were I to write as much, or as often as I have heretofore done, I wou'd not have half my necessary repose! I am under promise to you not to speak of politics, but to send you the papers. This I will do to some extent. I will at least send you some of them!

I am under promise to visit Philadelphia, and deliver a Lecture, which is intended to aid in building, a church, for the "Fire-men of Southwalk," where the late riots have taken place.[1] Many Senators, and Representatives have,[2] or will lecture for the purpose named. I did not wish [to] unite, but they have invited, and at last sent for me, and my friends urge me to go. It will take place in the "musical fund Hall, " on the 28 inst. What subject do you suppose, my dear, I have chosen for a lecture?[3] It is Indian Characters etc. This I thought, would be the best suited to a "border man." It [is] one too, that I understand, as well as any one can, and if I should not succeed in telling well, what I do know, there will be no one present, I presume, that would be able to criticize my facts. It was desired that I should lecture on Texas, as a subject, or the Incidents of the Revolution. I did not chuse this theme, because I must not either say "I" so often, or mean the same thing, and it would savor, of egotism, and since I became a son of Temperance, you have not imputed that to me.

I will try, and make a decent lecture, and I would be much more happy in making the speech, if you were here to go with me, and write the notes for me, preparatory to my speaking. You [have] done so, on other occasions, and if you were here, I wou'd be inexpressibly happy, that I might tax you again. When the matter is over, I will write to you, and tell you what I think of my effort, or send you the newspaper notices! I think that I stated to you in my last, that I have consented to address the New York Mother Society, on the 24th of February (if I live and have luck).

I wish you wou'd send me if there is time, after you receive this letter, a description of the summer dress, that you wish me to bring you. If you shou'd not, I will bring one to suit my own notions, and I hope it will suit you precisely.

I have heard that Charles & Tom Power, are, or have been recently at Galveston, but no farther than the fact. I have not heard from our kindred in Alabama, or in Tennessee only from Bro. Will. He sends for himself, & family all love to you, and our babies. I am at a loss to know why they do not write to us, or to me, in answer to my last letter, from Alabama. They may have written to you, as I requested them to do, in my letter. However, it does seem to me, that they had as well be located, in Irving's "sleepy hollow," as in that Cane brake region! Now, my Love, I will write as often as I can. To day I did not attend the Senate as I have been busy all day in my room. My love to all.

Thy husband truly,
Houston

[1]See Griffith Owen to Sam Houston, January 13, 1851. A. J. Houston Collection #3945, Texas State Archives, Austin, Texas. The invitation to lecture stated that the Church had been destroyed by a "violent tornado" on December 22, 1849, at a loss of over $2000.
[2]Henry S. Foote had previously spoken. Ibid.
[3]Owen suggested that Houston speak on "trials and difficulties of our frontier settlements, as verified in the history of Texas, and exemplified in your own personal experience, and observation, and then close your address with a declaration of Texas' devotion to the Federal Union." Ibid.

Washington
26 Jany 1851

My Beloved,

The sun of another sabbath has set, and I am seated to write you again in bad spirits. Only one letter from you, has reached me here. I am unhappy, as to the cause. You may have written many, or you may be ill, and not able to write, and no one is prepared to tell me of the fact. I know in my situation you will think my uneasiness is reasonable, and natural. To night I hope to receive several. I was at church, and heard Bro. [James] Huckins of Texas, make a very interesting discourse, on aids to the church of Texas. I hope he will succeed well. I intend to go again to night, to hear him, and then finish my letter.

My Dear, I did not go to church, as I thought when I paused. I was called on by company, from New York, and found when they left, that it was too late, for the sermon. When this letter is ended, I intend to read the Testament, for the balance of the evening. With the year I commenced the Testament, and have read a chapter, for every day, thus far. It is my intention, to read one every day of the year. It may be, that the Lord will bless my imperfect hopes, & prayers. All the attention, that we can give to the scriptures, is not wasted, tho. it may not profit us, as much as we desired. The whole evening has passed away, and the last mail has come in, for to night, & yet no letter from home. Indeed my Dear Love, I am unhappy, lest something may have prevented you from writing, of an unpleasant character! If I could, I would fly to our home! I count each day, with anxious feelings, and fervent prayers, for your happiness, and safety. Each day, only increases my solicitude to see, and be with you, at our own hearth! I will hope, my dearest, that you will not be annoyed, by vile enemies and the wicked, who have sought to harass you, and persecute you![1] Tis now past midnight, and I am much disappointed, by not getting a letter, or letters, that I feel as tho. I had slept. If I can find time tomorrow, I will try, and write to you. At all events, so soon as I can get a letter from you! No letters from Alabama. One thing affords me some consolation, and that is—no mail I think, has come from Huntsville, but one, since my arrival. I hope high waters are the cause, of my not receiving letters, and that I will soon get them, with good tidings. Present my love to mother, & kisses to the children!

Thy ever devoted Husband
Houston

[1]Houston was referring to the grand jury indictment and trial Margaret was facing.

Washington
31st Jany 1851

My Dear Love,

I was made very happy last night on my return from Philadelphia,[1] by the receipt of your letters of the 3rd & 12th Inst.[2] Indeed I was gratified, for I had been unhappy, or rather miserable, for fear something had happened, or worst of all that you were sick. From y[our] letter, I felt almost, as if I were with you all, while I was reading your description of house scenes.

But I must first write of business. Until I return, (if I live) I will pay mother, the same interest on her money, that she could get from any one else, if it is 10 percent. I hope to take home with me some two thousand dollars in cash, and leave no debts behind me. I hope my dear that no one will be allowed to ride my horse, and please say to Bingley, if the horse should attempt to rub his tail to grease it, so that he can not rub the hair off it. So soon as the oats are large enough to pasture, let the mare, my colt, and the mule colt run of the part, out of the garden part. My horse may at times be put on it. I am gratified, that the trade was made, by Col Yoakum, and hope you will say to him, how much I am delighted. The exchange was against the North, was the reason he did not draw on me! This was proper. I intend to write soon to him, but if I do not, ask him to get Mr Heath[3] to take such of the hands as are at home, & have my Thompson place[4] burned round, so that if the woods should be burned near the place my <u>fence</u> will be safe! I may have to cultivate the place, or a part of it this year. You did not tell me, my dear, that all the clearing was done, that I left for Prince, and Bingley to do! The Col. can give for me to Mr Heath, <u>five</u>, or <u>ten</u> dollars, to burn around my place. It is important that it should be done, and that stock shou'd not run on it.

My Love, I am happy that you have such agreeable company, as the young Ladies of whom you speak. I was much amused at Sam's financial tact, for I have been quite deficient, in respect to trading. I think my Dear, it is a little like Sam's long spear. You will recollect the "one about as <u>long</u> as six long trees." I do hope the Young Ladies may remain with you, so long as I am absent, and as long as they please after my return. I hope you will all be healthy and happy!

I send you many papers which you will find marked, and after you have perused them you can send them to my friend Col Yoakum, and he can retain them or return them to you, if you desire it! I will leave the whole matter to you. You will see what is said about the Lecture, in Philadelphia. It was as well done, as any thing, that you ever heard me do, unless it was to tell you how much I love you! You may be judge, if I ever let it appear!

I saw Albert Goodall, and he was anxious to see me. He is a clever fellow. I saw [Thomas] Gotts letter to Crawford,[5] which was sent to Albert [Goodall], and in a few days, he will send to me a copy of it, and a letter to you, which I will forward, so soon as they arrive. They will be a great consolation to you, but Mr Gotts will provoke you, and kill him off, if it is not done already. I told Albert everything, and he is gratified. You will be amused, at Mr. Gotts, important, and self-complacent letter.[6] He is a very dog! I have not time to read or correct this letter.

My love to mother. Kisses to the children, and the young Ladies.*

Thy Husband truly
Houston

[In the margin:] *I forgot, you dont love kissing!!

[1]For a copy of the speech see *Writings,* vol. 5, 267–81.
[2]Margaret's letters for these dates have not been located.
[3]This was probably Simon Peter Heath, who lived next to the Thompson farm. Carpenter, 2013.
[4]For information on this property, which Houston purchased from Andrew and Ellen Cummings Thompson, see Walker County Deed Book Vol. B-2, page 151.
[5]A. C. Crawford ran the oldest mercantile business in Galveston. Charles W. Hayes, *Galveston: History of the Island & the City* (Austin: Jenkins Garret Press, 1974), 880–81. Gott was attempting to recover money from the estate of Virginia Thorn's mother, Elizabeth Goodall Thorn Worcester. Virginia Thorn Papers.
[6]None of these letters have been located.

Washington
31st Jany 1851

My beloved,

To day I wrote to you, and was in good spirits, comparatively happy. To night I write again, in profound sorrow. This morning my friend [David] Kaufman arose from his home in health, & as usual, went to the House, was attentive to his duties, and called upon me in the Senate about two o clock. We conversed for a while, on business. I thought he looked pale, but did not think it worthy of remark. We parted, and I wrote my letter to you. About four oclk we adjourned the Senate, and I came down, and dined. I had risen, and stepped into the hall of the Hotel, at five o clock, when a messenger accosted me, and told me that Mrs Kaufman wished to see me. I said "Mrs Kaufman?" He replied, "Yes sir. Mr Kaufman is dead." I hastened to the scene of woe. He lay a corps [sic], still warm, and with his natural glow of countenance. There sat his bereaved spouse, in all the agony, of silent grief, and his little daughter[1] unconscious that she was an orphan. There is a dignity in silent anguish, and affectionate sorrow. It was not long before Mrs Cushman, and Mrs K.'s Sister were with her, but this only added to her anguish. Genl Rusk, Col Howard[2] & myself did, (and will do all in power,) to alleviate her distress. Col Kaufman had returned from the capitol soon after we parted, and complained of a pain, in the breast. He said his heart felt heavy, and was like lead. He lay down, and sent for a Physician. It was but a short time until he came, but he only arrived in time to see my friend expire. The last gasp was upon his lips! It was supposed to be a disease of the heart. This morning he had said to his wife, that he felt a slight pain in the breast, but seemed not to apprehend anything from it. How sudden, & solemn are such admonitions, to the living, and how little heard! It is another warning, to us, that "in the midst of life, we are in death." I will try, and redouble my exertions, that I may be ready, when the summons does come! It is in the power, of God, to give us hearts for preparation, and for this we can pray, & hope, and may the Lord keep us, from the power of Sin!

Thy devoted Husband,
Houston

[1]Six year-old Anna Kaufman. Carpenter, 1685.
[2]Indian agent, George Thomas Howard. For a biography see Frederick C. Chabot, *Genealogies of early San Antonio Families (The Makers of San Antonio),* (San Antonio, Texas: Privately Published by the Artes Graficas, 1937), 344–45.

Washington
8th Febry 1851

My Dear Love,

I write again, as I am seated in the Senate, & a dry posing speech is making by a bad speaker.

Since my last, I have nothing more to say. The time is passing while I may be detained here. I assure you my Dear, that I am most truly tired of this place! There is not one source of joy here, that I can find. There is a listlessness with Congress, that takes away, all interest in Legislation. So for as I am concerned, I feel fully bent, on staying with you, and our little chicks, while others are working on, in a way to suit themselves. I propose to try, and be rational, and reason, as well as truth says <u>love your family, and stay with them</u>!!! If I live, I surely will never again, come here to spend a long session without you, and Mother will not consent for you to come, and you will not come without our little ones. You say I may look out for a place here near the city for you, and the children, If I conclude to remain longer in the Senate. This I have thought on, and inquired about. That may be done. I will not resign, until I go home, if spared to do so!

My purpose is, to let you make an unbiassed [sic] decision. I will not seek to influence you in the decision, which you may make, on the subject. I assure you my Dear, that I would not exchange your society, for all the honors, of this world without it. In a former letter you bid me to forgive you for any bad temper, or unseemly expressions used by you! I will do so my Love, with great pleasure, provided you will forgive me at the same time. If you do, I will make the best of the bargain, for you will have more to forgive than I have! If you can be free to make this bargain, I will be delighted with it, and endeavor, never to break it, in word, or deed! Life is too short, to trifle with happiness, and it is a tender flower, and will only grow with the hearts culture!

Thine Ever,
Houston

The following letter is from the Temple Houston Morrow Collection of Houston Materials in the Barker History Center, University of Texas, Austin, Texas.

Huntsville
Feb. 8th, 1851

My ever dear husband,

I was greatly dissappointed [sic] at not getting a letter from you by last night's mail. There was a mail from New Orleans, but no letter from you. I am consoled by the reflection, that but a few weeks of our painful seperation remain, and if I could get your letters regularly, I would be comparatively cheerful, but whenever a dissappointment occurs, I am completely unnerved. Well I do hope, that I shall never again be required to exercise my fortitude in the same way. Not that I expect you to resign, for I find that your friends are so opposed to it, that I hardly think you will carry out your original purpose, but I do not think you will leave me again. As I mentioned to you before, I would like for you to select a pleasant boarding house for us about 8 or 10 miles from the city. There are many arguments in favour of a country home, one which would weigh greatly with me, is that at night I would have your company, without being so much interrupted by visitors. Many other arguments will suggest themselves to your mind.

I believe there is not much news in Huntsville that would interest you at this time. But one marriage has occurred lately. Miss Baker[1] and Mr. Scott,[2] the Presbyterian minister. They were married in the morning, and set of[f] for Cincinatti [Texas] to spend a few days. Mrs. Matthews[3] was to give them a supper. Mr. Baker[4] married them himself.

I have heard that bro. William was elected mayor of Memphis,[5] so I fear he has declined coming to Texas. If so I regret it exceedingly. But I would act towards him as I do towards my relations, would not take the responsibility of urging him to come. I hope however he has only post-poned coming and not given it up altogether. When you see him and sister Mary, tell them if they could see their little namesake,[6] I know they would be proud of her. I think she is very intellectual, and her beauty is the admiration of every one who sees her. Her beautiful hair is considered quite remarkable. The children are all well. Sam studies a little, but is more fond of play. Nannie and Maggie are as wild as antelopes, but I think they are very sweet children.

As this is my last letter but one, to Washington, I will remind you of my summer bonnet. If you have not had a dress made for me, when you get this, I expect it will be too late, so I will just get you to ask for the latest patterns. And now my love, let me beg you not to think of bringing these things if they will be at all in your way coming home. You can just send them round with your other baggage.

I send you a purse which I thought would please you, as it is rather unique. Mother is not well, and I fear her health is seriously failing.

The young ladies Miss Kittrell and Miss Goree are with me, and send their compliments to you. They say they realy wish you would come home, they had such a curiosity to see you. You can imagine from whose description it arises.

Thy ever devoted wife
M. L. Houston

[1]Theodorah Baker. Identified in Carpenter, 2004.
[2]Hamilton Scott. Ibid., 2005.
[3]Margaret is probably referring to Florah (Mrs. Robert) Mathews. Ibid., 2026.
[4]Daniel Baker, a Presbyterian minister and father of the bride. Ibid., 2004.
[5]No documentation of this has been located, so it is possible Margaret was mistaken.
[6]Mary Willie Houston.

The following letter is missing the first eight pages. It was filed in the original collection with letters from 1851. It is included at this point because of references to a speech in Philadelphia. However, it is also possible that the fragment is from a letter of June, 1846, as Houston also made a speech in Philadelphia at that time.

. . . it has been of service to his success. I hope he may succeed well, for truly we need help in Texas.

I learn that my speech in Philadelphia, had a most happy influence, and has given an impulse, to the purposes of the society, which it was designed to aid. Truly my object was not displaced, and if good has grown out of it, I feel richly compensated, for all my efforts. If I have rendered one human being more virtuous, more comfortable, & happy, I feel that I have only discharged the duty of a good citizen.

I know my Love, that you will rejoice, that it had fallen to my lot, to be useful, in a cause which affects the moral, or physical condition, of our fellow men! and may insure their improvement, or secure their bliss. I will never cease my efforts, to benefit the human race! I am no zealot, but I feel, that I am a man, & bound as such, to aid my fellow men!

My Love, I have returned from dinner, and will finish this page, before I start to church. I learn my Dear, that there are no less than thirty churches in this place. With a population of thirty thousand souls, you will suppose, they have at least the means of Grace, if they would only improve them. The people appear to me, as tho' it is matter, of form, or fashion. The heart does not seem to be engaged, and only the eyes. A few Sundays since I was amused at Mr <u>Sprole</u>,[1] when rebuking the Ladies, about their fashions. He said they were not satisfied, with the forms, & proportions, which their Creator had given them, but they must give themselves new ones, and by their fashions, had given themselves the shape of <u>wasps</u>! This I thought a delicate subject, and led to many reflections, more amusing, than appropriate for the sabbath. Indeed it would astonish you, to see the <u>bustle</u>-ing, which fills the pavements of the avenues, or the drawing rooms of the city. They keep others at a good distance I guess! I can only speak for myself, and I know, that I do not come, in contact with them!

By this time my Love, you would (or will) be tired reading, and I might stop, but I will continue to persecute you, by writing more! My Love I have been to church and witnessed the administration of the sacrament. The church of the Baptists, was shut, as there was no preaching this afternoon. I then went to a Presbyterian Church, where I had never been. There is one thing here, which I have noticed, and it is the rise of leavened bread, for the sacraments! It was not so, when I first witnessed the ceremony, nor do I recollect ever to have seen it, until I came here. It seems to me, as tho' the design was to do matters, in a cheap, & common way. I am sorry to see it! These things, ought to be, regarded in form, as well as in spirit.

Do not my dear think that I intend any reflection, upon the holy ordinance. No! Indeed my Love! nothing is farther from my design. I hope never to feel a disposition, while I live, but these are things, which can not pass unnoticed.

As usual my Love, the bag, at the end of the pole, was poked at me, and for the first time, I was found without one cent less than a $5 note. I do wish they would let me know, when they will make their singular collections. If they will do this, I will be prepared! and contribute "with pleasure," as our boy wou'd say. Dear Boy! I would rather see him now, and his dear mother, than to have the proudest sceptre, on the face of the Globe!

If I ever had ambition, I am now cured of it entirely. Fame may suit the young, and those who have not passed through so many various scenes, as I have done! If spared to pass down a lengthened vale of years, I hope to enjoy a tranquil evening, and be prepared, for the setting sun of life, and the dawn, of a happy immortality. I apologized long since, in my letter for its length, and yet I continued to write.

I will mention one fact. To day I had fire in my room, and fancied it pleasant. Now it is raining hard, and has been for hours. It is now about 9 o clock, and I must conclude on the 15th page.

You will please to present my love, to all the family. Give my respects to the Palmers, and the neighbours. Tell all the servants, that I expect them to do their duty, as faithful servants.

Give my Love to our Dear Boy, and tell him how much his Pa loves him, and is very happy to hear, that he is a good boy, and good to his Ma! He must do all that his Ma tells him, and he must pray to his good Father, for his Ma, & Pa, and his Grand Ma.

Thy faithful & devoted Husband
Sam Houston

301 : December 17, 1850–March 10, 1851

[1]Houston is probably referring to Presbyterian minister Thomas Sproull.

Senate Chambers
12th of Feby 1851

My Love,

I have just spoken in the Senate, on the subject of creating Genl. [Winfield] Scott a Lieutenant General.[1] I am opposed to it, & when my speech is published I will send you a copy.

I write a few lines only, that I may, send you this, with a letter of Cousin Columbus. You will like to see it, as it speaks well, of our relations prospects, of getting out of debt. You will too see what he says about politics.

I can only add, that I will write to you a long letter, so soon as I can.

Give my love to Mother and the children! Has Maggy learned her catechism? I would be delighted again to hear her, if she should ever place Sam before the flood in his origin.

You will please present me to the young Ladies, and I hope they will stay with you until I get home. If Miss Kittrell pleases you, I will let Sam have a cow to trade for her. You may advance him one, if you think proper, and I will pay you. Say so to him!

Thy devoted Husband
Sam Houston

[1]For a copy of this speech see *Writings,* vol. 5, 284–86.

Washington
15th Febry 1851

My Dear Love

Two days since I commenced writing, a letter to you, to say that I had been out shopping for you, that morning. I found a Miss Nesbit, from Georgia, whom I took to be precisely your size. She is the same hight [sic], and seems to be your person. If I had placed my arm around her, I could [have] told precisely, but as I did not ask the privilege, I had to risk the fit. I hope you will be pleased with the selection, which was made of articles! The summer dress, is silk plaid, and the morning dress, is a white muslin, or spotted muslin. It is very tasteful, and the silk has beautiful <u>sleeves</u>, very wide, and edging, on the dress. They are what I call "very <u>nice</u>." The Bonnet is of linnen [sic], and straw, with flowers on the side, and <u>inside</u>. It is trimmed with green Ribbon. You will have to wear, white sleeves, with the silk dress, and these I intend to take you. Now my Love, such other things, as I fancy, I will take to you, if spared, to reach my dear Wife!! A pair of plain Bracelets would be very pretty, but you will not wear jewelry! I will tell you, of a present sent to me from California. It is a large Gold Ring,[1] from a friend of my early days.

On friday morning the 20th, I hope to leave here for Harrisburg, Penna, where, I am invited by many members of the Legislature, and the Ladies of the place hearing of it, have invited me to Lecture for the Benefit of a church.[2] This I have consented to do. From thence I intend to visit New York to make a Temperance Speech![3] I am invited to many places, but have declined going. I hope I may do some good for the cause. It is worthy of better services than mine. I tell you about these matters because, I know you will derive pleasure from the facts.

You will feel assured, that any danger of a relapse has passed by, and that I will never decline, in my purposes, but endeavor by my example to stablish [sic] others in the principles, and practices of the Order of "Love, Purity, & Fidelity."

My greatest happiness, on this earth, is to assure you of whatever will promote your happiness. For indeed My Love, I am willing to confess, that I love you more, than I ever did, if such a thing is possible, but this is wasting paper, for I am sure you believe all this without its repetition. If it were not that a croaking speaker, is at <u>work</u>, I might convert this, into a <u>love letter</u>, but how can poetry, love, and politics harmonize? 'Tis impossible! Well, this is for your own eyes, and not to be seen by the young Ladies. If they see my letters, and they should ever marry, as no doubt they soon will, & their husbands do not write more love, than I do, they will sit down in the corner, and there the dear creatures will nearly cry their eyes out. It is to save them from any anguish that I would say, keep my letters from them. It is more easy to prevent sorrow, than it is to cure a canker, in the sweet bud, of affection. It will be a fine thing for me, if I live to resign, to travel with you, and Lecture on <u>love</u>, <u>courtship</u>, <u>& affection</u>, as well as <u>conjugal</u> <u>propriety</u>! If I lecture in Texas, you may promise the young Ladies "free tickets" for the course of lectures.

Present my love to Mother, and Sam, & kisses to our dear Babes! Respects to all our friends.

Thy faithful & devoted husband
Sam Houston

[1]The record for Margaret's estate lists a gold ring. Roberts, 371. It is unknown where the ring is now.
[2]The Episcopal church at Harrisburg. Friend, 213.
[3]The speech was for the Sons of Temperance. Ibid.

Washington
18th Feby 1851

My Dear Love,

I will try, and write to you acknowledging your last date, the 29th ultimo.[1] The receipt of the enclosure from you, of Bro Henrys letter gave me pleasure, because he is doing well. I do esteem, and love him much. He feels well about your case, or as he should do. Last night I received from A. G. Goodall the papers of which I spoke to you in a former letter.[2] I will enclose them to you so soon as I go to my room. I am now in the Senate.

You need not fear my Love, if I live, that all the whole earth, can keep me from court.[3] You must not intimate, that I intend to be home, but say that I may return by Galveston. It is true that I may do so, but it is not my intention now, to do so. You can say, that I have spoken of that route!

It is my intention to write to you from New York, or from some place East if I go as I intend to do on the 21st, and not return until the 26th inst. About the farming matters my Dear, dont think of them! Let them be. My heart leaps with the hope of seeing you all well, & happy.

It is true that I have been unhappy about the children, and servants not being <u>vaccinated</u>. I sent to Ransom, & Keenan,[4] matter years ago, and they ought to be <u>punished,</u> for their delinquency. I hope nothing may happen, of a disagreeable nature, from their <u>worthlessness</u>. There are certain kinds of neglect, for which I would punish men, as soon as for crimes!

I am glad that Miss Crawford & Miss Baker have called upon you! They may have been influenced, as you suppose! I pray my Dear, that you may have had a pleasant time, when I get Home, if Providence should be so kind, as to enable me again to embrace you, & the children! If you sell corn, you ought to have, the <u>current price</u>. No one will thank you, to let them have it cheaper than the market price. Remember my Raven Hill man! He did not feel under my obligations for my kindness. Others may be like Mr Terry.[5]

Let the mare and colts on the oats so soon, as it is fit for use; and the calves to go in the Garden portion of oats. Make them take care of my pig. It may be stolen! Let [it] be looked to!

Thy ever devoted Husband
Houston

I have not time to read this.

[1]This letter has not been located.
[2]See Houston to Margaret, January 31, 1851. These papers have not been located.
[3]Margaret's trial was set for April 3, 1851. Houston did not want his enemies to know that he would be present.
[4]Both men were Huntsville doctors.
[5]Ben Terry, who lived next to Thomas Palmer in the Raven Hill area. Carpenter, 1538.

Washington

19th Feby 1851

My Dear Love,

I send you herewith the Goodall papers before mentioned to you.[1] You will see the foot tracks of Madam Birdwell, and Mr Wilson. I say, "under clothes." This shows whose the diction was. The composition is a piece with Mrs Wilsons "diary" as I imagine. What do you think? Two things I request! One is that you will not let these things tro[torn] or mother, and the other [is] you will not be troubled, about the farm, or hiring the hands. I hope all will be for the best.

It is now half past one oclock in the morning, and I find myself busy. So my Dear Love, goodnight.

Thy devoted,

Houston

[1]These papers have not been located.

Washington

20th Feby 1851

My Dear Love,

It is past noon, and I found myself this morning at 2 oclock writing to you. Do not think me importunate by telling you how much I love you, or if I do not tell you, to evince it by writing, so often. While in my seat in the Senate, I often fall more in love, with my own fancies, than the talking of others.

It is probable, that I may not have it in my power to write until my return. In the morning, my intention is to start at six oclock, and go to York, Penna, and pass the night there. Next morning I propose to go [to] Harrisburg, where I am to speak for the Ladies, so that they can build a church, or buy a <u>parsonage</u>. Then I intend to visit Phila, and attend church on sunday. On monday I propose to go to New York, and make my Temperance Speech! On tuesday I am invited to see the people, or shake hands with them, at the city Hall in the Governors Room. Then I have sundry invitations to make speeches that night. I may, or may not, speak for some of them. Some are Temperance Societies, & others Literary. You know my Dear, that I have very little pride, in <u>literature</u>!! Now you can guess, if I do speak, what my subject will be!

I was glad that you, and our Son, keep count of the days of <u>hope</u>. I assure you my Love, that I do count the days, with deep concern! I regard all, and every thing, which seperates me from my family, as an impediment to my happiness!

I fondly anticipate the hour, when I can embrace you, and call you <u>mine</u>!! I hope you will not let this assurance provoke you to anger! If I had thought, that it would provoke you, I would not have impressed the assurance, for your love is more to me, than all the world beside.

I write in haste. My love to Mother, and the children!

Thy Husband
Ever truly
Houston

Washington
28th Feby 1851

My Dear Love,

I write with the more pleasure, because I have not enjoyed the pleasure for a week past. Last night I returned from my trip to the North. You will desire to know how it succeeded, and ended. Well, I went to York in Penna, and spent one evening, and looked in upon a Military Ball, was introduced into the Room, and walked round it after being given a general introduction, stood a while, walked around, and returned to my Hotel. The next day I went to Harrisburg, where the Legislature was in session. I was there received, most kindly, and waited on by many persons. I found that the members of the Legislature, the Sovereigns, and the Ladies wou'd conflict. A meeting took place with the Ladies, and it was concluded, to give the Ladies $300, for their Parsonage, and I was to address the community at large.

This was done, in the Hall of Representatives, and I need not tell you, that they were pleased, and to that effect, I sent you a paper to day. I have not seen the local Paper, but suppose they puffed me. From thence, I went by way of Philadelphia to New York. I was received by all, with the most flattering demonstration. The day was rainy, and for three hours, before seven oclock, the rain poured down in torrents. I expected as the hall was large, that there would be but few persons, and the <u>failure</u> <u>manifest</u> and the elite are not votaries of Temperance. With these matters upon my mind I entered the Hall, and to my astonishment, I found the most brilliant audience, that I have ever seen, and a fair proportion, of <u>the</u> <u>fair</u>. I was first presented on the stage, as I entered by a private door! So soon as I was seen, the applause began, and continued, for many seconds. Prayers were offered by an eloquent Divine. Singing, and other ceremonies, preceded me, when I was introduced to the Audience, by the President of the National Temperance Society, where the applause was long, and deafening. I made the speech! It occupied about an hour, and thirty minutes. When I was done, the applause was renewed, and when that ceased, three hearty cheers were given.

The handkerchiefs of the Ladies, were flourished with great spirit. The audience was said to be more numerous, and the hall more crowded, than it ever was, to Miss Jenny Lynds concerts. It was supposed that there were present from five to six thousand persons. When the meeting was over, two carriages were in waiting to take me to Balls. One the "Young Guards" (Whig) and the "Washingtonians." Each one contained, (Room, I mean) about from six to eight hundred persons! I was introduced to both assemblies by the Presidents of the respective associations. At each Ball, as I entered the Band played "Hail to the Chief." I would not stay for supper, at either Ball, but left as soon as I could leave without giving offence [sic]! You will see by the papers which I send you, what the next day brot forth!

Well my Love, I declare to you, that all this display, and all the manifestations of approval, or admiration, did not afford me as much pleasure, and joy, & felicity, as to press you to my heart, or either one, of our little <u>ones</u>! So you need not for a moment suppose that any thing on earth can seduce my affections from home, and its endearments. I am not writing a love letter, unless it is matrimonial, for if it were purely a romantic sentiment, such as lovers <u>express</u> (at least) I would not <u>allude</u> to <u>children</u>! If I thought you would like it better, I could drop the children. You will appropriate the assurance as you please, for really, I woud be willing, to say, that I would not give one affectionate smile of yours for all the <u>fuss</u>, which took place. I[t] was gratifying to me, but did not awaken the tender affections of my heart.

My love to all.
Thine Ever,
Houston

Washington
5th Mar 51

My Dear Love,

Do not suppose, that because this is a call Session of the Senate it will detain me. I will leave here so soon as I can pack my Trunk and Boxes. I am to day to go, & pay the milliner, for some articles, which I have got for my Dear Wife, who by the bye, I hope very soon to see. I send you my Love, two letters, one from Miss Tene [Serena Royston] and one from Young [Lea Royston]. You will see that Young is scared about "<u>Oregon</u>." About this, he need have no fears. There would not be one Single State, of the whole <u>South</u>, but S. Carolina, that would not go for me, if I am the Democratic Nominee. They could not go against me. If they do, it would be an unaccountable freak indeed!

I would be glad that Serena was with us, but I cant go by for her. I would be delayed, if it were even proper to do so, and my anxiety, to see, and embrace my Dear "Esperanza"[1] and the little ones, that the prospect of a Sceptre would not cause me to pospone the pleasure. You will recollect my Dear Esperanza. She was my Love of days gone by, but which I hope soon to find renewed.

My love to all.

Thy devoted
Houston

[1]At their first meeting, Houston called Margaret his "Esperanza," a star of hope.

Washington
6th Mar 1851

My Dear Love,

I am yet here as you will see, and have done all in my power to get off. If I live, I will get off by saturday next, and hope to be home by the first of April or before! Your articles are all made, and I must say, that I hope to take you dresses & finery enough to have you well trimmed for our wedding. The Bonnets, and two dresses, are quite pretty, and such, as I am sure you will be pleased with them. If I stay another day, I think I will get another dress for you! I wish by all means, not only to see you smile, but to keep you smiling. If I live to reach home, in the evening, and I think the stage arrives late, I do not intend to make a display of them, <u>during the night</u>, as I think they will show <u>better</u>, in day light. But <u>this</u> <u>matter</u>, I will leave <u>to you</u>, my Dear !! I am not sure but I may get a suit for Sam. You can guess the colour. I will wager a kiss! You need not tell him, for I may be disappointed in getting one! As for Nannie, Maggy, and Mary, I will let you select for them. My task is confined to Ladies & Lads, but not little Girls!

I thank you for the purse, and will do anything in my power [for] Mrs. Dawson.[1]

Thy Lover
Houston

I have not time to read this.

[1]Houston is probably referring to Antoinette's friend Mrs. N. A. Dawson.

Senate Chamber
10th Mar 1851

My Dearest Love,

This morning I intend to start for home, and will not on any account, stop a moment, that I can avoid. I do not expect to see bro. William, or his family, as I pass on my way home. I intend to write to him, if I can stop for half an hour, & ask him, and Sister to come, and see us. I send to you some seeds. You can soak them in tepid water, for twelve hours, or twenty-four, before planting. If this, should beat me home, I can tell you that I have filled your order fully! Oh! such finery!!!

I am so anxious to get home, that I can think of nothing else, only to say that the call session has detained me until today!

My love to all, and respects to the young Ladies. Tell Sam not to marry until he can have the pleasure, of courting by love letters!

I am thy devoted Husband
Sam Houston

Chapter V

May 8, 1851–October 18, 1851

When Houston reached home he found that Margaret's case had been continued until early fall. He wrote the following letter to his cousin John (Jack) Houston, which is now in the Sam Houston Correspondence in the Barker History Center, University of Texas, Austin.

Huntsville Texas
8th May 1851

Dear Jack,

From toil, and labors, I have a few moments to write to a friend, and say all are well! I have been hard at work in my farm since my return, that I have injured the old wound in my right shoulder. So much so, that I can only write with difficulty. I must take rest, I find, from necessity, or I may make my self a cripple!

The persecution of my wife was not carried out. It was ascertained by the Judge, as is believed, that I would be at home the day before the trial which was to take place, on thursday the 3rd of apl. So he adjourned the court on monday previous, on account of a sick wife, as he said, but others said, it was because I was to be home, and present. I was at home on the 2nd of april. On the former mistrial,[1] tho a <u>packed</u> jury, he had acted imfamously [sic], I learn! It was a malicious conspiracy, and intended to affect me! It will have an end!!!

I am anxious to hear from my God daughter,[2] and Mrs. H. is very anxious to hear, how she has got through, with her trial, of anguish, and peril. You may write to me forth with, and let me hear all that interests you, and the family. Give our love to all, and a kiss, and joy to my God daughter.

What is the matter, with our friend Tom Shankland? He is upon me, like a waggon load of bricks. Is he crazy? Do let me know, what has befell him? He is mad about "constructive mileage."[3] It was mine by law, as forty other reasons!! If I had not taken it, it would have been the veriest act of Demagogism, that could have been perpetrated in life. It was no [blurred] and whether others took it or not, I care not, for my course was plain, and I abhor a Demagogue, or the—ism, when it keeps money, out of an honest mans purse!

Poor Joe Lewis I suppose is scared at Toms fury. I like Tom, but he is a queer fellow! Tell Joe a thousand regards to him, and to write to me! Jack, I pray [you] to send me a News paper containing my speech on the River & Harbor Bill.[4] I cant see in the papers. See Mr Sutton, and ask him about it. I want it much!!! Dont fail to present our affection to Cousin, and all the family. Our little "red head" is one of the <u>finest</u> of the <u>fine</u>! They are all [blurred] children. Sam ate too many green plumbs [sic], but is better.

Thy friend & relative
Houston

[1]Houston is probably referring to Thomas Gott's suit against Nancy Lea which was dismissed March 29, 1851. Copies of Walker County Court records furnished by County Clerk James Patton.

[2]Mary Houston Garland was expecting a baby.

[3]Houston may be referring to his bill to the U. S. Government for $4,816 which included travel of 6,240 miles @40 cents each and per diem pay from December 15, 1849 to September 30, 1850. This bill is in the Franklin Weston Williams Collection at the Woodson Center, Rice University, Houston, Texas.

[4]For a copy of this speech see *Writings,* vol. 5, 288–92.

The following two letters from Houston's younger brother William are in the Franklin Weston Williams Collection at the Woodson Library, Rice University, Houston, Texas. Houston's answers regarding these matters have not been located. No evidence has been found that William Houston and his family ever relocated to Texas.

Memphis
May 13 1851

My dear brother,

A few days after you passed on your way home, I wrote to you at Huntsville. Nearly two months have elapsed, and I have received no reply. The letter must have miscarried or you may have been from home, as I see from the papers, that you have been at San Augustine.

Let me hear, as soon as convenient, and say if you received my letter.—A few days will determine respecting one important matter with me. Mr Ferguson who bought me out at the Hotel, died in an "apoplectic fit,"—life ceases instantaneously, of course nothing of the situation of matters is known except so far as was known, before the occurrance [sic]. A payment of $1330 is due 4th of June, next, and if any thing should prevent it; my calculations will be interfered with. I am told it will be paid, and I have hopes to that effect. I have let my matters remain as they were when you were here, waiting to hear from you, of which I am in daily expectation.

Mary and the little ones enjoy excellent health. Mary is rather giving in to the idea of <u>going</u> to Texas, but she must hear something more [blurred] that she would like it.—She wishes to be presented affectionately to Sister Margaret and the little ones; kiss them for her.

My love to Sister, hoping before long to see her, and the <u>weans</u>.

With affection
W. Houston

Memphis
June 9th 1851

My dear brother,

Your letter of 8 May was received in due time. I could not answer it sooner, as I wished to do so definitely.—Respecting the matter that formed the subject of my last, I am glad you look at it in so business a way. And I wish you to so still more, as this is strictly a business transaction, and your brotherly kindness only qualifies it, and enhances its merits.—I wish you to say distinctly how much cash you could spare, and at what rate of interest, and what security would be sufficient.[1] And how much land you would give me the use of, and what requirements must be performed by me. I want all these matters explicitly stated in order that I may see my way clearly before I let go my holds here. It is not because I lack confidence in your offer, but there is so much depends [sic] on my movement in the matter, that nothing short of a <u>positive</u> assurance will induce me to undertake the change. It <u>must be beyond the possibility</u> of a misunderstanding at some future day; or unpleasant reflections on either side! Death must before many years step between us, and your suggestions on that point, are just such as wisdom would dictate. So far as being pleased, or suited in a situation in Texas is concerned, there can be no difficulty, as I have waited for a suitable opportunity [to] make it my home. And I think I will be able to induce the <u>least willing</u> to leave with anticipations of a pleasing nature, alltho' [sic] there is much reluctance expressed at present.

I will expect an answer at your earliest convenience as I cannot leave for <u>Texas</u> in a few days notice; and I will hope to have the <u>matters</u> full as requested on the first page. And it is also important that I should hear soon, as by the middle of July. I must accept or reject a matter of importance in the way of business; please write soon.

The family are well, and as interesting as familes [sic] get to be. Our children are growing finely and you know they are good looking; they could'nt [sic] be otherwise! They collectively and individually join in affectionate greetings to be made by you to all concerned, reserving yourself for the last.

Affectionately
thy Brother
W. Houston

[1]William Houston would sign a note on March 1, 1852, to borrow $2000 from his brother. See Henry G. Smith, by B. B. Waddell, to Sam Houston, December 16, 1853. A. J. Houston Collection, #4047, Texas State Archives, Austin, Texas.

A copy of a letter from Houston to his cousin John Letcher is in the Franklin Weston Williams Collection, Woodson Research Center, Rice University, Houston, Texas.[1]

[Huntsville]
19th July 1851

My Dear Cousin,

I have time to thank you for your speech in Pamphlet on the white basis. I was much pleased with it, and so far as I can judge, you sustained yourself with fine ability. Go on, and you must fill a space large enough to gratify, the ambitions, of a proud, and honorable man.[2] You are coming on the stage when I am preparing for my political exit. I only regret that I will not have done more to sub serve, the great cause of freedom and happiness, than has fallen to my lot. Tis true in the outset, I found many obstacles in my path. I might have done more, but what I have done must stand, and all my hope is that those who come after me, may do more for my country than I have ever done. It was my intention not to return to the Senate, but as things now stand, I intend to return, if only a part of next session. In the meantime I will be happy to hear from you, and all the family. Write to me of your Father & Mother, and cousin Narcissa B. Hamilton. Is your health good?

A wife, a son, and three pretty daughters, embody my cares, and my wealth. We are all well. My dear wife & Sam unite with me in love to your Parents, your dear wife, and all the kindred.

Thy cousin & friend
Sam Houston

[1]Notes with the letter indicated that the original was presented to Texas Governor Allan Shivers on November 25, 1952, to be placed in the Sam Houston Room of the Governor's Mansion. Its current whereabouts is unknown.
[2]Letcher would serve as a congressman and later governor of Virginia.

319 : May 8, 1851–October 18, 1851

Houston's Cousin John Houston wrote the following letter to him before he left Huntsville for Washington. It is in the Franklin Weston Williams Collection at the Woodson Research Center, Rice University, Houston, Texas.

17th Sept. 1851

My Dear Kinsman,

When the publication of certain Correspondence made its appearance in the New York Herald on the 22nd August, (which you have no doubt seen,) I had a letter written that day for you, but the confident manner in which Mr Donelson[1] stated that you would be here, induced me to suppose that my letter would not reach Texas before you left. Supposing that it is still not too late, you have this hasty note.

The correspondence above alluded to, created some sensation for the moment, but that appears to be fizzleing [sic] out. Still, however, tho' I have said on all occasions that you had no hand in it, and that you should not be held responsible for it. And, moreover, that I had no doubt but that you would disavow it in toto. Let me suggest that it would be well for you so to do, and in your own way, and in good time.

Let me suggest to you to refer to my letter to you some time since, as every day convinces me that all in that letter will turn out to be prophecy. Every day confirms it. In that letter I strongly urged you, if convenient, to make a visit to the North, and I extremely regret that you will not probably be in N. York about the time of the fairs etc in that state. The death of Mr. Woodbury,[2] tho' a national loss, will insure to your chances, if properly availed of, and the sooner the better, as I am persuaded that you are the Second choice of most of those in N. England, who preferred him first. This spirit should be cultivated.

Many questions are asked of me. How comes it that Gen. [James P.] Henderson (not freindly [sic] to you) has been elected Lt. Gov? etc. etc.? A brief notice should be taken, for outside of Texas, is there such a person, (in reality,) as Donaldson? I have said I doubted it.

We hear from Mary often, and she and the babe are both well, always [blurred] remembering you. Tom is now in Boston, but he hopes the ship will be in Annapolis by the 1 Oct. when he is to be examined. All the family are well. It is probable that Gertrude may go to Fort Hamilton to see Mary, in all this month.

As you no doubt have heard all about the Cuban affairs,[3] I must refrain from a word on that subject for the present, tho' when I see you, I shall offer a hint.

Mr. [Stephen] Douglass is now fairly in the feild [sic], and do not be surprized [sic] if the freind, of Gov. Cass should make an ugly squint at him.

Mr Fillmore has gone to Boston, to be present at Rail roads fete, where you <u>ought</u> to be. He has, as he ought to become extremely strong in many localities. Still, I think the party organization is in favor of Gen. Scott, and if so, he will be hard to beat. Poeple [sic] will not beleive [sic] that he is not a great Captain, <u>though some may doubt it</u>.

Let me, I pray you, hear from you. All send their love to you, and the excellent Mrs. Houston, and to Sam and the babies, in which I cordially join.

Affy and truly yr cous.

John H. Houston

[1]Someone claiming to be C. H. Donelson had written to the *New York Herald* and various other papers. Houston (sometimes spelling the name Donaldson), denied knowing any such person. See Houston to the Editor of the *Texas Monument*, September 27, 1851, *Writings*, vol. 5, 309–10.

[2]Judge Levi Woodbury of New Hampshire had been a candidate for president. Ibid., 284. Many of Houston's northern backers felt Woodbury's death would give Houston new hope for the nomination. Larry Gara, *The Presidency of Franklin Pierce* (Lawrence, Kansas: University Press of Kansas, 1981), 29.

[3]There had been an unsuccessful attempt by Mexican politicians to overthrow Spanish control of Cuba. Many Democrats were interested in the acquisition of Cuba, and it was one of the issues of the 1852 campaign. Ibid., 279.

Houston's reply to the above letter is in the Sam Houston Papers at the Barker History Center, Austin, Texas.

Huntsville
7th Oct 1851

Private
Dear Jack,

Your letter was truly welcome, and particularly so, as it told me that my Dear God Daughter Mary was well, and the balance of your rich treasures of the heart. Unlike a Lady, I will tell you my most [blurred] in the out set of my letter. My family are well, and the little red head [Mary Willie] is a great girl. She will do to class with your children, and that is saying enough for her. Mine are all clever weans.

The Court affair of my wife, has terminated, by the Prosecutor causing, and charging the court to order a Nolli Pruseque.[1] I did not want it, but my counsel, as the other Party [blurred] thought I ought to yield. I wished it tried, as I intended to speak in the case. I pitied the wretches, as they had been used as tools, and were poor dependents. So soon as the nol pros was entered I asked leave of the court to make a few remarks, which was granted, and then it was that I exposed the conspiracy, and gave to the conspirators rich gass, of Jessey under the shirt, and thunder over the coat. The indignation of the community was rather fierce, but repressed.

Now I will [go] to other matters. The James W. Henderson elected Lient [sic] Gov of Texas, is, and has ever been my devoted friend. He is no relation to J. Pinckney Henderson of Nashville Convention meanery,[2] who at this time I presume could not get more than seventy five or one hundred votes in his county for any office.[3] He is my enemy, and ought to be, for I tried to make him a great man, and should be punished for such a piece of presumption. What I did for him would have made an ordinary man at least respectable, but I failed in his case owing to the worthless material out of which I undertook to fashion a clever fellow. He is a poor dog!

Well now comes the Donaldson hoax, or humbug. Well I have seen great men who have canvassed our state, in the late election, and not one has ever heard of any such individual, nor did I ever know, or believe, any such man has ever been in Texas, or that any such man is in the United States. When my friend Col Yoakum wrote to him, for me, it was believed that he resided in the city of N. York. They are welcome to all they got out of me! I suppose it was all done by Bennett,[4] to get excitement up about the [New York] Herald, and make money out of the transaction. All persons are welcome to publish all they get from me! If I write as honest as I feel, I care not a straw who reads my secrete [sic] affairs. It may be that it was intended to do me harm, but in this they will fail. I have written a letter to Mr F. Pitcher of the Richmond Enquirer, and I suppose he will publish it.[5] He ought to do so. In a few days, I will send you a copy of it, and if needful, you can have it published in the Union. Poor fellow, he was badly hoaxed by Donaldson, and feels sore about the matter. I am not to play Dr Cureall, to every one who gets burned as bad, or worse than myself. The present canvass my dear Jack gives me no inquietude, nor will I let it do so. What are all the great [blurred] and how is our friend Mr [James] Buchanan? How is his health? I have liked him, and regretted that efforts have been made (as I believe) to lessen his good feelings towards me, as an old friend of other days. Mine shall not be unkind to him. His long association, with those who were near to my heart will ever recall feelings of kindness towards him. What are the relations, of him and Genl Cass and their friends? I ask these questions, for indeed I see, and hear but little of what is going on, in the political world. News papers, are due here, if the mails would bring them, but when they reach here they are a month old, and who would read a news paper, a month old? No one! Do you see my friend Joe Lewis, and thank and bless him for me!

When you write to my dear Mary, give her, and all hers, my love! To the family commend us all, in true affection and I would be recreant, if I did not offer a double portion [of] my love to Tom and tell him that I have much staked, on his success and character.

Write to me soon, & often and make me happy. I have to leave home in a few days to defend a man in a case of murder. He has paid me $500, so I must make a fine defence. Salute all friends. Send me any papers worth reading. I cant look over this letter, for want of time.

Thy devoted Friend & Relation
Sam Houston

P.S. Your letter has just reached me of the 26ult.[6] I hope Poor Buck is now well. I will send you a synopsis of my speech, & you can have it published.[7]

You can publish the facts about Henderson being my friend. The question was not rash, & if it had been, there was but one side to matters.

---

[1]For more information see Walker County Minutes, Book A, 368, September 30, 1851. For an account of the trial and testimony see Henderson Yoakum's Diary, Barker History Center, University of Texas, Austin, Texas.

[2]For information about Henderson at this convention see Friend, 205.

[3]For biographies of these two men see *New Handbook of Texas,* vol. 3, 554–55.

[4]Houston is probably referring to James Arlington Bennett, a retired army officer in New York. Friend, 278–79.

[5]For a copy of a letter concerning this matter written by Houston to the *Texas Monument* see *Writings,* vol. 5, 309–10. This article spells the name Donelson.

[6]John Houston's letter of this date has not been located, but for Houston's reply see *Writings,* vol. 5, 316.

[7]Houston is probably referring to his speech of October 6, 1851, which was delivered at the Huntsville Presbyterian Church. In this speech Houston defended his congressional record, his reasons for supporting the Oregon Bill and the Compromise of 1850. *Writings,* vol. 5, 310–14.

On October 11, 1851, Houston again wrote John Houston sending him a synopsis of the Huntsville speech. The location of the original letter is unknown, but a copy is in the Madge W. Hearne Papers, San Antonio, Texas, and is printed in Writings, *vol. 5, 316.*

The following letter is to Sam Houston from C. Edwards Lester, a New York author who wrote Sam Houston and His Republic, *the first biography of Houston. At the end of the letter is the statement "A true copy from the Original," signed John McCreary.[1] This holo-*

graph copy is in the Sam Houston Collection at the Texas State Archives, Austin, Texas. The original letter has not been located.

New York
18 Oct 1851

Hon Sam Houston
My dear friend

I have been confused at having received no answer from my last letter to you (dated several months ago) that I can hardly believe you received it. It cannot be that you are laboring under any false impression about myself since I do not believe, that after the intercourse we have had together, any body could change your opinion about me except myself.

I have been contemplating pretty carefully the state of things throughout the country, in both political parties, and I am perfectly persuaded from present appearances, that in the conversation the nomination will be between you and Douglass. The last time we met, and in my last letter, I expressed the opinion, that it was necessary for you to show yourself throughout the United States, in order that you might come personally into intercourse with some hundreds of thousands of men. The prejudice which at one time existed against you, in consequence of the misrepresentation of your [blurred] has died away; and nothing more was required (in my judgment) to ensure your success than to shew yourself to your fellow citizens.

Your friends are very anxious indeed that you should travel through the country; and they all wonder why you do not do it. I find a growing insensibility among them to your political prospects on this account, for they seem to think that you are still more insensible on the subject than themselves. For this reason there is a rapidly growing sentiment in favor of Douglass. I have seen him many times since last spring, and although he is accused of being engaged in political intrigues against you and others, I do not believe one word of it. He told me [he] preferred to wait till Cass, Buchanan, Woodbury, yourself and other prominent candidates of superior age, had either been elected or defeated. I believe that in his heart of hearts he would to day prefer to have you preceed [sic] him. He has told <u>me</u> so, and many other persons. He knows what my preferences are as well as yourself. But he has grown popular because of his recent speeches, and visits to different parts of the Union. And still more so in consequence of his not having displayed in his conversation, or his public performances, any anxiety on the subject of the Presidency. I have scanned his operations very closely, and if I had found him working against you I would have exposed him, but I believe he is acting honestly.

Now in regard to yourself: Will you come to the North. You need not go to New England for you are now personally the most popular democrat east of the Hudson River. But will you travel through Pennsylvania, New York and Ohio? You can do it in four weeks and the consequences could not be measured. This is not only my opinion but that of many of your truest and most judiciary friends. I have been wasting a considerable time, with the hope of getting a response from your friends in reference to the printing of the publication we had under discussion last spring.[2] But with the exception of two gentlemen, Mr Horace Day and Mr George Law, not a man among them has given a cent, or proposed to give one. Mr Law gave me two hundred and fifty dollars, and Mr Day two hundred. With as much more, I could accomplish the publication; but I cannot get it—Nor have I got it in my own pocket, nor could I raise it now, except by a [blurred] sacrifice. I am afraid I shall have to give it up; in which case I shall sell the paper which I had bought (at a small discount) make up the balance, and pay it back to the donors; for I intend in this, as in all other matters, to act a manly, an honest, and a frank pact.

I have not seen [Thomas] Shankland for some weeks. I received duly the last document you provided me, and I shall be very glad to hear from you <u>directly</u>, in order that I may know what you intend to do, for I feel jealous of your fame, and hope to see the object I have had so near my heart for many years speedily accomplished.

Faithfully your friend
C. Edwards Lester

[1]John McCreary was a Huntsville lawyer who was Houston's close friend and sometimes handled business matters for him.
[2]Lester would succeed in 1855 in publishing the book *The Life of Sam Houston: The Only Authentic Memoir of Him Ever Published.*

Chapter VI

November 11, 1851–February 22, 1852

January 14, 1852: Margaret Houston to Sam Houston
January 16, 1852: Sam Houston to Margaret Houston
January 18, 1852: Sam Houston to Margaret Houston
January 19, 1852: Sam Houston to Margaret Houston
January 20, 1852: Sam Houston to Margaret Houston
January 23, 1852: Sam Houston to Margaret Houston
January 25,1852: Sam Houston to Margaret Houston
January 28, 1852: Sam Houston to Margaret Houston
January 28, 1852: Margaret Houston to Sam Houston
[late January, 1852]: Sam Houston to Margaret Houston
February 1, 1852: Sam Houston to Margaret Houston
February 4, 1852: Sam Houston to Margaret Houston
February 11, 1852: Margaret Houston to Sam Houston
February 13, 1852: Sam Houston to Margaret Houston
February 22, 1852: Sam Houston to Margaret Houston

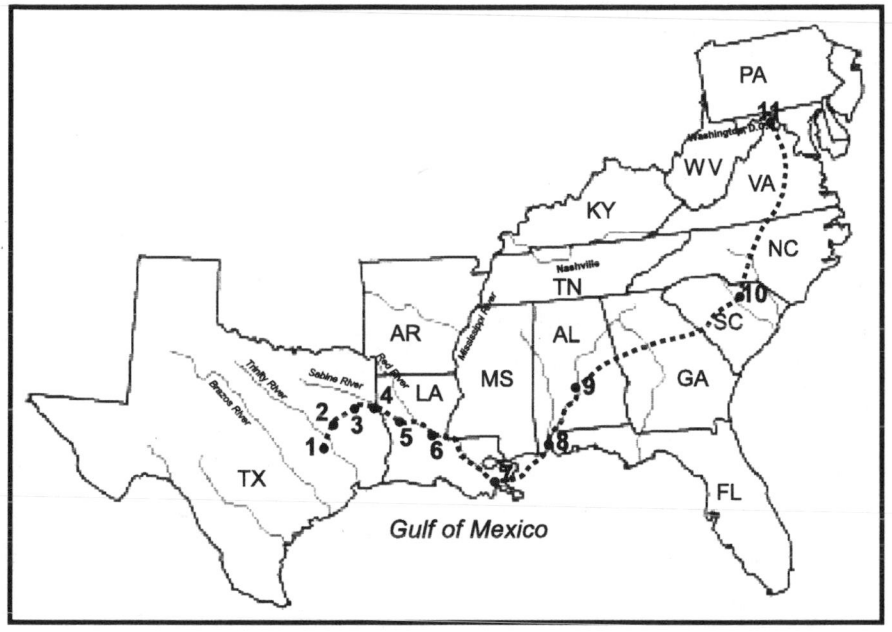

Houston's Southern Route to Washington, D. C.
November–December, 1851

1. Huntsville, Texas
2. Crockett, Texas
3. Nacogdoches, Texas
4. Sabinetown, Texas
5. Nachitoches, Louisiana
6. Alexandria, Louisiana
7. New Orleans, Louisiana
8. Mobile, Alabama
9. Montgomery, Alabama
10. Camden, South Carolina
11. Washington, D. C.

Houston began his trip back to Washington in mid-November, this time going by the southern route overland through Mobile, Alabama.

At Masters[1] 50 miles from Home
11th Nov. 1851

My Dear Love,

I did not expect to write to you, from this place, but I find the material & am happy to let you hear, that I am this far safe. Just as we left Town this morning, the rain commenced, and with slight interruptions, we have had rain all day. A more constant, and heavy rain, I do not recollect to have seen in my life, for the duration.

The horses <u>stawled</u> [sic], in a creek today, and we were detained two hours, and the poor driver was much exposed. Col [James] Reily, and myself got out, and <u>got wet</u>, tho' not badly. All the creeks, gullies and branches were almost swiming [sic.] We are now comfortable!

We met Mrs [Jane] Kaufman, & her sister[2] here. They came in the Eastern Stage, on their way to Washington, on Brasos [sic]. They are anxious to see you, and if they do not call, on their way out, it is their intention, to call on their return. I hope they will do so. The madam has lost her dear little Sam Houston[3] since I saw her last. He was the most interesting of all her children!

Gen Rusk is waiting for me! I hope to see him tomorrow night. I will write to you as often as I can my Love. If Col Yoakum cant sell Prince & his family, and Vernal wont take them, let the Col hire them to good and strict masters, or master, as far from town as possible. Where they will be well treated, well worked, and well fed!

You will find Miss Richardson a little <u>like a fair friend of ours</u>— Do you take?

Kisses and love to all the children, and remember me to Isabella,[4] & Jackson.[5]

Write to me love <u>once</u> a week! Do my Dear if you can without pain. May Kind Heaven sustain, & protect you.

Thy ever devoted Husband
Sam Houston

333 : November 11, 1851–February 22, 1852

Be very kind to Mrs Kaufman, & Sister. H

[1]Jacob Masters had a plantation in Houston County near the town of Crockett. Gifford White, *The First Settlers of Houston County, Texas* (printed privately by Gifford White, 1983), 8.
[2]Eliza Richardson.
[3]Sam Houston Kaufman died August 14, 1851. White and Toole, 21.
[4]Isabella Murry/Murrie, a British citizen, was interviewed and hired by Nicholas Dean of New York as a nurse for the Houston children. He described her as "so old, though still in the prime of usefulness, as not to be sought after as a wife, and clean and neat in her person and dress." For information about the arrangements see Nicholas Dean to Houston, February 22, 1851; March 12, 1851; and March 19, 1851. A. J. Houston Collection, #3950 and 3951.
[5]Jackson Paul, the Houston overseer.

Nacogdoches
13th Nov 1851

My Dear Love,

I have concluded to pester you, with another letter. I reached here safely, on last night, but the stage lay over a day. I found Genl Rusk had gone on, but expects me to overtake him, at Alexandria. To day I passed part of my time, in visiting our friends, all of whom send much love to you. It was reported, that you were coming on with me, and they were all agog to see you. With Col. Reily, I called a moment to see Betty Culp,[1] and she had been quite ill, but not enough so to hurt her speech. She would "talk all," as our daughter says. It is said that she had a "<u>misfortune</u>," which was the cause of her indisposition.

To day I gave Drafts to A. Huston[2] on me for $500.00, and took a Draft, on the Gen'l Post office Department, and also took a mortgage on a half League of land in Robertson County, on Walnut creek, which I will send to Col Yoakum, as collateral security for the same. I have got a Stage Driver, who promises to take to you a bag of Jamestown or (Gempson) burry [sic]. I hope he will not fail to do it. Oh Stramonium is what I mean.[3] Sub rosa, It may be that Mrs Harrison (late Mrs [George W.] Terrell)[4] Will become a citizen of Huntsville, and her husband established a Professor there.[5] He is right smart, & may make a good Editor. This may or may not be. If they go there, you will have to be on the lookout for I fear the Madam will find it difficult, to keep smoothe with people.

I will now tell you, my Dear some little of my feelings, about you, and our Dear little flock. I am miserable, because I am not with you, and I am constantly, when alone, and often in company, musing upon the pranks of our Dear wee ones. I think of Molly [Mary Willie], when I last kissed her in her Dear Mothers arms. She is as present to my vision, as tho. I were this moment looking at the little cherub.

My prayers, tho. feeble, and an unworthy offering, shall be for your happiness, and our Dear offsprings. You will infer from my writing so often, that you are always present to my mind, and to my heart, of hearts.

You will write to me every week, and if you cant my Love, please to get Mr Creath, to write for you. Dont oppress, or distress yourself to write, but you know my Dear, how miserable I am, if I don't hear from you, regularly. My heart is yours, and you ought to be kind to it, and pity it.

Give my love to the Dear little ones. Say to Sam I hope he will be a noble, & generous Boy, Loving to his Ma, & sisters, and trying to make them happy. Kiss all of the children, give Howda to Isabella, & Jackson [Paul]. I hope the servants behave well, and that Joshua takes care of the horses.

Thy ever devoted Husband

Houston

P. S. I will send my note on Pleasants[6] to Col Yoakum. I can't see him, and it is perfectly good.

Thine

Houston

[1] Elizabeth Thilman (Mrs. Daniel D.) Culp.
[2] Almazon Huston, *New Handbook of Texas*, vol. 3, 801–802.
[3] This was used as a treatment for Margaret's asthma.
[4] Ann Terrell married J. C. Harrison July 23, 1849. Helen Smothers Swenson, *8800 Texas*

Marriages, 1823–1850 (St. Louis: Frances Terry Ingmire, 1981), vol. 1, 63.
[5]At Austin College.
[6]Benjamin Pleasants of Nacogdoches. Carpenter, 1415.

Sabine Town
14th Nov 1851

My Dearest,

To day I travelled not less than 68 miles to day [sic], so that I slept none last night, and it is now 11 oclock P.M. and I am to start at 3 oclock A.M. so I do not expect to retire for more than an hour to night as company is waiting for me to write this letter, when we are to resume our conversation.

It may be that I will reach Genl Rusk, at Natchitoches, on tomorrow night. He was there this morning, and was to lay over a day, for conveyance to Alexandria, and he may not obtain it, until I arrive.

By the mail from here, a Deed for a half League of land in Henderson County will be sent to Colonel Yoakum [sic]. I can communicate no need to you of interest from this point. I am not determined as to what route, I may take to Washington. It is barely possible but not probable that I may pass thro Alabama. If I do, I may see Bro. Henry, as I think the Legislature is in session at Montgomery.[1] If I go there, and should be <u>provoked</u>, I will speak, and if I do speak, I will try, and <u>provoke</u> others.

To day our ride was not by any means disagreeable. Col A Huston came this far with me.

My dear Love, give kisses to all our dear little flock.

I am thy ever Devoted
Houston

[1]Henry Clinton Lea represented Perry County in the Alabama Legislature. Brewer, 492.

Natchitoches La.
Sunday 16th Nov 1851

My Dearest,

I reached here on last night and found that Genl Rusk had set out by hack in the morning for Alexandria. I hope to meet him there. The river has only risen here, a few inches, and I think we will have to go by land, as far as the mouth. I feel pretty well, after my trip to his place. To day has been the sabbath. I was but little out of my room, and to my astonishment when I did go out, I found all the stores, Groceries, and shops open. At the same time, the cathedral Bell was ringing, and its votaries were on their way to church. Such things are usual in all catholic countries. They look strange to me, tho. I have formerly seen them at New Orleans.

The stage starts in the morning at 2 oclock so tonight I must try, & get some sleep. Tomorrow night, we hope to reach Alexandria. I have met with a fellow traveller, who was originally from Georgia. He is very moral & genteel. I like him much. This moment, two other travellers have arrived, and one is on his way to South Carolina. I believe he is not a "fire eater." I think I will go by the Southern route, but will not say until I reach Orleans. My intention is to spend a day there, and hope to send you some <u>supplies</u>. If I do, I will send them to my friend [Archibald St. Clair] Ruthvens care.

I requested Col Yoakum to send Bro. Charley the Books he wanted.

I have to write with my Gold pen,[1] and really fear you can not make out my writing. No matter. I am sure you read, to some extent, the feelings of my heart. I do not allow myself to think of being absent from <u>you</u>, and our Dear Children, as long as the usual session lasts, if I live. I could not bear to think of a subject so painful. Often I wish, I could fly to you, and there remain. To be sure, I am kindly received, and at times, almost caressed, but this is a poor requital, for the vast sacrafice [sic], of conjugal, and domestic happiness, that I forgo.

I feel, if possible more that I have ever done at leaving home. At meal times, I get no kisses, nor do I see any bright eyes, or pretty

<u>curls</u> displayed. I feel that there is but one home, in this world for me, and that is where you are present.

To day, I have had some headache, but will take some Jaynes pills, ire I retire, if it is not better!

Give my love, and kisses to the Dear Children. Say something appropriate to each one for me.

Tell all Howdas.

Thy Faithful & Devoted
Houston

[1]This pen is in the Houston collection at the San Jacinto Museum of History, La Porte, Texas.

Mouth Red River
20th Nov 1851

My Dearest,

To day we reached this place. The trip was not very unpleasant, tho. somewhat tedious. We do not know yet whether to go up the River, or to New Orleans. We think we will go to Orleans. I wish to send you some stores from that point. I wish too to go, by Montgomery. I see that the Legislature is in session, and I will see Bro. Henry, if I go that route. But I heard the Alabama river is so low that Boats can't run in it. If I go to Orleans and find that the case, I must then ascend the Mississippi.

I have not my dear, mentioned to you, for Joshua, if there is any Rye left, after sowing the patches, to have it sowed, in the stable lot, where I had Peas sown last December. Let it be done!

It was my wish that you should get all the cotton seed that you wish. I have been told, that a half Gallon of cotton seed, twice a day to a cow is plenty for them, and a handful of meal on each feed milckows [sic].

Now my Dearest, I want you to manage, so as to be satisfied, and you may rely upon my being perfectly so. I doubt not but what you will do what you may think best, and you may rest assured, I will do everything in my power, to advance our material interests, and your happiness.

My intention is to write you from New Orleans. There I hope to be able to say how I will go to Washington.

Salute our dear, Dear Children. Write to me about them, and particularly about yourself. Howda to all.

Thy ever Devoted
Houston

Huntsville
Nov 22nd 1851

My dear love,

I have not recd another letter from you since my acknowledgement of yours from Master's & Nacogdoches, but I am in continual expectation of one from Sabine town. After reading your dear letters, I seem to have new strength for the trials attendant upon your absence. It is true, they are many and often severe, but when reminded that you love me, I am cheered by the sweet reflection and determine to bear every thing cheerfully for your sake. Our last parting dearest was surely the most painful yet. Oh the agonizing prayers that ascended from my poor heart that night for your safety! And oh what sweet qualities filled my soul on the reception of your first letter. I felt that the Lord had heard my prayers and a sweet encouragement was given to me, to ask yet [torn] whom my soul loved [torn] I also tremble when I think of the incessant toils and worldly cares by which you are surrounded. I fear nothing for the allurements of pleasures or fame, but oh the useless cares and occupation of a stateman's life, they too may cheat the soul! Dearest, do not forget to pray!

Our dear little ones seem more interesting to me each day, but although with a mother's pride and fondness I watch their youthful charms, it is often with a sad heart, because dear papa can not see them too. Often through the day little Mary falls on her knees and murmurs the sweet name "papa papa" again & again, and then springs to her feet and looks in my face with an expression so [torn] your absence, and seems very happy. Anne Goree is to be married next teusday [sic]. The family is so anxious for me to be present, if I can be sure of getting home comfortably and in suitable company.

Thy affectionate wife
[torn] Houston

New Orleans
24th Nov 1851

My Dear Wife,

This is monday, and I intend to set out by way of Mobile at 3 oclock P.M. On saturday, I arrived from the mouth of Red River, as you will get my letter from that point. I happened to get on the same Boat, with Dr. Ashbel Smith. He was in fine health and spirits. Yesterday (sunday) Mrs [Ellen] Reily took her departure for Galveston on the "Menco" Steamer. I went to the wharf, and saw her, but they were on the eve of departure. I could only hand, & speak, & present your love to her. She said she would call, and see you, and the children on her way to Nacogdoches, soon. Rev'd Mr Chilton[1] went over on the same Boat & said to me that Bowden,[2] his son in law, and his son[3] wou'd settle in Huntsville as lawyers. He says Bowden is sober, and says he will stay so. If so, I will be rejoiced indeed, for he is talented.

My Love, I have ordered us

1 Bll sugar cured Hams
1 Half Bll Buckwheat
1/2 Dozen jars Pickles
1/2 Bll Mackand No. 1
1/2 Bll Cero (marked Oil)[4]

1 Dozen assortive Preserves

1 Bll sides Bacon

1 Box Starch

1 Doz. Tomato Ketchup.

To be sent so soon as the full supplies arrive.

To Mrs. Margaret L. Houston

Huntsville

Care of Wm. Hendley Co.[5]

Galveston

To be shipped to Cincinnati on Trinity.

Orders will be sent my Dear to Cincinnati to let you know when the articles reach there. I think you had best get flour, and sugar from [Sanford] Gibbs, or [George W.] Rogers.

I send you a note on Mr. Raily,[6] who lives on the Brasos. He was here without money, and is a respectable man. He will pay it.

Now my Dear, I am thro with business, and will have time to write you a little of private matters. I found Christie, & family pretty well. I took soup with them yesterday. They were very kind, & spoke much of you, and the children. They send much love to you.

I may call at the Cane brake, and see our people.[7] If not I hope to see Bro Henry. I did not speak here. It is not needful. It may be that I will speak in Mobile & Montgomery, or not as it <u>suits</u> [torn] You will suppose that I intend to write to you, as often as I can. I am not anxious to be at Washington at the meeting of Congress.

I hope my Dearest, that you will have a peaceful time of absence, and be happy.

Do the best you can. I intend to be satisfied with what may be.

My love to our Weans and howda to all.

Thy Devoted Husband

Houston

[1]Reverend Thomas Chilton. Identified in Lois Smith Murray, *Baylor at Independence* (Waco, Texas: Baylor University Press, 1972), 16.

[2]F. W. Bowden. Identified in Brewer, 539.

[3]George Washington Chilton. He actually established a law practice in Tyler, Texas, in 1851. *New Handbook of Texas*, vol. 2, 83.

341 : November 11, 1851–February 22, 1852

⁴Wax.
⁵For a biography of William Hendley and information about his company see Hayes, 882.
⁶Houston is probably referring to John Railey, who lived in Jefferson County, Texas. Carpenter, 1185.
⁷The Royston family.

Mobile
25th Nov 1851

My Dearest,

This morning I arrived after a stormy passage of the Lakes. At 5 P.M. the Boat starts for Montgomery, and I wont detain. I did not tell you, that I have ordered a Barrel of beautiful apples from New Orleans for you! I did so, and hope they will reach you safe & soon.

I called a few minutes since, to see Mrs Levert,[1] with a cousin of hers, Mr Beers,[2] and for the first time I saw Dr Levert.[3] He was very clever, and she had a thousand kind things to say, and inquire of "Margaret"! Their eldest, and youngest children are living.[4] The oldest is fine looking. I seen [sic] Mrs. Nathan, who looks very much broke. I say now, my Dear, when I can do so in sincerity, and when you do not expect me to say so, that I have seen no children that will compare with ours. I assure you, this is my judgement [sic], but why not? I do not see any other mother, who will compare with theirs! The weather is so bad that I hardly think I will call by the Cane brake. Yet I may. Kisses to our dear children. Howda to all

Thy devoted
Houston

Mrs. Levert said, "when you write, send my warm love to Margaret." I do so, but it is <u>cold to mine</u>. H.

¹Octavia Walton LeVert. For a description see Sterling, 13.
²Oliver Sturges Beers of Mobile. For a biography see Owen, vol. 3, 125.
³Dr. Henry Strachey LeVert. Ibid.
⁴Octavia and Annette LeVert. A son and daughter had died in infancy. Owen, vol. 4, 1039.

Huntsville
Nov. 28, 1851

My ever dear husband,

Since I wrote last week, I have recd two letters from you, one at Sabine town, the other at Natchitoches. How very happy, I was made by them I will not attempt to describe to you, but leave you to imagine. I am sorry you have not fallen in with Gen'l Rusk, as your journey would no doubt have been much more agreeable. However, I ought not to regret as you would have had so many engrossing topics of conversation, that you would not have had much time to think of me, and I have no wish to be forgotten I assure you.

Since you left, I think we have had the coldest spell of weather I have ever seen in Texas, at this season. On last monday, we had a fine snow, and but for the dampness of the earth, I think it would have been some inches deep.

Mrs Kaufman spent last sabbath night and monday with me. She left compliments with me, for you, and requested me to say to you that you must not forget to send her documents.[1] Miss Richardson asked my leave to give you a kiss, when she next saw you. I did not say no, but I felt it. In these matters, I suppose I am rather selfish, but it is my weakness, and I can not think it an unamiable one.

Anne Goree and Mr. Barclay were married on last tuesday night.[2] I did not attend, as I could not make up my mind to come home in the night without any company, that I felt like trusting myself with. In fact I think my dear husband is the only suitable protector at this time. Owing to the bad weather I have had but little company since you left, and in truth, I am glad of it, for it leaves me more time for reflections that are very sweet to me. I believe Mrs Evans apprehends that I am going into confirmed melancholy, but I do not think so, for although I am very sad, I am not unhappy, and have no wish to be more cheerful.

My household matters move on more smoothly and harmoniously than they ever done since I was a house-keeper. I am astonished at my own success, and wish you were here to admire it. But I will give you a small insight into my arrangements. We all arise with the sun, and so soon as all are dressed, assemble for worship, an exercise in which the children engage heartily. When that is over, we proceed to breakfast, which Eliza is getting ready, while Perlee and Nash are milking. Soon after breakfast, Isabella and myself sit down to our sewing, while the children are engaged with their lessons. We do not confine them long to their books, but allow them an abundance of time for exercise. Thus one duty after another is taken in regular succession, and all confusion is avoided. We have supper before dark, that the children may be present at evening worship. After they are asleep, I often take a book and read until late. I promised myself a pleasant time last night from reading "Butlers analogy," but Sam took a fancy to sit up with me, and read aloud from the history of Queen Elizabeth,[3] and I became interested in that, for he reads quite well enough now to entertain me very agreeably. Yesterday he brought me a picture of Bonaparte's approach to St. Helena, and a new train of reflections suggested itself to my mind, which I trust enabled me to impart him some profitable instruction. The subject was a comparison between the two exiles of Patmos[4] and St. Helena.[5] For the first time, he seemed to look [upon the] unhappy Napoleon without the us[ual] adornments of his vivid fancy. After some time spent in comparing the two, I remarked to him, "My son, I can not account for your admiration of that man." He replied, "Well ma, I am just like yourself, I can not account for it either, and yet I do love to hear about him, and" (shall I tell you the rest?) "I think Pa wants me to like him, for he gets me images of him." This morning he commenced the subject again, and asked me if I did not think his papa inclined to "indulge him" (to use his own expression) in his fancy for Napoleon.

We are all well except little Mary Willie, who has had fever for two or three days, but I think she is better. The children all [torn] and improve in every respect. It is so cold today that I write with difficulty, but I can not forgo the pleasure of saying a few words to you.

Ever thy devoted wife,

M. L. Houston

[1]These were probably documents concerning a petition Jane Kaufman was presenting in Washington to have the stages cross the Trinity at Sabinetown instead of Strothers. Friend, 218.

[2]Anne Goree married John Barkley on November 25, 1851, with James Maxey officiating. Vick-Rainey, 10.

[3]Quite possibly he was reading from one of the two volumes of *History of England* by Macaulay, 1849. Both volumes have Houston's signature and are from his library. Margaret Rost Collection, Sam Houston Memorial Museum, Huntsville, Texas.

[4]The island where St. John is supposed to have been exiled.

[5]The island where Napoleon was exiled.

Montgomery Ala
1st Dec 1851

My Dear Love,

On friday night, I reached here, after a long trip from Mobile. This is monday, and I intend to leave to day for the East. In five days, I hope to reach Washington.

Since my arrival, it has rained more heavily, than you could imagine. The railroad was, as reported, torn up by the freshet, and caused me to be quiet here, until it should be repaired, and I am in no vast hurry, to get on.

On saturday, a Resolution was passed, by the H. R. to place the Hall, at my disposition, and I was invited to speak, which I did. Tho the evening was bad, I met a respectable audience.[1] Some ladies attended, but not very many. I have requested Bro Henry to write to you, what he thought of the speech.[2] He may not write, and I send you a paper to see how what [sic] a Whig Editor says of it. It was quite clever, and I think superior to my former one at this place. I had a bad cold or rather a hoarseness, that somewhat embarrassed me. To both parties it gave more satisfaction than Gen'l Footes delivered a few days before.[3] I was most decided for the Union, and nothing short of it. Bro Henry, I think, was much gratified. I have seen more of him, this time than I had ever done before, and put all my former acquaintance together.

He is a most capital Gentleman, and able at that. He was elected District attorney, of his old District. I find it is a situation most sought after. He was elected by a large Majority. He would have had Lucy Ann here if he had anticipated my coming. They are all well at the Cane brake, and Marion. He did not wish to run for the Legislature, nor Jack Cocke[4] either, but Columbus [Lea] & Young [Royston] broached their Disunion doctrine, and compelled him to run, by the wishes of his friends. Columbus has his couch pretty well trimmed. I am glad of it. I have seen many of your friends here, and they are most kind, in their expressions, & inquiries for your health, and the little ones. How many General have you? Only four! Is it possible and how many Girls? only three, and their dear Mother fancies them perfectly beautiful! And you? I think them very clever!

So the chat changes. Bro Henry supposes Sam smart, for he says he was the smartest fellow that he ever saw when here[5] of his age. I told him that you expected to come on in the spring to the city. He was very anxious for you to come this way. I told him if you did come, and it would be by sea, I supposed, and Vernal would accompany you. My mind is still the same, if I cant return, for my Love, I am not, I declare to you, happy from you, and the children, for one moment, tho. I may be cheerful, and apparently happy.

I want you, my Love, to write a long letter, to Sister Virilla, and complain to her mildly, about Martins[6] not coming to stay with you, and his Grand ma,[7] in my absence, and my inquiry upon his friends at Matagorda. This I wish done, as I am satisfied Tom & Sally [Power] have been telling mean, & base stories about the matter since they came here! I want you to write the truth, as tho you had no inclination, of any thing, or suspicion of meaness. Urge Serena (or Teen) to go to Texas. Bro Henry says she ought to go. Young & Bob[8] don't care, or think about any thing, but "Young & Bob," and Young belongs to Columbus! Poor Teen, and her mother, would they were happy, in Texas.

My Dearest, my paper is nearly out, and I must close with using expressions of Devotion, Love, and affection to you, and the children.

Thy Husband
Houston

[1]It was reported that "he addressed a large assemblage. . . . His remarks were mostly confined to an able defense of the Compromise, and of his own course and consistency. He also advocated the cause of the Union, as the only security for republicanism. On this point he spoke with animation and power, and occasionally reached eloquence of a high order. The celebrated Texan is well known as a popular orator, and when excited, or on topics in which he becomes impassioned, he speaks with much effect." *Montgomery Alabama Journal*, vol. 5, #215, December 1, 1851, p. 2.

[2]For Houston's comments about his speech see *Writings*, vol. 5, 332.

[3]Senator Foote spoke on the Southern Address, the Nashville Convention, the Texas Boundary Bill and the Fugitive Slave Bill. For a complete review of the speech see the *Montgomery Alabama Journal*, November 25, 1851, vol. 5, #209, p. 2.

[4]Jack F. Cocke defeated Columbus in the election for state senator. Brewer, 493.

[5]The Houstons visited Marion with two-year-old Sam in 1845, after the death of Andrew Jackson.

[6]Martin Royston, Varilla's son.

[7]Nancy Lea.

[8]Young Lea and Robert Royston.

Camden S. C.
4th Dec 1851

My Dear Wife,

After I left Montgomery I came directly to this place in two days. I did not go by Charleston, as you know I dislike going by water. The stage was so full last night, that I did not go on, but concluded to stay to day. I have had a quiet time, and find the people very civil to me. You know the <u>fire-eaters</u> are about <u>10,000 minority</u> in the state. It is curious to witness the madness of some here. I am convinced of one thing, and that is, if abolition is to be brot about during our day, it will be done by the <u>ultras</u> of the South. It seems strange to me that the conduct of these wretched fanatics, has not already produced fearful, if not fatal, insurrections in the South. I mean in this State particularly. The rebukes which the[y] have met with has only exasperated some of them, here as well as in Alabama.

At 6 oclock this morning I have to set out, and by staying to day,

I have secured the choice seat in the stage, but you know my Dear, if any Ladies should come, my Gallantry would transfer me to the worst,[1] which I do most <u>gallantly</u> hope, will not be the case.

As I said to you, I was not by any means anxious to be in the city, at the meeting of Congress. There will be trouble, & fuss and I, as you know, I prefer quiet. I may pass thro Raleigh N. C. but I am not determined. The Legislature is in Session there, and I have some old friends, which I should like to meet, but will not make it an effort to see them. My Dearest, I feel inexpressible anxiety about you, and the crisis which awaits you, in the coming month,[2] but have no forebodings [sic] to increase my solicitude. I will arrange matters so, thro Col Yoakum, & Col Christy that I may hear the result in four days. From Col Yoakum to Col C, in four days, and then by Telegraph, to me, in as many hours. Should the time be the "8th of January,"[3] and a Boy, why I will leave you in full possession of your wishes, but should it not be as you calculated, and is a Girl, why, you must welcome the little stranger, by a kiss from me, & reserve for me, to give it a name, as I hope it may be red headed! So my Love, I conjure you, not to think I will not be gratified, at the result. As Providence gives us offspring we ought to be gratified & thankful. For the sake of Sam,[4] we might desire matters otherwise, but our great Creator knows best what ought to be done, and we ought to learn submission to his will.

I think my Love, this is about the seventh letter, I have written to you, since we parted. That is pretty "punctual" is it not.

I will hope to meet on my arrival at Washington, (should I live,) at least one, or two letters. When I recur to home, as the day is declining, and think of our little ones, and the rural scenes, and all the associations of home, & family, my heart is sad, and I am pained, that I did not adhere to my resolution to remain, where I was happy. My love, and kisses to the children. Howda to all.

Thy Devoted Husband
Houston

[1]For an example of Houston's conduct towards ladies on the stages see Ester Mueller, "Trav-

eling Thru Texas on a Stage Coach with Sam Houston," *San Antonio Express*, July 17, 1932.

[2]Margaret was expecting a baby in January.

[3]Houston is referring to the national holiday on January 8th which celebrated Andrew Jackson's victory at the Battle of New Orleans, as well as his wish to name a son for Jackson.

[4]Sam had expressed a desire to have a brother instead of a fourth sister.

Senate Chamber
9th Dec 1851

My Dear Margaret,

On last evening, I reached here safe, and quite well. My first inquiry was for my letters, or yours, and soon obtained them. I was truly happy to receive two from you, including one from Sister. The Robt Gott[1] letter too came to hand, and gave me but little trouble. Pay no attention to it, and tell our Mother, not to heed it for a moment. You know I intended to see you in March by some means, if I live. Now I am settled, in my determination. No one will undertake a suit for Mr Gott, and if they did, I would not care. But of this, I will say more anon, when I send it back to you, to let our friends see the audacity of the fellow. Vernal ought to see him, and give him his orders, as I am absent.

As Prince, & Mary are hired out, that matter may rest for the present. I may sell them to Bro Charles if it suits here after.

I found my Cousin Jno Letcher, & his family here and was met by all my friends, with much pleasure. They kept me up to a late hour, but to day I feel quite rested, & fresh.

I think of you, and home, and all our dear little ones, if possible with more tenderness than ever. So soon as I can, I will write to you again. I have yet some fifty letters on my table, not read, and await my attention. I must render it.

Your letters made me feel, as tho. I were at home and could see, and speak to each one, of our dear little family. Your description of Mary Willies "little prayers" was truly graphic.

What are all the cares, and excitements of this place compared to home? They are idleness, vanity & sorrow!!

My Dear Love Kiss all the children, and a special message to our noble Boy, so that he will feel, that he has a <u>charge</u> upon him.

Howda to all

Thy Devoted
Houston

[1]The brother of Thomas Gott.

Washington
14th Dec 1851

My Dear Love,

I am truly culeapable [sic] for not having written you often, say at least three times instead of once, in the last week. To day is sunday, and I went to church morning, and evening. It was to hear my cousin Gallaher[1] preach. He is a great man, and I think truly pious. He has the same mind, that Mr Baines has, and is very intelligent I think.

I would blame myself more than I do for not having written to you oftener, were it that I never could get a room to suit me, until last night, since my arrival! I did not order my stationary [sic], to be sent to me, until I could get a room. Then again for several days past, my friend Genl Rusk has been quite ill, from bilious colic. He is now better, but not yet well.

I must interlace my letter with some matters, which may surprise you somewhat. But first I will promise that you know, I am a great hand to kiss. Well, the evening of my arrival, my cousin, Jno Letcher, would have me to go into the Ladies ordinary, when they were <u>all</u> at supper—a great [blurred] and gentlemen also. I had supped at the general table. I entered the room, and toured along, until I came to my cousin,[2] where she rose, so I <u>just kissed her</u>, as you woud expect me to do. And tho a week has passed, I have not called into the Ladies parlour, owing to my being so busy, & I declare to you, I did not retire last night, until 1/2 past 3 oclock. I will try, and change this, for I do not propose to lose my rest in this way. As it is sunday night, I will not write about politics, but I intend to give you a birds eye view of them, if I live this week. What do you suppose I did last evening? You could not guess, therefore I will tell you. I went to the Book Store, and purchased "Butlers Analogy" and intend to read it carefully. As I know My Love, it will gratify you, I assure you, I never retire to my bed, no matter [how] late, without reading in my Testament, and kneeling down to pray.[3] I trust God will bless my imperfect efforts, and convert my soul, in His own good time! I have found here the "History of Christ" by Rev'd Wells. Would you like to have it sent to you my Love? Say so, if you have the least desire, or for any other works. To day I met all the Houstons at church, and also Mrs. Nesbit and her daughter Margaret. They were all very kind in their inquiries, and regrets, because you did not come on, and I blundered out an awkward apology but did not say as usual, that "you were not in travelling trim." I suppose if I had, that they would have all left suddenly. They all sent much love to you! I told them if you did not come on in the spring, I wou'd most certainly, if living, go, and see you in, or near the month of March! The hope of seeing you in a few months, cheers me in the gloom of absence!

At times when alone, I think of you, and home, until my heart seems to sink in me, with a leaden weight. I am truly sorrowful, that my fate seperates us, for a moment. I will try hereafter to write often. Indeed I did expect to day to have had another letter from you. All my letters have not yet reached you, that I wrote on the way.

Give my love to the Dear children, and imprint a kiss, on their dear lips. I hope our noble boy is progressing well.

Thy devoted
Houston

[1]Reverend James Gallagher. Rev. Samuel Rutherford Houston, 111.
[2]Mary Susan Holt Letcher.
[3]Texas Congressman L. D. Evans occupied the room below Houston and reported he could hear Houston regularly kneeling in prayer. William Carey Crane, *Life and Select Literary Remains of Sam Houston, of Texas* (Dallas, Texas: William G. Scarff & Co., 1884), 240.

Washington
16th Dec 1851

My Dear Love,

Two days since, I wrote you a letter. Again I write, but only to write, and say I love you, and our little ones. Tis true, I think of you My Love, when I do not always think of the little brood. When I do think of them, it is with indescribable feelings, and they are never thought of but what you are in the foreground of the picture. I told you in my last, that my heart was heavy. I assure you my love, that all the pageants which I may see, will not requite me, for the pangs of absence.

It is true my Love, that I may visit Philadelphia, New York, & Buffalo, and for a while may feel the excitement of travel. To these places I have been invited, and to others. I do not know, if I live, how many places I may visit. Political matters may go on in their own way. Matters have changed since I arrived here. Douglass, & others seemed to take by storm every thing when I came here.[1] Now the matters seem at a stand, and I find that every day brings some new paper, with my name, <u>up</u> as the Democratic candidate! The <u>people</u> are for me. The politicians, or a majority of them are not with me, and the only question is "Can the minority rule, and control the majority"? I think not. The people are speaking out, and will be heard!

I will let you see, from time to time, something of weather, that you may have some excitement to drive away hypo [sic].

Thy devoted
Houston

[1]Houston had written his cousin John Houston on October 11, 1851, that there had been a good deal of matter about Douglas published in the *Union*, and only one piece about him. He wrote that "they had to make a long apology about that. It was done <u>because it was requested</u> by a friend!" *Writings,* vol. 5, 316.

Washington
19th Dec 1851

My Dear Love,

If I dont soon get a letter from you, I am fearful that I will wear out your last letter, by frequent perusal. I read it again, & again. It is to me sweet communion in your absence, to read something, which you have written. My heart is with you, and around it, cluster a thousand sweet memories, of happy home. What would I not give to be at home, surrounded by my domestic circle? It would be to me more precious, and delightful, than all, and every thing which can result to me here. Tis true of [sic] the 23rd I expect to make a speech in Phila, but this will be, only a momentary excitement, and leave me to sigh again for my home.

To day I expect to speak, if Gov. Foote[1] gets thro. He has only taken up <u>one</u> day yet. How long I will be absent to the North I cant say. I expect to be most constantly travelling. I will, if spared, write to you, from the various points, if I extend my trip on far as proposed.

<u>Every</u> <u>bod</u>y sends love to you, & Sam. My love to all

Thy devoted Husband
Sam Houston

[1]Foote had recently been elected governor of Mississippi.

Washington
21st Dec 1851

My Dear Love,

Owing to the annoyance of the Senate, by Foote[1] & Rhett,[2] I have not yet spoken as I expected to do. They have occupied the last four days, and tho. I was entitled to the floor, I did not claim my right, lest I be thought discourteous, as they were engaged in altercation. Tomorrow (monday) I expect to speak, as I have the floor. It is a time, & occasion when my duty to the country requires me to speak.[3]

I hope to be able to make my views, clear to the understanding of the Senate, and the country. My course has no demagogueism [sic] in it, and is clearly natural. This will satisfy you my Love, & that is what I desire.

To day I went to hear Mr Gallaher, who is now the stationed Preacher, in the Presbyterian church near my Hotel. We are intimate, and agree on all matters, except Baptism. He is as able a man, as Mr Baines, and that is saying much.

He is, on next sunday, to Preach on the dispersion & restoration of the Jews. I would be most happy to hear the sermon if possible, but I do not hope to do it.

To day I was in hopes to have heard from you, or Col Yoakum, but no letters have reached me, of later date, than the 28th of Novem. My Dear I will write as often, & as anxiously, as tho' I received them regularly. I assure you, that hope of seeing <u>you</u>, and our dear <u>chicks</u>, buoys me up, and will I trust, until I can (with the blessing of Heaven) see you in March. I would sooner resign than not enjoy the felicity, which a visit to my home would afford me. Since I have been here, I have seen Maj Donelsons family, & the Madam, as well, Miss Mary, are devotedly attached to you, & recall the memory of Sam, with much pleasure.[4] They desire their love to you, and Sam. Mary says she wants to see you in the "White House." My cousin Mrs [Susan] Letcher is still here, and in a short time my Cousin Narcissa B. Hamilton, will be here, to see her Cousin Letcher, as well as myself. I hope soon to be less annoyed, and to write to you more at leisure, than now. Mrs Gaines[5] is here, but I have not seen her yet. I go no where, and feel less like visiting, than I ever did.

Ever thine
Houston

[In margin:] My friend Cleveland[6] is here, and sends his best regards to you & Sam.

---

[1]Houston would speak against Foote on the next day. Friend, 283. For more information on

the debates between Houston and Foote see 216–17.

[2]R. Barnwell Rhett, from South Carolina, elected upon the death of John C. Calhoun. *Biographical Directory of Congress*, 149.

[3]For a copy of the speech see *Writings*, vol. 5, 317–36.

[4]The Donelsons had seen Sam in Tennessee at Andrew Jackson's funeral.

[5]Mrs. E. P. (Myra) Gaines.

[6]William D. Cleveland, a businessman from Houston. Jesse A. Ziegler, *Wave of the Gulf: Ziegler's Scrapbook of the Texas Gulf Coast Country* (San Antonio, Texas: The Naylor Company, 1938), 81.

Baltimore
23rd Dec 1851

My Dear Love,

It was one oclock last night, before my speech was revised for the Press. Indeed, my Dear, I had but little time to sleep, as I had to rise early, to take the cars, for Philadelphia. I did so, and when I reached here, the Train had left, and I cant be in Philadelphia to lecture to night. There has been here a great snow storm, and in part owing to that the cars were delayed. I telegraphed that the disappointment, might be attributed to the true cause, and some one else, might be obtained to speak, for the occasion. I intend, if spared, to lecture tomorrow. And from thence, if I can, and it is proper, to go North during the Holidays.

I spoke in the Senate on yesterday,[1] and as you will soon get it, I will forbear to say much, but I will say it was a rich scene, and others say Gov. Foote was for the first time completely floored. I was truly amused, to see him so perfectly chargrined [sic]. He writhed & raved and made quite a tyrade [sic], but all to no purpose. The laugh was on him, and the Senate gratified! I was calm, & pleasant throughout and suggested, that I had a better anecdote,[2] but would not tell it. It was called for, but I forbore to say any thing, which would wound his feelings. We came this far in the cars, but have no intercourse! He is a bad, & base man, & has no regard for truth or honour. He is now known as "Parson Means" & it will stick to him!!! For some time past his conduct has been ungentlemanly, & outrageous, in the Senate. Since my arrival he has occupied, two thirds of the time of the Senate! He evinces no respect for the Body, or its members. He says that he has gone home, to be inaugurated,[3] and then be elected to the Senate again. If the Senate had to select its own members, he wou'd not be chosen one of them! He may not get back, but if he does he has to see sights in Mississippi.

I am travelling with Mr McEwen[4] of Phila, a cousin of ours, once of Kingston Tenn. He desires to be presented to you, and Sam! My Dear, I want you to read Sam the anecdote of Parson Means, and render to him, the moral, as it is a good one.

Now my Love, Christmas is at hand, and what would I give, to pass it with you, and the dear children. My heart will be with you, and lavish upon you all the affection, devoted love. My feelings are really painful, often when I realise that I cant be with you. Heaven I trust will guard, and preserve us all to meet again, and then, I can tell you volumes, of the most lively, and devoted affection. I often wonder, that I could for one moment be absent from you, when it was possible, to be with, or near to you! These fancies, you may deem Poetic, and they may be the Poetry of love, but they are true also!!! What a contrast there is between the weather here, and my feelings. The rivers are all frozen over. Even the great Patomac [sic] at Washington.

My Dear I did not receive any letters from you recently, and flatter myself, that it was occasioned by mail failures, or the negligence of Post Masters. I will write to Love, whenever I can! Love to all. If I live to get to New York, I will see Isabellas friend![5] Tell her howda.

Thy devoted Husband
Houston

[1]For a copy of this speech of December 22, 1851, see *Writings,* vol. 5, 317–36.
[2]For Houston's anecdote on Parson Means see *Writings*, vol. 5, 333–34.
[3]Foote had been elected governor of Mississippi, and would resign his Senate seat on January 8, 1852. *Biographical Directory of Congress*, 152.
[4]Houston is probably referring to William McEwen. Identified in Byron and Barbara Sistler, *1840 Census Tennessee* (Nashville, Tennessee: Byron Sistler and Associates, 1986), 354, and in Roland Vern Jackson, et. al., *Pennsylvania 1850 Census Index* (Bountiful, Utah:

Accelerated Indexins systems, 1976), vol. 2, 1028.
[4]Houston is probably referring to Nicholas Dean, who recommended Isabella for the job of nanny to the Houston children.

Huntsville
Dec 23rd 1851

My beloved husband,

By last mail I recd yours from Montgomery Ala, and from Camden S. C. and at the same time a letter from bro. Henry, giving me an account of your visit. So that you will readily suppose that it was a happy season with me, and indeed you are not mistaken, for so many days had passed without a word from you, that I had become quite sad. Mrs [Frances] Creath came over soon after I recd your letters and told me, I looked so bright, that she could have guessed the truth, if I had not told her. Last saturday was my regular day for writing to you, but I was informed that the mail would not go out until thursday owing to an accident which happened to the stage coming up. So instead of writing, I borrowed Col Yoakum's horse and buggy and attended our church meeting. Do not look so frightened my love, for I assure you I felt very well, and although it was a cold day, I wrapped myself in my cloak, and had mother to drive me, and Joshua to walk before the horse. I did not know but that it might be the last time I should ever attend, and my feelings were solemnized by the thought. I do not think I ought to indulge any forebodings, for my health is fine, and I believe if I could take exercise enough I would be much more cheerful, but the weather has been damp and cold, and I have had a great deal of work to do for the children, so that I have spent too much of my time in sitting, but I hope I shall do better after this and exercise more. I often think if my dear husband were with me, he would scold me for sitting so much, and my conscience reproves me for doing any thing that he would disapprove.

The children have suffered a good deal from colds, but they are getting much better. Nannie had a violent attack of croup on friday night, but was soon relieved. She took medicine very readily with the promise that papa should be informed of it. She is a great girl, but I fear she will have a sad temper. Mag is as incorrigible a romp as ever. Little Mary Willie grows rapidly. We are no longer at a loss to know whom she resembles, for her features are growing singularly like a certain fancy face that hangs in our parlour, about 21 years of age. Sam talks a great deal about you. He often reads aloud to me, while I am sewing until late at night. He has cut one of his jaw teeth about which you were so much concerned. He complained a great deal while it was coming through. I suppose it was something like cutting a wisdom tooth. Isabella is quite cheerful and contented. Her health is much improved. She had been subject to attacks of bronchitis, but I think my skill and our climate are curing her. Ellen Kitrell is with me and sends her compliments to you. I saw that she did not wish to go over the river until after christmas, and invited her to stay with me, with the understanding that her beaux were not to visit her here. She is getting ready for a ball tomorrow night, but is to go from Mr. [A. P.] Wiley's. I think she will soon be married to a young man in Ala.[1] I hope soon to get a letter from Washington. Do not forget.

Thy devoted wife
M. L. Houston

[1]Ellen Kittrell would marry Joseph P. Herral on February 21, 1854. Vick-Rainey, 14.

New York
26th Dec 1851

My Dear Love,

I am here Christmas. I passed in Phila, and visited my two little cousins McEwen's. They were very happy to see me, and sent much love to you. They were children when we were in Kingston. I am glad that you have sent for Mother. I did not say any thing to you, I think about the way that she went off, and the mood in which she was. I supposed, that you were aware of the fact, and I did not wish to allude to it, as I thought your feelings would be mortified. I was truly full of regrets, and felt deeply. I hope there will be no more such feelings, or occasions. If your mother, my Dearest, were my own, if I know myself, I could not be more desirous to make her happy, or to serve her more kindly, & faithfully, than I now do. Her notions, and my own, I know run in the same channel, so far as, we wish to have our own way. I wish to save her trouble, and she will not let me. Well, we both mean well! I hope the matter is at an end, and neither will ever have cause, for unkind feelings, so long as we live.

Surely I have had none, and they would be most unhappy to see if I had! Well Dear, let this rest.

You did right my Dear, in sending as you did for Mother. I hope she will, or has arrived safe, long since. I will be uneasy, until I get your next letter, for I know the roads are miserably bad, from Huntsville to Bro Vernals. You tell me, that he has been Licensed to Preach. I am happy that it is so. My prayer is that he may be useful to the church, and the cause of Religion![1] I know, and feel, that I am not good, and that it is not fit, that I a sinner, should even express admiration for Holiness in others. The Lord is my God, and he holds me, by His Almighty power, and can, in an instant convert my soul, & open my eyes to His wonderful Salvation!

27th I closed the above last night at 12 M. The hour has come to night after a busy day. To night at eight, I was invited inside the "Columbian Order of Tammany."[2] On my admission, I made a pretty, & appropriate Speech, much to the satisfaction of the Brothers. It was not a public, but rather private exhibition. I am gratified that I came to the city. Matters are changed, and I find the "Donaldson correspondence"[3] has done me no injury! I have been invited to many places in the North, where the people think I can go, during the Holidays. I will enclose you one invitation which I have received, to give you an idea of the Telegraph. I can not explain it to you, but so it works. I intend to visit Hartford Conn't, on the 29th if spared, and from thence, I may go to Buffalo. On my return, I may make a public speech here, and Lecture in Phila, as I could not, on my way here. I have a serious intention to visit our great friend in Providence,[4] and should have done so, but for the lack of time.

I can only say to you my Dear Wife, that all our friends here regret much, that you did not come on, and our friends Col Mickle,[5] and Lady have read me a Lecture, for not bringing you, and all the little Houstons, to rusticate with them on Long Island, last summer.[6] They are a most worthy, & wealthy family. You, I hope my Love, will not suppose for a moment, that I can enjoy myself a moment, only when I can reach you, and our little ones, for I declare to you, there is an empty aching void which nothing but your presence can fill. If I laugh, it is not the laugh of pleasure, which I can feel, and enjoy as at little Mag's lisping blundering, and the singularity of sweet Nannie's. Nor can all the splendor of New York afford me the pleasure, which I realise, at the antics of Molly. Then add to these, the sweet smile of a Mother, which sheds on all these the perfection of bliss. Do not suppose, that our Philosopher is forgotten. No my Love, I feel for Sam, some thing more indefinable, than all I feel for them, but no less affectionate. Yet, he is a Boy, and I grant you, a noble Boy.

You can say to Isabella that her friend Mr Dean, & Mrs. [James] Auchincloss, are glad to hear from her. Mr Dean is not well at this time, but I hope will soon be restored. Kiss all the Dear Little ones, and present my affection to Mother.

Thy Devoted Husband

Houston

[1]No evidence has been found that Vernal Lea was ever pastor of a church, but he was often referred to as an "elder."

[2]The Tammany Society was a powerful Democratic political organization founded in New York City in 1789. Houston was initiated into the society as member No. 3322. Friend, 217.

[3]C. H. Donaldson was apparently a pen name of an unidentified person who wrote letters to the *New York Herald* using Houston's name for political purposes. Houston wrote to the editor of *The Texas Monument*, September 27, 1851, to set the record straight. See *Writings, vol. 5*, 309–10.

[4]Mrs. Alva Woods.

[5]Andrew H. Mickle of New York City. Identified in *Writings,* vol. 6, 239.

[6]The Mickles' home on Long Island was described as "a magnificent place near Oyster Bay." James Auchincloss to Sam Houston, April 20, 1851, A. J. Houston Collection, #3964, Texas State Archives, Austin, Texas.

Buffalo N. Y.
31st Dec 1851

My Dear Love,

I find my self on the Eve of the New Year 52, North of the city of New York some 480 miles, and to me it seems, an endless distance from you. I am in the midst of a snow storm, and if I live, I intend tomorrow, to wend my way south.

I may, or may not speak here, as the night will be so unfavorable. I spoke at Hartford, on the subject of the "Indians," on the 29th night,[1] and hundreds could not get in the House. It went off well, and the Ladies were much pleased, and I would have been inexpressibly happy, if a Lady, had been there, which I need not name. You know, my Dearest, you say, your infirmity is jealousy. I would not for all the world, be author of any act which could, with just cause, arouse such feeling, in your breast. Yet, I do know, that you are restrictive, of my admiration! I do not blame you, and candidly, I am not displeased that you are so. But the Lady to whom I allude, and to whom my affections are constantly recurring, is none other—and I may as well tell you at once—my own Dear Wife!! Now dont you think my Love, I would have been happy to have seen her? Yes, dont doubt it! If the snow storm ceases in time to day, I intend to see the falls of Niagra. From here they are 22 miles, and the cars run twice a day.

If I live to reach the city again, my first pleasure will be to read your letters, which I hope to meet there, and then write to you.

Many happy, happy New years to you, and Mother, and a thousand kisses to the children. May Kind Heaven shield, & protect you! May you be happy. Tell all Howda.

Thy devoted Husband
Houston

[1]For an outline of the lecture see *Writings*, vol. 5, 377. The notice, taken from the *Texas State Gazette* gives the date of the speech as January 5, 1852. Ibid.

My Dearest,

I am again at my post. I am well. Your letter has just reached me. Send Joshua to Buds,[1] and get Jim, & Nancy[2] to stay with you. Do in all things as you think best my Love. I desire you to be happy, and employ any means, which you may think fit. I am sorry to hear that Mother was injured. I was not willing that she should go, as I could not see that it was of any use. I hope she will soon recover entirely. I cant express any opinion, about her going to Mr [Charles] Power's, but if I were to do it, I would not be disposed to advise the trip.

Let Nancy & Jim come up. You will be more happy, and have good attention. About your health, and happiness, I am more concerned, than about all the property we jointly own![3] I only got in this morning, & was present to receive Kossuth[4] in the Senate. He was greeted <u>to an excess</u>. He is a Great man, but we cant go to war for Hungary![5] You will see all the news, for I will try, and send it to you. A speech has been sent to you. You must read it, or have it read. I read with pleasure Genl [Francis. L.] Hatch's[6] letter. Tis all right!!! I will write to you often. I intend my Love, if spared to see you, and our dear little ones, in the spring. Policy or politics, will not prevent it, and I hope duty (Imperious) will not interpose in the way of all my hopes, & wishes!

Dont fail to send for the servants to Vernals, & soon.

My heart swells, when I think of you, and the children as you describe them. Oh my Love, if [I] could only have been with you and them, to have given Christmas & N. Years kisses! My love to Mother & kisses as usual to the children.

Thy Devoted
Houston

Howda to Isabella, Jackson, & all. I fear you are blinded in Mary Willies charms, but I hope not.

[1]Vernal Lea.

[2]Slaves owned by Vernal Lea.

[3]Houston is referring to the property in Liberty County owned by the family.

[4]Louis Kossuth, a Hungarian patriot. Upon meeting Houston, Kossuth was reported in the *Congressional Globe* as saying, "I wish I had been as successful as you, sir." Houston replied, "God grant that you may yet be so." Crane, 210. For a description of Houston's attire at the meeting see Friend, 217–18.

[5]It is unknown how Houston would have voted on an earlier resolution extending hospitalities and a reception in the Senate to Kossuth. Houston abstained on the vote after pairing with an absent Rusk. Crane, 209.

[6]F. L. Hatch, the editor of the Huntsville *Texas Banner*.

Senate Chamber
6th Jany 1852

My Dear Love,

While I write this note, I feel that a crisis, is at hand with you, of deep interest, & solicitude to me.[1] I feel that I ought to be with you, and if possible, sustain you with my presence, and my affection. These I am not present to console you with. My prayers, & my hopes, are all that I can offer. They are as ardent, and sincere, as the human heart is capable of. I can not estimate the sacrifice which I would freely give to be present with you in your travail. I must be unhappy, & miserable until I can hear from you. Don't, I beseech you, my Dear, be unhappy at the event, in <u>any</u> case. I look for a Girl, but if it is a Boy, I will be satisfied, because Sam, will be very happy, and it will have a decided impression on his character, and I hope for the better. It is snowing much, & we have had more snow this season, than any two, since I have been here.

I hope you are <u>snug</u>, & comfortable this cold weather. I will not be happy until I can see you, and clasp you to my heart. Give to our Dear little ones a Fathers embrace, & many kisses. My love to Mother, & howda to Isabella, & Jackson.

Do write. In six, or seven days, I hope to hear from you by Telegraph, as I have before advised you, thro. Col Yoakum, & Christy.

Thy ever devoted Husband
Houston

[1]Houston is referring to the impending birth of their fifth child.

Senate Chamber
7th Jany 1852

My Dear Wife,

For two days past, I have written to you, and as a speech is making in which I feel little concern, I would rather converse with you, tho' thousands of miles intervene, to your smiles, only in fancy, than be idle. The <u>rage</u> here, has been for Kossuth. I think the fever has got to its hight, and will decline, in the scale of fancy.[1]

For the first time this season, I <u>dined</u> out, on yesterday. I have attended to no <u>Levees</u>, nor have I time, even to call, and see my [Letcher] cousins, in the parlour, more than once a week. I find myself pressed with company to a painful extent. Do not my Dear, suppose, that I am troubled about the pressing matters of the Presidency. Genl Scott will be run by the Whigs, and if the Democrats, wish to succeed they will have to run, a military man, or they will be beaten, as sure, as they were beaten before. So you see, my Dear, I am easy in my feelings, and will not be annoyed by any thing which may be done!

I can tell you little if any thing that will interest you. If I see any thing of import, I will send you the paper marked, so that I need not write it. My friends do not fall off, but stand by me, and wherever I go, the enthusiasm among the people is manifest, and none but the politicians are opposed to me. The resemblance, to matters now, and when Genl Jackson was first brot forward, is very striking. He had the politicians against him, and the people for him.

To day is a beautiful sunny day, and the snow is fast melting away. My Dear Love, I count on the approach of March next, and the great sustainer of my heart, is the hope of seeing you, and <u>all</u> our "<u>chicks</u>."

My love to Mother, & kisses to <u>all</u> the <u>little</u> ones.

Thy devoted Husband
Houston

[1]For information on how the American public received Kossuth see Parke Godwin, "When Kossuth Rode up Broadway," *Ladies Home Journal,* Vol. XIV, #3, February, 1897, n. p.

The following letter is in the Dorothy Loe Collection, at the Sam Houston Research Library in Liberty, Texas.

Huntsville
Jan 7 1852

My dear husband,

I must write by this mail, as it is my regular day, though I am hardly able to do so. I had an uncomfortable night, and it is so cold today, that I can hardly hold my pen. Since I wrote last week, I have recd your welcome letters of the 14th and 16th ult. I have felt more cheerful since their reception, particularly as you speak of coming home in March. My time will pass much more pleasantly, with the hope of seeing you soon, and yet it is my wish that you should weigh the matter well, and not do any thing that can possibly militate against your interest, or take any step that you may here after regret. I rejoice to find that in the midst of your many cares, and surrounded as you are by gay company, you still find time for your religious duties and for good books. I am not surprised that you see the nothingness and vanity of all around you. I can imagine but one attraction that the great city of Washington would present to me, and that is my husband's society, and that would be far sweeter in some wild-wood shade, for then I could have it all myself. On some subjects, I plead guilty to the charge of selfishness. I need not tell you what they are.

Our children grow more and more interesting. I can not say that one is more talented than another, but Nannie is the most remarkable. Her mind seems a mighty Niagara, that rushes impetuously over every obstacle. I sometimes almost regret that she has been taught to read, and wish that her genius had been allowed to slumber a little longer, but there is no possibility of confining such a mind as hers, for she learns things almost intuitively. I will give you a specimen of her reflection. She asked me a few days ago, what was the sin that caused Satan's fall from Heaven. I told her, it was pride. She then asked how pride could [torn] into the heart of a pure angel, and if God put it there. It is a subject she had never heard discussed, for you know I am not fond of taking up perplexing subjects, particularly in the presence of my children.

Yes she is a strange child and although her intellect is so masculine, her nervous system is so exceedingly delicate, that she can not bear the least harshness. If she should ever be deprived of a mother's care, and thrown upon your hands, my dear husband, let her always be controlled through her affections and judgement. But I trust I shall be permitted to tell you in person my reasons for saying so much about her. Sam is doing well. He surprised me this morning, a little after dawn, by the assurance that he did not want any more sisters, but a little brother to play with him. I do not know the cause of his sudden exclamation, and did not question him about it. Mag and Molly are as busy as little bees, and as sprightly as mocking-birds. Molly keeps up her devotions, and if any one talks while she is on her knees, she raises her head and shakes her fist at them, with a look of fury and indignation. Maggie still boasts of pap's forehead, and takes . . . *[The last part of the letter is missing.]*

Senate Chamber
9th Jany 1852

My Dear Love,
Yesterday I did not write to you, and therefore did not say that I

was at a Kossuth Dinner.[1] I was there, but did not speak.[2] I was at Dinner last night given by the Jackson Democratic committee[3] of this place. There I did not speak, but left at an early hour.[4] I will not sanction the Humbugging now going on. I have been and will be conservative in my votes, and my actions. There is a great furor, now in the community, but it will be like the Tempest which only leaves evidences of the fury of the elements, and ruined castles. There is a <u>rage</u> by some to make capital, & reach the Presidency. This may suit some persons, but me it will not. I would rather my children should have it to say, my "Father was a wise man, & patriot," than that "he was President of the United States." The relation which I am to bear to our children, must depend upon myself, and they must be satisfied with my discretion. My own country first, secondarily the cause of Freedom & humanity thro out the world! This I know my Dear, will meet your sanction. I agree with you, that "it is an agreeable thing to be generous, when it costs us nothing." Intervention in the affairs of foreign nations, might cost us a great deal. "Ill none [sic] of it."[5]

My Dear, I am not less anxious, than when we parted or when I last wrote. Give my love to Mother, & kisses to all the children.

Thy devoted Husband
Sam Houston

---

[1] For a description of the dinner attended by members of the Senate, House, Cabinet, and Supreme Court, see Nevins, 548.
[2] For a description of Houston's attire at the dinner see Friend, 283–84.
[3] The January 8th celebration of Jackson's victory at the Battle of New Orleans.
[4] For a description of the Jackson Day dinner and the speech by Senator Stephen Douglas see Nevins, 545.
[5] Houston is referring to the situation in Hungary.

Washington
10 Jany 1852

My Dearest,

I write to you to let you know that you are always present to my mind, and my affection is always ardent and sincere for you.

The constant inquiries for you, would keep memory alive, if it needed revival, which I assure you it does not. Day and night, you, and the little ones are present to my mind, and my heart. I look with consolatory pleasure to the spring, when I hope to embrace you, and resume, the agreeable task of nursing, the little fellows, and narating [sic] to Sam, something amusing, and instructive!

So soon as I can with leisure, I will write you a sketch on the subject of matrimony! I have, of late had fancies on that, which <u>liken</u> matrimony to a continued courtship. What do you think of this? You will approve of it, I think! I will look with intense anxiety until I hear from you. In three days, I hope to hear from you, by Telegraph, as I told you of my arrangement! I hope my Dear Love, you have received the stores from New Orleans.

In all matters, which concern your happiness, or comfort, dont take money into the account, but expend what you want, & I will not question the matter. Col Yoakum, will furnish you any amount that you desire. He has it in his hands, or can collect it of ours, when he chuses. Now dont fail in this. Do as seems best!!!

To day I was to see poor Mr [Henry] Clay.[1] He is fast sinking, and can only live a few weeks—March will limit his existence, I think! I have been to see him before, and can see the change! I told him at any hour, or time, to let me know, if I could be of use to him, and it would afford me the greatest pleasure to serve, or wait upon him. He seemed much gratified, and assured me, that there was no friend, upon whom he would more readily call, than on myself! My paper is nearly out.

My love to Mother, and kisses to <u>all</u>. Can Mary Willie talk?

Thy devoted Husband
Houston

[1]For a description of Clay's health at this time see Remini, 770. Clay lived until June 29, 1852.

Senate Chamber

13th Jany 1852

My Dear Love,

You would be provoked at me if I did not write you something in the form of a letter. I can only say how much I love, and how great my anxiety is about you. I have only received three letters since I came.

None arriving for two sundays, has given me increased anxiety, but as none has come from anyone at Huntsville, induces a hope, that none arriving is owing to the fault of the mail. The deep snows, may have an influence, South as well as North!

In my next letter, I hope to tell you something of a pleasant nature! Indeed my Dearest, I hope to have none, but pleasant incidents, to tell you of! I send you some Drafts which I paid you to day. I have funded my money, and it is drawing interest. I want to manage, my Love, that you will have as much as you chuse to expend. I hope my Love to be able to send you the sort of "steam loom," that you desire, as well as the matters which I spoke of yesterday.[1] If Mr Shaw can take charge of them, I will send them.

I am my Dearest,

Your devoted Husband

Sam Houston

[In the margin:] I have not time to read it over.

[1] No letter for January 12, 1852, has been located.

Huntsville

Jan. 14, 1852

My very dear husband,

I am greatly indebted to you for the treasures brought by the last mail, your favors of the 19th, 21st, and 23rd ult. I am distressed to learn that you have recd so few of my letters, and surprised that you have recd none from Col Yokum, for he told me not long ago, that he had written to you several times. It is all to be attributed to the condition of the mails. I recd a note from Mr [Joseph] Lewis, written at your request, after you had set off for New York.[1] I hope you will thank him for me. He mentioned that he would send me a paper containing your speech, which I have no doubt he did, but I have not yet received it. Of course you will know that I am exceedingly anxious to see it. I hope by next mail, I shall recieve a copy of it.

Since I wrote to you last week I have had a very sick family. Every member of the family, both white and black has had an attack of neumonia [sic] except Eliza and myself. Isabella has been able to assist me a good deal in nursing the sick, although suffering much from her bronchial affliction, owing to the repeated colds which she has taken. She had never before lived in a damp airy house, but endures it with great cheerfulness. The children all had very severe attacks, but they seem almost well again. What a mercy, that my strength has been prolonged to nurse them through their sickness! Mother's attack was very severe, but she is much better. Dr Evan's family were so afflicted with the same disease, that I did not send for him at all.

I am glad that you still intend to come home in march, though I still say to you that I do not wish you to do any thing that you may afterwards regret. It is an important year with you, and if you think it will be more favorable to your prospects to remain at your post, distressing as the loss of your society would be, I will try to summon fortitude and take care of our little ones at home, if my life is spared. If it should not be, your own feelings will dictate what you had best do. I could write volumes on this subject, but my strength is not sufficient and there is a pent up fountain within my heart, that I must not disturb. It is a time of deep feeling with me of course, when all that is dear seems dearer, when "the sensitive mimosa of affection trembleth to its root," but I forbear.

You must present me affectionately to your kindred, and also to Mrs Donelson and Mary. The children talk a great deal about you. Maggie says, "Ma tell pa to bring me some green shoes, and write me a little baby letter."

I shall be very anxious to hear from your northern tour. It is hardly probable that I shall write again shortly, but I can not tell. Antoinette & Charles expect mother to go down as soon as she can leave me. Antoinette writes to mother, that she will come up after her, if she will not go, otherwise send their carriage to Houston for her. Jackson Paul will write to you soon after his return. He seems to think he has pledged himself to you, not to leave us, until your return. I did not understand it so myself, and tell him, if he would like to go into business of some kind, you will not think any thing hard of it.

As ever, your affectionate wife

M. L. Houston

¹This letter from Houston's secretary has not been located.

Washington

16th Jany 1852

My Very Dear Wife,

For two days, I have not written to you, and I feel some what culpable for not have [sic] done so! It is true that I have but little to say that can amuse, or interest you. I intend to quit Browns, at which I have been staying for near thirty years. They treat me, and my friends as tho. we were dependent on them. This you may suppose I do not like. It will cause them repentance, for my friends will quit the House to be with me. I find that the change too, in point of comfort, will be an amendment. Tomorrow I intend to leave them.

I find myself so pressed to make <u>lectures</u>, on various subjects, that I am really annoyed. I will not consent to make any more than I can help.

As to political matters, they are going on smoothly, and my friends are well satisfied with the present, as well as the future condition of affairs.

To day I put up some things, among them, the articles, of which

I have written. In addition to them, I included a blue dress for you, and a patern [sic] also for Mother (brown). I hope you will both be pleased with them. I have procured for you, a piece of <u>muslin</u>, such as you told me of, but cant send it, as it is too large. I will now tell you of a fancy of mine. The Nullification Key (Gold) which Cousin Columbus [Lea] gave me, I had made into a large plain ring, for my third finger,[1] and what device do you think I had put in it. You could not guess, so I will tell you. It is "my Wife & children." How do you take this conceit? I like it!!! It is, I know, and feel very <u>homely</u>. Dont you think so?

Well, you tell me that Mary Willie is becoming much like a certain "wall flower" that hangs in the parlour, and that she grows more, & more beautiful. I thank you for this delicate compliment, and the more, because you seem not to intend it. I am impatient to receive the Telegraphic dispatch, which I expected before this time, but It may be that there has been some neglect, or that there was some miscalculation, that I devotedly hope, we will some day have time to rectify. Mr Creath wrote to me about some money matters. Until I reach home in March, if I should be spared, we need not take any steps in the business. Indeed you know my Dearest, that we have in all matters, been more liberal, than any other person, to our means. And <u>that</u> Burke[2]—a great pest—is at me again, to send him money, for Sunday School matters, I think it is. I will not trouble him to disburse any <u>cash</u> <u>for</u> <u>me</u>, as I do not desire, to be <u>under</u> <u>any</u> <u>obligations</u>, to him, in <u>that way</u>.

It is now nearly one oclock A.M., and I must retire to rest!

My Love to Mother, and I want you to embrace all the children, and tell them, it is for pa, and that he hears, they are sweet, and good children. Tell Nannie if I live to get home, that I will not <u>whittle</u>,[3] so that she can be more about me [sic]! It makes me very happy, to hear that they are learning so prettily under Isabella. And how sweetly they ought to obey her! Sam, I have heard from by a Gentleman who overtook him on the road, and had a chat with him. He wrote that Sam was a "smart fellow, and talked like a Book." He said too that he knew Sam by his likeness to me, before he heard who he was! By the bye, Sam has not yet written to me about his Pony, & the Puppy! It is time.

I am truly thy anxious, affectionate, and ever devoted Husband.

Houston

[1] In a photograph made from the Daguerreotype in the collection of Mrs. F. T. Baldwin, a plain gold ring is seen on the third finger of Houston's right hand. See Sam Houston, Donald Day and Harry Herbert Ullom, eds., *The Autobiography of Sam Houston* (Norman: University of Oklahoma Press, San Jacinto Edition, 1954), opposite p. 70.

[2] James Burke. For a biography see *New Handbook of Texas,* vol. 1, 833.

[3] Houston was in the habit of whittling while he listened to speakers. While in the senate chamber he was supplied blocks for whittling prepared by the senate cabinetmaker, Mr. Griffall. Christian F. Eckloff, *Memoirs of a Senate Page 1855–1859,* Percival G. Melbourne, ed. (New York: Broadway Publishing Company, 1909), 42–43.

Washington
18th Jany 1852

My Very Dear Wife,

To day I intended to have gone to hear my friend Gallaher, but when I rose, it was too late as I supposed to hear the whole Lecture. He has been with me to night, for more than two hours, and walked to my quarters more than a half mile, in a snow storm, for it has been snowing the livelong day, nor has it yet ceased, altho, it is ten oclock. For weeks past, every thing has been white, and some portion of the time, excessively cold!

My friend Mr. Gallaher retains much affection for his departed wife, and seems to be more happy, and cheerful [when] in [my] company than with any other person. His wife[1] was one of my favorite cousins. *[In the margin here there is a drawing of a hand pointing to the line which appears to be written with a different pen and begins as follows:]*

Well, my Love, I had hoped by my removal that I would have rest, for a while, but I fear it is not to be the case! Just as I had finished the last paragraph, a gentleman came in, and sat for two hours in conversation, so that it is now twelve oclock (midnight). Nevertheless my Dear, I will continue to write until my letter is of reasonable length, as I suppose you would be provoked, if I did not write, <u>a whole letter</u>. I must tell you some news. Well Kossuth is gone, and a happy riddance. Your Husband did not make a fool of himself, as others did. I have no more inclination to do so, than I had to play the fool about Jennie Lynd! Miss Celeste, the Dancer, has been here, and is gone! I did not go to see her. Catherine Hays, the vocalist is here, and I have not been to hear her. For this, you will perhaps blame me, but I cant help that, for I do not wish to go into a Theatre, and if I went for one purpose, I might wish to go for another!

It is stated that Lola Montes, is to be here, and she is said to dance very well. It may be so, but I do not intend to see her exhibit, with her <u>short dress</u>. For this you will <u>not blame me</u>, I am sure! I, will try and do, as near like you would desire me to do, as possible, or what I think you wish me to do!

All my leisure time, and what I may steal from sleep, I wish to devote to you, in writing letters! I was delighted to hear from you, of your admirable health. I pray that it may be perfect, and that you may be spared future suffering!

All that you write me about yourself, and the children has ten fold charms for me, and enhances my desire to be with you soon, and always. The news you write me about the visit of Dr Baker,[2] and his friend, has been matter of amusement to me, and as the day was suited to "a disguise" I doubt not, was convenient for your feelings, as well as graceful, for your person! As he had not seen you before, there was no necessity, for a comparison, in your appearance. My Love, you I know, can have some idea of my anxiety since no Telegraphic dispatch has arrived. Indeed my Love, I do not know how to account for it, but in one way, and that I must tell you. A friend was in here to night, and I was telling him of my anxiety, when he said (being a man of family,) "There is no calculating, if it should be a Girl, For Girls <u>do stick so</u>"!!! I am prepared for it, and dont you be distressed. I think it will be <u>one</u>, if not <u>two</u>! My Love I am only concerned about your health, & happiness. Love to all!

Thy Husband
Houston

[1]Lucinda Houston. Reverend Samuel Rutherford Houston, 111.
[2]It is unclear whether Houston is referring to Dr. Daniel Baker of Huntsville or Dr. G. W. Baker of Cincinnati, Texas.

Washington
19th Jany 1852

My Dear Love,

This morning at one A.M. I closed a letter to you, and as it is now late to night, I can do no better than to write again. I am at leisure too, for I believe every one else, has gone to the concert of Miss Katherine Hays. Thus far my Dear, I find my new home more pleasant than my old one, but neither as pleasant, as my Woodland home! I pine so much for it, that I am now devising some pretext to get off sooner than March, if it is possible, and see you. The Telegraph has not yet come to me, tho. I have for days hoped for it. The snow storm may have caused disorder, in the wires, from the falling of limbs, on them. I will look anxiously until they tell me some news, from you!

The political atmosphere is at this time, some what troubled! To some it will be more so, if I judge rightly of the signs of the times. There are some matters which I hear of in connexion [sic], with some of the Candidates, which will be relished worse, than the "Donaldson correspondence" was by me! Our country really has some things to deplore, which I regret, for we have to leave our children, in the country, when we pass off the stage, and I would be happy, if I cou'd hope that I could leave them in a Government, as incorrupt, as the one, which existed when my Father left me, in this world. Our Government must be like all which have existed, in the world. The extension of our limits, the enterprize [sic] of our people, and the intelligence of possessed, will pospone the evil day! Yet luxury is growing upon us, a pace, and where it exists, to a great extent, avarice will grow, and so sure as it exists, corruption will follow, with faithlessness in office, and public men. I have compared our present condition, with what it was, when I was first in Congress, and I am sorry to assure you, that the comparison is by no means gratifying, to my humble stock of patriotism! I know my Love, that you are not a Politician, but at the same time, I know you love your country, your Husband, & your children, & these reflections, interest all of us.

If the people chuse to elevate me, I pledge myself to eradicate, so far as I can, all abuses. But even this determination, does not cause me to place my <u>affections</u> upon the Presidency, so far that the disappointment, would wound my happiness. Since I have been blessed with you, and what you have given to me, I feel that I should be content & happy while Providence is pleased to share me the enjoyment, of <u>such</u> gifts!! My Dear, are you not half provoked, that I write so much to you? If I thought you were, I would go to repose earlier than I do, "that I would." As I cant be satisfied of the fact, I will have to write, just as often as I can!

You must my Dearest, make such a talk, from Pa, to each of the children, as you think fit.

The weather here, is very cold, and a prospect of much sleighing. I have not been in one this year, nor do I expect to be!

My love to Mother, and howda to Isabella & Jackson! Salute all friends

Truly & faithfully thy Husband
Houston

Washington
20th Jany 1852

My Dear Love,

Another day has passed, and yet no Telegraphic dispatch. The time has almost arrived, when by mail I should hear from you! My solicitude increases with every hour, and the excitement of this great world can not estrange my thoughts from you, & home![1]

To day I wrote to Sam, not to lessen your labour in reading, for I know you would have to read for him. I must write a letter to my Dear little Nannie, as I know it will make her happy for a while at least. I suppose Maggie would rather have one from Judge Hay![2]

You did right with my likenesses, and need not have rendered any apology for so doing. The card was sufficient. You set a greater estimate, on them, than what I do myself! The likeness in the Parlour, and the one at Col E Allens,[3] I think most of! They are fine of their day, and as you say Miss Molly so resembles the one at home, I hope you will become more partial to it, as it serves for an index, to new works.

Matters move on slowly, and the <u>candidates briskly</u>! I am un-moved, and as quiet as a Lamb! I say "let the physic work." In my native county, there will be a fuss ire long, so says my cousin John Letcher! The reason why it has not heretofore taken place, is because the old Dominion has been frozen up. So soon as the snow melts away, the people will move. The cold here to day is six degrees be-low zero, as reported. The sleigh bells are constantly tingling, and I suppose the riders happy. I do not envy them. I think more about going home, than I do about amusing myself here! I do not expect to be happy, until I can see you, and our little ones. I need not again assure you my Love, that all the pleasures, and honors, of this vast world are not sufficient, to requite, me for the happiness, of which I am deprived, by my absence from you, and our little prattlers. I thought they were some times, <u>rather noisy</u>, but I would be willing to endure now, tenfold, if I could only be at home, and hear the hearty laughs, and see the smiling faces, of the little urchins! I can now see Sam's astonishment, and surprize, when Mag said he was the "first man," and her vacant, and non-chalant [sic] look!

My Dear Love, it is late, and I will close this epistle with kindest remembrances to all, and to yourself inexpressible affection!

Thy Devoted
Houston

[1]The fifth Houston child, another daughter, was born on this day.

[2]Samuel D. Hay. Dickinson, 53.
[3]On April 5, 1852, Houston wrote Ashbel Smith requesting that this likeness be sent to him. *Writings,* vol. 5, 338.

Washington
23rd Jany 1852

My Dear Love,

Apprehending that I may not have time to write this evening, I now write a few lines. The place is without news, only such as you dont care about.

The snow, and the sleighs, are the only subjects of remark, and amusements, except the "assemblies" or Balls, which I hear by chance are well attended. I have not been to one of them, nor do I intend to be this season. Do you my Dear, believe me, when I assure you, that I have more pleasure, in writing to you, and of my scrolling epistles, that I could feel, in attending twenty Balls!

My Love, I see that the convention at Austin unanimously nominated me for the Presidency.[1] It reached me by Telegraph from New Orleans. I expected news, more <u>interesting</u> to me, for many days. To day I hope it will, for indeed I am impatient, & unhappy. The mails in consequence of the storms, have all stopped. I will hope, and not despair. I would be glad my Dear, if I could write you any interesting matter. I will try to night, and send you, and Sam, some Temperance matters, to amuse you! I was last evening, at an "exile supper," prepared for the occasion, of a committee, which waited upon the President, in favor of soliciting him, to ask the release of OBrian Mougher & other (Rebels) from captivity. I went with the committee of several hundred, from Boston, Baltimore, and this city, and was <u>pressed</u> to the supper! Things went off well!

I will if possible, soon write you something political, tho I know you dont much care about such matters.

Love to all
Thy devoted
Houston

I have not time to read this letter!

[1]For information about the meeting held January 8, 1852, see Friend, 281.

Washington
25th Jany 1852

My Dear Love,

I had hoped to day to [have] heard from you, as this is the day, on which your letters usually come. I am still distressed, that I cant hear from you. It is now many days since I had hoped to hear from my friend Col. Christy. Other matters have been telegraphed from Orleans, of vastly less interest to me, than to hear from you, and of your situation. I can in my distress, only rely upon a beneficent Providence, and His perfect wisdom. I have been to church to day, and heard a beautiful Lecture on the subject of Zeruiah and her sons. Oh, it was quite rich! Hereafter they are to be continued, and I hope to be able to attend to all of them!

The snow still lingers with us, far beyond all recent example! I have nothing to interest you, by writing more my Love, or I would be happy to write all night.

As I have said in former letters, I anticipate with great pleasure, the meeting, which I fondly hope, is in store for us in the spring. This reconciles me to my present condition.

I wrote to Nannie last night and sent Books to amuse the children, and sent love to you, in hopes that Nannie, would appreciate the regard implied, and I hope our son, will not begrudge the notice, taken of his sister. I sent the little <u>red</u> <u>frock</u> picture to Mary Willie. I hope they will do to amuse them, and make them cheerful, and at the same time, learn them to take care of Books. In so doing, it will be strange if Mary Willies, is not demolished in a day. Indeed I think Miss <u>Romps</u>, [Maggie] will not last much longer. Nannie will take care of hers, and keep it safe!

My friend Caleb Lyon,[1] of Lyonsdale, is with me, and sends to you and Sam much regard, and good wishes.

Give my regards to Mother, and hug, & kiss the children all!!
Salute the family, and commend me to our friends.

Thy ever devoted & affectionate Husband

Sam Houston

[1]Lyon was later elected as a New York representative. *Biographical Directory of Congress,* 157.

Washington
28th Jany 1852

My Dear Love,

Had I possessed wings, I would have been with you ire this hour. To day about 2 oclock P.M. I received a Telegraphic notice from New Orleans, announcing the pleasing intelligence "A fine <u>daughter</u>, at 4 oclock A.M. 20th inst. All doing well. W. C." By adverting to my letters, you can have some idea of the relief, which the news gave to my mind. I was truly happy, and as I spoke of it to my fellow Senators, each one congratulated me, upon its being a Daughter, with only one exception, & he said, he prefered [sic] boys. I was happy, and no matter for others choice. I had made up my mind for a Girl, and particularly so, since Mr Williams used his consolatory expression, "that it must be a Girl, for girls stick so." Meaning, as I suppose, that they were expected long ire they make their advent. Dont my Love, say a word about the name! You dont care about that, and moreover my Dear, you intend as I suppose, to keep up my right, to name the Girls. You and Mother can name the Boys! You had in our contingency, declared your right! I do not know why it was that I never thought of providing finery, for the young Lady, to hold her first "levee" in.

I am anxious to know, what Mother has to say, in relation to the matter. I do suppose she would have been better pleased, to have had occasion to use, the other <u>half</u>, of my "San Augustine Banner." You see my Love, what a fine pretext I will have, to visit you, (if I live) in Feby or March! To see my wife, & baby will secure me the good opinion, of all the good wives, in the nation. But if it made one half of them, mad, it would not change my determination!

It is now one oclock A.M., but I coud not forego the duty, and pleasure of writing to you, tho. my duties have kept me engrossed, so much to day, & night.

You would be astonished to see how much I have grown, since I came to the city. Travelling, should I live, and warm weather will reduce me again.

I want you my Love, to write to me all the particulars, and tell me how the little stranger was greeted, by all the household!

My love to Mother, and kisses to <u>all</u> the children. I do suppose, that Mary Willie, & Mag, will make a rare fuss. Nannie, will feel the responsibility of her charge, and Sam will find cause of reflection, & regret. I reckon Mother said Heh!

Thy devoted Husband
Sam Houston

My Dear Love,

I know you wish to call the Baby Antoinette, and if you do, let it be her name! If you do not desire to call her Antoinette, I will insist on keeping the name in abeyance, as one of my "reserved rights."

Thy Devoted
Houston

Huntsville
Jan. 28th 1852

My ever dear Love,

Col Yokum [sic] has written you the news, that another fair girl is born unto us.[1] She was a week old yesterday. I frankly acknowledge, that for your sake, I wanted a boy, but from the moment of her birth I was reconciled, and now I am very happy. She is so strikingly like you, that everyone who sees her, either says or looks "what a pity she is not a boy." You say dearest if she is red-haired, you have a name for her. I send you a specimen which I do not think at all <u>reddish</u>. In that case, have you selected a name for her? I do hope in the choice of a name, we will be perfectly united. If you have not fixed on one, I would suggest "Antoinette Power," and I hope my love, that you will be candid with me, and not give your consent, unless it is your choice as well as my own.

My health is improving. I have suffered a great deal with my breasts, but not more than usual. I have not sent for Jim or Nancy, as your letter did not come until after the birth of the baby. I recd your speech[2] by the mail of the 20th inst, and read it with great pleasure, (before night of course!) Indeed I read the whole proceedings, and was delighted with your course, and (shall I say it?) proud of my husband.

The children are all in good health again. Please send me some garden seeds as soon as possible. Beets, cabbages, radishes, snap-beans, cucumbers and sage. I could write more, if it were prudent to tax my strength farther.

Ever thy devoted wife
M. L. Houston

[1]Yoakum's letter has not been located.
[2]Margaret is referring to Houston's speech of December 22, 1851, in reply to Foote.

The first two pages are missing from the following letter written by Houston to Margaret shortly after the birth of their fifth child.

. . . Please Mother too, and as she will spoil her, as much as grand parents do their daughters offspring, she will have a fine excuse! Viewing all the [blurred] I think you will call her <u>Antoinette</u>. Sam, to[o] and his sisters, would I am sure decide in favor, of the name! Oh! how I do wish to be at home and see you my Love, and the children. My very heart, seems absorbed, in the hope, and expectation, of seeing you all! I could write all night, but must cease by letting you know how much love Mrs [Myra Clark] Gaines sends you. Her suit has been on trial in the Supreme Court for some days. I did not attend, but I learn that the Room was crowded with Ladies, all the time. I have been told that she must gain her case, and if she does, it will be worth twenty millions. It is very popular here, for every one that I have heard speak of it says she ought to gain it, and they hope she will![1]

I sent you a letter from Bro Will. You will see that he has changed his mind, and I lend him $2,000. He is to secure it by Mortgageing [sic] double the amount of real estate! He secures the money, tho. he says, he may never be able, to repay the <u>kindness</u>!! he is a noble fellow, and I would be rejoiced if he were in Texas![2]

Now see what a long letter, I have written my Dear, when I only began to write a note, and say "<u>I love you</u>"! Cousin Narcissa [Hamilton] has gone, not in good health, tho. But left some embroidery for you. A pair of slippers! My love to all & kisses.

Thy Devoted Husband
Houston

[1]Mary (Mrs. Clement Claiborne) Clay wrote a description of Myra Gaines and said, "her fearless pleading in the Supreme Court was the theme of conversation the country over." Sterling, 82–83.
[2]For information about the loan see B. B. Wadell to Sam Houston, December 15, 1853, Andrew Jackson Houston Collection #4047, Texas State Archives, Austin, Texas.

Washington
1st Feby 1852

My Dear Love,

To day the young Lady is eleven days old, and I hope she, & her Dear Ma, are well. I hope my Love, you have been careful of your health, and that you will remain so, that your health may be restored, and made perfect. Ere this you have received some of my letters apprising you, of my intention to visit you, in the month of March.

That is, I intend to leave here about the last of this month, so as to reach home (should I live) by the middle of March!

You will be sorry for me, when I assure you, that it is now quite late, and I have not had an hour to my self since I rose this morning. True I have been twice to church, & heard two most able Lectures! They were on the character, of David, & Jonathan. I really feel pained, that my situation is such, that I can not promise myself, some seclusion, from visitors. That is, I am determined, if spared, I will not receive, or make visits, any longer, on sunday. I think it due to myself, and if I can not transact my business, in six days of the week, I will not give away the sabbath!

My Cousin Narcissa B. Hamilton, and the Daughter of another cousin have come, on a visit to the city. They are at Browns Hotel, with my cousin, Jno Letcher. On my return from church, I called to see them, and in answer to a thousand kind inquiries for you, and the children, I let her know, that she had a new cousin, at which she expressed much pleasure, and bade me present you a thousand kind wishes for you, and give you great love! My Dear, Mr Gallaher was present the Sunday night, that I received your letter, detailing the visit of Dr Baker, and his friend, and has come in to night. He regards me as a friend, and relation. He is a remarkable man, for in our intimacy of thirty five years, revived, I have not heard him use, one sectarian expression! He is greatly devoted, to his vocation. He preaches every day, or night, and some times, three times, in twenty four hours. I want to say a great deal to you, but I dont know what to say, as Mr Gallaher, and a friend are talking, so busily, that it bothers me! You know my Dear, that I have promised to be at New York, on the 18th of this month (if I can) at the Great Temperance festival.[1] I will send you a programme, of the celebration. You will see, that I am to present a Medal on the occasion.[2] I may, if I live, make several Lectures soon, as I have been invited, by various societies, in different places! I have been invited to Lecture in Providence Rhode Island, and to see your friends.[3] I will try, and go there and Lecture! I will try and make a good one, so as not to cause you mortification. It is partly on your account, I assure you, that I wish to go!

I do not expect you to write to me for some time, but I hope to hear of you from others soon! I received a letter from Jackson Paul, and he tells me his debts are pressing upon him. Tell him to keep them off, until I can get home, (if spared) and to say to his creditors, that I will try, and make matters easy, or pay them myself, and wait, with him. Sam, has taught me to be generous. Talk to Sam, about matters in confidence. I would like to know his thoughts, on the subject. I do not know any thing more, to say to you!

It is late, but I do not intend my Love, [to] let it be long ire I write again! I suppose Sam will be glad to read the "Banquet of Banquets." Love [to] Mother, and all.

Thy Devoted
Houston

My dearest,

By way of a Post Script, I can assure you, that, <u>I would not be willing to swap our girl for a boy</u>! Would you?

---

[1]For a complete account of the Banquet see Louise Boyer, "Sam Houston at the First 'Dry' Dinner," *Dallas Morning News*, n.d. This article reproduces the poster, which was several feet high, advertising the banquet and noting that the speakers included Horace Greeley, Horace Mann, Reverend Henry Ward Beecher, and P. T. Barnum. Although it is not dated, it was probably circa 1927 as it speaks of the banquet being "three quarters of a century ago." A copy is in the Sam Houston vertical file at the Barker History Center.

[2]Houston presented the medal to Neal Dow, Mayor of Portland, Maine. The solid gold medal, two and one-half inches in circumference, weighed four ounces and was decorated with an eagle flying over a waterfall and mountain tops. Ibid.

[3]Dr. and Mrs. Alva Woods.

Washington
4th Febry 1852

My Dear Love,

I was greatly pleased by receiving your last letter of the 14th ult. It was written before the Telegraph dispatch, but coming afterwards, it seemed as tho it had followed it, from you. I thank Providence, that you have gotten through all the troubles of sickness which beset you, in your almost helpless condition. I am not yet, without most serious solicitude about your own health. I hope you have been careful, & thereby you may prevent a return of the asthma. You must have had a serious time of it when all were sick, at home as well, as in the neighborhood. Could I have realised what was passing, I should have been distressed beyond measure. I hope under the care of Heaven, it will highten our joys when we meet.

It is only eleven days, until I hope to leave this place. My intention, is to go to Baltimore, and hear Mr. Fuller[1] preach on the 15th, from thence to Lecture in Philadelphia on the 16th, and on the 17th to go to New York, and on the 18th to attend the Banquet, and from thence either to visit Providence R. I. and Lecture there, or from N. Y. to turn my face homeward, & pass by way of Columbus Ohio, as my nearest route. And I may on the 25th Inst attend the Great Banquet in Columbus. I mean another "Temperance Banquet" of the state, to be given on that day, in Columbus. You need not fear my Love, that I will delay my trip <u>home</u>. The word <u>home</u>, has too many charms for me, not to attract me at the earliest moment, possible. Just think my dear, what a field of Fancy, I have to roam over. First to fancy, how you will look. How each of the children, will appear, and if by day, where, & how, each one will meet me, and then the Baby—Oh, the Baby! and <u>I must say it is pretty,</u> <u>or</u> offend its dear Ma! Well, I fancy it is very pretty, and red headed! We will see how I guess. Now I would make a wager that its hair is auburn, and I have a reason, which I hope to tell you soon! I do not wish to write too long a letter, as I write so often. I send a scrap, to amuse Sam, & his little sisters. Love to all.

Thy faithful Husband
Houston

[1]Richard Fuller. For a biography see Thomas R. McKibbens, Jr., *The Forgotten Heritage: A Lineage of Great Baptist Preaching* (Macon, Georgia: Mercer University Press, 1986), 181–85.

My ever dear husband,

I do not expect to write any thing very entertaining today, for realy I am scarcely able to hold my pen. For a week I have suffered severely from inflamation [sic] of the face and neck (from the teeth,) and one cheek is so swollen today, that I am not very beautiful I assure you, and hardly think you would fall in love with me. I have determined however, to write a few lines, lest you should be uneasy about us. With the exception of myself, all are well.

I recd no letters from you by last mail. It was a sore disappointment of course, but as there was no mail from beyond Houston, it is easily accounted for. I am exceedingly anxious to know what you have to say about the new-comer. I have no fears that you will not love her, after you have seen her, (for she is such a charmer that "to see her is to love her,") but until then, I must acknowledge I have some misgivings.

The children are growing so rapidly, that you would hardly know them. You would be amused to see Mary Willie with her pencil and paper writing to dear papa to "come hum." The children all talk a great deal about you, and long for the time to come when you will be at home again. I hope it will not be long until you make one of our circle once more. But I feel that it is so uncertain, that I am trying to prepare myself for a disappointment. Do tell me if you can, when you will set off for home. Col. Yokum does not think you will leave until after the Baltimore convention, but I have some hopes that you will think it just as well to leave sooner.

I do not feel well enough to write more today. I shall be happier if I get letters from you by next mail. Do not my dear love, indulge any uneasiness on our account, for the Good Lord watcheth over us. Maggie just now says "Ma are you writing to pa about me so good?" Sam and Nannie have been very inquisitive to know what I would say about them, and I have just said enough to tell them they were mentioned. Jackson is still with us and doing very well. Mother sends her love to you.

Thy devoted wife
M. L. Houston

Washington
13th Feby 1852

My Dear Love,

Altho. I am pressed with business, I can not deny myself the pleasure, of answering a part of your letter of the 28th Ult. One part, I anticipated you in, and that was the Babys name. That is settled, "<u>Antoinette Power</u>." This is friday night, and on sunday morning, if I live, I intend to go to Baltimore, not as a start on my journey, but to hear Mr Fuller Preach, as you desired me to do. From that I intend to visit Philadelphia—speak on the Indians, and attend the "Banquet" at New York, and speak on <u>Temperance</u>.[1] From thence, I intend to start on my way home, and my anxiety, will increase, if spared, as distance, and space will diminish, until I can see you, and be at home! Had I not been nearly ready, to start for home, I would have sent Miss Mag, the "baby letter," she wished me to send her.

You do not wish me my Love, to do, nothing, which might cause me regret hereafter. My notions are all set on political matters, and in them, you know I am a predestinarian, and above that, I will not for any high, and national office, descend to the petty employment, of a Grog-shop electioneerer. Others may, but I will not. Moreover, my Love, I would be mean, if I did not prefer you, and our children to my friends, that I should be about, at this time, and when it will be known, that my absence, arises from affection for my wife, and children! So Dearest, feel no anxiety on this subject. Much, the largest portion of my life, has been bestowed upon mankind at large, and if it were selfish to love my family, I could claim exemption from blame, and as Congress will not transact any important business for months to come, I would have nothing to lose!

I am much gratified, that you approved my Speech, in reply to Gov Foote. It was more agreeable, because you are careful, not to compliment* me, which is all well enough! *[In margin: *You know my Love you are fearful of <u>exciting</u> <u>my</u> <u>vanity</u>. Is it not true?]* I did not provoke Gov Footes attack, tho. I was really glad that he assailed me! Some thought I had laid a trap for "Parson Means" but indeed I did not, for I had only heard the anecdote, a short time previous to using it in the Senate! He has to wear the Nick-name, the balance of his life, I think. He had been my secrete enemy as, I found out, and this was, just retribution for his duplicity.

It was a perfect triumph, in the eyes of senators, for he had rendered himself, unpleasant to all, and offensive to many. They were all, anxious to avoid a contest with him, and he had taken up, at least one half the time, from the commencement of the Session, up to the catastrophy [sic]! I was smiling and pleasant all the while, and in the best manner, I could command, provoked him, and seemed to regret, the occurrence. When at last I remarked, that "he was about to leave us, and I hoped he would have a pleasant journey, and that he might enjoy a life less <u>troublous</u> [sic], than it had been for months, and years past" he was out of all patience, and sunk, while those who disliked him, manifested their pleasure, in a vociferous laugh! Well now my Love, I had some regrets, and would have relented, and forgiven him, had I not recollected his hypocrisy, and to my self I said, let him writhe, under his own reproaches, as the guilty must do.

Col Yoakum wrote to me, of the death of my poor Niece[2] & of Major Kibble,[3] I was truly sorry to hear of the dear Girls end, for I loved her as a daughter! I hope, & pray that she, and her Mother,[4] are enjoying eternal felicity, in their Heavenly Fathers rest. We know not, what trials, they had to endure, in life. I even forgive Moore the infliction of the sad calamities which he has brot, upon my kindred. It seemed severe, yet it was the will of God, that it should take place, within his Providence, or it could not have happened!

My Dearest, give my love to Mother, and kisses to all the dear, dear children. Salute our friends that you may see!

Thy ever devoted
Houston

Mrs Donelson, Mary, and Mrs Gaines, with many other Ladies send their best love, and congratulations to you. Mary says Sam must wait for her! I have the <u>seeds</u> for you, and I have a handsome morning wrapper, in the newest style for you.

Thine ever
Houston

[1]For an account of the Temperance Banquet at Metropolitan Hall in New York City see *Friend*, 280–81.
[2]The date of Bettie Moore's death is unknown.
[3]Houston's neighbor, Albert Kibble. Identified in Carpenter, 2028, and in C. L. Greenwood, *Index of Death Notices* (Barker History Center). Kibble died January 24, 1852.
[4]Houston's sister, Eliza Moore.

Washington
22nd Feby 1852

My Dear Love,

I was on my way at West Chester Pa. when I met a letter, which called me back on business, and I returned on last night. Had I gone on, I would have been no nearer home than I am now, for I was to go thro. Ohio, and would have been detained some what, and might have found the River frozen, so that I could not descend on it. On the 24th, I intend to go the southern route. It was fearfully cold at West Chester. I intend, if spared, to go by Nashville & Memphis, as the quickest route from Atalanta [sic] in Geo. I think it will be the most speedy. It may be tho. that I will pass by Mobile, and Orleans.

You have no idea my Love of my anxiety, and deep solicitude to be with you, and the little flock at home. It is of vastly more concern to me, than to be <u>President</u>.

Dont think that harm will result to any prospects of mine by my absence from here! Nothing of Congressional business will be transacted until april! And I will not traffic, for influence. The Party are bound to nominate me, or be beaten, if Scott runs, and the Whigs intend to run him, and Gov Jones[1] of Tennessee! Tell Isabella, that Mr Dean, & her friends were gratified to hear me speak of her, and express the pleasure, which she gave you, & her care of the children.

My Love to Mother, & the children, with many kisses to all, and tell them all to kiss, little <u>sissy Antoinette</u> <u>for me</u>, and they are not to call her "Ann," but to call her <u>Antoinette</u>![2] I requested Col Yoakum to show you my letter to him, as I did not know that I would have time to write you to night. I hope this letter will have better than the usual trip, and that I may beat it home.

I have much love from many persons to you, and hope to present it, in person soon!

Thy ever devoted
Houston

[1]James Chamberlain Jones, senator from Tennessee. *Biographical Directory of Congress,* 153.
[2]Antoinette Power Houston would be called "Nettie" by the family.

Chapter VII

April 10, 1852–August 30, 1852

April 10, 1852: Sam Houston to Margaret Houston
April 12, 1852: Margaret Houston to Sam Houston
April 13, 1852: Sam Houston to Margaret Houston
April 23, 1852: Margaret Houston to Sam Houston
April 29, 1852: Margaret Houston to Sam Houston
May 1, 1852: Sam Houston to Margaret Houston
May 2, 1852: Sam Houston to Margaret Houston
May 4, 1852: Sam Houston to Dr. Alva Woods
[undated]: Sam Houston to Maggie Lea Houston
May 5, 1852: Sam Houston to Margaret Houston
May 7, 1852: Margaret Houston to Sam Houston
May 9, 1852: Sam Houston to Margaret Houston
May 14, 1852: Sam Houston to Margaret Houston
May 24, 1852: Sam Houston to Margaret Houston
May 26, 1852: Sam Houston to Margaret Houston
May 28, 1852: Margaret Houston to Sam Houston
[undated fragment]: Sam Houston to Margaret Houston
June 1, 1852: Sam Houston to Margaret Houston
June 4, 1852: Sam Houston to Margaret Houston
June 4, 1852: Margaret Houston to Sam Houston
June 11, 1852: Sam Houston to Margaret Houston
June 12, 1852: Margaret Houston to Sam Houston
June 14, 1852: Sam Houston, Jr., to Sam Houston
June 15, 1852: Sam Houston to Margaret Houston
[ca. June 1852]: Sam Houston to Margaret Houston
June 17, 1852: Margaret Houston to Sam Houston
June 20, 1852: Sam Houston to Margaret Houston

June 25, 1852: Narcissa B. Hamilton to Sam Houston
June 25, 1852: Margaret Houston to Sam Houston
July 2, 1852: Margaret Houston to Sam Houston
July 2, 1852: Sam Houston to Sam Houston, Jr.
July 4, 1852: Sam Houston to Margaret Houston
July 9, 1852: Margaret Houston to Sam Houston
July 11, 1852: Sam Houston to Margaret Houston
July 14, 1852: Sam Houston to Margaret Houston
July 18, 1852: Sam Houston to Margaret Houston
July 25, 1852: Sam Houston to Margaret Houston
July 31, 1852: Sam Houston to Margaret Houston
August 1, 1852: Sam Houston to Margaret Houston
August 4, 1852: Sam Houston to Margaret Houston
August 5, 1852: Sam Houston to Margaret Houston
August 6, 1852: Sam Houston to Margaret Houston
August 8, 1852: Sam Houston to Margaret Houston
August 8, 1852: Sam Houston to Sam Houston, Jr.
August 13, 1852: Sam Houston to Margaret Houston
August 16, 1852: Sam Houston to Margaret Houston
August 17, 1852: Sam Houston to Margaret Houston
August 23, 1852: Sam Houston to Margaret Houston
August 23, 1852: Sam Houston to Margaret Houston
August 26, 1852: Sam Houston to Margaret Houston
August 28, 1852: Sam Houston to Margaret Houston
August 30, 1852: Sam Houston to Margaret Houston

Houston made a short trip home during the spring of 1852. As he journeyed back to Washington he wrote Margaret from East Texas.

Nacogdoches
10th Apr 1852

My Dearest,

At half past six this evening we got here, and it is now past nine oclock. At 2 A.M. we will set out for Sabine Town, and hope to reach there tomorrow night. I do not expect to sleep much on my seat in the stage. The corps[e] of Judge Sterne reached here to day, and is to be interred at eleven tomorrow![1] I did not call to see Mrs Sterne & family, as I thought it would only aggravate her sorrow, and I hear it is deep, and solemn. What ruin does these gambling, & drinking "Halls" bring upon families here, not estimating, the ruin of souls. There must be some remedy for them devised and enforced, or the devastating influence will increase, and dissolve the social system. My face is against them, with all my influence while I live.

I only write my love to let you know, that I am here safe, and that I love you, more than I do sleep! I called at Col Raguets[2] for a few minutes, saw the family, and presented you to all, and your message to Miss Augusta[3] in her Ma's[4] presence which was very gratifying to them, and for which all the family send their most kind regards to you, and the children. She says if she can go, she will be greatly delighted!

The papers, which were in the hands of Col Raguet, originating in the "Committee of Vigilance, and safety" of which Col R. was chairman, and connected with the Revolution,[5] will be held subject to the order of Col Yoakum! About these Col. Y. had great desire.[6] I am well, and to day ate two of my biscuit[s], and gave two to Judge Reese of Ala, a great friend of bro Henrys. They served in the Legislature together.[7] He will move, to Texas, and I think he will live next year at Vernals old place! If you have any trouble send for Vernal, and Thomas Palmer—dont fail my Love, if needful!

You can write to me as, often as you can obtain leave, from Miss Antoinette. Her fame, had preceded me here, as "a beautiful child."

What think you of this My <u>Love</u>? Is it not strange, what rumour can do, when it tries? Well, I think she is a fine baby!

Present me affectionately to Mother. Kiss the children & howda to all! Tell Sam, to spend his idle hours, in writing to me, and I will write to him.

Believe me ever thine
Houston

[In the margin:] P.S. I send you a receipt for Benj. Pleasants note. Take care of it my Love.

[1]Adolphus Sterne died March 27, 1852, in New Orleans. *The New Handbook of Texas,* vol. 6, 95.
[2]Henry Raguet. For a biography see *The New Handbook of Texas,* vol. 5, 408.
[3]Augusta Raguet. Identified in Carpenter, 1405.
[4]Marcia Anne Towers. Identified in *The New Handbook of Texas,* vol. 5, 408.
[5]For more information about this subject, see *The New Handbook of Texas,* vol. 3, 855.
[6]Henderson Yoakum was writing a history of Texas.
[7]George Reese and Henry Lea served in the Alabama Senate in 1839. No evidence has been found that he actually moved to Texas. Owen, vol. 4, 1420–21.

Huntsville
April 12th 1852

My ever dear husband

As it is only the 4th day since you left us, I have little news to give you, but I know you will be glad to hear that we are all well. The little ones were deeply grieved on awaking, to find that dear papa was gone. My own heart was for a few hours like some desolate spot over which the whirlwind had passed, and blighted every thing that was bright and beautiful, but hope soon whispered of joys to come, and as in other days, I will listen to her voice and be comforted.

Yesterday I recd yours from Crocket [sic],[1] and will as nearly as possible comply with your directions. The ground is so wet, that we have not commenced planting corn yet, but hope it will be dry enough this afternoon.

I enclose Mr Gillette's[2] letter to you. He also wrote me a few lines, which I will send to Mrs Cann.[3] It was a lesson to me on punctuality. If I had written a few days sooner, he would have given Mrs Cann and her two daughters a situation in his school, as he had needed just three teachers, but had now employed that number.

My dear love do not take it unkindly if I urge once more upon you the importance of your soul's salvation. Let me ask of you dearest particularly to remember the 3rd commandment. Read it over again and again, and meditate upon it very often. For my reasons look in Hebrews 12th ch. 1st and 2nd verses.

Ever thy affectionate wife

M. L. Houston

P. S. Mother and Sam send their love to you.

[1] This letter has not been located.
[2] Henry Flavel Gillette had a school in Cold Spring, Polk County. *The New Handbook of Texas,* vol. 3, 170.
[3] Mrs. Mark Cann, who had been a member of the music faculty at The Marion Female Seminary in Alabama. Identified in the *Marion Herald*, December 1, 1841.

Nachitoches [sic]

13th Apl 1852

My Dear Love,

As I expected, I reached here last evening, and soon after my arrival, a Steamer landed. It will leave this evening, for N. Orleans, & I intend to go on board, as far as Baton Rouge. From thence, take a Boat for Nashville, or Louisville, but rather think the latter place. Two young men of old French families, will go on, under my care, to the Geo. Town College in the D. C. They are very genteel, & feel much gratified on the occasion [torn] pleasant opportunity, as well as their kindred, tho. they are Whigs. So you see "a Prophet is not without honor, save in his own country." I have yet no news. You may rely on what I have told you. If the Democrats, are not wise in their nomination, they will be beaten worse than at any former period of the History or parties, in the U. S. The query is, will they have sense, to perceive the fact? I will remain on my oars, if I live. It would not be seemly for me to enter the armies of <u>contestants</u>. If my services, and capacity do not commend me to the country, I will be most happy, with you, and our dear little brood, at home, if we should be spared! I sent you a receipt of the Raguets, for the note on Pleasants. If the letter containing it should be lost, this will impart the fact, and that is all that I intend. If I were you, I would keep no money, at home, more than a few dollars. If Vernal wants to pay you any money, or Cleveland, let Col Yoakum* loan it out, on real estate Security, or let them, for the present retain it! [*In the margin:* * I have written to him about this business.]

You need not my Love, suppose that I will forgit you, for I have been so long, & constantly in the habit of cherishing thoughts of you, that if I were to try, I could not cease to think of you, constantly, and love you dearly!

You will please present me to Mother, & kiss the weans. Talk to them of me, and tell me what they say. That will furnish you matter to write about. Tell Jackson, so soon as he can, to get in the sweet potatoes.

Thy ever devoted
Houston

Please send Nash over for Genl [F. L] Hatch to [blurred] and set out my Mchemys [?] etc. I buried them, and Nash can shovel them. The Genl promised to do it for me. It should be done soon.

Huntsville
April 23rd 1852

My dear Husband,

I intended to have written you a long letter today, but have been compelled to postpone writing until it had become so late, that I must hurry in order to be ready for the mail. Maggie was attacked this morning with diarrhea and vomiting very much like the cholera, and I was quite alarmed, but she is now well enough to be at play. The baby too has suffered much with the thrush, but I hope she is getting better. So you will imagine that with my household cares, I have not been idle.

I have recd your several favours from Nacogdoches, Sabine town,[1] & Nachitoches. I thank you sincerely for thus caring for me, on your fatiguing journey.

Mother left us on the morning of the 21st, in the stage for Houston. I heard from her at Montgomery, and she was getting on finely. She had not determined how she would go from Houston, and could not until she should get there. I do not know when she will return. Indeed I think she felt as if she would never get back again.

We have made a beginning in the way of farming. On saturday evening (the 17th) we finished planting corn. The first half is coming up very finely, but Jackson [Paul] thinks the yellow corn is rotting in the ground. I do hope he may be mistaken.

We will have to incur some expense in repairing our spring. It has left its bed and is flowing into the lot spring. I sent for Col. Yokum to look at it, and he says it can be arranged very neatly, but would cost 30 or 40 dollars. I told him I knew you would rather pay that much than lose the spring.

I have not read many newspapers, since you left home, but to be candid, if we may infer any thing from their tenor, I do not think you will get the nomination, and if you wish to know my feeling on the subject, I must frankly acknowledge that I should not be very sorry. If you should be nominated and elected, it would only carry me into scenes for which I had no relish and surround me with people whom I could not love. And your life—but so much has been said upon the cares and perplexities of such a life, that I need add no more. I do not think you are very anxious on the subject, else I might say more.

The Gen'l and Mrs Hatch dined with us yesterday. He would have planted your shrubs, but could not find them. You did not tell me where you had buried them. Gen'l H. says they should not have remained in the ground more than two or three days. He expects to set off with his family for California in a few weeks. Several persons are going with him, from this county and from Polk. The gold fever is raging so, that I fear our young state will be depopulated.

Sam and Nannie are studying pretty well. Sam is deeply grieved that you do not wish him to draw. I will not suffer him to do it unless I find it is the only way in which I can indeed turn to get his lessons, and then he shall only spend a few minutes at it. Or if you think it best to prohibit it altogether, I will do so.

Mary Willie improves rapidly in talking. I used every effort in my power to get her to sleep with me, after you left, but could never succeed, and last night she came to me of her own accord. She and Isabella had had a falling out during the day, and her nurse had given her a slap which I do not think she relished much. I hope Isabella is getting over her singular affection. I find that her temper is easily subdued by telling her she can leave whenever she wishes, if she is not contented. Mary and Prince[2] have been over once since you left. She seemed so humble and so homesick, that I could not find it in my heart to forbid her coming again. The servants at home are doing very well. My health is tolerable.

Thy affectionate wife
M. L. Houston

[1]This letter has not been located.
[2]Houston-Lea family slaves.

Huntsville
April 29th 1852

My dear husband,

I have recd no letter from you, since you left Nachitoches, and I am becoming very uneasy about you. I had bad dreams about you last night, and today I am <u>considerably</u> <u>hyppoed</u> [sic]. Fortunately, I have so many duties, to keep me employed, that I find but little time for melancholy, but fears for you and your safety will continually obtrude themselves. The loss of the Glencoe has made me more uneasy than I would have been, lest a similar disaster should occur as you go up the river. After all the only stay at such a time, is a sure reliance upon the goodness and mercy of the Almighty. This indeed is an anchor to the soul, both sure and steadfast. Without this trust what is life? Ah, how soon would my poor heart be crushed beneath its burden of anxieties!

On yesterday I recd two letters from Charles Power and one from Antoinette. They wrote from Galveston, having bought a place and settled there. Charles gave me his reasons, which I thought were very good. I do hope that mother heard of their removal at Houston, as it would have been a sad trip for her to go all the way to Cany, and find them gone.

I hear fine reports of the Raven hill neighborhood. It is said to be improving greatly, and I must acknowledge that I have a great inclination to go there, if it should be your choice. I would make one suggestion to you. If you find that you are to have the privilege of withdrawing from politics, (which I think highly desirable,) I would advise you to get one of the mills that you were speaking of, for sawing plank, and have it sent to Raven hill, provided you determine to settle there.

I am more and more in love with a quiet rural life. My health has been so much better than I have been able to attend a great deal to my household affairs, and I find it very pleasant, and truly every thing does much better with my constant attention. Apropos, I commenced today, packing away butter for winter use and put 10 pounds as a beginning.

Col [Almazon] Houston brought the fine filly yesterday, but she is so badly foundered, that I suppose she will hardly ever get over it. He says if she should not, it is his loss. I can not quarrel with you for you know I predicted that you would buy a horse before you returned and thus staked my reputation as a prophetess upon it. Indeed, if you do not buy one or two more before you get back, I shall be very satisfied. I believe Jackson wrote to you, that Sam's pony was at home again. We heard of him on the Bedias[1] and Jackson went up after him. He came home in tolerable order.

The children are all well. The baby grows very rapidly. I think I mentioned to you, when you were at home, that I was fearful Maggie would be deaf. I am still distrest about it, and wish you would consult some physician about her. Her ears are continually filling with harce [sic] dry scales, which if not removed, form themselves into a hard lump larger than an english pea. I sometimes drop sweet oil into her ears and take out the scales, but I am almost afraid to tamper this much with them.

I have just received a visit from Miss [Mary] Wiley and Ellen Kittrell. Ellen requested me to send her compliments to you.

Ever thy affectionate wife,
M. L. Houston

[1]Bedias Creek is located a few miles west of Huntsville.

Washington
1st May 1852

My Dear Love,

On last evening I arrived safe here. I passed the mountains in the night, and felt somewhat ticklish. On my coming here I found all matters, looking very well. That I was away, has been a good thing, as my friends suppose. I find them all in good spirits. It is admitted by my opponents, and asserted by my friends, if I am nominated, that I will be elected. To me it looks this way, but whether I will be nominated, or not, is not certain. My friends are becoming sanguine, of success. My feelings, & my wishes shall remain, as I have always expressed them to you! I will not stake my happiness upon the issue of the election. If I were to consult my happiness, in after life, should Heaven prolong it, I do not by any means believe, that it would be, so far as I am personally concerned, increased. Well, when I arrived I learned there was to be a <u>levee</u>, at the Presidents—as it was said to be the last this season, I went to it. Until I went in, it was not known, that I had arrived, to more than a half dozen. I have not on any former occasion, seen so much satisfaction, expressed, at my presence. All persons, of all parties, seemed gratified to see me! Well, this was agreeable to me, but I was not induced by the friendly manifestations, of the people, to believe that they all wished to see me elected President. Many, very many, inquiries were made for "Mrs Houston and the children." "Genl, how many have you? only five yet." How many sons, and how many daughters have you? One son & four daughters!" "What a pity, there was not another son." "Yes, but it is possible that we may have — —, as much consolation from our daughters, as if they had been sons!" So you see my dear, people feel an interest in our family matters!

So soon my dear, as I can see our friends here, I will speak to you of them. Jack Houston, and many others have been to see me! The Senate did not sit to day, as it was Saturday. It is my intention to speak in a few days on the subject, of Kossuth.[1] Should I do so, I will send it to you! I expect, if I live, to be much employed, for I declare to you, that I am unhappy, indulging regret at my absence, from you! On former occasions, I felt enough, but as our treasures have in-creased, my cares have multiplied. Do embrace all the children for me! Howda to all.

Ever thy Husband
Houston

[1]For Houston's feelings on Kossuth see an excerpt from his speech on the subject. Crane, 210.

Washington
2nd May 1852

My Dear Love,

Tis true, I wrote to you last night, and thinking you will not be angry with me for it, I have concluded to write again. To day, I went to church to hear my friend Mr Gallaher, as he was to preach on the Providence of God. He did not satisfy me on the subject of "free will," and he said he would come down to night, and sit with me. I hope he will tho. it is now, ten oclock. He is a great man, and we are as guileless, as we were in early life with each other!

Monday 3rd May

My friend Mr G. called down, and sat with me until after 12 M. and we talked much, on various subjects. To day I attended the Senate, and was very cordially greeted by all the Body, and among others by Hon. W. R. King,[1] & presented your respects to him. We conversed a good while, and he spoke of your Father in terms, of great admiration, of his moral, social, & intellectual qualities. He is yielding fast to the influence of time.[2] We must all pass as a summers day, the shadows may lengthen, but night must close the scene. Mr Clay is yet living, but his friends say he can hardly survive a week! I learn that he suffers much, and is somewhat impatient of delay! What strange beings we are!

As to political matters. I can to day say to you, so far as I can judge the feeling, is becoming general, that no democrat, can beat Scott but myself, and it is probable, that this necessity, acting upon the Convention, may control their action. And moreover, the candidates, or their friends, have not been harmonious but discordant. They can only be brought together, by some understanding, such as I would not enter into, for twenty high offices.

All the solicitude, which I feel, is about your feelings, in the event that I should not be nominated, with the chagrin of my friends. For indeed my Love, the more that I reflect, the more thoroughly satisfied am I, that in private life, I should be most happy, with our little flock, and their dear Mother to join me, in loving them, and assisting her in training them for future usefulness, if we should be all spared, for years to come.

Thy Houston

[1]William R. King, of Alabama, the president pro tempore of the Senate. *Biographical Directory of Congress*, 151.
[2]Ill health caused King to resign his Senate seat. He died April 18, 1853. Brewer, 213.

The following letter from Houston to Dr. Alva Woods is from the Alva Woods Papers in the Rhode Island Historical Society Library, Providence, Rhode Island.

Washington
May 4, 1852

My Dear Sir,

On the 30th Ult, I returned from a visit to my dear Wife, and all the little ones. While I was at home tho. but about fifteen days Mrs Woods, and yourself in memory were often present, and formed a theme of conversation, and could only have hightened the pleasure by your presence. Mrs H. I found in pretty good health, and surrounded by no less than Master Sam, and his four little sisters. This forms quite a family circle. Their dear Mother says they are very pretty, except Sam, and he fairly "good looking," as he is opposed to being thought handsome. My own opinion, so far as expressed, was in accordance with that of my wife, as I think it is the part of a good husband, or amiable gentleman, never to contradict a Lady. But really, they are pleasant & promising children! Previous to my visiting home, and when I was at New York, my intention was to afford myself the pleasure, of visiting you at Providence! I intended a trip home, and I knew, it would gratify my Wife to inform her, that I had see Mrs Woods & yourself, so recently, as it would have been!

I can not enter into the [blurred] of matters here! I have not engaged in political contests here, nor do I intend, to depart from a rule of my own—<u>Tis the rights, and duty of the American People to elect, as well as select, their own Rulers</u>, <u>and I will not muddle, with their prerogative</u>. I send you a "life" said to be of myself, which I assure you, I have never read, but which I intend the first leisure. It is said to be cleverly written, and correctly also.[1]

At all times I will be happy to hear from you often, for your letters, answer a two fold purpose. So soon, as I have meditated upon them, I send them to Mrs Houston.

You will be pleased to present the regards of Mrs H. and myself

to Mrs Woods, and accept them for yourself. Commend us also to
Doct M Woods[2] & his Lady.

Truly thy Friend
Sam Houston

[1]This is probably *Sam Houston and His Republic* by Charles Edwards Lester.
[2]Marshall Woods.

*The following letter written by Houston to his daughter Maggie
is in the Sam Houston Hearne Collection at the Barker History Center, University of Texas, Austin, Texas. It is not dated but appears to
have been written during this time period.*

Dear Maggie,

You are a sweet little Girl, and I love you much. You must be
good, and love your Dear Ma & sisters, as well as brother Sam.

You must love Miss Isabella for learning you so many pretty
Hymns. Do you still fancy Mrs Evans, & Judge [S. D.] Hay as much
as ever?

Kiss Ma, brother, & sisters for Pa.

Thy father Sam Houston

Washington
5th May 1852

My Dear Love,

I have only written to you two letters, since I arrived, and that is
one less than I would have written you, had I not written to our Sister
Antoinette. When I returned, I found a pretty letter from her, dated
the 5th of Feby, and as it deserved an answer, I wrote her four pages.
Well I owed our friend Doct Woods a letter, and paid him.[1] I gave
him an out-line of our family matters, and sent them much love for

you. Ought not, you my Love, to write to Madam? It wou'd gratify them much. I have seen most of my immediate friends since I arrived, and I find them as cordial, & happy to see me, as on any former occasion. The parties are casting about, and to me, they appear, to me, as a mariner, at sea without a compass. They are all, in the Democratic Party, as it would seem, satisfied that they can succeed, with me, if I am nominated, and if neither of the others, whose names have been talked of, should be run, that the success of Party will be doubtful.

Now the question is, all the merits, and claims of any one, such as to cause the convention, to risk the success of Party, and its principles to recompense him, with a compliment, which would keep the Whigs in power, for four years longer. These reflections, seem to be pressing upon the leaders, as they would be, of the Party. They are smart enough to know, that leaders, unless the people go with them, present rather a shabby exhibition at the polls, on an election day. As the Frenchman said, in announcing an exhibition, "We shall see what we shall see." The Delegates, have not yet made their appearance, unless a very few. The Convention is to meet, on the 2nd of June, and on the 3rd it is my intention, to be at Richmond, at the "National Temperance Convention," where it is said my presence is much desired. So you see my Dearest, that I intend "to stick to that which is best."

My Love, I assure [you] that I would be more happy, than on any former occasion here, if I could only turn my face homeward, for I find, where my earthly treasure is, there my heart is also. I think so very often of the home scenes, which I enjoyed when there, that I am lost in the midst of scenes here, which [I] would once have enjoyed, and which all others seem to delight in now. I would rather be at home, and see Miss Mary Willie in one of her vast tantrims [sic] of temper, than to be here at the gayest Levee, or Soiree. I know my fancies are rustic, and my taste plain, but I do not wish to improve it, now, according to modern taste, & fashion. You my Dear, will I am sure, credit me, when I tell you that my own fancy, has not since our union, lead me to political life, but the contrary. It is true, on your account my Dear, I did with more freedom consent, a second time, to go into the Presidency [of Texas]. You, had a wish in that matter I think, for the reason, that it was told your relations, that I "could not be elected a constable," and for contradiction to this, you my Dear, I think were quite willing, that I should run, a second Term! Well, my Dear, you know, I was at home, and had no aspirations, when I was elected to the Senate! Then when two years elapsed, I was again called on, when the condition of Texas affairs, left me no alternative, but to serve again, as I have done to this time.

Every day, has only increased my desire, for private life, & home!!!

Business has pressed upon me my Dear, and I must close.

Mother I suppose has gone by this time. I will not fail if I live, to take her mantle.

Hug the Dear Weans, for me, and howda to all!

Thy ever devoted Houston

[1]See Houston to Alva Woods, May 4, 1852. Alva Woods Papers, The Rhode Island Historical Society, Providence Rhode Island.

Huntsville
May 7th 1852

My ever dear Love,

Since I wrote last, I have recd yours from Baton Rouge.[1] It was a great source of pleasure to me I assure you, as several days had passed without a word from you. I shall look anxiously for a letter from Louisville or Nashville, as the steamboat trip is a great terror to me.

Every thing at home is doing finely. The corn is growing rapidly, and if we can have a good season, I trust we shall make a fine crop. The peas and pumpkins are doing well, and I think we will have a great abundance. Jackson has the hands out soon after day-light, and works well himself. I rarely leave home. Indeed, I am so occupied with the children's lessons and other duties, that I have little time and less inclination to go out. They are both learning very finely, and I hope they will make good scholars. Sam sings exceedingly well, and I hope Nannie will soon sing well. It will require great perseverance on my part to teach them, for I do not think any of your children have a talent for music. Sam says I must tell you that he can recite the books of the Old and New Testaments perfectly.

My last news of Mother was from Houston and she was to set off for Caney (by way of Richmond) the next morning in Mr Ruthven's buggy, not having heard that Mr Power was living in Galveston. My only hope is that she may have ascertained the fact, the night previous to her expected departure. I have had great anxiety about her and shall be unhappy until I hear from her again. I was opposed to her undertaking the journey so soon, and if she could have waited until the time which you fixed upon in your letter to Antoinette, the mistake would have been avoided, but it is done, and my great concern now is for her safety and comfort.

Our little ones are all well except the baby. She still has the thrush, but grows finely notwithstanding. I think I could have cured her before this with number six, but disliked to use so severe a remedy, and have been trying milder ones, until I have become uneasy about her. I have at length resorted to number six, and find that her mouth is getting better. Mary Willie is more interesting than ever. I think she will be able to recite a rhyme before you get home, as she repeats after me very distinctly. Maggie is as great a romp as ever, and so opposed to getting her lessons, that I do not confine her to them. Isabella seems quite contented. I think I have given you my meager store of news. I hope in a very few weeks or months at most, you will be with us again. My health is becoming quite good again.

Ever thy devoted wife
M. L. Houston

P.S. Please remember the "New York Recorder" and also the "Mother's Journal".

---

[1]This letter has not been located.

Washington
9th May 1852

My Dear Love,

Twelve years, have been this day completed, since you were pronounced to be my dear Wife, & I am free to confess, that I love you more than I did at that hour. I <u>thought</u> I loved you then. I <u>know</u> I love you now!!!!

My Dearest, Col Yoakum sent me a letter which Mr. Wheeler[1] wrote in relation to Mothers going to Caney. She wants to go. I[f] she does not go, she will be unhappy. Dont <u>think</u> of the money. My endeavors will be, to make her happy, if I can! I know it is your first wish, and I desire to see it carried out. She will soon, wish to return, and if we live, we will see that the means are afforded for her to do so.

<u>Dont let a few dollars interpose</u> to her gratification or happiness. Unless she can be there by June, my Love, you know she will be miserable! I will write to Col Yoakum to let her have what money she <u>may</u> <u>want</u>! I got a letter from Jackson Paul to day. He says all are well, and he writes in fine spirits! My Dear, I have only received one letter from you, dated the 14th Apl. I think your letters are delayed.

I intend to write, in a day or so, but write to night, to put mother at ease!

My Love to Mother, and kisses to the children. Howda to all!

Truly thy devoted
Houston

[1]It is unclear whether Houston is referring to Judge Royal T. Wheeler of Galveston or Houston merchant Daniel A. Wheeler. Carpenter, 631, 937.

Washington
14th May 1852

My Dear Love,

Tis true that I have not written to you for a few days, tho I have sent you papers, seeds, etc. I will tell you the reason of my silence, and I am sure you will excuse me! I never get to bed until after midnight, and I sleep until breakfast. From that time until 12 N. if I am in my room, I have company. Then I go to the Senate, and remain there until 1/2 past 4 P.M. By the time I get my dinner, it is between five and six oclock. If I then go to my room, I find company there, and to tell you candidly, I do not sup, once in three, or four days. I enjoy good health—better perhaps, than if I were to eat oftener. You used to think I lacked appetite at home, but if you were to see me here, you would not think, I had found it in this city. I regret my Love, that your household cares have been so great, and that our <u>antie</u> daughter [Antoinette], has been unwell. Of course, I am happy, that she is again well! I can fancy Mary Willie, pet with her Nurse. She has not by any means disappointed me, in my estimate of her <u>will</u>! There is my Dear, a great deal of <u>Moffatt</u>, in our children, & it will take a Moffatt to control them. Dont you think Dear, that you had better, <u>resume</u> the <u>Moffatt</u> in your name? I am happy to hear, that our Son, & Nannie study well! You can my Dear, do as you please about Sams drawing. I only suggest that you have it in your control, and let him know, that he is dependent upon you for the indulgence, and let him have stated hours to draw. I think it a good thing, to teach him method, when young. Teach him to dispose of his clothes at night, so that he could get up in the dark, lay his hand on them, and dress. This is very important, to my mind. You can regulate the time, and duration of his drawing! I want him to send me specimens of them, and let him have paper to draw them on. To practice, he ought to use his slate. All artists first use chalk, or craon [sic] on boards, and he should use a slate, where he can rub out & correct any fault, or blunder!! I have promised to <u>sit</u>, for an artist tomorrow and he uses no paint, but a pencil and makes fine likenesses.

Cousin Columbus Lea, is here. He arrived yesterday, and left all well! He says Tene is well married,[1] and all our relations doing well. I sent copies to our kindred of my life[2]—Aunt Eiland and indeed all! How do you like it? Columbus will spend some weeks. I am very attentive to him, and laugh about his "Goats," and your "apprehension, of his ridicule."

I went to Baltimore, on last sunday to witness, a Grand Catholic Convention of Priests, Bishops, & arch Bishops.[3] I will reserve my opinion of them, until we meet, and if spared, I will tell you my opinion, but in the meantime, I will say, that I was not charmed, with the display! It was gaudy, beyond any thing, I have ever seen! All this had no charms for me, when I reflected, that the Almighty, inhabiteth eternity, and is not confined to Temples made with hands! All that I saw was such display, as I had fancied necessary to give importance, to an Idol, which had no power over humanity, but such as arises from a display of pomp, and ceremony! There was more gold, and embroidery, than I have before seen, in my whole life. The ceremony lasted some five hours, during which time, I was confined in the house, and did not understand one word, except a sermon of an hours length!

Now, my Dearest, I will tell you of politics! The days [sic] is drawing nigh, when the Baltimore Convention is to decide the fate of the Democratic Party—not mine, for I declare to you, that my pulse does not quicken at its approach! If Deity builds up, and pulls down nations, it follows, that He selects the nationals, and designs the means! If Providence wills, I will be selected, if otherwise, all my anxiety, could not reverse his purpose, and therefore I will not allow myself, to be disturbed, in the reliance which I place upon my Wife, and home, for earthly happiness. You can have no idea, of the indifference which, I feel about the results, only as to my party wishes. If I am not nominated, we will be beaten. Of course this is for you only! All say "if Houston is nominated he is sure to be elected." Then why not nominate him? Because others are intriguing, and he will make no bargains! So the people are to be defrauded out of their choice by the management of politicians, who control the Convention. My friends are sanguine and C. Lea thinks the signs good. During the convention, I expect, and <u>intend</u> to be at Richmond Va. representing Texas, in the Grand National Temperance Convention!!! Does this look much like, I felt uneasy? All that I desire my Love, is that you should feel as indifferent to result, as I do, and hope to do!

I know you dont think the Presidency would add to <u>our</u> happiness, or it would do more for us, than it has done heretofore! One thing I may say to you without egotism. My standing with the people at large, and the nation, I would not exchange for that of any man, who may be selected by the Convention. I am regarded as above intrigue, or corruption, and this I know you would vastly prefer, to my getting the Presidency!

Kiss our dear children for me, and give howda to all

Thy ever Devoted
Husband
Houston

[1]Serena Royston married James Patton on February 11, 1852. Family Adventures, compilers, *Early Alabama Marriage Records, Grooms' Surnames Beginning with "P"* (Shreveport, La.: J & W Enterprises, 1991), 64.

[2]Lester's *Sam Houston and His Republic.*

[3]The First Plenary Council. For more information see J. Thomas Scharf, *History of Baltimore City and County* (Baltimore: Regional Publishing Company, 1971), 530.

24th May 1852

My Dear Love,

I am happy that I have, an opportunity to send you the shoulder brace. You can see how to <u>fix it</u>, so as to relieve the pressure on your breast. You will see how it works and I hope it may be of real benefit to you.

Mr. Atwood,[1] the Gentleman who bears it, is on his way to Texas on business, and has promised to call, and see you. Please to extend to him the kind civilities of our cabin, and show him our children.

Thy affectionate Husband
Sam Houston

[1]A. Atwood of Washington County, Texas. Identified in Carpenter, 2063.

Washington
26th May 1852

My Dear Love,

The Delegates are coming in, and many appliance is made, by the candidates, and their friends. All that they can do, does not change the impression, that, if I am nominated, I <u>will</u> be, and <u>can</u> be elected, while there is only a "hope," that others <u>might</u> succeed, if nominated. For my own part, I will remain in the position which I have occupied, and already indicated to you, in former letters.

Now I only have to request of you, should I not be nominated, that you may feel, as I will! Not that I have <u>been neglected</u>, but that it is for the best. My chances, to all appearances, are the best, as regarded by my <u>friends</u>, and <u>they</u> are not a few. The main rally, as I have learned, has not been made by the friends of the parties! For my own part, I have not lifted my finger, nor intimated "place," to any one to secure influence, in behalf of my nomination. Of this tho. I have already spoken to you!

Columbus [Lea] has not yet returned, but I look for him daily. Come what may of all this tussle, for place, I am Resolved that my pulse, shall not give one discordant beat. My feelings without the nomination, if my friends fail, will be such, as I would not, I assure you, exchange for those of the candidate, who may be chosen. The convention, can <u>nominate</u> the Candidate, but the <u>masses</u> must <u>elect</u> the President. If this is reflected upon, as a matter of influence there is no doubt as to the result!!!

This is to be dreaded. If a weak nomination, is made by the Democrats, the Whigs will name, but one man in their Convention —Genl [Winfield] Scott, and unanimously nominate him. With the cry of "union in the Whig ranks," they will open the campaign, and the display of flags, and the prestige of success, at last election, with drums, & music, the Democrats will wilt in a fortnight, and cease to make fight. This is what I fear, and this is realy to be feared by our Party!

Well my Love, my heart is with you, and all the dear little ones, in your slumbers, for I am sure you have long since, been consigned to the arms of Morpheus, and I would be infinitely happier, if I were with you. Kiss, and hug all the Dear children, and say it is for Pa!

Thy devoted Husband
Sam Houston

Huntsville
May 28 1852

My ever dear Love,

By last night's mail I was made very happy, for it brought me your precious favours of the 9th and 14th inst. I think it was 10 o'clock, before I could get your letters, and therefore I had a quiet time to read them. The little sleepers around me did not know that letters had come from papa, or the scene would have been very different. I believe my recent affliction has been a blessing to us all. The children and servants seem more attached to me than ever, and more obedient. My great concern is that I may rule them all in the fear of my God.

I glanced over the papers which you sent me, and of course was curious to know what they said about you, for every thing relating to my dear husband must be interesting to me. But even with my woman's sagacity, I can not tell what will be. One thing gratifies me exceedingly, the spirit of calm reliance which your letters breathe, upon the decrees of the Almighty.

Every thing around us is prosperous and happy. We have had fine rains, and the corn, potatoes, peas, and pumpkins are flourishing. Jackson is doing well, but says he would go to California, but for his engagement with us. Isabella seems quite contented, and I hope will remain so. Her health is much better, and I suppose that will account for the change. The servants are all well and behave well. I suppose Col Yokum has told you that Albert is at home. They could get no lumber in Independence, and therefore as there was no work for him to do, bro. Baines thought it best to send him home. I do hope my love you will not blame bro. B. for it, as I do not see what else he could do. No one here wants Albert except Dr Kittrell,[1] and as he is not willing to give more than 20 dollars per month, I told Col Yokum I would keep him at home, for the present as I did not think you would be satisfied with that.

Poor John Lehr has been expected to die for several days. I hardly suppose he is alive at this moment. Mary, I am told is deeply afflicted. Poor child of sorrow, it will be a desolate world to her!

My health is much better, but I am still feeble. Last not least— our dear little treasures. They are all well and interesting of course. Sam and Nannie have not studied much lately, on account of my being unable to attend to them, but they are resuming their lessons again, and I hope they will learn well. Sam says I must tell you there is a mocking-bird's nest in one of the tea rose bushes, with four eggs in it. I proposed that he should write it himself, but he is more modest about his writing than drawing. I pray you will think the girls are terrible romps, but you must be very charitable towards them, as they inherit their mirthfulness from dear papa.

I have just written a note to Col Yokum to explain what you meant by Mr Wheeler's letter, money for Mother, etc, but he was at his farm,[2] and I am therefore at a great loss to know your meaning. Mother left here shortly after yourself, as I informed you, but took with her a hundred dollars of her Smith deposit, and never authorized anyone to call on Col Yokum for money. I do not know who Mr Wheeler is. It is all a perfect enigma to me. Mother was in Galveston when I heard from her last, and very well.

I hope soon to see you my dear Love, and be happy again. The baby has grown so much you would not know her. Her head is shaped like yours and her eyes are very much like yours.

Thy devoted wife
Margaret Moffette Houston (as you insist on it)

Yes dearest the 9th was the 12th anniversary of our wedding day. Oh how changed are my feelings towards you! Then I loved you—but now alas—I love you so much more that, I am not happy when you are absent from me!!!

[1]Pleasant William Kittrell. For a biography see *The New Handbook of Texas*, vol. 3, 1134.
[2]The Yoakum's farm was in Shepherd's Valley, 7 miles southeast of Huntsville. *The New Handbook of Texas,* vol. 5, 1035.

The first pages for the following letter from Houston are missing.[1] It was probably written in late May or early June of 1852. It speaks of Nancy Lea's trip to Galveston to visit the Powers and then continues:

. . . At this point I was interrupted, in writing, and have seen a number of persons. Among them, my Cousin Letcher[2] (who by the bye, is one of the most sensible men in Congress,) and Genl Rusk also. They are sanguine, that I will be nominated. There is in these matters, no certainty, and I do not allow, the prospect to elate me, and if not nominated, I assure you, I will not be depressed, by the result, for I assure you dear Love, I think more, and much more intensely about you, than I do about the Presidency, or any thing else in this world. Our young Barbarians, come in for a share of my thoughts, and affections.

Recently the Politicians, started a plan, to address each Candidate a letter, asking their opinions on some <u>grave</u> subjects. Rusk, & myself answered promptly, and without consultation. I met it as has been my habit, <u>openly</u>, and <u>directly</u>. Rusk did likewise, and told them he was <u>no candidate</u>, but would support me, by every manly means in his power. If I cant send you a copy in print tomorrow, I will send you a written copy of my correspondence, where you will judge of my course!

You can then send it to Col Yoakum. The general, if not the universal sentiment is if I am nominated, that I will easily beat Genl

Scott, and the only difficulty is, that each clique thinks, or says, that the Democracy is strong enough to elect any Democrat, who might be nominated. I have no clique, nor have I made any promises, of place, or favor. It is said that all others have. If this is true, it is a reason, why the hope of place, will cause those, who have to make the nomination, hazard the success of the Party. It is fallacious to think, that any civilian, can beat a General of renown. I adhere most scrupulously, to my principles, never to compromise my honor, by any intrigue bargain, or promise, of place, either directly, or indirectly. I will leave, (if nothing else) to my family, an unsullied escutcheon. I know my Love, you would prize this far above place, or power. I often jest, with my friends about having, <u>the doors of the "White House" widened</u>, and yesterday I was there, and told the <u>doorkeeper, that he must keep the House in good order, as I might have to take it for the next four years</u>. He is an Irishman, and was much delighted. He played it off, quite handsomely. So you see my Dear, I am not very sensitive, on the subject, turn out as it may. I comment at times, about the <u>pretty playground for children</u>! I never think of our humble home, but what emotions, of deep, and abiding affection swell my heart.

Thy Devoted Husband
Houston

[1]This fragment is part of the Sam Houston Hearne Collection, Barker History Center, University of Texas, Austin.

[2]John Letcher was a representative from Virginia. *Biographical Directory of the United States Congress*, 154.

Washington
1st June 1852

My Dear Wife,

Today I rec'd from Jackson Paul a letter of the 11 ult. I was truly gratified because it came from home, and told me of you, and the children. I regretted to hear that you had been unwell, and it was pleasure to learn that you were again, nearly restored to health.

You were the only one of the family mentioned, particularly, but Sam, and he told me of Sam's troubles about his "mustang pony." I am willing that you let Thos. Parmer trade it, <u>without giving</u> <u>boot</u>. My Love, you can say to Jackson to call on Col A. Hustons driver Mr Saxton,[1] and he will repay the two sacks of corn, as they were only loaned, and promised to be <u>returned</u>. It had best be done soon.

I hope you will say to Jackson, that I am delighted, to hear of the condition of the crop. I hope it may turn out well. I hope if my various seeds, which I planted have come up, they may be kept clean, and taken care of. The two fields in which I had Rye, and Barley, I want planted in peas* in rows about two feet and a half a part, or it may be three feet would be better!
[In margin: *The Goose peas I wanted planted in best land.]

The Baltimore Convention met to day, and will organize tomorrow. I have seen a Gentleman to day, from the scene of action, and he says there is no one who can tell, what will be the result of the election, or <u>nomination</u>. No voting will take place, until the 2nd, if then. I will with pleasure send you intelligence, as you will wish to put your mind at rest. Our cousin Columbus [Lea] is at the convention. He went there some three days since.

Rely on what I have before written to you, as to <u>my feelings on</u> <u>the subject</u>. I see that poor Davy G. Burnet, has come out with a vulgar publication against me, at which I had a most hearty laugh.[2] You need not read it, or suppose me plagued by it, for I am not. It is a poor impotent attempt to wound me, but it cant affect me for a moment. I see my friend Stuart[3] has been after him with a sharp stick. I intend to write to Sam, & Jackson, in a few days. Dr [Ashbel] Smith wrote me, as he went to Baltimore that Mother had reached Galveston safe, and was well.

I am drowsy, and will only say, that I love [you] more than ever. Kiss our children, and give my love to them. Tell all howda.

Thy Husband
Houston

[In the margin:] If the Pumpkin seed reached you from Baton Rouge which I sent let them be planted with the <u>peas</u>!

[1]Houston is probably referring to William C. Saxton. Identified in Carpenter, 1158.

[2]Burnet's *Review of the Life of General Sam Houston* was published in Galveston, Texas, by the News Power Press Print in 1852. Mary Whatley Clarke, *David G. Burnet* (Austin: The Pemberton Press, 1969), 189, 288. Although bitter enemies in earlier days, Burnet and Houston apparently eventually forgave each other in later life. The Houston children were not aware of the earlier feuds, and Burnet in speaking of the death of his son in the Civil War and the wounding and capturing of Sam, Jr., reported to historian John Henry Brown that it "would have been a great pleasure to me if the boys had known each other and fought side by side." Ibid., 210.

[3]Hamilton Stuart, the publisher of the *Civilian and Galveston City Gazette. The New Handbook of Texas,* vol. 6, 133.

Washington
4th June 1852

My Dear Love,

To day I am quietly in my room, as the Senate adjourned and on yesterday, (thursday) until monday. I presume in Baltimore,[1] all is hustle, and excitement. Treating-kissing open Houses, to influence members, of Convention, and it is said that 100,000 Dollars, are there for the purposes of bribing. I do not know whether there is, any truth that bribery has been resorted to, nor will I give myself any trouble, on that scene. I have just written to Genl Rusk, if he should at any time discover, any practices, or acts, inconsistent with the honor of the Body, to protest in my name, or <u>behalf</u>, and withdrawing my name, declare that I would accept no nomination coming from, any Body whatever, obnoxious to the suspicion of corruption. I will not soil my escutcheon—It is for our children, my Dearest, and your happiness, as well as my own honor, that I am acting. Offices, obtained by dishonorable means, would be no cause of pride, or gratification to me, or my friends.

The <u>universal</u> opinion is, "if Houston is nominated, he will be elected," and of all others, there is doubt, or a <u>hope</u>, that they <u>might be elected</u>!

Now my Dearest, the only thing which would cause me regret, is that if I should be nominated, it would afford me, an excuse, at any time, to leave, so that I could be with you, and our weans. I will consider the failure of my friends in my nomination, as no discredit to me. My enemies, and my opponents all declare, and believe me the most popular man in America, so that nothing, but intrigue, and corruption, can defeat the universal conviction. Genl Jackson, at a more advanced age, was <u>defeated</u> by similar influences, though never defeated by his countrys enemies. So I can not for a moment suppose, that my fortune will be superior, to one so deserving, as Genl Jackson.

In view of the influences which are at work, I can not <u>see,</u> <u>how I can be nominated</u>! So my Dearest, I am prepared for the result. I am also, prepared to see the Party beaten! I would regret such a catastrophy [sic], but I have witnessed it once already, from similar influences defeated. If it is now beaten, I think it by no means improbable, that power may pass from it, for the next twelve years, unless some Providential circumstance, should give direction to events!

If I am not nominated, I beg you to care <u>nothing</u> <u>for the result</u>! <u>I will myself feel no regret</u>, and I will have the more time to love you, and our children, than if I were nominated, and elected. I write to prepare your mind, and fortify your feelings for the events.

Give my love to the children, and kisses, very many kisses give them, and to you my Dear, my most ardent, and devoted affection. Howda to all.

Adieu thine
Houston

[1]For information about the Baltimore Convention see Klein, 219–20.

Huntsville
June 4, 1852

My ever dear husband,

It is my regular letter day, and as I recd nothing from you by last mail, except a little note about the olive seed, it devolves on me to reply to Sam's letter. I was quite disappointed for I have indulged fond hopes of getting a letter myself, but next mail I hope will bring me quite a bundle. I suppose just now you are much occupied and I ought not to complain if you should overlook poor me a little, but I must acknowledge that it requires more philosophy than I can command to be willingly forgotten by him who I love so dearly. The time of your return is so uncertain, that I am in painful suspense about it. When oh when shall I see you again! My health is good and every thing is prospering around us, but I am so lonely without you. I am thinking seriously of making a visit to bro. Vernal and Sister Katherine shortly, if I can hire a comfortable conveyance, in which I can take all the children. Jackson says he will look after every thing. The roads are said to be good, and I believe I would enjoy the trip finely. Missy [Goodall] staid with me last night, on her way home from Independence, to spend her vacation. She is much improved, and I think will make a very pretty and interesting woman.

Mrs Yokum was badly hurt on wednesday by one of Mrs Stone's[1] horses. Mrs S. had called to see her, and the horses had been brought into the yard. On going into the yard Mrs Yokum observed one of the horses approaching a pan of vegetables in the kitchen window and attempted to drive him away. He immediately threw up his hind legs and one hoof struck her right cheek and fractured the bone. She lay senseless for three hours, and at first was supposed to be killed. She had partially recovered her reason before I could get there, but I never saw any thing like the distress of the family. Col Yokum was at his farm, and it occurred about 11 o'clock A.M. so that it was near 4 P. M. before he could get home. I believe they sent a servant that had some difficulty in finding the way. I was with Mrs Yokum this morning, and we hope she is mending, but she is very badly hurt. In addition to the broken cheek-bone, one eye is entirely closed, (but I trust not seriously injured,) and one side of her nose much bruised, the inside of her mouth so much bruised that she can not swallow a morsel of solid food. Col. Yokum requested me not to give you a very gloomy account of matters, but I do not know how I could write more cheerfully. Mrs Y. seemed much inclined to sleep. I fear it is not a good symptom. The poor Col seems as humble as a little child. He has been a kind and precious friend to me, in sickness and in health. May the Lord spare me to her helpless family!

I recd a letter from Antoinette recently. They were all well, but Mother had heard of my sickness, and was much distrest. You will receive Sam's interesting epistle. He insists on enclosing it seperately, so that he can select a motto for it. I do not know what the motto will be.

Thy affectionate wife
M. M. Houston

P.S. I had sealed my letter and opened it to tell you that I had just heard from Mrs. Yokum, and she has been sitting up a little.

[1]Mrs. Richard (Grace) Stone. Carpenter, 2008.

Senate Chambers
11th June 1852

My Dear Love,

I have only a minute to say to you, how anxious I am to hear from you again, and say that I have paid the included Draft. Get what money you want my Love. Do not hesitate in want of any thing!!!

I shall be unhappy until I hear from you again. Write to me about the <u>Babe</u>, but I have to say, better get some one to write for you, than to run any risk, by attempting to write when you are not able. My Love, kiss the children and hug them for me!

Howda to <u>All</u>. Give my thanks, and gratitude to those dear Ladies, who have so kindly waited upon you. I will always feel kind to them.

Thy devoted & affectionate Husband
Houston

Huntsville
June 12th 1852

My dear Love,

I intended to have written you a long letter today, but Mrs Evans[1] and Josephine[2] have been with me all day. I will try to write in a day or two. Not a line from you last mail. What can be the matter! We have heard of Pierce's nomination. God grant it may turn out well! Sam's interesting letter, I need not say it is all his own, as that is very evident [sic]. I have not time to correct it for him, as the mail will soon close.

Thy devoted wife
M. M. Houston

[1]Mrs. J. W. (Manura) Evans. Carpenter, 2023.
[2]Josephine Duncan. Ibid.

The following letter is in the Sam Houston Papers in the Barker History Center, University of Texas, Austin.

June 14, 1852

Dear Pa,

Mamma has just read what she wrote about me and I will try to be a better boy. My little mocking bird which I told you about is dead. My poney [sic] is doing well

God Bless you. You[r] affectionate son.

Sam Houston Jr.

Washington
15th June 1852

My Dear Love,

I am truly happy, that yours of the 28th reached me to night, for

I was very miserable, and you will find by my last letter, that my forebodings, were of a distressing character. I have not for days past, thought, or cared, about politics. My heart was with you, and the children. As I told you, my thoughts, and heart, were not set on politics, & I find it so. <u>I have not felt one pang of disappointment</u>.[1] Had it been an election by the people, and I had not been elected, I would have been mortified, but when a new man was selected that no one knew, as a candidate, I felt that I lost nothing. He is a clever man, and I will support him, and the party in all good faith!

It is said that, the night before the nomination, was made, that a large majority of the states were ready to go for me, and that Genl Cass sent his son in law,[2] to Baltimore, & by him sent word to his friends to go for Genl Pierce. I suppose this was what prevented me from being taken up, and nominated. I cou'd by one promise, have (as I believe, have secured the nomination!)!! I would not violate my principles for all the honors, of the world! So my Love, you and the children are well, and I thank my God. <u>I do not care a straw for the nomination</u>!! I fear you will feel chagrined, at the result—be as I am, and let it pass.

You cant understand the <u>Wheeler</u> <u>letter</u> <u>money</u> etc. It was Mr Wheeler who wrote to Mother about the carriage, in Mr Ruthven's absence. That is all, and if Mother wanted money, I wished her to have it, and not, to let the cost of the trip deter him from it, as I am willing to pay any price, rather than she should be disappointed, as I knew she would be miserable if she did not get to see Sister Antoinette. It was <u>Mr Wheeler</u> who wrote about the carriage, and the cost of the trip. Tell our son, that I am glad the pretty Birds have chosen his Rosebush to nestle in, and rear their little songsters! Tell him to love them, because they are innocent, and harmless!

I am happy too, that our dear Nannie, is attentive to her lessons. She will make as good a scholar, as her dear Ma, and I hope Sam will be superior to his Pa. I am happy, very happy to hear the babe is well, and tho. I would have been happy if she had resembled her Ma, I can not be displeased, that she resembles me. I thought she was Paxton, when I left home!

Congress has adjourned to let Whig Delegates attend their Convention. I intend to go there for a day or two! We are idling our time here, and I think half the members, would rather be here than at home. I assure you my Love, I am not of that half. If ever a mortal panted for home, I do to be with you, and our chil<u>ren,</u> (as Sam would say.)

If Albert, is to be hired, or if Kittrell, wishes him to work about Town, and not at his place let him have him at $20, as I suppose he is of no use at home, until fodder taking time. Indeed I suppose, Joshua, or Bingley, cou'd be spared, as the crop is laid by, or soon will be. The fodder, and Peas, are all the crop we have to gather this year, with the Pumpkins! If they are hired out, or any one of them, I do not wish them, to be out of the reach of <u>Doct Evans practice</u>. I have written to Col Yoakum to direct, the fixing of the spring, in a handsome manner! King & Green[3] may wish [to] hire Albert. He may go to them, but <u>not</u> <u>about Machinery</u>.

My heart is sorrowful, at the news touching the situation of John Lehr. He was a noble man, and one that I loved much. I begged him to call on Dr Evans, and was sure, that he could cure him, but he would listen to others I fear. I think he was a good man, and hope God may receive him, to that rest, which is prepared for His children!

Poor Mary, will indeed be desolate, and her miserable Father, will be an annoyance to her, I fear!

You see Dearest, tho. it is late, and I want to start at 6 A.M. that I am inflicting, a long—long letter upon you! I will only ask you to read it all to our dear weans. Such things make them think, and gives them notions of business. And creates in them self respect.

My Dear, I see you have taken back a part of your name,[4] (perhaps in jest.) I was amused at Mary Willies disposition, after getting the "slap," not to forget it. I think this is more Moffatt, than Houston. Come from where it may, I like it. It is a proper feeling. Wrongs inflicted should never be <u>forgotten</u>, tho. they may be <u>forgiven</u>! All our children, seem to have that disposition, and I think it is more of yours than mine.

Kiss them all for me. Howda to all.

426 : CHAPTER VII

Thy affectionate

Houston

Present my affectionate respects, to those dear Ladies, who were so attentive to you, in your illness!!!

---

[1]Houston is referring to his not receiving the nomination for president.

[2]Henry Ledyard. Identified in Philip Shriver Klein, *President James Buchanan: A Biography* (University Park, Pennsylvania: The Pennsylvania State Press, 1989), 275. For information about balloting see McLaughlin, 282–83.

[3]J. W. Green. Carpenter, 2009.

[4]Houston is referring to Margaret's use of "Moffette" when signing her letters to him. See Margaret to Houston, May 28, 1852.

The following letter was written sometime in June of 1852, but the exact day is unknown.

Washington

June 1852

My Dear Love,

To day I hoped to have received from you a letter, telling me that you had recovered, and again were well. Such has not been the case, and I hope my suspense is owing to the irregularity of the mails. I will hope, and pray for the best. Truly my anxiety, and solicitude, have been inexpressible. All other matters are merged in my affection for you, and interest for the restoration of your health, for it seems to be with that, my happiness would be complete. All my happiness, appears to hang upon that alone. 'Tis true that many other things are necessary to its perfection, but they are all dependent upon you, and my affection for you absorbs all other matters.

Our dear children, are present also to my mind, but never, only when associated with you. The affairs, of politics, business, and all things are subsidiary to my love, of you, and a desire for the promotion of your happiness, with that of our children, both here, and hereafter! Until I can hear from you, I will feel no happiness, and to be candid my Love, I have not felt one emotion of true happiness since we parted. I have experienced momentary excitements, but none of happiness. The excitement of debates, and the meeting of valued friends, whom I had not seen for long years, have excited me, but then you were not present, and there was no one, to whom I could turn, and hope to meet, from them, a look of sympathy.

Without affection, I hold this world of little value. We may love our friends, as friends, but we can not love them as "our better half," nor as our children. Pure affection can only exist where spirits are congenial, and impressed by certain influences, to which all may be subject, but which few, if any, can explain. The merchant who freights, all his wealth, on a single bark, will not be liable, to feel the risk of his adventure, while the sea is smooth, and the wind fair, but let the storm arise, and threaten to engulf his vessel, and then he awakes, to a sense of the danger, by which all his hopes are surrounded. And so my Love, it seems to me in relation to yourself.

Whatever endangers your health or happiness causes me instant, and intense anxiety! I will hope for the best, and imperfect as my prayers are, they have been nightly, or daily offered for your health & happiness, and that our dear children, may be brot up, in the nurture, and admonition of the Lord!! For some time I have been no where, on visits, but to see my small friends. My God daughter, Mary Houston that was, and now (Mrs. [John S.] Garland) has been here a month, and I have seen her, but once, and her red haired baby not at all! She sent her to the Senate the other day, and I did not see her! They always (by Jack, who calls every day on his way to the office) make the most affectionate enquiries for you, and the children. They are a family, you would love if you only knew them. They always send their love to you! I will write of her. My love to the children. Howda to all

Thy ever devoted
Houston

Huntsville
June 17th 1852

My ever dear husband,

Tomorrow is my regular letter day, but as I was to have dined with Mrs. Leigh[1] today, and disappointed her the third time from having company to detain me at home, I have thought it was best not to postpone the visit any longer. I will therefore begin my letter to you this morning, with the expectation of finishing it tomorrow. My last mail brought me your dates to the 1st inst for which I thank you sincerely.

The result of the Baltimore convention has astonished the Democratic party, as far as I can learn. I hope you will agree with me now, that it is not based upon republican principles. The thing has always presented itself to my mind in this way. The delegates are chosen from amongst the most active politicians in each state, and consequently are men aspiring to office, and not a portion of the people. It is true each delegate is apprised of the wishes of his constituents, but he is not bound by any pledge, and in such a case three fourths in any body of men will go for the candidate most available to himself. The recent affair at Baltimore is a clear illustration. All the promises of promotion had been given at the North and none at the South, and hence the compromise that ensued. I hope my dear Love, you will not imagine that I write in any spirit of pique. Ah no, if you could only see the feelings of my heart on this subject, you would be satisfied that so far as you are concerned individually, I am pleased at the result, and if the whigs will nominate Mr Filmore [sic], I shall be pleased every way, for I know he will be elected and make us a good President. Now you have my politics. Who was the one man that clung so faithfully to the name of Houston?

I suppose you have heard of the death of John Lehr.[2] He was much lamented by a large circle of friends. He has left Mary a fine estate, but it is so situated, that she has it in her power to wrong his mother almost out of her support, and if [Mary] will be advised by some of her family she will certainly do it. Her father[3] began to assume authority before John's death, and immediately after it talked largely of his fine corn and cotton on the place. Mother Lehr[4] says that she wants to see you and tell you her troubles, for all your predictions have come to pass.

I just recd a letter from Charles recently. They were all well except himself, and he was suffering from boils. Mother does not speak of coming home yet.

Four of the preachers took dinner with us on last sabbath, on their way to the convention at Marshall.[5] Bro Burleson[6] was amongst them, and requested me to present his compliments to you.

Friday morning 18th

We are enjoying our usual health. The children grow finely, and talk a great deal of you, but I fear you will think they are [blurred]. We were all delighted to see your picture. Mary Willie recognized it at the first glimpse, and Sam exclaimed after looking at it thoughtfully, "It looks so much like pa it makes me feel strange!" Sam has been lazy about his books lately, but I hope he will do better. The next picture papers, I think had better be sent to Maggie & Nannie.

Thy devoted wife

[no signature]

[1]Rebecca Shannon (Mrs. Walter) Leigh. Identified in Vick-Rainey, 12.
[2]John Lehr died June 5, 1852. Lucy Alice Bruce Stewart, Verna Baker Banes, and Anthony V. Banes, comps, *Walker County, Texas, Cemetery Records* (Huntsville, Texas: Walker County, Texas, Genealogical Society, 1992), 144.
[3]Samuel Moore.
[4]Lucilla Lehr. The name is also listed in various records as Trecilla Lehr.
[5]Margaret is referring to the Fifth Annual Baptist State Convention of Texas. Murray, 337.
[6]Rufus Burleson. *The New Handbook of Texas*, vol. 1, 839.

Washington
20th June 1852

My Dear Love,

Since I wrote you last, I have been to Baltimore, as I told you I intended to go there, to pass my time. A time it was, for it was all confusion, and uproar.[1] The good Whigs, are worse off, than the Democrats were, for they could agree, on some one, but the Whigs, can agree, thus far, on no one. They have been four days in Convention, and stand as they began the balloting. Tomorrow they may be able to make a choice. It is thought, on tomorrow they may take an outsider, as the Democrats did.[2]

I was surprised in Baltimore on stepping into the Ladies Parlour, (preparatory to Dinner, as I had been taken to the Ladies ordinary, owing to the crowd in the Gentlemens Dining room) not knowing any Lady, as I supposed, when the first thing I knew, a lady jumped at me, and took me round the neck exclaiming, "aint you going to kiss me?" Who do you suppose it was? It was none other than Samuella Andrews,[3] of Houston. She is nearly as tall as my own dear Wife. You recollect when we last saw her, she was a little girl. Betty Culp[4] was with her, and claimed a kiss also! Poor Betty, she wept freely, as I had not seen her, since her husbands death![5] They came to the city, with Mrs. [Ellen] Reily, who was on her way to see Mr Clay, and remain with him while he lives, as he can only live a few days.[6] He is so feeble that he can not turn in his bed! Such are the passing Glories, of this world! I fear he can realise no change, in his "inner man," so far, as I can hear. It [is] in the power of the almighty Ruler, to change the heart, without any visible manifestations, and so I hope, it is with him.

To day I walked home from church with Mrs Reily, and nearly, all the way, you were the subject of conversation, & I can tell you, that she is as much your friend as ever, and partly so, I discover, for making me, as she believes, a Clever man!!! She says no one else could have done it. She, with Mrs Culp, & Samuella, send much love to you, and promise to visit us ire long! Tomorrow morning Mrs C. and her Sister, go to their relatives in Virginia,[7] and then to Lexington Ky, where Ella, has been at school, and where, she intends to return for another year!

If I live my Dear, I intend hereafter to attend the Baptist Church only. My friend Gallaher, has left here, and to day for the first time, in years, I went to hear the Episcopalians, and I declare to you, I can discover hardly any differences, between them, and the Catholics. My opinion, is, they will unite at some period not remote from the present. I hope there are good people, in all Christian denominations.

I have began a new leaf, and as some days have passed, in which I did not write to you, I feel like inflicting, a long letter upon you. If you are provoked at it, my Love, and are disposed to quarrel about it, we are at a most proper distance, but if you are gratified, I can assure my Love, I would be most happy, to be with you, to greet your smiles, and if you weep to kiss away your tears! or if you sigh, to soothe your breast!

You do, I doubt not fancy that I have some pleasure, in my absence from home? If you do my Love, and it deludes, you, into happiness, I wish you to think so, but if not, I will vindicate truth, by declaring to you my dear, that I have not realised, one moments happiness since I said "farewell" to you, and kissed our sleeping children, nor do I ever expect to be at rest in hope, and feeling, until we meet again!

There is not a night in which I kneel, at the altar of prayer but what (sinful as I am) I invoke our Heavenly Father, in behalf of, the spiritual welfare, of my beloved Wife, and children! I know my Dear, that I am unworthy, but we are all commanded, to pray, to, and ask of our Heavenly Father, who knows how, to give us good gifts.

Jack Houston's family to whom, I only paid two short visits since my return, send by him every day or so, their "love to you." When it was understood, that you were indisposed, all persons who heard it, made the kindest enquiries for you! And since your last letter, they have been much gratified, to hear of your recovery!

Now Dearest, I can only say, that I hope to be home in August, but I do not care for certain reasons, that you should say when you expect me. When asked, you can say <u>truthfully</u>, "I can not tell." You may say "I hope soon." If we live to meet, I will tell you why, I suggest this thing!

I have <u>forgotten</u> <u>politics</u>, my Love, and find that I knew myself, in part, at least! Had I been nominated, I would have been miserable about your dream, which had caused me some unhappiness, as you know I am superstitious. You see my Dearest, eight pages are filled. Dont be provoked! My love to our dear children. Howda to all

Thy husband
Houston

[In the margin:] Dearest, I think I told you of the Moffatts in my cousin Letchers [Congressional] District.[8] I hope to see them, in the month of July. Should I do so, I need not say, I will write about them.

[1]Houston was referring to the Whig Convention.
[2]For more information see "Report of Nominations," *The Daily Republic* (Washington), vol. IV, No. 13, June 25, 1852. A copy is in the DRT Library, San Antonio, Texas.
[3]Samuella Andrews was the daughter of Margaret's friend Eugenia Andrews of Houston.
[4]Betty Culp and Samuella Andrews were sisters.
[5]Daniel D. Culp.
[6]Ellen Hart Reily was the niece of Henry Clay. Hugh Best, *Debrett's Texas Peerage* (New York: Coward-McCann, 1983), 334.
[7]Their mother, the former Eugenia Price had been reared on a Virginia plantation between Richmond and Norfolk, Virginia. Marguerite Johnston. *Houston: The Unknown City, 1836–1946* (College Station: Texas A & M University Press, 1991), 22.
[8]John Letcher represented Lexington, Virginia. *Biographical Directory of Congress*, 154.

Huntsville
June 25, 1852

My dearest,

Last night, I was relieved of a weight of anxiety by your dates of the 5th, 7th, 8th, and 9th.[1] You can imagine my Love, how long a time has passed without hearing from you. True it is not quite two weeks, but what an age when filled with surmises, fears, apprehensions, anxieties and every thing gloomy! I learned from the news papers, that you were surrounded by a throng of gay admirers, and this thought was beginning to fix itself in my mind, "perhaps in that brilliant throng of heartless flatterers, he scarcely remembers his plain wife and rustic children!" But I believe now, you do realy think of us sometimes.

I rejoice to see that you are unmoved by the recent affair at Baltimore. Oh I long to tell you how I feel, since that important decision! Strange and wonderful are the ways of Providence, and I humbly pray that it may be for our mutual spiritual good. Yes I believe that it will be, and that the Lord assigns better things for you, than more earthly promotion. And now my dear Love, my best beloved, from the depth of my devoted heart, I will make one request of you. Never never again profane the name of our Creator and Redeemer! We are far far apart, and may never meet again. God only knoweth, and through his mercy, I trust we will meet again, and spend many happy days together. Oh if our hearts could be united in the love of God, and we could walk together in the ways of righteousness, I feel as if my life would pass like a sweet spring-day. May the Lord hear the prayers that day and night descend from my poor heart, in behalf of him whom I love so fondly! I will not attempt to describe to you, my great joy on learning that you would soon resign, and become realy an inmate of home, and a sharer of our humble joys. As parents we will have many, very many cares, but should not one gleam of intellect or one word of fondness from our little ones dispel a multitude of cares! It is true the management of their young hearts and minds will require great care and caution, and often when our hopes and expectations are brightest, they will be disappointed, and our poor efforts seem to fall powerless, but let us remember that we are dealing with frail earthly beings, and not Glorified spirits, and in studying their various traits of character, let us gently "seperate the good from the bad," continually imploring the help of our Heavenly Father, and he will bless our feeble efforts.

[In margin:] Sam was opposed to your nomination, lest it might keep you from home.

I recd a letter from Antoinette last night. I do not think Mother is happy in Galveston. I should not be surprised to see [her] at home soon.

Miss Sally Wiley and Mr Eskridge Goree were married last night. It is thought Miss Crawford and Mr Gibbs will be soon. Sam expects to write to you today. He was very anxious for me to assist him, but I have thrown him upon his own resources, and we will see what he will do. The children are all well. Baby looks so much like you, that I love to look at her. Jackson and Isabella are well and contented. The servants are all doing well. Dr Hamilton[2] called a few days ago, to see if you would take charge of his son & daughter[3] as you come home. Please do so, if you can conveniently. They say he is such a good Houston man, and I feel for their Mother.

Thy devoted wife
M. M. Houston

"The New York Recorder" and "Mother's Journal" [are] both published at New York. Do think of them if you please and pay them I entreat you. Ever thine M. M. H.

---

[1]None of these letters has been located.
[2]Dr. Calvin S. Hamilton. Carpenter, 2019.
[3]Edward and Emogene Hamilton. Ibid.

The following letter was written to Houston by his cousin Narcissa B. Hamilton. It is in the Sam Houston Papers, Barker History Center, University of Texas, Austin.

Female Collegiate Institute
June 25th 1852

My Dear Cousin,

I have contemplated writing to you for some time, but concluded to wait until the adjournment of the Baltimore Convention. I am more and more disgusted with the intriguing politicians that manage the convention, and stifle the will of the people. I do rejoice in my heart of hearts at the prospect of the defeat of the Democrats next November. I fully believe the hour the Baltimore convention made their nomination they virtually elected Gen. Scott. You must not conclude that I have gone over to the Whig party, oh! no, far from it, but I want the intriguing politicians of the Democratic punished, and I think that would be the best mode possible of affecting that purpose.

My dear cousin, I do hope that you will find it convenient to visit us this summer. You can surely do so now without any ulterior motive being ascribed to you. I should be more than delighted to see you here on the second tuesday and wednesday in July. That is the time of our commencement, and it is always an interesting time. Vast crowds assemble here on such occasions. As I write, I feel a tear upon my cheek that tells me that you will not come. I will give you one excuse to come if that will serve as an inducement. Misses M. and L. Houston wish to come and they lack an escort. Is not this an appeal to your gallantry? Now, cousin, if <u>you</u> cannot come will you send the Hon. Mr. Dunham,[1] or any of the Congressional beaux that can leave with them, for I am anxious to have them here. Where is John W. Harris?[2] If he is in Washington, give him my respects and tell him I have no inclination to release him from his promised visit, and I would be glad if he could come at that time and bring the Misses Houston with him.

I have made every effort to recover the lost daguerreotype but with no success whatever. It is forever lost to me. But I shall not tell you how painful the conviction is, you might think me very foolish.

Since I saw you, a friend of mine has had my portrait [painted] for the Lyceum Hall. The artist has made me magnificent eyes and brows; he has shaded the right cheek gloriously, it looks as glad as if an angel's breath were kissing it; or as if I were looking at you, ha! ha!

Dear cousin, I know not whether I shall ever see you again, but be assured of one thing, I shall ever cherish thy memory and deck thy friendship with thoughts most pure and as holy as the whispered prayer at eve. I hope that you left your beloved wife and dear children well. Remember me most affectionately to them when you write.

My love to cousin John [Houston] and all our dear relations. Your relations here sent you much love and most earnestly wish you to come.

Please write to me and accept my best love.

N. B. Hamilton

[1]Congressman Cyrus Dunham of New Jersey. For a biography see *Biographical Directory of Congress*, 936–37.

[2]John Woods Harris, originally from Virginia, resided in Brazoria County, Texas. For a biography see *The New Handbook of Texas,* vol. 3, 476.

Huntsville
July 2, 1852

My dear Love,

By last night's mail, I recd three letters from you and was more delighted than I can express to you. Your dates were the 15th[1] ult. and one which I was left to guess, I presume must have been the 12th or 13th. Yours of the 4th ult. which had been mis-sent also came to hand. I see from that, that you were prepared for the decision of the Baltimore convention. You know I do not approve of quoting scripture except in a religious sense, but on this occasion, I can say with deep feeling, that I trust our party may not "<u>pierce</u> themselves through with many sorrows!" If the Whigs will nominate Mr Fillmore, I shall feel no anxiety, for he would make a good President, but may the Lord preserve our beloved country, from the evils with which it is threatened in the event that some others should be, or rather, have been nominated. You will have learned before this, from my letters, that my feelings at your being left out were not those of mortification or unhappiness. Ah no! It has been to me the promise of better things, and the assurance which you give me, that you are now taking leave of politics, has given me new life. But I will not attempt to tell you how delighted I am until you get home.

Bro. Vernal is to be ordained on the 3rd sabbath in this month, and he writes to me, that he will bring two gentle horses for me, if I can get a conveyance to take myself and the children down. I do hope I will be able to do so, for I am exceedingly anxious to be present. The ladies of our church give a supper tonight, the proceeds of which are to aid us in purchasing a bell for our church, which I hope will be finished by the first of Jan. I do not know that I have ever mentioned to you that [Benjamin] Wilson had refunded our money 31 dollars.

The old Presbyterians are holding their Synod here at this time,[2] and have about seven ministers with them. Mr. McCoulough[3] is here with a pretty young wife,[4] and has been out to see me once, in company with the Revd Mr Fairbairn[5] recently from Penn. I was so unfortunate as to mistake the former for Judge [Daniel] Toler, and addressed him as such. But I hope he excused me. It has been so long since we saw him. Isabella is gone to meeting today, and our little flock are all upon my hands. So you can imagine what a fine time I have for writing.

Our crop looks finely and has never suffered for rain. It has been laid by some time and for weeks, the hands have had nothing to do, so that I rejoice at your permission to hire them out. They have however, behaved well, and have been obedient and submissive. I am very tired of Jackson. He is so lazy & conceited, but he is good humoured and as happy as a king, and any one who has lived through the reign of his predecessors[6] can endure him for a few weeks. The children are all well, and I am much flattered about them. I hope their dear father will not be too vain of them. You forget my love, that it was at your suggestion that I resumed the M. in my name.

Thy devoted wife

M. M. Houston

[In the margin:] New York Recorder & also the Mothers Journal.

[1]This letter has not been located.

[2]The meeting was cancelled because no elder was in attendance. For more information see William Stuart Red, *A History of the Presbyterian Church in Texas* (Austin: The Steck Company, 1936), 98.

[3]John McCullough of Galveston. For background see Earl Wesley Fornell, *The Galveston Era: The Texas Crescent on the Eve of Secession* (Austin: The University of Texas Press, 1961), 81.

[4]Margaret Jane Riddell. For a biography see *The New Handbook of Texas,* vol. 4, 389.

[5]Alexander Fairbairn. Identified in Red, 142.

[6]Margaret is referring to the problems with overseers Thomas Gott and Anthony Hatch.

Washington
2nd July 1852

My Dear Son,

For sometime, I have not heard from you. While you wrote to me I was happy to read your letters.

Children, can never know, or feel how anxious their Parents, are for their well being. Your Dear Ma, and our children, occupy my thoughts, and command all my affections. While this is the case with me, I feel, that your Dear Ma, feels no less, for her children than I do. You know my Son, what I have told you about the affection, and obligations of children for their Mother. I am sure you have not forgotten, the reasons which I gave you, on this subject. To be truthful, to be honest, and pious makes a perfect character. One that will last, and be bright, not only in this world, but the world to come, when all things which amuse, and please us here, will fade away, and be remembered no more! Be good, and love your Creator, my Son!

You will tell your Dear Ma, that Congress, has agreed to adjourn the last of this month. I intend to leave a few days before its adjournment. I have heard from Jackson Paul, that his Father[1] is dead! Poor fellow, he has much trouble. I am sorry for him. We ought to be as kind to the poor, as we can.

Give my love, & kisses to your Dear Ma, and Sisters. Tell all howda, and say to the servants, that I am glad to hear that they behave well. It makes me happy.

Thy Father affectionately
Sam Houston

[1]Andrew Paul. Identified in Carpenter, 2022.

New York
4th July 1852

My Dear Love,

We have gotten this far on our way to Lexington [Kentucky], with the remains of Mr. Clay.[1] The public demonstrations, of sorrow, or respect, are great,[2] and detain us much. I hope on tomorrow we will get off, and not again be detained. I wish to see the memory of a great man honor'd, but pomp and display, on such occasions, looks idle, and ostentatious. Col [James] & Mrs [Ellen Hart] Reily, had left Washington, owing to the indisposition of their child. Here we overtook them, and found the child better. They will go on to Boston & return west, perhaps by the time we reach Lexington. Mrs R. has talked much about you my Dear, and expressed great desire to see you, and cherishes great affection for you. I think she has lost much relish for the world, & is more devout, than formerly. So is the Colonel!

To day my Love, I went with Mr Anderson (the Father in law of Mr Samson, who is with us, as assistant Sergt of Arms of the Senate) to the Baptist church to hear Mr Magoon. I was not greatly pleased with him, tho. he is an intelligent man. He preached from the 8 C. & 12 V. of John. "If the Son make you free, you shall be free indeed."

I have not seen my friend, Col [Andrew H.] Mickle & his family. He is at his residence on Long Island, and he has recently lost a grand child. I look on all things in this city, as vanity, & a constant effort at display. I pity those who are doomed to live here, & maintain the round of display, which must to a great extent be heartless.

I know it is <u>heartless</u>, because I find my <u>heart</u>, does not enter into it, but <u>is at home with you, and our little ones</u>. I need not prate about home, for fear you think it idle prating. In confusion, in Philadelphia, I wrote a letter to you, and then tore it up—so you will credit me for one more letter than you receive, from me! I will write as often as I can my Love!

I want you to hug all the children, & kiss them for me. Take care of Mary Willie's "big hide," & dont let her strike you with it again, in so delicate a place, as she did before! Salute our friends, and give howda to all!

Thy affectionate Husband
Houston

[1]For information about the funeral procession entourage see Remini, 782–83.
[2]Some one hundred thousand New Yorkers viewed the casket. Ibid.

Huntsville
July 9th 1852

My beloved husband,

I expect Martha Ransom today, and will try to write you a few lines, before she comes, though I have little to tell you, that would interest you much, except that we are all well. I need not tell you, that we still love you dearly, for that you can not doubt, but my own anxiety to see you increases daily, and I trust you will be with us soon.

By last night's mail, I recd yours of the 20th ult. and also your letter from your cousin Miss H.[1] She is certainly very enthusiastic about you. I thank you sincerely for both. I mentioned to you in one of my letters, that bro. Vernal was to be ordained on the 3rd sabbath in this month, and that I had some hopes of getting down. I now expect to set off on tuesday morning, and go as far as Thomas Palmer's the first day.

Saturday 10th

Soon after Martha came yesterday, Thomas Palmer and Mrs. [Rachel] Palmer came in and remained until evening, and then left for home, so that I had no opportunity of finishing my letter. I am expecting Mrs [W. A.] Leigh today, so with company and my preparations for bro. Vernal's, I am much occupied. Eliza Yokum [sic] was married to Mr Campbell,[2] night before last. I believe for the present they are to remain at Col Yokum's.

Maj Connor[3] has made a profession of religion, and I believe he expects to join the baptist church. It is said he is much changed. Until yesterday, I have not seen Thomas Palmer, since the nomination. His disappointment is very great, but this you will expect. Martha R. is as much your friend as ever. I recd a letter last mail from Antoinette. Mother seems more cheerful than she was at first. I think her unhappiness was partly owing to my bad health. I am rather better than usual, but excessively weak, from the warm weather and nursing. By the Bye, Antoinette Power has two teeth. She is so fat & rosy, that I never suspected such a thing until they made their appearance. The children are all well. Isabella is doing better than ever. Jackson has been several days with his father, who is dangerously ill. He had not attended to any business of importance for us, since the middle of June, but indeed there has been scarcely any thing to do.

Before you come home, if you should purchase your wife a neat comfortable carriage, that would carry a lady, gentleman, & five children, I do not think she would quarrel with you.[4] A match of gentle horses too would grace it finely.

Ever thy devoted wife
M. M. Houston

[1]Narcissa B. Hamilton.
[2]Duncan Campbell. Vick-Rainey, 11.
[3]David Connor. Carpenter, 2021.
[4]Within a year Houston did indeed purchase a large yellow coach. The family would travel in it to Independence in October, 1853. R. Henderson Shuffler, *The Houstons at Independence* (Waco, Texas: Texian Press, 1966), 15.

Lexington Ky
11th July Sunday [1852]

My Dear Love,

This is the only time, I have attempted to write you, since I wrote you from New York. Ten days since, we reached here. On yesterday, the funeral took place. There was much display, and a vast multitude. To day I went to church three times, Baptist, Episcopalian, and Methodist churches, I visited. The regular Baptist minister was absent. In two days we intend to return to the city [Washington, D. C.]—by the most direct route.

I have not visited much here, tho. we are all treated with the greatest kindness, and warm distinction. You will excuse this scrall, as I have to write with a metalic [sic] pen! To summarize things in a word, I love you devotedly, and am each day, more anxious to see you! I intend to write soon again. Love to our dear little ones.

Ever thine
Houston

Cincinnati [Ohio]
14th July 1852

My Dear Love,

I am this far on my way back to Washington. Here I had the pleasure to receive yours of the 17th ult., and our sons letter. They were forwarded by a friend in Washington. They made me happy, tho. I would rather my son had been more studious, than it appears he has been. In future, I hope he will do better. He says he will, and I take it, he will not tell me, who loves him so much, a story. I will be happy at all events, in the hope, that he will keep his word. I have not time to write him, for when ever I stop people gather around me, and I have to leave them abruptly almost, at times, to write to you, my Dear! I hope to reach the city in two days, & a half, and if I live, I will write you at length, and to each send a letter. By this time you have rec'd quite a batch of letters for the family. I have many invitations for you to visit Lexington Ky, next summer if we live, and I have partially promised to do so, but <u>provided</u>, the <u>usual contingency</u>[1] does not happen. You know that we cant always start from home when we propose to do so. This <u>hindrance</u> is a <u>contingency</u>!!! Well my dear Love, my mind is made up, for me to quit the Senate, if I live. This is "sub rosa" for certain reasons.

Your reflections are very just about conventions, and if I am spared, <u>I will crush them for the future</u>! Had I been nominated, there would have been no contest in the elections. I am happy, that I was not nominated. Happy because if spared, I will live, with, and for my family. You know, my devotion to duty, and you know, you do not like to see me abstracted & absorbed in things, which are apart, from <u>your dear self</u>. Your reflections about conventions, would well become a statesman! If Providence had required, me for his purposes, I would have been called. The means are always prepared for the end! Many can now deplore, the result of the convention. Kisses, and love to the children, and howda to all.

Thy devoted Husband
Houston

I sincerely deplore the death of John Lehr. I pity old Lady,[2] and will do all I can for her, in justice to Mary and her child.[3]

[1]Another baby.
[2]Trecilla Lehr.
[3]John Lehr, Jr. Madge W. Hearne Collection of Family Papers, San Antonio.

Washington
July 18, 1852

My very dear Love,

I have just landed from my tour to Kentucky. I wrote to you last from Cleveland,[1] and meeting a letter from you, on my arrival here, I could not deny myself the pleasure, of replying to your letter. And too, I had the happiness to receive [one] from our dear Boy. Tell him, I intend to answer it soon. To day I received a letter from Emmet Lea, who thanks me for two plain Rings which I enclosed to cousin Columbus & Betsy.[2] I suppose he wished to let me know, that he could write. He says he will soon write a letter to Sam. They are all well, and his Pa will soon write to me! I will send the letter, so that Sam, can compare it with his own writing.[3]

My dear Love, your reflections, in relation to our family are most just, and becoming, as well as those which relate to Eternal things. While riding in the cars, to day, I had more serious reflections, than I recollect to have had, on any former occasion, and I assure you, I did not desire to banish them from my mind, but on the contrary, I try to cherish, and encourage them. My judgment is right, but my heart is not renewed by the Holy Spirit.[4] This must be done or no one can be saved! To obtain this, I will never cease to pray, as I am direc[ted] in the Holy scriptures. Nor will I, so long as I enjoy the use of reason, cease to use the means appointed for salvation. I fear my dear, that you imagine, that I am chagrined, at the late political result? Do not think so, my Love, for I declare to you, I am not!!! I understand the whole machinery, and I hope ire long to explain it to you in person. I will send you two out of many letters, which I receive, that you can see my friends are true, whether I have favors to bestow, or not! They came to me from all quarters. On my late trip, had you been present, every where, you would have seen, who had the public heart, tho. I could not be induced, to make any display, but demeaned my-self befitting the occasion, on which I was. I would rather be a christian, and religious man, than to be President, for a hundred years. All things are merged in death, but the immortal soul! If unregener-ate, thus I regard Religion, how happy must I be, if I were a christian, or true Disciple, of the son of God.

I am very happy to hear all are well! Kiss the children, & Howda to all.

Thy devoted
Houston

P.S. I hear with much concern, what is attempted with Mary Lehr by some people. I will try, and be at home so soon as I can! She must, & shall be protected in her rights!!!

P.S. My Dear, none of the Branches will do,—not even Toney [sic]![5] They are all mean, and false. I hear news of them from friends. They are friends of the "Item."[6] They wont do!!!

---

[1]This letter has not been located. Houston may have mistakenly referred to the Cincinnatti letter.

445 : APRIL 10, 1852–AUGUST 30, 1852

[2]The parents of Emmet Lea. Pauline Jones Ganrud, *Alabama Records* (Easley, South Carolina: Southern Historical Press, 1958), vol. 182, 97.

[3]Emmet Lea was a few months younger than his Cousin Sam. Ibid.

[4]Houston is referring to his struggle to reach a decision about joining the Baptist church.

[5]Houston is referring to John and Anthony Branch. Carpenter, 2010, 2004. Houston's opinion of Anthony would later change and he would serve as one of the executors of Houston's will. *The New Handbook of Texas,* vol. 1, 699.

[6]A Texas newspaper.

The following evening Houston wrote Sam a letter. The original is in the New York Public Library, and it is printed in Writings, vol. 5, 347–48.

Washington
25th July 1852

My Dear Love,

Yesterday, I was very happy, by the receipt of your letter, of the 9 Inst. To know that you, and the dear children are well, & happy makes me very happy, so far as I can be, when absent from <u>you</u>! I do believe my dearest, as I write this, that you are a little selfish, and do not wish me to be too happy, when absent from you! If this is so my Love, you may console yourself by realization, for I again, and again assure you, that, I could not be happy, with all mortal appliances, or means when absent from you! I could be happy with you alone, if I knew, that the children were all well, but if I were with them, and you were absent I could not be happy, but be as I now am, miserable.

To day I attended church, and heard a sermon, from a Preacher, whom I did not know. He preached from the 16 c. & 18 v. of Matthew, "before this rock, etc." I listened with more than common attention, and from the context, with the text, taken, I thought that he was not clear, in his apprehension of the Saviour's meaning, in His reply to Peter, but in this I may be wrong. Peter had given evidence of his <u>faith</u>, in Christ Jesus, and of His Divine origin. From this it seems to me, that the Rock refered [sic] to, was <u>Faith</u>? You can no doubt render me light on this point, if we live to meet. My remarks, only amount to an enquiry, and it would seem that Peter, himself, would not be substituted, for a principle, when the principle, must exist in all who are to be saved! Dont think my Dearest, that I by any means feel controversial, for I have mentioned my reflections to no human being, nor do I think the point, important enough, to raise any dispute about. I do not think with our Catholic friends, on this text! nor that Peter was more, than any other of the Apostles. I think my Love that the season, is as warm here, as in Texas. To night we had a fine rain, and it I hope, will cool the weather!

As Jackson Paul says, "I have no circular news." In my last, I wrote to you, that I suffered "palpitation of the heart," or some functional derangement of that organ. Since I wrote I have been much relieved, and I do assure you, that I think it was in part, owing to my anxiety to see you. I asked Dr Sheppard,[1] as he is here, to bleed me. He did not do it, but if I do not get relieved entirely soon, I will lose some blood. I have not bled for years, & it might be well, to lose some blood! I have commenced to day to take the shower bath! I intend to keep it up! It is fine and healthy when taken in the morning. While talking of water, I recall Sam's sickness last summer, and would say to him, not to go into the water, or dabble in it, or he may be taken sick again!

I presume you went to see bro. Vernal ordained. If you did, it was all right, and I only regret, that I was not there to have accompanied you. I am happy, truly happy, to hear that he has "chosen, that better part." I have uneasiness, lest you did not go safe, and you know my Love, that I always think I can do things right so that you would have been safer, with the children, under my care, than any ones else!

You have not yet told me, whither [sic], Antoinette is as "smart," or "pretty," as the balance of the flock! You say, she looks very like me, and that her head is like mine. That gratifies me, but if it were precisely like her Dear Ma's, I would not be less gratified. While on that subject, I think Miss Nannies like her Ma's, as much, or more than either of the others. My Dear, you have not written, as much about the children, as I thought you wou'd have done! I am fearful my Dear, that you have been chagrined, at the result of the <u>Convention</u>. If so, be assured I am not. I feel that I am a happier man, than if I had been <u>nominated</u>. What of reputation, I have, is not dependent, upon Jugglers, and their tricks! Well this is a prosy letter, and you will be tired reading I am sure! Give kisses, and love to the dear Children for Pa! When you write to Mother, Give my love to her, Ann, & Charles [Power]!

Thy devoted
Houston

[1]Dr. William H. Sheppard of Washington County, Texas. *The New Handbook of Texas*, vol. 5, 1015.

Washington
31st July 1852

My Dear Love,

As the Senate did not sit to day, I have been unusually engaged in writing letters of business, for I write no political letters!!! I was much opposed to adjourning over, because it seems to postpone my getting away from this place where, I will never be contented, and my feelings, my hopes, and my desires can never be gratified, or delighted, because you my Love, and our children are not here. I see around me, persons who have families at home, but who seem to be contented here, and seek pretexts to remain. They may be happier here, than at home, and if so, this may furnish them a satisfactory reason for remaining. This certainly is not my case, and I desire to get off so soon as I can. You will, I doubt not, approve of my conclusion, and will sanction my reasons. I would be so happy my dear, if I could only be seated beside you this evening, and had no apprehension, that we would soon have to part again. I could enjoy, not only your dear society, but the pranks, and antics, of our children. You will not fancy, that this is romance, but a veritable sketch of real life.

I assure you my Love, that I feel as tho every hour spent here, is an hour lost to you, to me, & happiness. The sacrifice which I make is made to our mutual interest, and that of our children. It is my duty, if Heaven wills it, that I should do all within honor, and the compass of my power to place my family, above want, or inconvenience, when I can not remain with them. Well to this, I yield submissively to my detention here. You need not fear, that I will ever desire to remain in public life! I do assure you my dear, that I do not pass an hour, that you are not present to my heart, and thoughts. At times I fancy, that I can feel your breath, and hear your words, as well as see the children playing around us, where we are seated! Never have I laid myself to rest, since we parted, that you are not present to my mind.

Now my Love, since I have told you this much, you will not suppose, that I can be very happy, when I am absent. I send you a "New York Herald." You will see in it, a dreadful catastrophy![1]

Give my love, and kisses to the children, and howda to all!

Thy devoted Husband
Houston

P.S. There is confusion in the pages of this letter,[2] for I was interrupted by company, & I was sorry that they had not kept away. I may write again tomorrow if I live. I am half provoked at times to say funny things. I believe I will have to do it.

Thine Ever
Houston

[1]Houston is probably referring to the massacre of U. S. Troops under Capt. Randolph B. Marcy by Comanches at Ft. Arbuckle, Oklahoma. The *Montgomery Alabama Journal*, July 29, 1852, vol. VI, #149, p. 2, reported that over 80 men were killed and that "It is believed that an Indian War is inevitable." Marcy, who had served in Texas during the Mexican War, was not killed, and later fought in the Civil War. For a biography see *Dictionary of American Biography*, VI, Part 2, 273–74.

[2]Houston had skipped the second page. He went back and finished the letter on this page.

My Dear Love

To day, as usual I attended the Baptist Church, and the present Pastor preached, from the 1 C. & 15 v. of 1st Timothy. It was rather a fancy, than a practicle [sic] sermon. He finished the whole chapter.

Well my Love, I really hardly know, what to write with a hope of interesting you. There is nothing but my duty here, that <u>interests me</u>, and I do not suppose for a moment that the details of my duties could interest you. If I tell you, how much I love you, and the children, and how anxious I am to be with you, it will only be repeating, an oft told tale, and you may begin to doubt my sincerity, upon the principle, that persons who swear vehemently, to facts, implicate their own veracity. Well as I have nothing else to write about, but such things, if you will, you must suspect my sincerity, while I must do you the justice, to believe you would not be pleased, if others were to suspect my truth on these subjects. If I were now present with you my love, I am satisfied that few words would convince you of my devotion. Yes, my perfect devotion to you, and a good liking for the children.

At home, the sabbath has been to me a pleasant day, but here it is the reverse. You know, I do not visit on the sabbath, nor do I desire, others to visit me. Here I can not avoid it entirely. I like my friends to call, upon me, but not on sunday.

Were I at home with my flock, I could read the Bible, and look upon you and our children, and feel, that I should be grateful to my Creator for happiness, and all this would not make me, a worse, if it did not make <u>me a better man</u>! Tis true that my exterior, and all my actions compart, with all, that I profess to you to be, but our attention must be called to the subjects, which are discussed in our presence, unless we are drawn by affection, to those objects at a distance, whom we love most affectionately.

Under these circumstances, how much more gratifying, and delightful, it would be to me, if I were in a situation, where I could look affection, and <u>whisper</u> love! I may be fanciful, and censorious, but I declare my Love, I do believe, that I love my family more than any one that I know here. Yea, twice as much. I can only account for it on one of two principles, either, that I am capable of loving more, than other men, or that I have, a more <u>lovely</u> wife & children, than other men, or it may be that both these facts exist? Dearest I will leave you to settle this point as proposed, and let me know your conclusion. You may consult Sam, & see what he will say?

I did not write to you as often last week, as usual, & one reason was ridiculous enough! I thought you would be at bro. Vernals, as your last letter announced the fact of your departure, on the next day. Well was not this a sage notion, as if you would be absent when a letter was written a few days since, would reach Huntsville? I will tell you when to quit writing my Love, to me at this place, and where to write to me. I will write to you as often as I can, and will try, and quit complaining! If I do not, I will sit in, and write, proper, and sincere love letters, if they should be ever so trite, or common. I fear I am becoming common place any how, for loving, as I do, my Wife & children. Well, I will stand it, until we can settle it, face to face!

Thy devoted Husband
Houston

Washington City
4th Aug 1852

My Dear Margaret,

I find myself in my seat, and a dry debate going on. This being the case, I will lose nothing by writing you a letter. This week I received none from you, or Sam. I attribute this to your absence to Vernals. I hope you are now safe, at home, after a pleasant visit. To day I am not so well, as usual. Last night I set up with Genl Rusk, who has had a violent attack of Bilious cholic. He was attacked at 12 M. yesterday. It was a fierce attack, and for some hours he was sinking fast. Indeed it was most probable, that he wou'd not be able to react. No cause could be assigned, for his indisposition. For years, he has not indulged in any excess. It may have arisen from the state of the weather. The mercury fell from 98 to 60, and is now at that. To day I found it convenient to day to put on Broad cloth, and my cloak. I have never before seen any thing like the present season, is here! Fire would be very agreeable. I am all impatience, for a few days to run by, until I can get off, to embrace you, and the weans. I dare say no more than this subject, as I fear, to run into a long love letter, and compel [sic] you to read it. But I will say in all sincerity, that I do love you most ardently, and would say much more, but will defer farther declarations until, I adjust them, as <u>proposed</u>, in the conclusion of my last letter. In the meantime I will say to you, that in consideration, of a small amount of my love for you, I have felt myself compelled to run the risk of a scolding for buying sundry dresses for you. Such as will suit my fancy, and I hope your taste. They are of various kinds, and all I ask in return is, that you be pleased with them, and with me for getting them for you! I have ordered Mother's mantillo [sic], and hope to get one that will please her! "Sams Hat" too, is on the way, and will be placed on his head, if he will be studious. I do anticipate, vast happiness, should I live to reach home from pressing my Dear Wife, & children to my heart. Do my Dear Love, hug, & kiss the dear children for Pa! Howda to all!

Thy devoted Husband
Houston

Washington
5th Aug 1852

My Dear Love,

I wrote to Sam a, note of this date,[1] and as I have nothing to do, but listen to a dry speech, I will write you a few lines in hopes, that I may cause you an hours cheerfulness.

My friend Rusk, is much better, but still feeble. Tis true I have no need to write, and my dear to repeat, the old tale of love, you know, to save you, I ought to eschew that. If I were to tell you one tenth part of how much I love you, I am sure you would laugh at me, so I must wait, and make my professions *[the word* declarations *is crossed out here]*, so that I can qualify, my declarations, so as to suit your mood & avoid ridicule. If I were to say that I love you more than I have ever done, would you believe me? Well, I honestly declare I do, so far as I can judge, and I hope ire long to tell you my reasons, for my belief. One is, that sleeping, and waking, you are present to my mind.

On the 14th Inst. if I live, I intend to be in Carlysle Pa, the land of my ancestors, to speak at a great Democratic meeting. Then on the 20th if I can, I am to be at New Market Va, as I have mentioned in a former letter! Then I intend to return, and start for home, about the 24th or 6th of this Inst.

My mind is as restless as a chained Bear! I reflect at times so intensely, that I am almost crazy. I can assure you, I do wish you were with me, or I with you. I am sure my Dear, that you can not be more anxious to see me, than I am to see you. If ever man suffered by absence, I do, and as to my ever returning here, if I live, will depend on consultation, with you, my Love.

Kiss the children for me! Howda to all!

Thy devoted & faithful Husband
Sam Houston

I fear you cant make out this letter.   H.

[1]This letter has not been located.

Washington
6th Aug 1852

My Dear Love,

Dont be alarmed at my writing so often, for I will relieve you by writing a short letter. I send you some "puzzle Grass" seed, so that you may have it put in a bed by its-self. I have not any news to write to you.

There is news of cholera etc. on the North-State of N. York. I can hardly be confined in this <u>sink</u>, with any patience. I am happy that my home and family, are far remote from this city, and I hope my children, may be so situated that they may never be within the hateful influences, which are every day becoming worse, not only in the <u>social</u>, but the moral, and political condition, of this place! Tomorrow, I intend to send you a Resolution, which I have offered, in Senate, that strikes at official corruption. I can not stand it any longer! My God, has placed it in my power to abstain, from the vices, which are around me, as a man, who has a hope of a happy immortality!

Business prevents me from writing more. I am in the Senate chamber.

Thy devoted & faithful Husband
Sam Houston

Washington
8th Aug 1852

My Dear Love,

Another sabbath has passed, and as usual, I went to the Baptist Church, and heard the same Preacher. The people here seem to think they are good enough to stay at home. I judge this from the fact, that few attend church, unless there is a new preacher to be there. I did intend to have gone to day, and heard Bishop Andrew[1] of Ky, who was to preach here to day, but did not attend. You may rely my Dear, that I do not go to church, either to criticise or cavil. To you I am indebted, for giving my mind a direction, <u>anti</u>-<u>controversial</u>. I think it unprofitable, to discuss points of scripture, which are abstruse, or misterious [sic], when we have our duty, so clearly pointed out, in a manner so plain, that if we give heed to, what we are taught, there can be no doubt as to the course which we should pursue. If we only practice, what is manifestly our duty, we will enjoy more happiness, than if we seek to find out, that which our Creator, has not imparted to us, but has reserved, from us, for wise, & gracious purposes. To enquire [sic] into sacred things, beyond what has been clearly given to us, to know, is vanity, if it is not crime! This my Dear, is my conclusion.

To day another member of Congress paid the debt to nature. Mr Ro. Rantoul,[2] one of the ablest members of the House of Representatives, died of Aresypilus.[3] He had his family here. They left to day with his remains for Boston, his place of residence! He was a temperate, moral man, and I think a professor of Religion. There is some sickness here, and a tendency to cholera. The weather is singularly cool. For days past, I have put on my winter Garments, and find them pleasant even in the sun! Genl Rusk is still mending, but he was so ill, that it will be some days, before he can resume his place, in the Senate! He is an able, and useful member!

Cousin Jno Letcher receives letter[s] from his wife often, and she always directs her love to you, and the children. I told her, that she reminded me, of you—It was true, and she is said to be handsome, which in my estimation, adds, to the resemblance. She was very popular with all the Ladies, who became acquainted with her while here, and here the paralel [sic] holds grace again! I have written to you much of late, and one reason is that I am more happy in so doing, than at any other employment.

Thy Devoted
Houston

Letcher, evinces his love for his wife, by his conduct in her absence. He is one of the most remarkably proper men, I have seen in my life, for propriety of conduct, tho. not religious. His wife is a member of the church, and I think truly pious.

Last night I put up some Peas for you, and send them with this letter. I send our Boy some Clover (Verbena) seed! I put in this letter some of the clover—smell it.

Give love and kisses to the children. Write to meet me at Memphis, and San Augustine!

[1]Methodist Bishop James Osgood Andrew. For a biography see *Dictionary of American Biography,* vol. 1, Part 2, 277–79.
[2]Robert Rantoul, Jr., died August 7, 1852. For a description of his death and funeral see Congressman Timothy Jenkins to Harriet Jenkins, August 8, 1852. Timothy Jenkins Collec-

tion, Hamilton College Archives, Colgate, New York. Copies in the possession of the editor.
[3]Houston meant the infection Erysipelas.

The following letter to Sam Houston, Jr., is from the Sam Houston Hearne Collection in the Barker History Center, Austin, Texas.

Washington
8th August, 1852

My Dear Son,

I write you a few lines, because I love you so much, as I hope you are a good Son, and obey your Dear Ma, and love [your] little sisters.

I intended to send your Ma some of the clover, but sealed her letter, and did not put it, in the letter. It is said to have a pleasant perfume, when dry. The seed you need not open at present, as it will be more safe, to remain, until it is time to sow it in the spring.

I do not expect you to write again, unless you write to me at Memphis, or San Augustine, as I have requested your Dear Ma. If I live to meet you my Son, I hope to find you all that will make my heart glad!

Thy Father
Sam Houston

I have a beautiful Testament, for some one of our "smart Child<u>ren</u>." Kiss Ma & Sisters for me, my Son!

Washington
13th Aug 1852

My Dear Love,

To day I intend to set out for Carlysle Pa, to make the speech proposed in my former letter. I hope to be back on monday, three days hence. While absent, as I will be going from home, I may not write to you until my return. Any change for the time, seems to hasten my departure, for home, and for you, my Dear. The meeting is of great importance, to the Democracy of Pa, and may decide the votes of that state. You see my Love, that I feel anxious for party success, whe[ther] I lead, or am under the saddle.

Last night in the parlour of the Hotel, I met with Mrs Genl Ruben Davis,[1] (bro. of Genl James Davis)—also Dr Sykes of Miss,[2] and his family. Your cousin Judge Rogers[3] married a Niece[4] of his, and I think they will all remove to Texas. Your cousin Capt Rogers,[5] who removed to Texas, settled in Washington [on-the-Brazos] as they inform me! There is no recent news here, that seems at this moment to command attention. I have just received the "Globe" of to day, and send it to you, as it contains some remarks of mine about Indians, etc.[6] It was made at the instant, I had not time, and was in a hurry.

My Dear, I have to start and I know, you will excuse a letter much shorter than usual.

My Love to the children, or as much of it, as you are willing to spare to them, of the vast amount which you command. You know my Dear, that I charged you, that I was fearful, you would be jealous of Sam, when he was a baby! We have so many to love now, that we must enlarge our hearts, or by some means increase the stock on hand—Dont mistake me Dearest, and get angry at me. I mean, the Stock of love, not the stock of children!!! hem!!

My Dear Love,
Truly thy Husband
Sam Houston

[1]Mary Halbert Davis.
[2]Dr. William A. Sykes. Identified in Irene S. and Norman E. Gillis, *Biographical and Historical Memoirs of Mississippi* (Irene S. and Norman E. Gillis, 1962), 600.
[3]Houston is probably referring to Judge James Harrison Rogers. For a biography see *The New Handbook of Texas,* vol. 5, 663–64.
[4]Barbara Hogue. Ibid., 664.
[5]Captain William Pelag Rogers. *The New Handbook of Texas,* vol. 5, 665.
[6]For a copy of this speech, taken from the *Congressional Globe,* see *Writings,* vol. 5, 349–54.

Washington
16th Aug 1852

My Dear Love,

As I proposed, I spoke at Carlysle on the 14th and this morning found myself in the city again. The Speech was a very good one, and as others were pleased with it, I ought to be. I had travelled all the night before, and did not make as good a speech as I could have done under other circumstances. On the 20th if possible, I am to be (as stated before) at New Market. My Cousin Letcher, is to go with me, and I hope to meet some of your kinsfolk, the Moffatts. I send you a letter, from Bro. William, which I wish you to take care of!! I am sorry that Sister Mary is not well. I will write to Bro William, and tell him not to let Sister use "Quinine." That I would wager is the cause of the symptoms of which he speaks.

A few more days, will close the Session, and if spared, I will not sleep much, until I can embrace you, & the little Houstons.

I hear often from Bro Henry & family. Mr. Baker from Marion left there, several days since, and left all well, but Henry, who is not so well. He caught cold last winter at Montgomery, and it still lingers with him. He has some uneasiness. I will write to him, if he can, to spend the winter in Texas. Do you write also my Love. To day I wrote to Jackson Paul. For weeks my Love, I have had no letters from you, or Sam! Kisses, and Love to the children for Papa!! Howda to all, and regards to friends.

Thy devoted
Houston

Washington
Senate Chamber
17th Aug 1852

My Dear Love,

It is now eleven oclk at night, and we are still in session. We are constantly engaged in business, day and night. And such business!! At the close, or near it, of each session, the members either from fatigue, or a great thirst, are in the habit of using <u>something</u>, in their water, which has a tendency, to increase their loquacity. The effect is to keep, members who wish to attend to business, in a very unpleasant state of mind. We have to stand boring, and have no other resorce [sic], than to endure, the most prosy, and impertinent speeches. This is the situation in which I am confined, and my only relief is, to think of you, and the children, and fancy, that you are all reposing sweetly, and securely, in our "wild-wood" house. My fancy, or imagination, is all that is left to comfort me, until with a hope, that ire long I will get home, to embrace the treasures of my life, and the joys of my heart.

Maggy Trimble[1] arrived today in bad health, and I have only seen her, for a moment. She sends kindest love to you. She was most happy to see me! I am fearful she will not live long! I must close, as I hope we will soon adjourn.

Thy devoted Husband,
Sam Houston

I cant read for correction.

[1]Margaret McEwen (Mrs. John Trimble) was the daughter of Houston's cousin Robert McEwen. Samuel Rutherford Houston, 204.

23rd Aug 1852

My Dearest,

Last evening I returned, from New Market, where there was a great <u>rally</u> of the Democracy, and where <u>they said</u> I electrified them with a speech! Well, it was a very good one, I suppose. There were about 10 or 14,000 thousand people, about 3,000 Ladies it was said. I saw your relations,[1] as I believe they are. What was your Grand Pa's name. If it was Henry,[2] there is no doubt of the relationship. Our cousin Susan Letcher came to meet her husband, and I would have been the very happiest man on earth, if my Dear wife could have met me there. I wou'd have forgotten, that I had made a great speech, only as you, my Dear wou'd have been gratified with the fact.

The Session will soon be over, and I on my way home, if Heaven wills it. I will not try to describe my anxiety to see you. No letters have come of late, and I hope, it is owning to the reason suggested in my former letter. I will still write or send letters, or if not letters, News papers. Love to the children.

Thy husband
Houston

[1]The family of Philander B. Moffett of New Market. Identified in Roland Vern Jackson, et al., *Virginia 1850 Census Index* (Bountiful, Utah: Accelerated Indexing Systems, Inc., 1976), 390.
[2]Margaret's grandfather, Nancy Lea's father, was Henry Moffette.

23rd Aug 1852

My Dearest,

I send you a very important Recipe. Cant you send it to Mrs Norwood or Mrs. Rucker[1] that is, in Washington. It may cure her little Daughter[2] of deafness. I have been in the Senate from 11 A.M. until seven P.M. and eat nothing. We are still in Session, and I do not know when we will adjourn. My Dear, Judge Johnson & Tilly[3] are here on their way north. They look well, and say they will stay a few days.

I forgot to tell you how much love Cousin Susan Letcher & Jno. wish me to give you for them. The Houstons here send you great love. I have just seen Jack here and he reports all well.

Thy devoted Husband
Sam Houston

[1]Adeline Norwood (Mrs. B. J.) Norwood at Washington-on-the-Brazos, Texas. Identified in Carpenter, 2063.
[2]Mary A. Rucker. Ibid.
[3]Judge Robert D. and Matilda Maffit Johnson of Galveston. Tilly was an old friend of Margaret's.

Washington
26th Aug 1852

My Dearest,

This you see, is drawing to the close of the session. I am <u>busy</u>, beyond any former example, from various causes, and I assure you I do not regret, that it is the case. I say so because it employs my mind, and to some extent, prevents my anxiety, being so painful as it otherwise would be! For several weeks, I have received no letters from home, and you will fancy, my infelicity. You see my Dearest, that I have not sought to retaliate upon you, by silence.

I am unhappy, because I have not heard from you since your visit to Vernals. You know <u>I</u> fancy, that you are always safest, with me for a <u>driver</u>. I can only hope that your trip was gratifying and pleasant, and that you returned without accident to yourself, or children.

I can tell you no news of interest. I can tell you a fact, my Dear! If I can judge, correctly, I do believe I am much more anxious to see you, than any other husband in Congress is to see his wife. This I might account for, if we were face to face! I hope it will not be long, until we may have leisure to talk, and tell all our cares, as well, as to realise, happiness in mutual sympathy.

I am in the Senate, & will conclude, with kisses to the children, and howda to all.

Thy devoted Husband
Houston

Washington
28th Aug 1852

My Dear Love,

I wrote to you last night, and was so fortunate as to get to rest, at

1 oclock and rose early this morning to resume my duties at half past Nine. When we are to get off from the capitol to day, or to night, no one can tell. Tomorrow is the sunday, and I hope to get some rest. On wednesday I hope to set my face, towards home, where my heart has been so long <u>set</u>! There are no matters here, which I could relate, that would gratify you, that I now think of. I send you such news papers, as I think will gratify you. Cousin Letcher sent you a paper to day, which has always been opposed to me. All the Democratic papers of Va, are now puffing me! Who thanks them? Extorted praise, calls for no thanks! You will see that the scamps call me "old Houston" who never, saw me, nor even a <u>picture</u> of me. I may if needful, suppose the epithet, arises from the fact, that I have been so long <u>distinguished</u>, or to say the least of me, <u>notorious</u>, that people suppose, in the ordinary course run, that I must be <u>very old</u>!

Well my Love, if you do not quarrel with them, I will not, I can assure you. Read to Sam the <u>epithets</u>, and Nannie, also, and see what they say, or how they estimate it.

Indeed writing about you, and the children draws me, home with cords of inexpressible force. I feel as tho. I have wasted ages of happiness by absence, from you my Dear, and the little ones. You have them around you, and do not feel my absence, with the same force, that I do yours. They are never present with me, but what you are associated with them. You and them, are the same to me, for you are mine, and they are yours!

Kiss them for me & tell them love from Papa!

Thy ever devoted Husband
Houston

Washington
30th Aug 1852

My Dearest,

This is the last night of the session, and I rejoice, that it is so. I hope to get off, on the day after adjournment, say on the 2nd Sept. I have for you all that I think you will want in the way of <u>dress</u>. I found that Mothers Mantillo could not be had here, and sent to N. Y. for it. It has not yet been received. & I am in pain lest it shou'd not come. If does not, I will hope to get a fine one in some of the cities through which, I may pass, on my way home. I will have one if it <u>can</u> be had!

I do not know that you will fancy the finery, which I have chosen for you. I hope to have, a good laugh with you, about some portions of it. I have not yet got any thing for our Daughters, & Sams Hat is not yet done. I hope to be able to get it yet! If I do not, the fault will be that of the Hatter. But I hope Sam, will not have reason, to make that same remark, which he did about the "red Boots" to wit. "He was a strange man, for he must have known, that you were a <u>very great</u> man!"

If I fail in the mantillo, and the Hat, it will not be my fault, but my misfortune. We will sit all night I suppose. I hope not!

Give love, & kisses to the children! Howda to all!

Thy ever devoted Husband
Houston

Appendix A

The following letter was written to Margaret Houston from her former teacher, Joseph McLean. It was on a school outing to New Orleans in 1836, with Professor McLeans's group, that Margaret first saw Sam Houston. A very faded note from Mrs. McLean is on the first page. Andrew Jackson Houston Collection (#3944) at the Texas State Archives.

Jackson Miss
Oct 14 1850

Dear friend,

We have removed from the beautiful city, Columbus, and we are now residing in Jackson. Mr McLean says his next move will be to Texas where you reside. *[The next two lines are blurred and faded.]* I would be very glad to see you and your husband, and children, and other relations. Jackson I find a pleasant place. The steam cars go and return from Vicksburg every day. We have a view of the governor's Mansion from our window, and of the Capital from the other. Jackson is situated on Pearl river, a stream navigable except in autumn. The number of inhabitants is about four thousand people of every nation, and every religion. Remember me affectionately to your Mother, and to Antoinette. Do write again. We are ever so pleased to hear from you.

Yours truly,
L. P. McLean

Dear Mrs Houston

After the lapse of many years I take the liberty of writing to you. I recd several letters from [you] & replied to them, but I know you did not receive them. Just as I was on the eve of leaving Columbus

Miss I recd your notice of the Baylor College for which accept my thanks. I see occasionally printed documents from Gen Houston (whom of all men living I would rather see and be acquainted with), for which also present him my warmest thanks. How often & how fondly I think of long long ago, those halcyon days of yore, when you were young, & studying under my supervision, the happiest days of my life were spent in your father's family & beneath his hospitable roof. The paternal admonitions I recd from him have never been effaced from my memory nor do I think they ever will. It is a green spot on memory's page, which nothing can obliterate. After ten years residence in Columbus I find myself in the city of Jackson. I am not as yet much pleased with the place, however I will remain in it at least one year. It is my determination then to go to Texas & spend the residue of my life, be it long or short. My life appears at least to me, to have consisted of long very long years. Since I left my parents' roof, appears to me to be about four score years & ten, although it has been only 25 years. I do not however yet, feel the effect of old age. Mrs McLean & myself have excellent health, wife weighs about 190 & I about 160. Neither of us had any serious sickness.

At a Camp Meeting held recently not far from Columbus, I had the pleasure of seeing Capt Kennon's family & amid the group I saw Mary Moffet, the widow Kennon. I was again [torn] it reminded me of days gone by & of her father[1] & Margaret Langdon.[2] She is a gay widow very large & I thought very handsome. She was dressed in full fashion & it appeared she wished particularly to attract attention. She lives in her father in law's house. I did not see Mrs Lea.[3] She lives near Selma. I saw her last winter but once in Mobile. She was broken considerably. I had the pleasure of seeing one of her sons, whom I thought bore a great resemblance to his dear father, who was my earliest & best friend. Mrs McLean's sisters & her brother are all married & doing well, they live here is Miss. Her mother died a few years ago & her father is married again, he did not suit himself as well as he might have done. I wish I could see you all once more, & talk with you & your Mother about days of yore & times gone by. I hope I may yet have that indescribable & joyful pleasure. Give my love to your Ma & Antoinette & Vernal & to all, everyone of the family who are there.

Remember me kindly & affectionately to Gen Houston. I have a young man, a protégé whom I wish to send to West Point if I possibly can. He is an amiable boy whom I took from the cruelty of a step mother & adopted him myself. He is handsome & accomplished, a southerner named Joseph M. Thompson. His father will do nothing for him, & the boy's aspirations are for West Point, if he has a fault, except a notable pride & a thirst for glory I have never been able to ascertain it. I hope as a boon to me, & as a rich gift to a noble boy, that you would prevail on Gen Houston to excerpt himself in his behalf. I trust you will when opportunity presents itself reply to this letter. If Col Baylor[4] be convenient to you, present him my respects, also to Mr [James] Maxey my dear old pupil & tell him I am determined to go to Texas. I only regret I did not go earlier. Gov Quitman has issued a proclamation to convene the legislature on the 18th proximo.[5] I expect some pleasure then. Miss is indignant at the treatment which Texas & the South has received at the hands of the federal government. Gov A G Brown[6] made a grand speech on Saturday night in the representative's hall. There is great excitement here on the subject all nullifiers [blurred]. How it may terminate God knows. I hope however that the Union will be preserved. Still I do not wish nor want the South to succumb to imposition from the North. I remain for ever your affectionate friend & Tutor Jas A McLean.

[1]Mary and Margaret Moffett were the daughters of Gabriel Moffett, Nancy Lea's brother. Madge W. Hearne family papers.
[2]Mrs. Levi Langdon. Ibid.
[3]McLean is probably referring to Margaret Moffett Lea (Mrs. Green Lea) who was the sister of Nancy and Gabriel Moffett. Ibid.
[4]For information about Robert Emmet Bledsoe Baylor's early life in Alabama see Brewer, 554–55.
[5]For information about this incident see Nevins, *Ordeal of the Union: Fruits of Manifest Destiny 1847–1852*, 362, 365.
[6]For more information about Albert G. Brown's views and the views of Mississippi politicians see Ibid., 365.

Appendix B

The following notes and memoranda are from Henderson Yoakum's Diary.[1] *The dates mentioned are very confusing. The Court Record Books for Walker County for 1850 through 1851 indicate a different series of events: On September 25, 1850, Margaret was indicted for "assault and battery upon Virginia Thorne." On September 30, 1851, a mistrial was entered and the case was dismissed. In addition, Houston discusses in his correspondence of 1851 the coming trial,*[2] *and depositions were taken in July of 1851.*[3]

Huntsville, Texas
Nov. 8, 1850

General Houston returned home from the late long session of Congress, a few days since. He is somewhat troubled about some domestic matters. It seems that some eight or ten years since, Vernal Lea, brother of Mrs. Houston, became the guardian by appointment of the Probate Court of Galveston, of the person and estate of Virginia Thorne, then a little girl of some seven years old.[4] He took her to his house and kept her till his wife [Mary] died, when he transferred her person to the care of Mrs. Houston, where she resided till October, 1849, as one of the family. About a year previous to that, General Houston had procured an overseer by the name of Gott, who had lived in the family, and among other things had formed an intimacy with this girl. Loose conduct on the part of the girl met with the rebuke of Mrs. Houston, which so offended the girl that she became insolent and ungovernable. As she had some time before that united herself with the Baptist Church of which Mrs. Houston was also a member, the latter laid the whole matter privately before Mrs. Evans and Mrs. Birdwell, also members of the same church, and asked for their advice. They advised her not to bring the matter up before the church, but to correct the girl privately at home. This Mrs. Houston did. The girl made her complaint to Gott, the overseer. About a month after this time, Virginia eloped with Gott, who put her to board, and had himself appointed her Guardian by the Walker County Probate Court. At the last fall term of the District Court, Gott took Virginia before the Grand Jury and procured that Mrs. Houston be invited to appear before the Grand Jury. The testimony follows:

The State vs Margaret Houston
    Indictment for Assault and Battery against Virginia Thorne.
    This cause came on for trial on Monday morning, Sept, 30, 1850, S. D. Hay, Dist. Attorney for the state. H. Yoakum and A. P. Wiley for defendant. The jury were accepted by defendant without a challenge.

<u>Virginia</u> <u>Thorne</u>, witness for the State, sworn and examined, says, that on the last of the last fall court, she was up stairs at Mrs. Houston's, had dressed little Sammy, a child of Mrs. Houston's when Mrs. Houston came up and told her to bring the child to her; she led the child along; it cried a little; Mrs. Houston said "Don't hurt the child." Virginia said, "I am not hurting it." Then Mrs. Houston slapped witness and knocked her up against the bed post. Witness said, "Don't kill me." Then Mrs. H. struck her many times with a cow hide—perhaps twenty strokes. This was in the night about bed time in Walker County. Witness did not know her age.[5]

<u>Cross Examined</u>. There was one wound on the witness's right wrist, and one on her elbow; no others were made. Witness never told Mrs. Baines or Mrs. Creath that she was mad when she led the child to Mrs. H. Never said that Mrs. Houston had treated her kindly; was not advised to go before the Grand Jury by Mr. Gott; Mr. Gott took her to the Grand Jury. Gott had notified her a day or two before that she would have to go before the Grand Jury.

<u>Thomas Gott</u>, witness for the State, swore and examined, and states that on the said Monday morning of the last week of last fall court Virginia Thorne showed him a bruise on her right wrist. Afterward Mrs. H. said to Virginia in his presence, "Virginia, be careful how

you behave, remember what you got last night. That cowhide is still here." Mr. Gott thought that the girl was about nineteen years old.

Cross examined. He was the overseer for General Houston. He had been there about 11 months. Had not always been treated kindly there. (Quest by defense counsel. Did Mrs. Houston object to you and Virginia sitting up too late at night? Objected to by the state. Objection sustained by the court.) Virginia left General Houston's about the last of October, 1849. Witness went with her, and took her to Cincinati [sic] in Walker County.

Vernal Lea, witness for the defense, examined. Was appointed guardian for Virginia at Galveston in 1842; was still her legal guardian so far as he knew, though he had lately heard that Gott had procured himself to be appointed her guardian by the Walker County Court. Witness kept his ward at his home for five or six years until his wife died,[6] when he entrusted the care of his ward to Mrs. Lea, his mother. The latter went to live with Mrs. Houston; Virginia went with her, and remained there till she was clandestinely taken away by Mr. Gott last fall. Witness said that Virginia was like all children not raised under the eyes of parents, rather hard to manage.

Mrs. Creath, for defendant, sworn and says: Virginia frequently staid with her; showed her a mark on her arm; told witness that last fall Mrs. Houston had corrected her; did not say whether Mrs. Houston had been severe or not. Witness inferred from what Virginia did say that the correction was not severe. Witness knew Mrs. Houston to be a mild kind-hearted woman.

Mrs. Baines, witness for defendant states that last spring Virginia told her of the affair—said "she hated the two oldest children of Mrs. Houston, of which Sammy was one, that she loved the baby—that she was trying to get Sammy to sleep and Sam would not go to sleep but cried. Mrs. Houston came up stairs and told her to bring Sammy to her. She was mad and jerked the child down, and Mrs. H. whipped her for it." She said that she had done wrong, and that Mrs. H. was a lady and a Christian, and that she had forgiven Mrs. Houston.

(Mr. Gott recalled and asked by defendant's counsel if he had taken

Virginia away without Mrs. Houston's consent? Question objected to and objection sustained by the court.)

Mrs. Evans examined by defendant's counsel. Said that she had known Mrs. H. for many years; her mode of family government was mild and forbearing; had been much and often at Mrs. Houston's home and never anything harsh or unpleasant had occurred in the family. Mrs. Houston had informed her and Mrs. Baines of Virginia's conduct, and had asked their advice as members of the Church (of which they as well as Mrs. Houston and Virginia were members) as to the course she should pursue. They both advised her to correct Virginia at home and not to take the matter before the Church. The witness showed a part of a communication between Josephine Duncan, her niece and Virginia in which the latter said that Mrs. H. was a perfect lady and a Christian. This was after the affair referred to in this case.

Mrs. Ransom, witness for defendant stated that she had been often at Mrs. Houston's and knew well her mode of family government, and confirmed what Mrs. Evans had said in favor of it.

Thomas Parmer, examined for defendant. Said he had been often at General Houston's. Mrs. Houston was a mild and forbearing woman; he had never seen anything unkind in her family.

(Defs's counsel here offered to prove by witness that Gott had said to him that he had always been kindly and well treated by Gen H. and family—objected to; and objection sustained by the court)

Mr. Holliman, examined for the defendant, had known Virginia since 1843; had lived near Vernal Lea; was often there; knew Virginia's disposition; she was hard to govern; required strong discipline. She was well treated at Mr. Lea's.

The evidence here closed, after argument and the charge of the court, the jury was unable to agree, so a mistrial was entered.

After court closed the Baptist Church took up the matter, and after a lengthy investigation of all the facts—fully acquitted Mrs. H. of all blame in regard to Virginia.

It was only at the close of this last investigation that Gen. H. returned home & found for the first time what had been done. It is understood that the matter has been urged on at the instance of some of his enemies for the purpose of affecting him.

[1]Henderson Yoakum Papers, Barker History Center, University of Texas, Austin, Texas.
[2]See Sam Houston to Jack Houston, May 8, 1851, and Sam Houston to Henderson Yoakum, March 3, 1851, *Writings,* vol. 5, 292, and Houston to Yoakum, July 19, 1851, Ibid., 304.
[3]See Appendix C.
[4]In the summer of 1842 Vernal Lea had consented to act as trustee for Virginia, and her step-father C. F. Worcester had placed Virginia in the hands of Nancy Lea. See James P. Goodall (Virginia's half-brother), to Judge Robert D. Johnson, August 8, 1842. Elizabeth R. Worcester Estate File, Galveston County Court House.
[5]Virginia was born on November 11, 1834, according to the Gott Family Bible and Virginia's tombstone. Thorn-Gott Collection, Mrs. Virgie Looney.
[6]Mary Lea died in late 1845.

The following documents are a series of depositions taken in July of 1851, for the Walker County District Court pertaining to the assault trial of Margaret Houston brought about by Thomas Gott. Unfortunately three pages are missing in the middle and an unknown quantity at the end. A search of the court house records has failed to locate them. The handwriting is believed to be that of Henderson Yoakum:

Depositions taken by counsel in pursuance of the defense of accused [Margaret Houston]

James T. Sims being first examined.

Int.1. Are you acquainted with the parties? Ansr. I am.

2. How long have you been acquainted with Susan Virginia Thorne? Answer: About four years.

3. Is she married or single? Answer: She is reported to be married to Thomas Gott.

4. In whose family did she live when you first knew her? Answer. When Gen Houston and family came up here in 1847, they boarded at my house some 4 or 5 weeks afterwards. Mrs Lea & Susan V.

came also. The latter remained there till Gen H. & family left my house, & then went with them.

5. How long did she remain with Houston's family? Ansr: She remained there till Gott took her off—I do not know how long that was. I think it was between two & three years.

6. In what capacity did she act in Gen H's family during the time she stayed at your house? Ansr: I do not know. I never saw her only at meal times.

7. Do you know whether she was regarded as an equal in the family? Ansr: I do not know any thing about that. So far as we were concerned she came to the table with our children. Gen H's children ours and Virginia all eat [sic] together.

8. Do you know her age? Ansr: I should think about 17 years of age or may be over.

9. When was she reported to be married to Mr. Gott? Ansr: Some three or four weeks ago.

Cross interrogs by Vernal Lea—

1. So far as you saw was she treated kindly by Gen. Houston & family? Ansr: Yes sir, so far as I know.

Sworn & subscribed before me this 18 June 1851 J. T. Sims

[signed] H. M. Crabb Chief Justice Walker County

Paul J. Simons[1] being next examined by [blurred]ictors to settlement

Int. 1. Are you acquainted with Mrs. Gott?: Ansr: I am.

2. Where did she reside when you first became acquainted with her? Ansr: At Gen Houstons.

3. In what capacity did she live there? Ansr: I don't know—when I saw her she seemed to be more engaged in taking care of the children than any thing else. In fact I only saw her passing about out of doors.

4. How was she dressed? Ansr. She was dressed rather homely I thought. I do not remember what she had on.

5. In what did she seem to be engaged when you saw her? Ansr: When she was not engaged with the children she seemed to be employed in various little domestic affairs about the house.

6. How old is she? Ansr: I should judge her to be some 18 or 19 years old.

7. What is a good house servant of the age of Mrs Gott when you saw her at Gen H's worth per month? Ansr: About five or six dollars per month.

8. What is the board of a child from five to seventeen years old worth per mo? Ansr: From four to five dollars.

9. What would the board of a girl from five to 17 years old including her services be worth? Ansr: I would not charge any thing.

10. Would not the services out weigh the board in such case? Ansr: If it were a boy the services would perhaps out weigh the board —if he was smart & according to the circumstances, but a girl is not worth so much as a boy.

11. Has this girl been to school any while she was at Genl Houston's? Ansr: Not to my knowledge. I saw her at Sunday school.

Cross examination by Vernal Lea

1. How long were you at Gen Houston's? Ansr: Some two or three times & two or three days at a time.

2. Did you see her at the Sunday school? Ansr: I did.

3. Do you know whether she was a good scholar or not? Ansr: No sir.

4. Had Gen Houston any negro women about his house, if so, how many? Ansr: He had some three or four negro servants about the house. There were perhaps two girls he kept about the house all the time.

5. Had he any negro boys about the house? Ansr: Two.

Re examined

1. State the size and age of the two boys. Ansr: Nash was about 5 or 6 years & Pearl about 7 or 8 years old.

Cross examined again

1. How old were the women? Ansr: They were grown women.

Re examined

1. Do you know whether those girls were not frequently hired out? Ansr: I believe they were sometimes.

Re cross examine:

1. To whom were they hired? Ansr: I cannot say. I do not recollect

2. Do you know of your own knowledge that they were even hired at all? Ansr: I do not know of my own knowledge. I do not recollect.
3. When you were at Gen Houston's did you not see negro servants enough to perform the services of a family of the size of Gen Houston's? Ansr: I should think so.
P. J. Simons
Subscribed & sworn before me this 18th June 1850.
H. M. Crabb Chief Justice Walker County

Benj. S. Wilson being next examined by adjuster Thos Gott.
Int. 1. Are you acquainted with Mrs Gott? and if so, how long. Ansr: I am—about three or four years.
2. Where has she lived during that time? Ansr: She lived at Gen Houston's, Mrs Goodman's in Cincinnati, & at my own house.
3. How long at Gen Houston's? Ansr: Some two or three years.
4. In what capacity did she live at Gen Houston's? Ansr: I considered her as a waiting maid in his family—I viewed her as such upon a passing acquaintance without having any introduction to her, or particular knowledge on the subject.
5. What are colored servants worth here by the month—I mean familial servants? Ansr: They are worth ten dollars per month.
6. Did you hire a servant during this time, if so from Whom? Ansr: I did hire one from Mrs Houston.
7. How long did Virginia, now Mrs Gott stay at your house? Ansr: 12 months.
8. What would you consider her services as a servant worth per month? Ansr: That would be very difficult for me to answer. She was very handy with her needle, and ready and cheerful, but as we were not accustomed to hire white servants in this country, I cannot say what they would be worth.
9. At what rate could a white servant of her age and sex be obtained here per month? Ansr: There is not settled compensation for white servants in this country—They are either had for nothing, or they are more [blurred] costly than negroes.
10. Are white servants more or less valuable than negroes? Ansr:

They are either much higher or they are beneficiary altogether.

11. What do you mean by <u>beneficiary</u>? Ansr: I mean that they are permitted a house gratuitously, also clothing comforts etc & the services received as a compensation.

12. Did you see Mrs Gott frequently at the house of Gen H.? Ansr: No sir.

13. How much did you give Mrs Houston for her servant? (This question is objected to for illegality) Ansr: Ten dollars per month.

Benjamin S. Wilson

Subscribed & sworn before me this 18 June 1851.

H. M Crabb Chief Justice

Mrs Jane C. Wilson next examined. Questions by Gott.

1. Are you acquainted with Mrs Gott? Ansr: Yes.

2. How long have you known her? Ansr: Four years.

3. Where did she live when you first knew her? Ansr: She boarded at Mr Sims. She stayed then with the Houston family. I don't know on what terms she lived there.

4. Where has she lived since that time? [Ansr:] She went home with Gen H's family—from Sims & remained there for some time & went on a short visit to Vernal Lea's, & remained there a month or so.

5. In what capacity did she live in Gen. Houston's family: Ansr: I tell you conscientiously that I looked upon her as a servant.

6. Were you ever acquainted at Gen Houston's at that time? Ansr: I went there as often as any place, but I cannot say I was well acquainted.

7. What sort of a servant would you regard her? Ansr: I used to think when I first went there she was a very bad one, but I thought so from what Mrs Houston told me. I had her word for it. But I afterwards found this to be false, for a better girl I never saw than I afterward found her to be.

8. Where did she live after she left Gen Houston's? Ansr: She went from there to Mrs Goodman's. She then came to my house.

[Three pages are missing]

Sam Houston being next examined—

Quest. 1. by V. B. Lea. Are you acquainted with the parties to this suit? Ansr: I am.

2. Please state how long you have known Mrs Gott? Ansr: Since sometime in 1841 or 1842, I think in 1841.

3. Please state as far as you know, where she has been since that time? Ansr: At that time she was living with Mrs Lea at Galveston. Sometime in 1842, Mrs Lea moved up on the Trinity to Vernal Lea's. I think Virginia preceded her up there by a few days. She staid at Capt [William] Bledsoe's sometime. I do not know how long, and then went to live at Vernal Lea's. She staid there until sometime in 1847, when I moved to this place. Some weeks after I moved here Mrs Lea, my mother in law came up here to live with me and brought Virginia.

4. Please state the age of Virginia at the time you first saw her in 1841 or 1842, and under what circumstances she came to live with Mr Lea. Ansr: She was a very little girl, I suppose about four or five years of age when I first saw her. When I first saw her at Mrs Lea's she had her head bandaged, as I understood from falling from a steamboat which affected her skull for sometime, but from this she afterwards recovered. After her mother died she was taken to Maj. [James] Cocke's in Galveston, who kept her some short time. When Dr. [C. F.] Worcester her step father brought her to Mrs Lea, stating that he had none but young men about him, and could not take care of her. Mrs. Lea took her and I thought always treated her with peculiar kindness, as she was treated by every member of the family.

5. How long did Virginia remain at Vernal Lea's? Ansr: About four years, with the exception the time of a visit made by Mrs Lea to Alabama in 1845, when she staid at Mr. Bledsoe's.

6. Please state the position occupied by Virginia in your family, while she lived there—the style in which she was clothed and boarded? Ansr: She was treated as a junior member of my family, eat with the children—as to her clothing I understand she had seven or eight dresses at the time she went away. I paid no particular attention to her dress. I always saw her very genteel.

7. What was her occupation in the family? Ansr: Until we came to this place, I think she could not have learned to sew. She was about that time learning to sew very well. She was previously playing about with the children when not instructed by Mrs Houston. She had learned to read very prettily. From the fall of 1846 to the spring of 1847 she was down at Vernal Lea's with Mrs Houston & my children. In 1845 or 6, she was sent to school to a lady teaching at Mr [Howell] Holliman's near Vernal Lea's. She was entered for the session. Towards the latter part of the session a difficulty took place between her & the school mistress & she was sent home, I don't think she went the whole session. That was the only school I ever knew of in the neighborhood during the time she was there. She was at Bledsoe's and part of the time at Lea's. She was exceedingly sickly, & had the ague a good while. She suffered for many weeks with an abscess on the thigh. Physicians were called in, perhaps one from Liberty, and every attention given to her that could be given to a child until she recovered.

She was at times a little obstinate, and if Mrs Houston ever admonished her, Mrs Lea would say to Mrs Houston, "Margaret she is an orphan, and don't say any thing to her." This having repeatedly occurred it became unpleasant, and I importuned Mrs Lea to send her or to let me send her to her relations in Alabama, but Mrs Lea objected upon the ground that the girl had been given to her, & she wanted to keep her as a comfort to her old age. I met with a relative of hers Mrs. Dyer in Washington City, and understanding she had no children, I recommended her to send for her, telling her she was one of the smartest children I had seen, but she declined it.

8. While she lived at your house here, were her services necessary to your family? Ansr: They were not necessary. We had three negro women almost all the time. They were sufficient to do the work about the house. One of them was occasionally hired out, as they had not employment at home. I am satisfied she never milked a cow, went to the wash tub, cooked a meal of victuals or put down a piece of bread to bake while at my house.

9. Did she have any fires to make? Ansr: None. She never made on a

fire, unless it was put up when the wood was laid down at the fire place in her room. She may have kindled a fire then. I never heard of her making up a bed unless she had slept in it. I never saw her engaged at it.

10. Do you know any thing of her having to make fires in Miss Lucinda Paul's room while the latter was at your house?

11. [sic] I was not there at the time, Miss Lucinda was hired by Mrs Houston to help her quilt. They slept together as I understood. If they made any fire, it must have been in their room when they slept. The wood and pine was always provided & laid down at the fire place. They may have made up a fire to dress by, for when they were ready they came down into the parlor. I am sure I never saw her perform any menial services and I am satisfied Mrs Lea would not have permitted it.

12. Taking into considerations her age was she dressed as well as your children? Ansr: I can't say. She always appeared genteel. My children never were dressed extravagantly.

13. State if any pains were ever taken with her education while living here with you? Ansr: Mrs. Houston, so far as I can judge, took the same pains with her as she did with my son Sam. She would frequently sit up with her and assist her in getting her Sunday school lesson.

14. While at your home, what have been her services compared with her nurturing and raising? Ansr: I can form no estimate on that point. I was exceedingly anxious she should leave Texas, and had it not been for fear of disobliging Mrs Lea, I would not have kept her.

15. Was she of any service to Mrs Lea? Ansr: None that I know of. I do not know what Mrs Lea had for her to do. Mrs Lea had part of the time, a negro woman, a boy some 15 years old, and a small negro girl. Mrs Lea was herself a member of my family.

16. What was the treatment shown of her by your family, while at your house? Ansr: When we were in Nashville in 1845, Miss Kitty Hoffman's father requested Mrs Houston to take her and raise her. Miss Kitty remained at Vernal Lea's after we brought her out here, and until about the time Virginia left. I suppose, for I was not at

home when Virginia left. I state this as a reason why we did not need Virginia's services, as Mrs Houston had become responsible for Miss Kitty, & if we had need the services of a girl we could have had Miss Kitty's. I cannot state particulars further about the treatment of the family towards Virginia unless you suggest something by shaping your question differently.

17. What was Virginia's reported age in December 1849? Ansr: I should think she was in her fifteenth or sixteenth year at this time, though that can perhaps be ascertained in Galveston.

I will make another statement. Virginia was frequently disposed to go without her shoes. I noticed it, especially when company was present & rebuked her for it, and also for carelessness in dress. I will further state that in addition to the negro woman at my house while Virginia was there, we had two negro boys that worked about the house. One of them is now in his thirteenth year, the other is ten years old. In addition to these, Mrs Lea's servants were there all the time, so far as I know.

Sam Houston

Subscribed and sworn before me this 19th June, 1851

H. M. Crabb Chief Justice Walker County

Mrs M. L. Evans next being next examined—

Int. 1. by Vernal Lea—Are you acquainted with Mrs Gott? If so, how long have you known her? Ansr: I am & have known her about 3 years.

2. Where did she live during your acquaintance? Ansr: At Gen Houston's part of the time, and part of the time perhaps three or four months at Vernal Lea's.

3. In what capacity did she live at Gen Houston's? Ansr: I don't know. She was there under the charge of that family.

4. Were you intimately acquainted there, were you there frequently? Ansr: Yes I was. Sometimes two or three times a week. When any of the family were sick I was there very often. I visited there often enough when they were well.

5. How was Virginia treated by the family? Ansr: When I was there

she was treated a member of the family.

6. Were you there when Lucinda Paul was there? Ansr: I was there at one occasion . . . *[Additional pages are missing.]*

[1]The son-in-law of Thomas Birdwell.

Bibliography

for Volume III

Interviews:

Grant, Ruth. Lufkin, Texas. A relative of the Thomas Birdwell Family.

Hall, Elizabeth. Tuscaloosa, Alabama. A descendant of Henry Clinton Lea.

Looney, Mrs. Virgie. Gonzales, Texas. A descendant of Virginia Thorn and Thomas Gott.

Patton, James. Huntsville, Texas. County Clerk, Walker County, Texas.

Sandlin, Carolyn. Marion, Alabama. A descendant of Henry Clinton Lea.

Sneed, Joe Weldon. San Antonio, Texas. A descendant of Virginia Thorn and Thomas Gott.

Manuscript Collections:

Birdwell-Wilson family papers in the possession of Ruth Grant, Lufkin, Texas.

Burch-Remick-Roberts Collection of Sam Houston letters, San Antonio, Texas. In the possession of the editor.

Greenwood, C. L. "Index of Death Notices." Card file at Barker History Center, University of Texas, Austin, Texas.

Hearne, Madge W. Collection of family papers, San Antonio, Texas. In the possession of the editor, San Antonio, Texas.

Hearne, Madge W. Collection of Houston Correspondence. Barker History Center, University of Texas, Austin, Texas.

Hearne, Sam Houston. Collection of Houston materials. Barker History Center, University of Texas, Austin, Texas.

Hearne, Sam Houston. Collection of Houston Materials. Sam Houston Research Center and Library, Liberty, Texas.

Houston, Andrew Jackson. Collection of Correspondence. Catholic Diocese Library, Austin, Texas.

Houston, Andrew Jackson. Collection of Correspondence. Texas State Archives, Austin, Texas.

Houston, Margaret. Collection. Barker History Center, University of Texas, Austin, Texas.

Houston, Margaret. Vertical Files. Barker History Center, University of Texas, Austin, Texas.

Houston, Sam. Letters. Daughters of the Republic of Texas Library, San Antonio, Texas.

Houston, Sam. Collection. Barker History Center, University of Texas, Austin Texas.

Houston, Sam. Vertical Files. Barker History Center, University of Texas, Austin, Texas.

Houston, Sam. Vertical Files. Daughters of the Republic of Texas Library, San Antonio, Texas.

Jenkins, Congressman Timothy. Collection. Hamilton College Archives, Colgate, New York.

Loe, Elizabeth. Collection of Houston Correspondence. Sam Houston Research Center and Library, Liberty, Texas.

McDonald, Mrs. R. E. Collection of Houston Correspondence. Dallas, Texas.

Morrow, Temple Houston. Collection of Houston Materials. Barker History Center, University of Texas, Austin, Texas.

Rost, Margaret. Collection of Houston Materials. Sam Houston Memorial Museum, Huntsville, Texas.

Sneed Collection of Thorn-Gott papers in the possession of Joe Weldon Sneed, San Antonio, Texas.

Thorn-Gott Collection in the possession of Virgie Looney, Gonzales, Texas.

Williams, Franklin Weston. Collection. Woodson Research Center, Rice University, Houston, Texas.

Williams, Franklin. Collection of Houston Correspondence. Sam Houston Memorial Museum, Huntsville, Texas.

Woods, Alva. Papers (Mss 816). Manuscript collection of the Rhode Island Historical Society Library, Providence, Rhode Island.

Worcester (Elizabeth R.). Estate File. Galveston County Courthouse.

Yoakum, Henderson. Diary Collection. Barker History Center, University of Texas, Austin, Texas.

Court Records:

Walker County Deed Book, Vol. B-2.

Walker County Minutes Book A, 274, September 25, 1850.

Walker County Minutes, Book A, 368, September 30, 1851.

Printed Sources:

Best, Hugh. *Debrett's Texas Peerage.* New York: Coward-McCann, 1983.

Biographical Directory of the United States Congress, 1774–1989. Washington, D. C.: United States Government Printing Office, 1989.

Boyer, Louise. "Sam Houston at the First 'Dry' Dinner." *Dallas Morning News*, n.d., circa 1927.

Brewer, Willis K. *Alabama: Her History, Resources, War Record and Public Men from 1540 to 1872.* Spartanburg, S. C.: The Reprint Company Publishers, 1975.

Carpenter, V. K., transcriber. *1850 Census of Texas,* 4 vols. Huntsville, Arkansas: Century Enterprises, 1969.

Chabot, Frederick C. *Genealogies of Early San Antonio Families (The Makers of San Antonio).* San Antonio, Texas: Privately Published by the Artes Graficas, 1937.

Christman, Margaret C. S. *1846 Portrait of the Nation.* Washington, D. C.: Smithsonian Institution Press, 1996.

Clarke, Mary Whatley. *David G. Burnet.* Austin: The Pemberton Press, 1969.

_____. *Thomas J. Rusk: Soldier, Statesman, Jurist.* Austin: The

Pemberton Press, 1971.

Coit, Margaret L. *John C. Calhoun: American Portrait.* Boston: Houghton Mifflin Company, 1950.

Crane, William Carey. *Life and Select Literary Remains of Sam Houston, of Texas.* Dallas, Texas: William G. Scarff & Co., 1884.

Crews, D. Anne, ed. *Huntsville and Walker County, Texas: A Bicentennial History.* Huntsville: Sam Houston State University Press, 1976.

Dabney, Virginius. *Virginia: The New Dominion.* Garden City, New York: Doubleday & Company, Inc., 1971.

The Daily Republic (Washington, D. C.). Vol. IV, No. 13, June 25, 1852.

Dickenson, Johnnie Jo.*Walker County, Texas 1850–1860 Census.* Huntsville, Texas: Dickenson Research, 1989.

Dictionary of American Biography. Edited by Allen Johnson and Dumas Malone. 11 vols. New York: Charles Scribner & Sons, 1964.

Eckloff, Christian F. *Memoirs of a Senate Page 1855–1859.* Percival G. Melbourne, ed. New York: Broadway Publishing Company, 1909.

England, Flora D. *Alabama Notes.* 4 vols. Baltimore: Genealogical Publishing Co., Inc., 1978.

Ericson, Carolyn Reeves. *Nacogdoches—Gateway to Texas: A Biographical Directory, 1773-1849.* Nacogdoches, Texas: Ericson Books, 1991.

_____ and Frances Ingmire. *Walker County, Texas Marriage Records 1846–1856.* Nacogdoches, Texas: Ericson Books, 1985.

Family Adventures, comps. *Early Alabama Marriage Records.* Shreveport, Louisiana: J & W Enterprises, 1991.

Fornell, Earl Wesley. *The Galveston Era: The Texas Crescent on the Eve of Secession.* Austin: University of Texas Press, 1961.

Friend, Llerena. *Sam Houston: The Great Designer.* Austin: University of Texas Press, 1954.

Galveston Weekly News, February 11, 1850.

Ganrud, Pauline Jones. *Alabama Records.* Easley, South Carolina:

Southern Historical Press, 1958.

Gara, Larry. *The Presidency of Franklin Pierce*. Lawrence, Kansas: University Press of Kansas, 1981.

Gillis, Irene S. and Norman E. *Biographical and Historical Memoirs of Mississippi*. A reprint of the original work published in 1891 by the Goodspeed Publishing Company of Chicago. Printed privately by Irene S. and Norman E. Gillis, 1962.

Godwin, Parke. "When Kossuth Rode up Broadway." *Ladies Home Journal*, Vol. XIV, #3, February, 1897.

Guthrie, Keith. *Texas Forgotten Ports*. Vol. 3. Austin, Texas: Eakin Press, 1995.

Hayes, Charles W. *Galveston: History of the Island & the City*. 2 vols. Austin: Jenkins Garrett Press, 1974.

Heitman, Francis B. *Historical Register and Dictionary of the United States Army, from Its Organization, September 29, 1789, to March 2, 1903*. Baltimore: Genealogical Publishing Co., Inc. 1994.

Houston Chronicle, July 23, 1939. "Many a Story is Found in These Old Papers on Famed Leader"

Houston Press, April 21, 1936.

Houston, Sam. *The Autobiography of Sam Houston*. Donald Day and Harry Herbert Ullom, eds. Norman: University of Oklahoma Press, 1954.

Houston, Samuel Rutherford, comp. *Brief Biographical Accounts of Many Members of the Houston Family*. Cincinnati: Elm Street Printing Company, 1882.

Hudson, Winthrop S. *Religion in America*. New York: Charles Scribner's Sons, 1981.

Jackson, Roland Vern. *Pennsylvania 1850 Census Index*. Bountiful, Utah: Accelerated Indexing Systems, 1976.

_____. *Tennessee 1850 Census Index*. Bountiful, Utah: Accelerated Indexing Systems, Inc., 1977.

_____. *Texas 1850 Census Index*. Bountiful, Utah: Accelerated Indexing Systems, Inc., 1976.

_____ and Gary Ronald Teeples. *Louisiana 1850 Census Index*. Bountiful, Utah: Accelerated Indexing Systems, Inc., 1978.

_____ et al. *Pennsylvania 1850 Census Index*. 2 vols. Bountiful, Utah: Accelerated Indexing Systems, Inc., 1976.

_____. *Virginia 1850 Census Index*. Bountiful, Utah: Accelerated Indexing Systems, Inc., 1976.

Johnston, Marguerite. *Houston: The Unknown City, 1836–1946*. College Station: Texas A&M University Press, 1991.

Kennedy, Imogene Kinard. *Polk County Marriage Records, 1845 through 1880*. St. Louis, Missouri: Frances Terry Ingmire, 1984.

Klein, Philip Shriver. *President James Buchanan: A Biography*. University Park, Pennsylvania: The Pennsylvania State Press, 1989.

Krisch, Lucille. *1850 Census and First Taxpayers of Angelina County, Texas*. St. Louis, Missouri: Frances Terry Ingmire, 1981.

McGuire, James Patrick. *The Hungarian Texans*. San Antonio: The University of Texas Institute of Texan Cultures at San Antonio, 1993.

McKibbens, Thomas R., Jr. *The Forgotten Heritage: A Lineage of Great Baptist Preaching*. Macon, Georgia: Mercer University Press, 1986.

McLaughlin, Andrew C. *Lewis Cass*. New York: Houghton, Mifflin and Company, 1898.

Marion Herald, December 1, 1841.

Montgomery Alabama Journal, Vol V, #209, November 25, 1851.

Montgomery Alabama Journal, Vol. V, #215, December 1, 1851.

Morrell, Z. N. *Flowers and Fruits in the Wilderness*. Dallas: W. G. Scarff & Company, 1886.

Mueller, Ester. "Traveling Thru Texas on a Stage Coach with Sam Houston." *San Antonio Express*, July 17, 1932.

Murray, Lois Smith. *Baylor at Independence*. Waco, Texas: Baylor University Press, 1972.

Nevins, Allan. *Ordeal of the Union, Volume I: Fruits of Manifest Destiny 1847–1852*. New York: Charles Scribner's Sons, 1975.

New York Daily Tribune, Monday, February 21, 1887.

"Old Timers Recall Sam Houston as Admirer of Red Hair—Whittler—Grand Speaker." *Houston Press,* April 21, 1936.

Owen, Thomas McAdory. *History of Alabama and Dictionary of the Alabama Biography.* 4 vols. Chicago: S. J. Clarke Publishing Company, 1921.

Perry County Historical and Preservation Society. *Perry County Heritage.* 2 Vols. Marion, Alabama: Published privately, 1991.

Pippenger, Wesley E., comp. *District of Columbia Marriage Licenses Register, 1811–1858.* Westminster, Maryland: Family Line Publishers, 1994.

Polk, James K. *Polk: The Diary of a President 1845–1849, Covering the Mexican War, the Acquisition of Oregon, and the Conquest of California and the Southwest.* Edited by Allan Nevins. New York: Longmans, Green and Company, 1929.

Ray, Worth. *Tennessee Cousins.* Baltimore: Genealogical Publishing Company, Inc., 1994.

Red, William Stuart. *A History of the Presbyterian Church in Texas.* Austin: The Steck Company, 1936.

Remini, Robert V. *Henry Clay: Statesman for the Union.* New York: W. W. Norton & Company, 1991.

Roberts, Madge Thornall. *Star of Destiny: The Private Life of Sam and Margaret Houston.* Denton: University of North Texas Press, 1993.

"Sam Houston: Property Bought and Sold by Sam Houston and Wife, Margaret, Period from 1847–1858." Information from Deed Records, James D. Patton, County Clerk, Walker County, Huntsville, Texas. Typescript, 1989.

Scharf, J. Thomas. *History of Baltimore City and County.* Baltimore: Regional Publishing Company, 1971.

Shuffler, R. Henderson. *The Houstons at Independence.* Waco, Texas: Texian Press, 1966.

Sistler, Byron and Barbara. *1850 Census Tennessee.* 8 vols. Evanston, Illinois: Byron Sistler & Associates, 1976.

_____. *1840 Census Tennessee.* Nashville, Tennessee: Byron Sistler & Associates, Inc., 1986.

Smith, Elbert B. *Magnificent Missourian: The Life of Thomas Hart Benton.* New York: J. B. Lippincott Company, 1958.

Smith, Elbert B. *The Presidencies of Zachary Taylor & Millard Fillmore*. Lawrence, Kansas: The University Press of Kansas, 1988.

Speights, Virgie. *Old Timers of Sabine County*. Nacogdoches, Texas: Ericson Books, 1983.

State Guard (Wetumpka, Alabama), November 10, 1849.

Stein, R. Conrad. *The Story of Mississippi Steamboats*. Chicago: Childrens Press, 1987.

Stewart, Lucy Alice Bruce, et al., comps. *Walker County, Texas, Cemetery Records*. Huntsville, Texas: Walker County, Texas, Genealogical Society, 1992.

Swenson, Helen Smothers. *8800 Texas Marriages, 1823–1850*. St. Louis, Missouri: Frances Terry Ingmire, 1981.

Tatum, Bowen C., Jr. "Henderson King Yoakum." *Texas Bar Journal* Vol. 33, #8 (September 1970): 719–24.

Thrall, Homer S. *A Pictorial History of Texas*. St Louis, Missouri: N. D. Thompson, 1879.

Trammell, Camilla Davis. *Seven Pines: Its Occupants and Their Letters, 1825–1872*. Houston: Published Privately, 1986.

Vick-Rainey, Mary E. *Marriage Records of Walker County*. Huntsville: Walker County Genealogical Society, 1979.

Walker, Donald R. *A Frontier Texas Mercantile: The History of Gibbs Brothers and Company, Huntsville, 1841–1940*. Huntsville, Texas: Texas Review Press, 1997.

Wallis, Johnnie Lockhart and Laurance Hill. *Sixty Years on the Brazos*. Waco, Texas: Texian Press, 1967.

White, Edna McDaniel and Blanche Findley Toole. *Sabine County Historical Sketches & Genealogical Records*. Beaumont, Texas: LaBelle Printing Company, 1970.

White, Paul R., Sr. *Taproots: A Virginia & Carolina Legacy*. 2d ed. Nashville, Tennessee: Terrell's Bindery & Graphic Industries, 1986.

Williams, Amelia. *Following General Sam Houston*. Austin, Texas: The Steck Company, 1935.

Wisehart, M. K. *Sam Houston, American Giant.* Washington: Robert B. Luce, Inc., 1962.

Ziegler, Jesse A. *Wave of the Gulf: Ziegler's Scrapbook of the Texas Gulf Coast Country.* San Antonio, Texas: The Naylor Company, 1938.

Zuber, William Physick. *My Eighty Years in Texas.* Austin: University of Texas Press, 1971.

Index
to Volume III

62, 193, 398–99; intelligence of, 21, 44, 127; naming of, 113, 131, 183; number of, 403, 457; reports on, 22; status of, 7, 155

Chilton, George Washington, 341n3

Chilton, Thomas, 340

Christy, Catherine Drieder Baker, 13

Christy, William, 143, 249, 348, 363, 379

church, 71, 240; activities, 228; affiliation, 445, 446n4; Baptist Church, 431, 445, 446n4, 468; Bible class, 104, 105; communion, 204; division in local Baptist, 29, 47, 268; fashion at, 300; Sam Houston's views on Episcopalian Church, 431–32; trial and acquittal of Margaret Houston, 471

Churchville, Maryland, 258

Cincinatti, Texas, 105, 146, 160

civic responsibility, 245, 247

clairvoyance, 55–56, 68, 274

Clapp, Elisha, 170, 171

Clark, Myra, 383, 383n1

Clay, Henry,
addressing the Senate, 130, 132, 151, 187; compromise report of, 184; declining health of, 368, 433n6; dislike for Benton, 214; dislike for Taylor, 12; funeral of, 440, 441n1, 441n2, 442; Houston and, 225

Cleveland, Louis, 211

Cleveland, William D., 354, 355n6

Cobb, Howell, 112n1, 115, 228

Cobb, Mary, 228

Cocke, Jack F., 346, 347n4

coffee, 132

college, land for, 120, 122

Comanche, 448, 449n1

commencements, 197, 436

Committee of Vigilance and Safety, 395

communion, 228

compliments, Margaret's lack of, for Sam Houston, 388–89

Compromise Bill,
defeat of, 238, 239; obstacles to, 216, 230, 237; report of Mr. Clay, 184; Sam Houston's support for, 196, 206, 208, 324n7, 347n1

Connor, David, 441–42

Cordova, Jacob de, 26, 30, 62

corruption, 375, 413, 420, 454

corsets, 134

court deposition of Sam Houston, 477–80

Crawford, A. C., 107–108, 110n2, 294–95

Crawford, Rouwanah, 240, 305, 434

Creath, Frances, court testimony of, 470

Creath, Joseph Warner Dossey, 11, 29, 43, 47, 63, 139, 335, 372

crops, 183, 192, 415; condition of, 408, 419, 438; corn, 148; health of, 399; instructions on, 398; tobacco, 51, 56, 74, 91; and weather, 193

Cuba, attempt to overthrow, 321, 321n3

Culp, Betty Thilman, 22, 334, 431, 433n3, 433n7

Culp, Daniel D., 431

Cushman, George L., 118, 119n5, 127, 204, 228, 244

Cushman, Mrs., 150, 296

Daingerfield, William Henry, 150, 150n2

date of homecoming, 153

Davis, George A., 90–91, 91n5, 119

Davis, James, 95, 260, 261n1, 457

Davis, Ruben, 457

Dawson, N. A., 310

Day, Horace, 326

Dayton, William L., 213n1

Dean, Nicholas, 334n4

Deane, Euincy Lea, 239n1

Deblane, 97

Democratic Party,
Houston speaking at a party meeting, 453; nominations for Presidency candidates, 378, 435; on the question of the Presidential nomination, 364, 407, 412, 414

dogs, Newfoundland, 195, 214

Donelson, Andrew J., 121, 173, 174, 354

Donelson, C. H. (Donaldson), 320, 321n1, 375

Donelson, Catherine (daughter), 174, 175n1 (174)

Donelson, Elizabeth, 121, 174, 175, 354, 370

Donelson, Mary, 121, 174, 354, 370

Douglass, Stephen, 321, 325, 352, 352n1

Dow, Neal, 385n2

dreams, 46, 48n3; map, 59, 118, 137; Margaret Houston's, 33, 34n3, 400, 433; Sam Houston's, 9, 27, 270n1

dresses, 181, 184, 218, 374, 463

drunkenness in the Senate, 86

Dun, William S., 278n1, 278n1

Duncan, Josephine, 424, 471

Dunham, Cyrus, 436, 437n1

Dunlap, Mary, 150, 150n2

education, Sam Houston, Jr., 209

Edwards, Thomas G., 192

Eiland, Ovid, 285

Eldridge, Joseph P., 189

Eliza (slave), 167, 183, 202, 344

Ellis, Joseph, 17, 29, 35

Ellmore, Franklin H., 202, 203n1

enemies of Sam Houston, 46, 91, 201, 421, 472

entertainment, 374, 375, 378

Episcopalian Church, Sam Houston's views on, 431–32

Esperanza. *See* Houston, Margaret

Evans, Jemmia, 35, 141–42

Evans, L. D., 351n3

Evans, Lemuel, 203

Evans, Mrs., 105, 172, 343, 406, 468

Evans, Mrs. J. W. (Manura), 14, 424

Evans, Mrs. M. L., 471, 480–81

Evans, Oresumus, 203, 204n3

Evans, William F., 35, 45, 141–42, 286, 370, 426

Fairbairn, Alexander, 438

faith, 53, 61, 73, 221, 446–47

family, Houston's devotion to, 13, 20, 54, 76, 205, 209, 446, 450–51

Ferguson, Mr., 317

Fifth Annual Baptist State Convention of Texas, 430, 430n5

Fillmore, Abigail Powers, 287, 288n3

Fillmore, Mary Abigail, 288n4 (287)

Fillmore, Millard, 321, 437

financial matters
Houston's attention to, 63, 372, 385; loans, 317–18, 398; Margaret's access to money, 167, 416; Margaret's frugality, 199–200, 209, 234, 368, 423; mortgages, 334; Nancy Lea's travels, 410, 425

Finch, Sarah, 261n1 (260)

Fitzpatrick, Aurelia Blassingame, 46, 48n4, 50, 56, 63, 66, 74

Flacco (Lipan-Apache Indian Chief), 184, 184n3

Fletcher, John, 7

Foote, Henry S.,
addressing the Senate, 290, 292n2, 345, 347n3, 353; duel on Senate floor, 178; Houston surprising, 355–56; speech in reply to, 388–89

foreign policy, 367

Fremont, John C., 96

Fugitive Slave Bill, 263, 347n3

409, 458, 460; of Sam Houston, 24, 60, 248, 267, 278, 381, 411; vaccinations, 305

Heath, Simon Peter, 294

Hemphill, John, 263, 263n1

Henderson, 91

Henderson, James Pinckney, 25, 208, 210n1 (208), 244n2, 320

Henderson, James W., 322, 324

Henderson, Lawson, 68, 68n2

Hendley, William, 342n5

Henry, John K., 35

History of Christ (Wells), 351

History of England (Macaulay), 345n3

Hoffman, Kitty, 184, 478; behavior of, 211, 239; Daniel Johnson and, 260; education of, 220; father of, 175; gifts for, 207, 224, 269; habit of lying, 200; and the Houstons, 175n4

Hoffman, Mr., 211

Hogue, Barbara, 457

Holliman, Harmon, 97

Holliman, Howell, 471, 478

homesickness of Sam Houston, 4–5, 58, 87, 93, 102, 115–16, 117, 128, 143, 171, 223, 232, 233, 375, 448

horses, 94, 159, 401; carriage and, 92, 442, 442n4; Powhatan (Sam Houston's horse), 220; Sam Houston, Jr. and, 419, 424; Yoakum's accident, 422–23

Houston, Antoinette Power (daughter of Margaret and Sam), 380, 411, 447; gender of, 381–82, 385; hair color of, 382, 386; naming of, 381, 382, 388, 391, 391n2; Sam Houston's thoughts on, 387

Houston, Elvira Margaret Walker, 182n2 (181)

Houston, James (Buck), 48, 53, 70, 324

Houston, John (Jack),
correspondence with, 320–21, 322

24, 352n1; visiting Houston in Washington, 287, 403, 432

Houston, Lucinda, 375n1

Houston, Margaret (wife of Sam Houston), 10–11, 213. *See also* pregnancy; adoption of Moffett surname, 411, 416, 426, 427n4, 438; anxiety of, 67, 143; depression of, 67, 140, 140n1, 195; described, 133, 470–71; difficulties with overseers, 183, 192, 438, 438n6; on faith, 15–16; health of, 37, 112–13, 123, 143, 219, 234, 241, 246, 249, 365, 382, 386, 387, 413; Houston's devotion to, 151–52, 187, 216, 231, 427–28, 452–53; Houston's nickname for, 309; jealously of, 90, 361, 457; loneliness of, 10, 29, 42, 54, 71; love of home and Huntsville, 124, 401; on politics, 15–16, 407–408; pregnancy of, 349n2; on religious devotion, 415; on Sam Houston's legislative responsibilities, 153, 154–55; stature of, 196; suicide ideation, 158; timidity of, 17–18; Virginia Thorne issue, 322, 468, 469–72, 470. *See also* Gott, Thomas (overseer); Thorne, Virginia)

Houston, Margaret Lea (daughter of Sam and Margaret), 13, 16, 90, 113, 401–402

Houston, Mary Ball (Mrs. William), 174n2, 250, 251n, 317

Houston, Mary T. (god daughter of Sam Houston), 247, 253, 253n2, 321, 322, 428

Houston, Mary William (daughter of Margaret and Sam), 266, 377; beauty of, 282, 372; birth of, 178; crying, 267; dowry for, 271; gender of, 380; hair color of, 190, 225,

lation concerning disunion, 187; legislation concerning Texas, 230, 245, 261, 262, 263; legislation on boundary Bill for Texas, 252; legislation on River and Harbor Bill, 316; legislation on various issues, 263; participation in, 458–59, 460; per diem pay, 316n3; responsibilities of Sam Houston, 83, 87–88

Lehr, John, 63, 72, 416, 426, 429–30, 430n2, 444

Lehr, John, Jr., 444, 444n3

Lehr, Lucilla, 430

Lehr, Mary Moore, 43, 63, 71, 72, 105, 176, 445

Lehr, Trecilla, 430, 444

Leigh, Rebecca Shannon, 429, 441

Leigh, William D., 220

Lester, Charles Edwards, 324, 327n2, 406n1, 413n2

Letcher, John, Houston's visits with, 349, 350, 364; public offices in Virginia, 319n2, 418n2; sending newspaper clippings for Sam Houston, 462; speech of, 319; traveling with Sam Houston, 458

Letcher, Mary Susan Holt, 350, 354, 459

LeVert, Annette (daughter of Henry and Octavia), 342n4

LeVert, Henry Strachey, 342

LeVert, Octavia (daughter of Henry and Octavia), 342n4

LeVert, Octavia Walton, 342

Lewis, Joseph, 212, 287, 289, 316, 323, 370

Lincoln, Abraham, 34n1

Lind, Jenny. *See* Lynd, Jenny

litigation concerning V. Thorne, 153, 285, 293, 315, 322

livestock. *See also* animals; birds (canaries raised by Houston) horses,

189, 247, 272, 277, 279, 293–94; pigs, 102, 139, 147, 188; pony, 373

loans to William Houston, 317–18, 318n1, 383

Lockette, Napoleon, 218n1

Long, John, 102, 120, 139, 170

Louisiana, tragedy of, 101, 103n2

love letters, 216, 248, 451, 452

Luther, Martin, 21–22

Lynd, Jenny, 266, 288, 308, 374

Lyon, Caleb, 379, 380n1

Maddox, T. W., 185

Maffitt, John Newland, 23

mail contracts, 203; delays in, 50, 53, 61, 135, 157; failures of, 73, 218–19, 370, 465; length of, 122, 374, 432; problems with, 375, 378, 427; rained on, 63, 66

Marcy, Randolph B., 448, 449n1

Marion, 346

Martin, Mary, 267–68

Martin, Peter W., 267–68

Mary (slave), 349, 400

Masters, Jacob, 334n1

matrimony, Houston's views on, 368

Matthew, Theobald, 118, 119n2

Matthews, Florah, 298

Maxey, James, 7, 43, 104, 147, 156, 345n2, 467

Maxey, James Jr., 104, 106n1, 118n1 (117)

Maxey, Virginia, 14, 112

McCown, Jerome, 35

McCreary, Jesse, 12, 13

McCreary, John, 324, 327n1

McCulloch, Ben, 79

McCullough, John, 438

McDonald, 288

McDowell, James, 157

McEwen, Robert, 175, 287

McKinney, Sam, 280
McLean, Joseph, letter from, 465–67
McLean, L. P., letter from, 465
McMillion, Caroline, 29, 35
menopause, 177
Mersfelder, Mary, 236
Mersfelder, Paul, 167, 171, 225, 236
mesmerism, 40, 55–56, 68, 82
metaphysics, fondness of Sam Houston, Jr. for, 220
Mickle, Andrew H., 440
Miles, Polly, 239n1
Miller, Washington D., 25, 145
ministry, aspirations of Sam Houston, Jr., 214
Mississippi river, 338
Moffet, Margaret, 467n1
Moffet, Mary, 466, 467n1
Moffett family, 433, 458, 460n1
Moffett, Gabriel, 467n1, 467n3
Moffett, Philander, 459, 460n1
Moffette, Henry, 459, 460n2
Moffitt, John, 161
Molly. *See* Houston, Mary William (daughter of Margaret and Sam)
Montes, Lola, 374
Moore, Bettie, 390n2
Moore, Eliza, Houston's estrangement from family of, 101
Moore, Eliza (wife of Samuel Moore), 43, 71, 172, 173n1, 173n2, 181, 217, 390n4
Moore, Isabella, 15, 27, 43, 170n2, 177n1
Moore, Samuel A., 43, 43n5, 389, 430n3
Moorman, John J., 181
Morris, Elizabeth, 108
Mosely, Mrs., 285
Mother. *See* Lea, Nancy
Mother's Journal, 409, 435, 438
Mougher, OBrian, 378
mourning, 184, 199, 217–18

Murry (Murrie), Isabella, 333, 334n4, 344, 370, 400, 406, 415–16, 438

Nancy (slave), 362
Nash (slave), 114, 344
Nashville Convention, 322
Nathan, Mrs., 342
National Temperance Society, 308
Neal, Lucy (slave), 114
Nesbit, Margaret, 351
Nesbit, Miss, 302–303
Nesbit, Mrs., 351
New Orleans, 282
New York Mother Society, 291
New York Recorder, 18, 105, 124, 234, 409, 435, 438
newspapers, account of Sam Houston, 462
Norwood, Adeline (Mrs. B. J.), 460, 460n1
nullification, 137, 149, 372, 467

opium, 61
Oregon Bill, 324
overseers. Margaret's difficulties with, 438, 438n6. *See also* Gott, Thomas; Hatch, Anthony; Johnson, Daniel; Paul, Jackson.

Palmer, Othaniel, 158
Palmer, Rachel, 4, 158, 441
Palmer, Thomas, 4, 147, 158, 287, 395, 441, 442. *See also* Parmer, Thomas
Palmer, William, 79
parenting, Sam Houston on, 19
Parish, Elam, 29
Parish, Katherine, 15, 27
Parley, Peter, 286
Parmer, Thomas, 277, 279, 419, 471. *See also* Palmer, Thomas
Parson Means. *See* Foote, Henry S.
patriotism, 222

compared to Presidency, 445; support for Houston's nomination, 321, 321n2, 325, 402–3; Zachary Taylor, 69. *See also* Baltimore convention.

Price, Eugenia, 433n7

Prince (slave), 43, 62, 277, 333, 349, 400

property, 96–97, 120, 294

public domain, resolution on, 150, 150n1

public office

    election to Senate, 408; offices held by Sam Houston, 408; resignation from, 434; retirement from, 437, 443; Sam Houston on, 432–33; Senate term, 259, 268, 297, 319

public opinion of Sam Houston, 198, 245, 413

Rachel (servant), 109

Raguet, Augusta, 395

Raguet, Henry, 395

Raily, John, 341

Ransom, Devereau, 194n6

Ransom, John (Dr.), 201, 248, 260, 305

Ransom, John (son of Dr. Ransom), 194n7 (193)

Ransom, Martha (Mrs. D. J.), 125, 248, 254, 441, 442; court testimony of, 471

Rantoul, Robert, 455, 455n2, 455n3

reading, 21–22, 37, 51–52, 62, 75

Red Church Maryland, 257

Red River, 272

Reese, George, 395, 396n7

Reeves, William, 29, 35

Reformation, gift book on, 51

Reily, Ellen Hart, 340, 431, 433n6, 440

Reily, James, 124, 333, 440

religion

    baptism, 354; beliefs of Houston, 32, 82, 177, 210, 300; Christian fellowship, 74; religious nature of Houston, 243; religious practices of Houston, 292; religious services, 301

remedies, 201, 246, 260, 338, 447

Renfro, E. D., 47, 48n4

resolutions in legislature

    on Austria, 129, 129n2; on corruption, 454; on nullification and abolition, 137; speaking on, 145, 145n1, 150, 150n1, 151, 152n3

retirement, Houston's plans of, 186, 188, 242, 247–48, 437, 443

revivals, 211

Revolution, 395

Rhett, R. Barnwell, 355n2

Richardson, Eliza, 118, 119n6

Richardson, Jane, 170n3

Richardson, Miss, 333, 343

Richmond Enquirer, 323

Riddell, Margaret Jane, 438

River and Harbor Bill, 316

Roark, Reed W., 254

Robb, Benjamin F., 255n1

Robb, John, 255n1

Roberts, Ester Jane (Mrs. Phillip Sublett), 93

Roberts, I. J., 279

Rockbridge county, Virginia, description, 179

Rogers, Colonel, 247

Rogers, George W., 169, 178, 341

Rogers, James Harrison, 457

Rogers, John, 51

Rogers, Judge, 239

Rogers, Mary, 15, 27

Rogers, Timothy, 239n1

Rogers, William Pelag, 457

Rose, Robert, 119

Roundtree, 35

Royal, Peter, 47

Royston, Martin, 280, 281, 287, 346

211; relationship to Houstons, 8n6, 472–73; residing with the Wilsons, 200, 236n1; role of, in Houston's home, 473, 476, 478, 480; taking residence near the Houstons, 210; Vernal Lea as trustee of, 472n4

Thornton, F. G., 200

tithing, 241

tobacco. *See* crops

Toler, Daniel, 438

Towers, Marcia Anne, 395

traveling

safety, 461; travel pay, 316n3; travel problems, 153, 278, 280–81, 282, 338, 342, 345; travel route illustrated, 166, 331

treason, 206

Trimble, Mrs. John (Margaret McEwen), 459, 459n1

Tripler Hall, 288

Újházi, László, 140, 140n2

Union

compromise, 222; "disunionism," 185, 186, 190, 214, 224, 250, 254; preservation of, 207, 231, 467; Sam Houston's loyalty and dedication to, 116, 126, 206, 231

Union, 116n4, 352n1

Utah Bill, 263

vanity, 389

Wade, John W., 15, 114, 124, 132

Wadkins, Cloana (Mrs. Henry M.), 15

Wallace, Daniel, 251–52, 252n2, 264, 265, 265n1

Wallace, Mary Houston, 8, 156, 168, 173, 174, 176, 177n1

Wallace, William, 176

War Department, 264

"Washington on the Brazos," 333

"Washingtonians," speech given for, 308

Watson, Elizabeth (daughter of Thomas and Elizabeth), 45, 67, 236

Watson, Elizabeth (Mrs. Thomas), 31, 236

weather, 154, 343

affects on pregnancy, 172; hurricanes, 193; inclement, 18, 375, 452; seasons, 205; in Washington, 149, 270, 376, 377, 378

Webster, Daniel, 76, 225, 237

wedding anniversary (Sam and Margaret Houston), 54, 153, 186, 410, 417

West Point, 467

Wheeler, Daniel A., 410, 410n1, 416

Wheeler, Royal T., 410, 410n1, 416

Whigs, 138, 148–49, 364, 390, 397; Convention of, 414, 431; presidential nomination, 407, 426, 437

White House, 125, 418

whittling, 373n3

wife of Sam Houston. *See* Houston, Margaret (wife of Sam Houston)

Wigfall, Louis T., 210n1 (208)

Wiley, A. P., defending M. Houston, 469–72

Wiley, Mary, 402

Wiley, Sally, 434

Williams, Mr., 380

Wilmot Proviso, 44, 45n2

Wilson, Benjamin S., aligning with Gott and Virginia, 193; correspondence, 5–6, 30, 70; court deposition of, 475–76; financial matters, 38, 47, 437; Gott and Virginia boarding with, 200, 210, 288

Wilson, Jane C., 154, 236, 285–86, 476

Wilson, Sam Houston, 6, 7, 18, 38, 49, 62

Wood, George T., 160

Wood, George W., 182, 244n2

Woodbury, Levi, 320, 321n2, 325
Woods, Almira (Mrs. Alva), 38, 213, 385n3, 405
Woods, Alva, 213, 243, 385n3, 405–406
Woods, Marshall, 406
Worcester, C. F. (stepfather of Virginia Thorne), 472n4
writing instruments, 86, 216, 443
Wyley, A. P., 186, 187n3

Yoakum, Eliza, 441
Yoakum, Henderson,
    assistance with domestic issues, 144, 277, 279, 280, 287, 294, 333, 337; assistance with financial matters, 368, 398, 410, 416; correspondence with, 178, 203, 226, 290, 323, 381, 389, 391, 417; as defense counsel of Margaret Houston, 469–72; delivering news of birth of child, 348; farm of, 417n2; injury of wife, 422–23; journal entry on Margaret Houston's trial, 468–81; land deal with Houston, 286n1; legal/land matters, 336; managing law business for Sam Houston, 63; mentioned, 354, 363, 370, 387; news of Texas Bill to, 262; using Sam Houston's legal references, 184; vaccines sent to, 201
Yoakum, Mrs., 144, 226, 422–23
York, Pennsylvania, 306, 307
"Young Guards," 308